The 2 × 4 Model

Over a quarter century of studies have shown that addictions, mental illnesses, and their combinations (*dual diagnoses*) are pervasive in the general population. Meanwhile, emerging neuroscience is revealing that the neurodevelopmental basis of major mental illness and addiction diseases are tightly interconnected and often unified pathologies of the brain. This science calls into question the profound split between the addiction and mental health fields that define our fragmented research, professional training, and treatment delivery systems—a split that leaves most patients out of reach of adequate professional expertise and evidence-based standards of care. The 2 × 4 Model, as described in this translational textbook of Addiction Psychiatry, is the essential blueprint and operational manual for the fully integrated, expertly staffed, Dual Diagnosis clinic—a clinic that is maximally capable and efficient in treating the full spectrum of addictions, mental illness, and their comorbidities, through integration of psychotherapies and medications, *by one team under one roof.* Replication of 2 × 4 Model clinics into a national system would allow widespread access to excellent, transparent standards of Addiction Psychiatry as a decisive measure against mass incarceration and the exploding health care crisis of untreated addictions, all while rebuilding brain health as a core public health, social and economic imperative of modern society.

R. Andrew Chambers, MD is Director of Addiction Psychiatry Training at Indiana University School of Medicine in Indianapolis. He is a graduate of Centre College (chemical physics/mathematics; 1991), Duke University School of Medicine (MD; 1996), Yale University Psychiatry (2000), and Basic Neuroscience Programs (2002). After completing the IU Addiction Psychiatry Fellowship (2012) and earning certifications in Addiction Medicine (ABAM) and Addiction Psychiatry (ABPN), Andy has practiced and taught Addiction Psychiatry at Midtown Mental Health Center in Indianapolis. His research, supported by the Veterans Administration, the American Psychiatric Association, and the National Institutes on Drug Abuse (NIDA) and Alcohol Abuse and Alcoholism (NIAAA), has pioneered rodent models of dual diagnosis, contributing to our understanding of neurodevelopmental mechanisms that drive addiction disease in adolescence and mental illness. Andy's basic, neurocomputational, and health systems research aims to translate to a better future of integrated addiction and mental health care and professional training.

The 2 × 4 Model

A Neuroscience-Based Blueprint
for the Modern Integrated
Addiction and Mental Health
Treatment System

R. Andrew Chambers, MD

Routledge
Taylor & Francis Group

NEW YORK AND LONDON

First edition published 2018
by Routledge
711 Third Avenue, New York, NY 10017

and by Routledge
2 Park Square, Milton Park, Abingdon, Oxon, OX14 4RN

Routledge is an imprint of the Taylor & Francis Group, an informa business

© 2018 Taylor & Francis

Library of Congress Cataloging-in-Publication Data
Names: Chambers, R. Andrew (Robert Andrew), author.
Title: The 2 x 4 model : a neuroscience-based blueprint for the modern integrated addiction and mental health treatment system / R. Andrew Chambers.
Other titles: Two times four model
Description: First edition. | New York, NY : Routledge, 2018. | Includes bibliographical references.
Identifiers: LCCN 2017036720 (print) | LCCN 2017037379 (ebook) | ISBN 9781315154466 (ebk) | ISBN 9781498773058 (hbk) | ISBN 9781138563858 (pbk.)
Subjects: | MESH: Behavior, Addictive--therapy | Delivery of Health Care, Integrated—organization & administration | Mental Disorders—therapy | Diagnosis, Dual (Psychiatry) | Mental Health Services-organization & administration | Models, OrganizationalClassification: LCC RC564.68 (ebook) | LCC RC564.68 (print) | NLM WM 176 | DDC 616.86/0651—dc23
LC record available at https://lccn.loc.gov/2017036720

ISBN: 978-1-498-77305-8 (hbk)
ISBN: 978-1-138-56385-8 (pbk)
ISBN: 978-1-315-15446-6 (ebk)

Typeset in Galliard
by Florence Production Ltd, Stoodleigh, Devon, UK

This work is dedicated:

to my parents, Hank and Peggy,
    who gave me my education;

to my first addiction psychiatry trainees, Kalyan, Ayesha,
Camila, Emily, and Jason,
    who helped inspire this book; and

for patients and families suffering with mental illness and
addictions
    throughout the world.

Contents

Figures

Boxes

1 Introducing the 2 × 4 Model

The 2 × 4 Model Blueprint

This book describes a simple, evidence-based design for the modern behavioral health clinic that fully integrates *addiction* and *mental health* diagnoses, treatment, clinical expertise, and professional training under one roof, as provided by one treatment team. This design, called the 2 × 4 Model, provides mental health and addiction care in a fully integrated and yet individually flexible way, even as these illnesses present in many different comorbid combinations across many different individuals. When implemented in a single clinic, or, if replicated in multiple clinics across a region or nation, the 2 × 4 Model clinic can be transformative because it reduces or eliminates the segregation, fragmentation, chaos, and lack of adequate service provision that has so long and pervasively existed in the wide gap between the mental health and addiction fields. A network of 2 × 4 Model clinics could form a new and strengthened backbone for a modernized behavioral healthcare system that provides a *physician*-led integration and team approach to mental health and addiction care at an explicitly stated standard of care, as implied by declaring fidelity to the 2 × 4 Model design. Such a system of 2 × 4 Model clinics holds considerable potential for generating much greater access to high standards of addiction/mental health care, encompassing the full range of Substance Use Disorders (SUDs) and major mental illnesses (MIs), while enhancing the cost-effectiveness, preventative, and therapeutic power of addiction psychiatry. Rebuilding and renovating general psychiatric care based on a new backbone of 2 × 4 Model programs that fully integrate psychiatric and addiction expertise holds considerable potential for enabling behavioral health to have the decisive public health and social impact that it is capable of delivering, which is so desperately needed.

The Context: The Split between Mental Health and Addiction Care

The U.S. and other nations are suffering from under-resourced, highly fragmented and overtly failing mental health and addiction treatment systems. Serious domestic public health, social, and economic costs are mounting as a result of this breakdown, ranging from the disgraces of mass incarceration and homelessness, to the growth of an unsustainably expensive health care system. While built and incentivized for deploying highly technical, procedure-based care for the treatment of terrifically expensive medical diseases and injuries that result from *untreated addictions*, the U.S. health care system mostly ignores the diagnosis and treatment of addiction itself. Paired with the ballooning costs of mass incarceration, the exploding health care costs of not treating addiction have significant consequences for state and federal government budgets. While paying for prisons and non-preventative medical care, government budgets have increasingly retreated from supporting public, university, and post-graduate education, making it increasingly difficult for middle class families to afford and participate in higher level education needed to sustain and grow our society's intellectual and scientific capital.

At the heart of this crisis, which undoubtedly impacts our whole health care system across all its specialties, lies a fundamental flaw specific to the behavioral health system: *Mental health care and addiction treatment are almost totally segregated from one other.* This means that in most places in the U.S. and other developed nations, if you have a mental illness and an addiction (i.e., if you have a *dual diagnosis* disorder), and you are seeking treatment, you generally cannot find adequate or expert treatment for one or both of these illness components, especially as provided by one health center and one treatment team. This is a serious problem because, as will be described in greater detail in Chapter 2, most patients suffering with moderate to severe mental illness have one or more addictions. Similarly, most people suffering with multiple and/or severe addictions, have one or more types of mental illness. In other words, the majority of patients who need behavioral health care, actually have both mental illness and addictive disease; yet, our current behavioral health system, which generally separates mental health from addiction care, is primarily built to treat only the minor fractions of the whole behavioral health population that do not have comorbid Substance use disorder (SUD)/Mental illness (MI) conditions.

The negative consequences of this set-up are far reaching both for individual patients trying to get expert, evidence-based care, and for the operations, costs, and effectiveness of behavioral health as a whole. Ignoring the diagnosis and treatment of a substance use disorder in a mentally ill person, can reduce and even eliminate the total effectiveness of mental health care. Similarly, ignoring mental illness strips the quality and effectiveness out of addiction treatment. Our segregated behavioral health care system is ridiculously complex; it is geographically and financially fragmented and yet needlessly redundant in ways that do not support efficacy. Patients typically encountering clinics or hospitals that treat only mental illness or addiction, but not both, get referred to an endless merry-go-round of different buildings, different providers, and different cities—sometimes simultaneously, sometimes sequentially—because of their dual diagnosis comorbidity. Across these siloes, no one behavioral health professional, or center of care is actually willing or able to be 'where the buck stops' in providing comprehensive, longitudinal care for the patient—to actually take clinical responsibility for what is ultimately wrong with them (e.g., a complex dual diagnosis syndrome)—because these siloes don't effectively treat a major portion of what the patient actually has. All this is happening, while psychiatrists and behavioral health treatment centers and funding are already in seriously short supply. A true case in point, is illustrated by the de-identified story of Mr. M as presented in **Case Vignette #1**.

The kind of chaos this scenario illustrates, happens in part, because of a number of false assumptions implied in the structural design of our divided behavioral health system. First, as previously mentioned, there is the false assumption that people with addictions or mental illness are largely separate populations, and that only a minority are dual diagnoses cases. Second, there is the inaccurate assumption that patients who do not currently have a dual diagnosis, for example, those with mental illness (but not addiction), or, those with addiction (but not mental illness), will remain stable in their diagnostic lanes. Actually, it is more accurate to understand, and expect, that there are considerable conversion rates of going from having an underlying mental illness to acquiring a comorbid addiction, and conversely, going from having an addiction only, to developing a concurrent mental illness as well. Third, for patients who are accurately recognized by our fragmented system as having dual diagnosis conditions, there remains the usual failure to see them and treat them as having *one brain and one syndrome that has multiple illness components.* Instead, the segregated addiction and mental health systems patients are often referred to (if they have access to both), seem to operate as if the patients have two brains, each occupied by a different discrete illness: An addiction in one brain, and a mental illness in the other, so that it does not seem to matter in the least that two totally different sets of therapists, treatment cultures, and psychopharmacological prescribers, (who often don't communicate well with one another) are working on the patient.

The split between mental illness and substance use disorder expertise and treatment has been long-standing. It is also fairly deeply engrained across all the key professional subcultures and endeavors of behavioral health including research, professional training, and clinical care. Accordingly, although this problem has been recognized and discussed as a major challenge among many experts in behavioral health for several decades (as exemplified by the outstanding body of work by Robert Drake), it has remained remarkably stubborn to change. Clearly, the roots of the problem are many, and they go very deep. Traditionally in Western medicine, we have relied on biomedical research to *translate* into clinical innovation and improvements in health care, especially for resolving very difficult medical challenges. But with respect to this core fault line running through the heart of behavioral health, a wealth of clinical, epidemiological, and neuroscience research, that supports the integration of mental health and addiction expertise and treatment, has simply *failed to translate.* In essence, as discussed in detail in Chapter 2, we have a seriously deficient and inefficient behavioral health care system that has been unable to adapt or respond to the scientific evidence that:

Case Vignette #1

Mr. M. was a 42 year old man who presented to the psychiatric ER in crisis, as he was being treated simultaneously on an outpatient basis at three different centers, by three different psychiatrists, separated geographically by a total path of some 25 miles. Aside from the fact that he had great difficulty in complying with this complex treatment array (due to time demands, lack of reliable transportation, child care coverage, etc.), he was not being effectively managed by the treatment he could get to. His garden-variety opioid/benzodiazepine addiction/anxiety syndrome was being treated as follows: First, at the methadone clinic where he was being treated for his opioid addiction, but where they do not treat other addictions or mental illnesses, he was referred out to another psychiatry clinic where he could get his anxiety addressed. In this second clinic, where the psychiatrist does not treat addictions but focuses on anxiety, he was put on a rapid acting benzodiazepine for anxiety. After some time, back at the methadone clinic, he was noted to be unusually over-sedated; they drug tested him and found the benzodiazepine in his urine. After more time and clinical confusion that was produced by the general lack of (and barriers to) communication between the methadone clinic psychiatrist and the anxiety disorder psychiatrist, it was decided that he should no longer be on methadone and benzodiazepines. But now, given the fact that the methadone clinic does not want, or, is not able to address what may now be a co-occurring benzo-diazepine use disorder, and the outpatient psychiatrist is also not comfortable with, or able, to do an outpatient taper of the benzodiazepine, the patient is referred to the third psychiatrist, at the third site, whose job it is to do outpatient detoxes from alcohol and benzodiazepines, but is not responsible for treating the addictions to these drugs. This happens in a clinic that is not near either the methadone clinic or the outpatient psychiatric clinic. Now, in the context of being treated by three different prescribers, (who normally don't have time to talk to one another), none of the doctors or treatment sites can fully grasp what is happening with the patient in terms of the interactions between his mental illness, his addictions, or the therapeutic vs. detrimental combined effects of the drugs he is being prescribed to treat these problems. So he ends up being brought to the ER by ambulance after overdosing.

1. Mental illness and addictions typically occur in the same patients;
2. The brain pathologies, genetics, and environmental risk factors of these disorders are intimately interlinked (and may often be one biology);
3. Optimal clinical outcomes and efficiencies in treating mental illness cannot be achieved when addictions are ignored or dismissed and vice-versa.

The 2 × 4 Model, by design, aims to fulfill the translational implications of these evidence-based principals. Its design and operation rejects the clinical status quo in behavioral health, calling into question the traditions and cultural forces that are keeping mental health and addiction care separated. The 2 × 4 Model is what we create after we go back to the drawing board and say, instead of keeping the broken, fragmented system we now have, let's create a system of behavioral health clinics that each are comprehensively, and expertly capable of:

•   Treating any major mental illness(s) and any addiction(s);
•   In any comorbid combination or stage of progression;
•   By *one* treatment team;
•   Under *one* roof; and
•   For as long as it takes to get the patient better and keep them better.

The following chapters will serve as a basic and clinical science-informed blueprint and functional description of the 2 × 4 Model Integrated Dual Diagnosis Clinic. It will describe the overarching scientific basis, design-concept, organization, staffing, and operation of the 2 × 4 Model clinic as exemplified by its working prototype built at the Eskenazi Health Midtown Community Mental Health Center in Indianapolis, also home of the Indiana University Addiction Psychiatry training program (2012 to present). The aim of this manual, first, is to assist and guide clinicians, clinical educators, administrators— and addiction psychiatrists especially—in the replication and operation of 2 × 4 Model clinics nationwide and internationally, to form a core network and higher standard of behavioral health care that expertly integrates addiction and mental health diagnosis and treatment. Second, as these clinics become more widely replicated, they will serve as key professional workforce training sites where multidisciplinary team members, including psychiatrists, nurses, and therapists (PhD and masters level therapists and social workers) can be fully cross trained in both addictions and mental health care. Finally, as 2 × 4 Model clinics become more mainstream as a backbone for behavioral health, they will drive a *reverse translation* in clinical and basic science, where the research missions of pharmaceutical companies and the behavioral health institutes , such as NIMH (National Institute of Mental Health), NIDA (National Institute on Drug Abuse), and NIAAA (National Institute on Alcohol Abuse and Alcoholism), will become much more focused on developing new integrative/ parsimonious treatments for comorbid addictions and mental illness, which so many real-world patients in behavioral health need.

Why Call It the '2 × 4 Model'?

The '2 × 4 Model' is named not just in honor of the well-known 2 × 4 inch (cross-section) wooden beam used as a universal building block in building construction. The '2 × 4 Model' refers to its design as a two dimensional conceptual grid: A two component (vertical) *Illness* dimension, and a four component (horizontal) *Treatment* dimension (i.e., forming a 2 × 4 unit grid, **Figure 1.1**). In the vertical, *Illness* dimension, the two components represent a balanced, co-equal, and integrative focus on both (i) mental illnesses, and (ii) addictions. As will be discussed in Chapter 3, both categories of brain disorders (mental illness(s) of whatever kind, and addiction(s) of whatever kind) are given equal, and, as is often clinically indicated, simultaneous priority for diagnosis, monitoring, and treatment. In the horizontal, *treatment* dimension (Chapter 4), the four components represents how the clinic *routinely* employs an array of (i) diagnostic, (ii) psychotherapeutic, (iii) pharmacological, and (iv) professional communications in the care of patients. Not only are *all* of these components valued as crucial and equally important in the provision of care, but an eclectic array of tools and approaches *must* be routinely available and used within each of these components (detailed in Chapters 5–8). This is not at all to say that every patient must be given the entire spectrum of all the diagnostic tools and treatments that are available. *In fact, a key design feature and operational goal of the 2 × 4 Model clinic is that it is built to be able to individualize the care of different patients according to their unique needs that arise from their diverse demographic, social, and diagnostic circumstances.* What allows this flexibility, is the presence and relatively frequent use of not one or two, but many tools from the tool boxes within each of the treatment dimension components. In this way, the 2 × 4 Model is most definitely not a 'cookie-cutter' model of behavioral health care delivery. When the clinic honestly accepts the challenge of expertly diagnosing and treating so many different mental illnesses and addictions that may occur in so many different combinations within the patient population, there cannot be a dominance of 'one-size-fits-all' or 'pill mill' approaches in the clinic. This philosophy of individualization, as something that would seem desirable by patients and important to elevating standards of care, is a major shift away from the way many treatment clinics in behavioral health, and particularly within addictionology are currently operating. For example, many 'abstinence' based treatment clinics offer only 12-steps. They literally and figuratively offer just one path or 'dogma' to success. In these models, patients who fall off the recommended narrow path are too often seen as failures, rather than being understood as having diseases that are too complex and refractory for so narrow and simple a treatment. Similarly, methadone maintenance clinics, as important and greatly needed as they are, serve a quite narrow mission with a very limited set of therapeutic tools. Too often, stand-alone, for profit methadone clinics operate disconnected from psychiatry or general health care as 'opioid treatment by government algorithm', which is perhaps ironic given that government-based insurance programs (e.g., state

Medicaid programs) often refuse to reimburse the care they provide. In many methadone programs, tight adherence of the facility to a laundry list of state and federal regulations serves to make up for what is often lacking in expertise, formal training, and individualized clinical decision-making in addiction psychiatry on the part of the physicians who staff these clinics. This design can be practical, beneficial, and extremely efficient for some patients, because there is essentially only one pharmacological treatment—daily methadone dispensation —that is deployed to keep patients healthy (and the clinic economically profit-able). Nevertheless, stand-alone methadone maintenance is often not optimal for many because it cannot expertly treat other co-occurring mental illnesses and addictions that are so frequent in opioid addicted patients.

The 2 × 4 Model clinic thus represents a design and operational approach for integrated addiction and mental health care (that can be conjoined to methadone clinics), which can expertly and longitudinally treat the full spectrum of addicted, mentally ill, and dual diagnosis patients. And it does this in a highly individualized way regardless of the specific combination of mental illness and addiction a specific patient may have at any one point in time, or how that comorbidity may evolve over time. In this way, because of its broad applicability to the entire spectrum of behavioral health patients in need everywhere, the 2 × 4 Model clinic has the potential to be a universal building block of a modernized system of behavioral health clinics in a given region, nationally or internationally.

Who Operates in the 2 × 4 Model Clinic and How Does It Work?

Patients seeking treatment in a 2 × 4 Model clinic will be expected to not only have a range of different combinations of comorbid mental illnesses and addictions, but also a range of severities of these conditions. Accepting and embracing this complexity (which we as professionals ought to do, since it *is* the clinical reality we are facing) means that embarking on integrated dual diagnosis care is a *team* activity. Although this is certainly made necessary by the patient population itself (these patients require a diversity of approaches and clinical time commitments that only a team of people can deliver), the team approach also makes the work more fun. The well run 2 × 4 Model team is psychologically supportive to all its team members, who are collectively working together to treat a quite sick and tragically downtrodden patient population. Chapter 9 describes the essential professionals and roles of the key 2 × 4 Model team members with a discussion of how they should interact and practice to flexibly deliver the best care together. This description includes an outlining of the physical infrastructure that a 2 × 4 Model team needs to operate in.

The 2 × 4 Model is designed to operate primarily as an outpatient program. This is because (get ready for another reality that we must face) the mental illnesses and addictions that patients need care for are typically chronic diseases that require long-term professional management. Accordingly, the therapeutic activities that generally produce substantial and sustained clinical improvement should themselves be sustained over the long-term (e.g., months to years). Short-term inpatient stays (e.g., the 30 days 'rehab'), even at really posh facilities and, despite their expense, often do not have sustained clinical efficacy. This is due to a number of reasons including, first of all, the fact that successfully detoxing a patient from a given drug (usually requiring days to a few weeks) does not really treat the addiction itself, or the mental illness that goes with it. Second, patients obviously cannot live in rehab units forever, where, although they may be relatively well-sheltered from the drugs they are addicted to in the short-term, they are unable to work and live their lives with their families. For these and other reasons, as discussed in greater depth in Chapters 9 and 10, the 2 × 4 Model approach has to be understood and implemented primarily as an outpatient endeavor that is supplemented by the inpatient service or supervised rehab setting. This does not mean that the concepts and design features of the 2 × 4 Model shouldn't also be applied in inpatient settings, or that the 2 × 4 Model approach calls for even more reductions and closures of inpatient psychiatric settings and beds (producing even more of the unintended detrimental consequences of deinstitutionalization). Instead, the 2 × 4 Model emphasizes the primacy of the outpatient setting, located in geographical proximity to where patients live, as the core structural element of integrated dual diagnosis care, where most of the therapeutic action will happen. Actually, this is also quite a bit of a paradigm shift from the current status quo, because so much of the public, and even many professionals in the behavioral health field, still tend to think of addictions and integrated dual diagnosis treatment as something that should happen in short-term inpatient settings. Indeed, this thinking is close to the reality we face. Truth is, these inpatient systems are too costly, too short-term, too rare in number, too geographically distant from where patients live, and frankly, too ineffective, to be the back bone of the system we really need. These inpatient units are typically isolated or disconnected from outpatient dual diagnosis programs, or built as supplements to longitudinal outpatient services that don't deliver integrated dual diagnosis care. In other words, these inpatient settings unfortunately don't do a lot of good because they don't have the 2 × 4 Model outpatient programs that they need to be linked with. This is not to say that we don't need inpatient dual diagnosis and detoxification services; indeed we clearly need even more and better ones. However, inpatient detoxification programs and psychiatric hospitals that are mental illness/addiction sensitive and accepting should be adjunct services for, and supplements to, more ubiquitous longitudinal outpatient dual diagnosis programs that should form the primary foundation of integrated dual diagnosis care.

Putting it all together, Chapter 10 describes how the tools, the team, the setting, and the practices of the 2 × 4 Model are integrated into one functional unit in the care of a very diverse mentally ill and/or addicted clinical population, composed of patients with different short- vs. long-term needs, clinical severities, and stages of disease progression. At the heart of this description we are striving to create, in the most clinically effective way, the best blend of mental illness and addiction treatment services. In essence, we want to retain and merge the best tools and practices from either field (Chapters 3, 4, and 10), while limiting or discarding those things, practices or habits from either field that are of equivocal value, or are even damaging to care in the context of the integration. For example, if there is a certain practice that is widely adhered to in the addiction treatment culture or tradition, which would nevertheless be unhelpful or detrimental to apply to a patient with mental illness, then we should probably significantly reduce or discard that practice altogether in the 2 × 4 Model. Alternatively, a given practice from the tradition of addiction treatment might also be really useful in mental health care too, even though it is not widely used in mental health settings, just as an artifact of there being two different clinical traditions. In this situation, by all means, we would want to embrace this practice in the 2 × 4 Model.

Closing out this book, Chapters 11 and 12 cover a range of special topics that extend from the clinical implementation of the 2 × 4 Model. This includes addressing how 2 × 4 Model programs should be involved in professional training and research, how they may be replicated across regions and checked for construct fidelity, and (along with Chapter 8) how they may be financed and connected to the rest of health care.

Target Readership and Limitations of This Book

This book is a design and operations manual that will have several audiences, including most directly, addiction psychiatrists in and out of academia, and fellows who are training in addiction psychiatry. For the latter group in particular, it can serve as a core textbook and training guide. In many respects the well-executed 2 × 4 Model clinic would be the ideal venue for building, supporting, and leveraging the uniquely broad skill sets of addiction psychiatrists (see Chapter 11), which is the only type of physician that is formally trained and board certified by the American Board of Medical Specialties (ABMS) for diagnosing and treating *both* mental illness and addictions. However, addiction psychiatrists will likely remain in short supply for some time, requiring, in addition to addiction psychiatrists, the clinical participation of dedicated psychiatrists who are not ABMS certified in addiction psychiatry, or boarded in addiction medicine by the American Board of Addiction Medicine (ABAM). Also, 2 × 4 Model clinics will need to be equipped with an array of non-physician clinical professionals and administrators (Chapter 9), who all will be critically important in building and operating these programs. Accordingly, all professional groups involved in behavioral health care will likely find value in this book. To the extent that 2 × 4 Model clinic designs may be viewed as providing good or desirable standards of care that should be promoted for more universal access, a range of non-behavioral health professionals and organizations involved in supporting and collaborating with behavioral health care services (e.g., researchers, public health agencies, insurance companies, criminal justice teams, and child care professionals) may also find interest in the 2 × 4 Model blueprint.

This book cannot supplant the many hundreds of textbooks and published manuscripts already available that describe how mental health or addictions diagnosis and treatment may best occur according to the evidence base. It is not a substitute for formal residency training in psychiatry or fellowship in addiction psychiatry, and it does not represent a comprehensive textbook of psychopharmacology for mental illness or addictions, or the many psycho-therapies for these conditions. It also is not intended to serve as a complete resource covering the clinical phenomenology, epidemiology or neuroscience of dual diagnosis disorders. Instead, it is an integration and translation of all these fields, intended to inform a clinical design and approach that has the potential to create a much higher standard of behavioral health care, professional training, and research that is important to our public health and well-being as a society.

For a deeper and highly detailed description of the many scientific and clinical subfields of knowledge discussed in this book, the professional trainee and practitioner should look to other sources, including the key and representative references listed at the end of each chapter. My hope is that this book will introduce and advance the 2 × 4 Model as a coherent, conceptual, organiza-tional, and operational strategy that binds all these subfields together to help patients. This book is more about how the knowledge and parts of fully integrated dual diagnosis care should fit and work together, more so than an in-depth description of the evidence base supporting each piece. Accordingly, for the sake of efficiency in writing, and to some extent, to enhance the read-ability of this book as a practical design and operational manual, in-text cita-tions are not used. Nevertheless, to the best of the author's knowledge and clinical experience, this book is founded on where the weight of evidence exists as represented by the references listed at the end of each chapter, except in areas where the evidence base remains too under-developed, or where the art of medicine must come into play. Please note that each of the 250 background sources listed in this book are used once and only once, but have relevance for multiple chapters other than where they appear. These sources and their authors are not the only ones that have contributed to this field. I know the readership will appreciate the impracticality of exhaustively listing all sources and authors that might in some way inform this book, given that virtually any research paper or textbook on the topic of either mental illness or addiction could in some way be relevant to the topic of dual diagnosis.

Background References and Further Reading

Chambers, R. A. 2007. "National conference on dual diagnosis: A meeting of minds on a specialty topic that defies specialization." *Journal of Dual Diagnosis* 3 (2): 3–7. doi: 10.1300/J374v03n02_02.

Charney, D. S., J. D. Buxbaum, P. Sklar, and E. J. Nestler, Eds. 2013. *Neurobiology of Mental Illness.* 4th ed. New York: Oxford University Press.

Galanter, M., H. D. Kleber, and K. T. Brady, Eds. 2014. *Textbook of Substance Abuse Treatment.* 5th ed. Washington, DC: American Psychiatric Publishing.

O'Brien, C. P., D. S. Charney, L. Lewis, J. W. Cornish, R. M. Post, G. E. Woody, J-K. Zubieta, J. C. Anthony, J. D. Blaine, and C. L. Bowden. 2004. "Priority actions to improve the care of persons with co-occurring substance abuse and other mental disorders: A call to action." *Biological Psychiatry* 56 (10): 703–713.

Sadock, B. J., V. A. Sacock, and P. Ruiz, Eds. 2009. *Comprehensive Textbook of Psychiatry.* 9th ed. New York: Wolters Kluwer/Lippincott Williams and Wilkins.

2 Clinical and Neuroscience Basis for the 2 × 4 Model

This chapter will provide an essential overview of the scientific foundation and rationale for the integration of mental health and addiction services as implemented by the 2 × 4 Model design. Reviewing this evidence-based argument, *which enacts a translation of science into practice*, is crucial not only to inform the reader of the value of the 2 × 4 Model design as applied in a specific clinic, but to instill broader understanding and motivation among clinical professionals on why integrated mental health and addiction treatment should be a much more available standard-of-care in behavioral health. This chapter will outline science from areas of psychiatric research that most directly point to the unmet need to more fully integrate mental and addiction care: epidemiology, clinical, and basic neuroscience.

To begin this discussion, it is worthwhile to first consider these questions: If fully integrating mental health and addiction care is so important, why isn't it already the norm? Indeed, why is it so rare? If the science is so compelling for justifying 2 × 4 Model clinics, why hasn't this science been translated?

There is a growing recognition that plenty of excellent basic, clinical and health services science has failed to translate into changes and improvements in clinical practice in behavioral health. This is a general problem that seems to bedevil behavioral health and psychiatry to an extreme extent like no other sector of health care; this may be attributable to the usual suspects of stigma and lack of funding in behavioral health. Although the general *failure in translation* in behavioral health is too big a topic to cover in detail in this book, it is important to consider this failure with respect to the lack of integration of mental health and addiction services and clinical expertise. Understanding some of the causes of this particular failure help us understand the key barriers that have to be overcome in order to make the science we cover later in this chapter translate, so that 2 × 4 Model clinical systems can become more of a reality. Understanding the history of the field of 'dual diagnosis' helps us contextualize the science of it, which in turn should help us better use this science to improve clinical practice.

Why the Split between Mental Health Care and Addiction Services and Expertise?

Much of this problem is about the steady grip of culture and tradition. In many respects, the services and professional development cultures in mental health care have grown up quite separately from that of addictionology. While since the early twentieth century it has been known and accepted within medicine, and in much of the public's mind, that different varieties of mental illness are brain-based illnesses, similar conceptualizations about the disease model of addiction have lagged far behind. Only in recent decades, due in part to accumulating science, and perhaps more suddenly in the context of the contemporary iatrogenic prescription drug epidemic has the disease model of addiction become more clear in our society. It took a crisis of mass over-prescribing of addictive drugs beginning in the late 1990s that has produced an unprecedented outbreak of addiction and secondary illness and death, for physicians to recognize that they were woefully uneducated about the pathophysiology of addiction as a biomedical disease process.

Alcoholics Anonymous and other variants of the 12-step peer group tradition, while certainly deserving of their status as representing some of the first effective approaches to healing from addiction, originated and matured fairly independently from psychiatry. A strong emphasis of this tradition on the re-orienting of motivation away from addiction toward the "higher power" also led many people both within and outside this movement to equate recovery with a religious awakening, or as a reformed personal relationship with Jesus or God. Perhaps as a side effect of this interpretation, many people have then come to understand addiction as essentially a spiritual matter, not a biomedical one. Certainly, the proof was in the pudding for so many people who have successfully recovered from their addictions while being a part of Alcoholics Anonymous (AA) or Narcotics Anonymous (NA). And, like many religious movements, an emphasis on purity of approach and dedication to the process of the 12 steps, and the higher power, led many (but not all) to believe that psychotropic medications represented crutches, pathological substitutes, or even conveniently deniable relapses to addictions. Even one-on-one psychotherapies were often not deemed necessary or core to the 12-step recovery movement; while ability, willingness, and dedication to participation in the group were deemed as essential markers for success. Thus, rather unfortunately (and to be sure inadvertently for many of its early proponents), the 12-step movement as many people understood it—and identified it as being synonymous with addiction treatment—originated almost like an antipsychiatry movement, where the core ingredients to psychiatry, including medications and individual psychotherapies were not valued, and the core theory underpinning it was a spiritual rather than biomedical idea.

As AA began to take off and thereafter, there was a vacuum of attention and emphasis on addiction in main stream psychiatry, spanning its early development and middle maturational stages, for example, from the 1800s up to the 1980s, when the full impact of deinstitutionalization began to be felt. Across the seminal works of the great theorists and clinicians that founded psychiatry, from Freud on down, there is a notable lack of content and exploration pertaining to substance use disorders and addictions, despite the elaboration of many clinically applicable theories of mind, motivation, emotion, and developmental stages, that still to this day inform our understanding of much of the spectrum of psychiatric disorders. At the same time, much of real-world psychiatric practice, occurring outside of academia, and serving other than wealthy clientele, was focused on the moderately to severely mentally ill as embedded in the formerly massive institutionalization system. In this extensive system of long-term hospitals, the patients, who would later be discovered, post-deinstitutionalization, to be the most vulnerable to addictions, were largely (and often forcibly) sheltered from access to addictive drugs, except nicotine. Of course it was only by the 1970s, when deinstitutionalization began to happen in full force, when tobacco use was beginning to be widely understood as an addiction and a major public health problem.

So you have this early segregation not only of patients, but of clinical approaches and cultures that by the 1970s had become heavily entrenched. So then, concurrent with deinstitutionalization and the youth and civil rights revolutions of the 1960s and early 1970s, politicians began to respond strongly to the fears of the voters, that 'all hell was breaking loose' especially with respect to the behavior of nonwhite folks, young people, and their proclivity for 'sex, drugs and rock-n-roll'. Perhaps picking up a bit from the lack of involvement of psychiatry in understanding and treating addictions, but also from the over-framing of addiction as a lack of correct spiritual orientation from the 12-step community and politicians, with most of the American people in full agreement, thus unleashed the 'war on drugs'. Initially, this seemed to make sense while reviving our past cultural tendencies for extreme puritanism, as in abolition, when we attempted to make it not only illegal but *unconstitutional* for an American to drink alcohol. While forgetting the lessons learned from the 1920s of suddenly deciding that fairly common behaviors, and large portions of the citizenry are criminals, the 'war on drugs' also picked up on the morality and spirituality perspective that some in the 12-step community also espoused. If recovery was synonymous with finding the higher power, asking for forgiveness, making amends, and shepherding others into following of the higher power, then being in a state of actively using drugs, especially while unattached to 12-step groups, was the same as being in a state of immorality and sin. For the large number of people who could not have their behaviors helped by religion or the 12-step community, their drug use would have to be understood as representing a state of criminality, best dealt with via punishment, including mass incarceration and its associated economic and educational deprivation.

The consequences of these dynamics were of course far-reaching in terms of making it even harder for psychiatry to accept its role, and the challenge, of treating addicted patients. It's hard enough being the only sector of the medical profession that focuses fairly exclusively on a population of patients that tend to be poor, have weak political representation, and are highly stigmatized, precisely because of the mental disorders that psychiatrists are trained to treat. Admitting and dealing with the fact that many of these patients are also addicts—essentially 'criminals'—in the eyes of much of the medical profession and society, would be adding insult to injury for our patients and for psychiatrists. A double dose of stigma, a double dose of economic deprivation, not only in the patients we serve but on behavioral health professionals—potentially spelling, after the near elimination of psychiatric hospitals, the final doom of psychiatry.

Within the halls of academic psychiatry, a somewhat different set of dynamics have persisted to keep mental health and addictionology apart not only at the level of clinical care, but in terms of physician and allied professional training and basic and clinical research. First, the culture of academia demands of its faculty members, in the interest of their own survival in a highly competitive arena, a great deal of hyper-specialization. Professional advancement and tenure, especially at the most prestigious schools, requires fame (not among the public, but among other academics in one's field) and money (not personal wealth, but ability to acquire major grant support). Really, the only way one achieves these things is to be regarded among peers as being a leading expert, to know a whole lot, more than only around 50 other people in the world, about either quite a narrow list of topics, or one topic. Typically, this kind of specialization is focused on a single disorder or method of approach, such as the expert in bipolar disorder, or the expert in PET imaging of dopamine systems. What this means is that, on the whole, psychiatric faculties are relatively impoverished of members that are interested, or can find resources to support their interests in how different disorders are interrelated and comorbid, and how such comorbidities can be treated in an integrated way. Although a diversity of interests are easier to maintain for a closely related set of conditions or methods (e.g., the expert in posttraumatic stress disorder (PTSD) and depression, or the expert in fMRI neuroimaging of schizophrenia and dementia), the cultural divide between the addictions field and the mental illness field, which are each very large in their own right, is basically too broad for many faculty members to successfully bridge within the academic culture. This results in the training and role modeling of medical students, residents, and other graduate students that promotes the segregation and compartmentalization of clinical interests, even for those who do not stay in academia. Just as teaching centers have so few faculty members or clinics engaged in treating mental illness and addictions in an integrated way, so we may expect that very few trainees, who will leave academia and enter practice, will feel supported, motivated or informed to treat mental illness and addictions in an integrated way.

A second set of issues more specific to the research side of academia has also persisted to maintain and even worsen the split between the mental health and addiction fields. Much of biomedical advancement in the last quarter century, including that in psychiatric neuroscience, has been guided by an emphasis, and many critics might say even *extreme* emphasis, on a form of reductionism which strives to isolate disease causality to the level of single genes or molecules. This strategy works very well if a disease is actually caused by a single molecular aberration. Or, it might work in the case of a more complex but still limited set (e.g. 10) of molecular factors, if there is support for the work of scientists who can integrate this limited set of factors into a mathematically complex systems model of the disease process. Unfortunately, neither of these conditions are readily met with respect to understanding many forms of mental illness and their comorbidities, especially those involving the intersection of mental illness and addictions, because these syndromes are usually the result of very complex combinations of hundreds of genetic determinants and a wide range of environmental experiences.

There are two important scientific principles that are particularly relevant to understanding the pathogenesis of dual diagnosis disorders that are not in line with the primary emphasis on the search for simple molecular models of psychiatric disorders (or phenotypes) that have been heavily prioritized in recent decades. One is *equifinality:* This is the situation where you have two totally unrelated causal ingredients (e.g., different genes or even different environmental experiences) that each can lead, either independently, or in combination, to the same disease or phenotype. Two is *multifinality:* This is where one causal ingredient can lead to two or more different diseases or phenotypes. Not just one, but both of these dynamics are likely in play in the pathogenesis of most patients with mental illness and addiction. For example, in terms of equifinality, either a certain combination of genes, or a traumatic experience, might lead to an impulsive behavioral pattern in adolescence leading to alcoholism (two different causal factors both produce same phenotype). Or, in multifinality, a traumatic experience alone, such as sexual abuse at age 8, could lead to a personality disorder, major depression, and an opioid addiction by age 25 (one causal event to three phenotypes). Real world complexities such as these are very unsettling for NIH grant review committees. Nevertheless, research efforts on these kinds of complexities are likely integral to understanding the pathogenesis of mental illness and addiction comorbidities (and necessary for supporting academic faculty members who are interested in these comorbidities), while, unfortunately, they antagonize the supremacy of molecular determinism, which has in recent years been central to the culture and investment of NIH-funded behavioral health research. The point here is not that the study of single genes, or single neurotransmitters, or single brain regions, or single environmental stressors, or single DSM diagnosis are not important, but a lack of support of research that integrates several of these domains has hindered our understanding of addiction and mental illness as integrated diseases processes, which should be researched and treated together.

Few people outside of academic psychiatry recognize the great intellectual and economic power that the behavioral health focused National Institutes:

NIMH (Mental health); NIDA (Drug Abuse); and NIAAA (Alcohol Abuse and Alcoholism) have in setting the agenda not only for psychiatric research but for professional education and clinical practice in the U.S. This is because the $2.5 billion in annual grants awarded from these agencies to medical schools and departments of psychiatry across the country, are a primary support to the economic vitality, prestige, and even existence of many psychiatry departments. In turn, the interests and expertise of most faculty members of these departments (who are in turn responsible for driving research and providing psychiatric education to medical students and residents) are heavily influenced by the agendas of the institutes. Thus, the program officers of the institutes will report, quite accurately, that the types, approaches, and focus areas of the grants that are awarded, are determined by the specializations and interests of the academics who are invited in from the universities, to evaluate the grants.

Notably, these institutes are split significantly by having a mental health vs. addiction focus, and even in the case of NIAAA vs. NIDA, by focus on *type* of addictive drug. These splits thus contribute to, and reinforce the over-specialization and splitting of academic faculties along mental health vs. addiction lines of interest. Because the institutes must guard their assigned turf and budgets very closely, they have a tendency to avoid awarding grants that seek to understand how their primary disease processes of interest, may overlap or be interactive, or should be modeled, diagnosed, or treated together. The realization that this situation may be hindering the advancement of our understanding and treatment of real-world behavioral health patients, who typically have multiple comorbidities that span the interests of more than one of these institutes, led to the interesting recent proposal, that at least two of the institutes should be merged. In this case it was a proposal for a merger of NIAAA and NIDA, which seemed straightforward given that both institutes were focused on addictions, and given the clinical reality that the great majority of patients with alcohol addiction also suffer with one or more other substance use disorders. However, fears of losses in total funding dedicated to each of the missions of the two institutes and other politics within academia and the government, as influenced by stakeholders who benefit from the segregation, prevented the merger. Merging NIDA and NIMH would likely be an even greater improbability.

The bottom line is that to a very large extent, the split between the mental health and addiction fields, is quite deeply culturally rooted and financially reinforced from academia to the clinics, from bench to bedside, from the NIH to industry, to clinicians, to patients. Remarkably, the split seems to have even hardened in some ways over the last 30 years, even as an accumulation of research that we consider later in this chapter (ironically much of it also funded by the split institutes), has grown to illuminate the fallacy of the split, and its detrimental impact on patient care. This hardening of the split has occurred, and/or been reflected by, the widespread adoption *of the self-medication hypothesis*, widely held by researchers, professional educators, and clinicians, as the "go to" explanation for the comorbidity of mental illness and addiction.

Self-Medication: A Hypothesis of the Split, by the Split, and for the Split

The self-medication hypothesis holds that people with mental illness use drugs at high levels because for them (because of their illness), there is some good, beneficial, therapeutic, or essentially *medicinal* advantage provided to them from the drug use. This hypothesis has been, for many decades, very popular as the predominant explanation among scientists and clinicians for why mental illness and substance use co-occur, that it has reached the level of dogma, becoming almost synonymous with (i.e., just another term for) dual diagnosis itself. Like dogmas that persist in other disciplines, where explanatory belief systems are stubbornly held on to despite abundant evidence against them, and sometimes with negative consequences, there are aspects to the self-medication hypothesis that are appealing. In terms of being some kind of explanation . . . or any kind of explanation . . . for dual diagnosis, self-medication was the 'first game in town'. Its origins and momentum were built in the context of two major trends, one being de-institutionalization and the second, the declines of tobacco smoking in the general population, happening in the 1970s and 80s. In this era, mentally ill people, no longer relatively sheltered from mass exposure to addictive drugs (while living in long-term hospitals), began to show very high rates of substance use disorders involving a range different drugs when they emerged into the community. They also smoked more cigarettes, which became increasingly obvious as the more mentally healthy majority of our population stopped smoking in increasing numbers.

So in the 1970s and 80s, how could one explain all this drinking and smoking and drugging in mentally ill people, when at the same time, we were beginning to understand ever more clearly, that for people without mental illness, heavy drinking and smoking and drugging was by and large not beneficial or healthy? In the absence of a coherent neuroscience of addiction as a disease (this would not really emerge and mature until the 1990s and later), and without a generally accepted clinical formulation of addiction as an involuntary disorder of motivational control and compulsion, it was almost a matter a certainty that psychiatrists and other behavioral health experts would conclude that there must be something especially good about drinking and using drugs for *mentally ill people,* some special benefit that only having a mental illness could allow for. This idea of course had great appeal not only for psychiatrists and other clinicians, but for patients and researchers. For the care givers and patients together, 'self-medication' offered a way to not double stigmatize and blame the patient for having both a mental illness and a 'despicable' substance use disorder. So, clinicians and patients could say to each other and themselves, "*Don't blame them (us) for it, they (we) are just trying to cope, the best way possible, with all these horrific symptoms.*" Another big benefit for the clinicians was that with the self-medication explanation, one doesn't have to actually diagnose and treat the drug use itself, because the drug use is being framed not as a disease but as an act of medicine-taking.

So, with self-medication, drug use is not regarded as a treatment target, rather it is viewed as a treatment in and of itself, as a reasonable, helpful, and in some way beneficial response to having a mental illness, that anyone in their right mind might do if they were that mentally ill. From this perspective, why would a caring clinician want to directly stop a mentally suffering person from gaining relief from 'self-medication'? Also, according to the self-medication approach, if we (the mental health team) can just treat the mental illness symptoms, then patients will naturally stop their use of those other 'medicines'.

This logic, which essentially conflates the properties of addictive, mind-altering substances with medicines *specifically in the context of mental illness*, has been quite alluring for clinical and basic science researchers whose careers often depend on being awarded grants that seek out new therapeutic agents *for the mentally ill*. Thus, given the widely held assumption that nicotine, alcohol, cocaine, amphetamines, opioids, marijuana, etc., are in some way medicinal for mental illness, all we need to do is push for research grants that figure out how and when, and under what specific clinical or biological circumstances they are medicinal. For corporate interests (e.g., tobacco companies, or pharmaceutical companies that make opioids and stimulants) that would rather keep the attention of the clinical and scientific communities (and by extension the public) fixated on their drug of interest as being a therapeutic commodity rather than a disease causing agent, the self-medication hypothesis is a win-win for them and the academics they support.

So, the self-medication hypothesis is an explanation for dual diagnosis that emerged in a context where there were basically no alternatives. Then, it grew and became dominant in the field because of certain other advantages it gave clinicians and academics who applied it. This is not to say of course that self-medication does not exist at all; it definitely does (e.g., most of us at some point have taken a nonsteroidal anti-inflammatory medication for a headache, or an antibiotic for an infection). There certainly are addictive drugs that can sometimes be therapeutic (e.g., opioids for acute pain; stimulants for ADHD; THC for nausea and anorexia). *The key problem arises from the widespread application of the self-medication hypothesis as the dominant, guiding theory to specifically explain substance use disorders in mental illness.* In essence, this specific application of self-medication arose from an original lack of integration of our understanding of mental illness and *addiction* that, to the extent that it continues to be the dominant theory, actually continues to reinforce the segregation of the mental health and addiction fields. This happens because at their very cores, self-medication and addiction are completely opposite concepts:

Self-medication: The rational, discriminating, voluntary choice to take a drug to achieve benefit, where via its psychoactive profile, and during intoxication, the drug alleviates specific symptoms and increases well-being.

Drug addiction: The irrational, indiscriminant, involuntary compulsive behavior, to repeatedly seek out and take a drug regardless of its psychoactive profile, benefits or detriments, as experienced in either intoxication or withdrawal, and pursued to an extent that produces specific symptoms and degrades well-being.

So, when applying the self-medication rational to explaining drug use in mentally ill people, we are actually specifically representing or sub-typing substance use *in mentally ill people* as a behavior that is essentially *the opposite of what addiction is*. In effect, and unintended or not, the self-medication explanation dismisses and replaces the possibility of addiction with something very different. So then, when we are systematically ignoring or dismissing addiction in mentally ill people, then where else would addiction exist? Why it must be in mentally *healthy* people! That's right: It's in the mentally healthy people where addiction happens, and where addiction treatment is needed! The mentally ill—well those people are just self-medicating mental illness. They just need more mental health treatment. Thus, the segregation between mental health and addiction treatment cultures is perpetuated.

A remarkable aspect of the self-medication hypothesis that reflects its status as a dogma, is that it persists in its popularity, despite plentiful contradictory evidence that is also actually quite widely accepted and popular. This strange reality renders much of the dual diagnosis literature illogical and conceptually incoherent, and thus of doubtful value in the eyes of many behavioral health experts and researchers who remain safe and secure in their mental health or addiction silos. For example, it is quite the norm for a research paper on a given kind of dual diagnosis comorbidity to start out by saying that the presence of X type of substance use is detrimental in Y type of mental illness, and that the X-Y comorbidity is a significant public health problem. This allows the paper to state the health importance of its topic. Then, after the data presentation, the paper inevitably confirms the close association between the substance use X and the mental illness Y, only to conclude with the usual discussion of what causes X to occur so frequently in Y: Patients with Y are self-medicating with X! In this way, readers of the dual diagnosis literature are often left dazed and confused:

> Let me get this straight . . . So it's important for us to figure out why drug use happens in mental illness because the drug use is so frequent and harmful for their mental and physical health, and, yet we conclude that the drug use is medication?

In some instances, the conceptual incoherency arising from trying to stick with the self-medication dogma at all costs, can seem to take on comically bizarre proportions in the literature. For instance, a certain review paper that comes to mind outlined the clinical science literature exploring why a given substance N was so commonly used in mental illness. In this review, 100 percent of the studies that were cited, and the language of the paper itself, authoritatively supported some variation of the self-medication hypothesis to explain why substance use N was so frequent in mental illness, with absolutely no presentation of alternative theories or questioning of the self-medication view. Then, the paper went on to take an interesting turn. It went on to cover the facts that, however, not only is substance use N devastating for mentally ill patients, but this devastation is so great in part because clinicians are not treating this substance abuse N in their patients, *apparently, because clinicians had gotten the impression that the substance use was like a medicine.*

To the extent that the self-medication hypothesis is a seriously flawed explanatory model that has nevertheless persisted in its popularity, it is also buttressing a behavioral health system that is flawed in part due to its divided approaches to mental health vs. addiction treatment. The following five points highlight how the self-medication hypothesis is actually not empirically well supported, and how in many ways it is contradicted by widely replicated and ubiquitous clinical data and anecdotal clinical experience.

Fact #1: Addictive drug use overwhelmingly does not operate as medication for mental illness. The weight of the evidence is clear that the intoxication and withdrawal profiles of drugs that are abused at high frequencies by mentally ill people, generally produce psychiatric symptoms in otherwise healthy subjects, and worsen or add to pre-existing psychiatric symptoms in people with mental illness. The association between drug use (including illicit and legal substances) and worse clinical trajectories of mental illness has been conclusively demonstrated and replicated across the full array of measurable outcomes, including rates of suicide, risk of homelessness and criminal incarceration, premature medical illness and mortality, risk of accidental injuries, need for psychiatric hospitalizations, and financial destitution. Well controlled, objective measurement studies conducted in human subjects with and without mental illness have never conclusively demonstrated *differential* benefits of commonly abused drugs (including nicotine) in mentally ill vs. heathy brains to a level that indicates a special medicinal utility of a given drug that is unique to any mental illness.

Fact #2: Cessation of drug use in mentally ill people produces clinical improvement. The weight of the evidence is clear that cessation of chronic drug use including all those types used at high rates in mental illness (spanning nicotine, alcohol, cannabinoids, cocaine, methamphetamines, and opioids) is associated with improved clinical outcomes in terms of measures of medical and psychiatric morbidity and mortality, on par with improvements seen with the introduction of psychiatric medications.

Fact #3: Self-medication is more likely in mentally ill people who do not use drugs compared to patients with dual diagnosis. Patients with mental illness who actually do self-medicate most consistently and effectively, with drugs that have been objectively proven to reduce mental illness symptoms (e.g., lithium, fluoxetine, and aripiprazole), are actually *less likely* to have comorbid addictions. Conversely, patients with both mental illness and addictions are *least* likely to self-medicate with drugs that are actually objectively measurable to medicate psychiatric symptoms.

Fact #4: Effectively treating psychiatric symptoms does not treat substance disorders. Successful reduction of psychiatric symptoms with psychiatric medications generally does not produce an impact on co-occurring drug use behavior, especially when that behavior is not being recognized and treated as a disorder.

Fact #5: Differential drug types do not naturally segregate among patients according to different types of psychiatric illnesses. In contradiction to the self-medication view that the unique psychoactive profile of one type of drug should co-segregate with a particular mental illness (and its particular target symptom set), mental illnesses of different types generally produce increased rates of drug abuse involving many drugs, including all of the same ones that are abused at high rates in the general population. In general, increased severity of mental illness and certain pervasive features of mental illness (e.g., impulsivity), that are not unique to any one type of mental illness, are the key predictors of substance use risk, and this risk is pervasive across different types of addictive drugs.

Moving forward form Fact #5, which begins to consider epidemiological data in terms of considering the causes of dual diagnosis, we now turn to the related issue of understanding the depth and scope of the dual diagnosis phenomena in the general population, and how this information should inform our approaches to treatment within and across behavioral health clinics.

Epidemiology of Substance Use Disorders in Mental Illness

A key question is this: For people seeking behavioral health care of some kind, what proportion of patients have current, or history of, both mental illness and a substance use disorder? The answer is, if you include all the major forms of mental illness and all the major addictions, including to nicotine: *the majority.* The majority of patients with significant mental illness, seeking treatment in a mental health treatment venue, also have a past or current substance use disorder(s) *of some kind or combination*, and the majority of patients needing help with addiction, and seeking treatment in an addiction treatment venue, also have mental illness(s), *of some kind or combination*. A bird's eye view of this public health challenge for people with moderate to severe levels of illness can be represented as a simple Venn diagram as in **Figure 2.1A**, where roughly 50–60 percent of patients who need professional treatment are actually 'dual diagnosis' patients. That is, they have one or more forms of mental illness with one or more types of addiction (note that this book uses dual diagnosis to mean any combination of mental illness and addiction(s) in the same patient). In contrast, much smaller fractions of the whole, roughly 20–25 percent, have only mental illness without addiction, or a substance use disorder without mental illness. Unfortunately, this clinical reality stands in contrast to how our behavioral health system has long been arrayed as two big siloes that inaccurately assume that mentally ill vs. addicted people are two different and largely unrelated clinical populations (**Figure 2.1B**).

As previously mentioned, it is vital to understand that the epidemiological overlap between mental illness and substance use disorders is not only massive, but, as a first rule of thumb, it is also pervasive across different categories of mental illness, and different types of drug use. This means that if you select a subpopulation enriched with any one type of mental illness, say PTSD, the odds of finding addictions to nicotine, or alcohol, or opioids, or other illicit drugs in that sample will *all* be elevated compared to the general population. If you select out a subpopulation of people with nicotine addiction, you will find a much greater likely hood of encountering not just PTSD, but schizophrenia, bipolar disorder, personality disorders, in that same population, etc., than you would in the general population. In general, overall illness severity (or multiplicity of diagnoses) in the mental illness domain predicts (or goes along with) greater severity and/or multiplicity of diagnoses in the addiction domain, and *vice versa*.

These prevailing aspects of the dual diagnosis epidemiology operate fairly independently from, but simultaneous with, the long-recognized observations that differential forms of mental illness do occur at differential frequencies in the general population, and similarly, that differential drug addictions occur at differential frequencies as well. So for example, nicotine addiction, by far the most common addiction, occurring in about 20 percent of the general population, is about three times more common than alcohol addiction (~7 percent) in the general population. Similarly, in a given mental illness, let's pick major depression for example, where rates of nicotine addiction are substantially elevated (about 2-fold above the general population), rates of alcohol addiction are also quite considerably elevated, say 2–3-fold, but still occurring less frequently than nicotine addiction. So, even as multiple types of substance use disorders are elevated in the context of major depression, these elevations happen in a way that tends to preserve the relative proportions of those addictions (with respect to each other) found in the general population. The same is generally true across the mental illness spectrum: The frequencies of addiction are elevated 2–8 times above that found in the general population, while at the same time, regardless of mental illness type, nicotine tends to be the most common, followed secondly by alcohol, followed thirdly by marijuana and opioids, and fourthly by other illicit drugs.

A second rule of thumb, that goes along fairly well with the epidemiological trend that likelihood of having one or more addiction is greater with greater mental illness severity, is that the frequency of a given type of mental illness in the general population, tends to be inversely related to the degree of vulnerability to addiction that the particular mental illness seems to entail. That is to say, the more severe forms of major mental illness, which thankfully, are rarer than the milder, less debilitating forms, tend to show greater addiction vulnerability. So, severe forms of mental illness, which tend to be identified in patients with schizophrenia, schizoaffective disorder, bipolar disorder, and severe forms of antisocial and borderline personality, are very highly comorbid with substance use disorders, and are among the more rare varieties of mental illness (e.g., each occurring in about 1 percent of the population). In these types of mental illness,

SUD rates can occur at rates 4–8 times that found in the general population across all the addictive drug types. Then, the more moderate forms of mental illness, typified by the PTSD spectrum (and softer forms of cluster A and B personality disorders), which are several times more common than schizophrenia (~ 5 percent of the population), also have elevated rates of various addictions (e.g., 3–6 times the rates found in the general population) but not *as elevated* as in the most severe mental illnesses. Then in the lower third tier of MI severity, we tend to encounter the more garden variety unipolar (major) depressions, anxiety spectrum and adjustment disorders (e.g., mild PTSD), that are by far the most common forms of mental illness (e.g., lifetime prevalence of up to 20 percent). These disorders still have their elevated risk rates of co-morbid addiction involving the usual suspects (nicotine, alcohol, opioids, marijuana, and stimulants), but happening at elevated rates that are only a relatively 'mild' (2–3 times) that found in the general population.

There are several important implications of these epidemiological realities. First, is the inescapability of encountering addictions in mentally ill people, even when mental health professionals (or treatment systems) might hope to avoid substance using patients, by limiting their work to treating certain forms of mental illness. Whether one treats a small population of patients with schizophrenia (80–90 percent of whom are likely to have an addiction), or a larger population of patients with depression (50 percent of whom will have an addiction)—either way, one will be confronted with a great deal of addiction. Second, there is the inescapabilty of frequently encountering multiple types of addiction within a given diagnostic population (or even within a given patient). One cannot hope to frequently encounter just one type of addiction (e.g., perhaps one they are most familiar with), just because they are specializing in treating one type of mental illness. In all the major mental illnesses where rates of nicotine addiction are elevated, so too are rates of alcoholism, opioid, cannabis, cocaine, and methamphetamine addictions. This reality is likely to be a major driving force for why multiple drug addictions also frequently occur together in the same patients (e.g., nicotine with alcohol; alcohol with cocaine; opioids with nicotine, etc.). Like a particularly massive celestial object that can pull not just one but many smaller bodies into its orbit because of its powerful gravitational pull, mental illness tends to collect multiple addictions in its orbit, thus bringing those addictions together, actually *coalescing them* in the same population, and often in the same patients. These forces create what is known in epidemiological circles as Berkson's bias: where if you select a subpopulation of people to study who all have one type of disease, that population will also inevitably be enriched with other diseases and disorders at rates above that found in the general population. Following through with the astrophysics analogy of Berkson's bias in understanding the epidemiology of dual diagnosis, we can observe that the more massive the celestial object is (i.e., the greater the severity of the mental illness), the more capable it is of attracting other secondary objects (e.g., addictions) into its orbit, and the larger (more severe) those secondary objects might also be.

The bottom line here is that addictions (of all kinds) are totally hyper-concentrated in mental illness. This means that the major portion of all the premature medical illness, injury, and death that is happening as a result of addictions, is happening primarily in mentally ill people. If we connect the dots of this reality with the additional fact that addictions collectively represent the leading root cause of premature illness, injury, and death for the whole, *general population*, then it becomes clear that addictions *in mental illness* is the leading source of disability, illness, and death for all of us—for our entire population!! Yes, you read that right: the comorbidity of mental illness and addiction is by far the number one public health problem we face (and probably the biggest driver of unnecessary/preventable medical costs), and yet our health care system is totally unprepared and ill-designed to deal with this reality, *because we do not adequately diagnose and treat addictions where they most commonly occur with their greatest ferocity—in the context of mental illness.*

Both the lay person and the medical professional might take pause here and say:

> Wait a minute! This is an outrageous and unreasonable claim! Everybody knows that the major types of disease in the general population, the big killers, are *medical* in nature, not psychiatric or behavioral—like cancer, heart disease, strokes, lung disease, infection, and dementia.

A medical school graduate can easily have this view, if he does not take into account the question of what other disease process most commonly led to, or caused the cancer, the heart diseases, the stroke, the chronic lung disease, the infection or the dementia? The answer is addiction, which most often occurs (and is untreated) in mental illness. To illustrate this relatively under-appreciated dynamic further, let's look at the situation with nicotine addiction. Nicotine addiction all by itself, is by far the #1 root cause of medical illness and death in the U.S. general population. Its disease footprint is so big on a public health scale that in the U.S., about half the population who die before the mean life expectancy, die because of nicotine addiction. This morbidity and mortality is bigger than that caused by any one of the separate categories of cancer, or coronary artery disease, or chronic lung disease, because nicotine addiction is the major preventable cause of all of these. Thus nicotine addiction is not only the major cause or contributing factor of many types of cancer beyond lung cancer, it is the root cause of about half of all cancer deaths. It is startling to put this fact together with the epidemiological reality that half or more of all people with nicotine addiction in the U.S. have a mental illness of some kind, which is true for only 10–15 percent of the general population. This means that the great weight of illness and death (and preventable medical expenditures on disease that result from untreated nicotine addiction) happens dispropor-tionately, and to a very great extent, in mentally ill people. In mental illnesses, particularly for those like schizophrenia, where addiction to nicotine is extremely prevalent, the carnage related to these facts has become quite clear. In schizophrenia, nicotine addiction on average produces decades of years of life lost per person. In schizophrenia, nicotine addiction is not only the leading cause of early death, it is the cause of death for most people. To a less severe but still significant degree, this same carnage is happening across the entire spectrum of much more common forms of major mental illness.

Certainly, we should not limit this discussion to nicotine, since this is not the only drug used at excessively high rates in mental illness, even though most readers will agree, nicotine alone goes very far in making the point. But to ram it home, let's consider alcohol and opioids as well. In considering alcohol addiction, again we acknowledge that it is the norm for this disorder to occur in people with some form of comorbid mental illness, and for it to occur in mentally ill people at rates that are 2–4 times that in the general population. Now consider the public health destruction due to alcohol addiction: Heavy/chronic alcohol use is a causal factor in about one third to half of all cases of suicide, homicide, assaults, domestic violence, injuries, and deaths by falls, drownings, fires, motor vehicle accidents, liver failure, pancreatitis, gastro-intestinal bleeds, and traumatic brain injuries . . . just for starters. Or let's take opioid addiction, again which in the first decade of the twenty-first century had risen to epidemic proportions. Again, as with nicotine and alcohol, opioid addiction, including its most common prescription drug variety, has most intensively impacted mentally ill people. In a phenomenon adeptly termed 'Adverse Selection', doctors unaware of the elevated risk of addictions in mental illness (and in people with non-opioid addictions), have shown the unfortunate tendency to specifically select mentally ill/addicted patients as being the most likely recipients of their most dangerous opioid prescribing practices. In turn, overdoses on prescription drugs have become a major cause of injury and death in mentally ill people, while on a general population scale, it has eclipsed suicide, homicide and car accidents as a leading cause of early death. Furthermore, all this still does not include the wide range of infectious diseases including HIV and hepatitis B and C, bacterial endocarditis, etc., which together (and they often can happen together) attack the brain, heart, lungs, liver, and immune system, producing other secondary cancers and infections, and multi-organ failure.

All this general medical morbidity and mortality is happening *predominantly* in, and as a result of, mental illness comorbidity with addiction. Yet all of us will bear the unsustainable *medical* expenses, human and moral costs of this, until we get serious about treating addiction at the heart of where it occurs—and in an integrated way—in the context of mental illness. In the next section of this chapter, we describe the brain basis for the tight causal connection between mental illness and addiction. In this new field of psychiatric neuroscience focused on explaining why dual diagnosis happens, we are beginning to see how mental illness is a biological vulnerability state for addiction, not as a matter of choice, but as an inevitable result of mammalian brain design and development. This science then translates to compel us to understand that addiction and mental illness, in many cases, actually represents one state of brain illness with two manifestations, rather than being two distinct brain illness that just happen to overlap.

Neuroscience of Addiction Vulnerability in Mental Illness

As we have now considered 'self-medication' in some depth, if it is an inadequate, and possibly even a clinically harmful explanation for substance disorder comorbidity in mental illness, then what is our alternative? How do we explain why so many mentally ill people use drugs so much? Our initial approach to this question, started with realizing that the conceptual and empirical problems inherent to the self-medication hypothesis could be easily avoided if we just look at substance use in mental illness, not as 'taking medicine' but as quite the opposite, as a disorder, a disease process, just like the way we view it in relatively mentally healthy people—*as a disorder called addiction.* And, as we have already reviewed, the vast weight of the empirical literature largely supports this view. If the core disease process we are thinking about in addiction is one where the brain acquires compulsive drug-seeking and use despite objectively observable adverse consequences, it is logical (and fairly well validated empirically) that already mentally ill people might meet this disease definition even more readily than mentally healthy people (e.g., because the adverse consequences of drug use are often even more dire for them, than for someone with a healthy brain). But, if compulsive drug use is even more of a problem for mentally ill people than it is for mentally healthy people, then why do they do it even more frequently and with heavier patterns? Answering this is where the disease concept of addiction is so important. They do it *not* because there is a sound logic to it, or because it is good in some way. They do it because it is a disease that drives compulsive behavior. It is pathological, counterproductive, and unhealthy. It *is a disease.* And the thing is, mentally ill brains acquire it, are even more vulnerable to it as *a disease process* than are otherwise healthy brains. Sure, healthy brains can get addiction too, but mentally ill brains are 2–8 times more likely to get it!

It is in the same way that we can and should understand the disease comorbidity of dual diagnosis that we already routinely understand the confluence of many other medical diseases. For example, consider how we understand the relationship between HIV and AIDS-related infections. When we see a lot of tuberculosis in patients with HIV, we don't say: *"HEY! All these patients with HIV, they must be self-medicating with TB bacteria! Gosh I wonder if somehow acquiring TB makes HIV feel better to have, or if it's some kind of coping skill?"* Instead, what the immunologists and infectious disease experts initially understood (and what we have all readily accepted) is that *both* HIV and Tuberculosis are diseases, and that while anyone could contract TB (if exposed to the right amount of bacteria), a person with HIV is many times more likely to get it, *because they are biologically predisposed, not because they are making a choice to get TB.* Thus at the heart of our understanding of why HIV patients become more susceptible to TB, is our understanding of how the biology of

HIV infection introduces a mechanical/biophysical/pathological vulnerability to TB infection.

So, as paralleled by the example of how one biomedical disease (e.g., HIV) predisposes to another (e.g., TB) we can do research that explores how mental illness introduces a mechanical/biophysical/pathological vulnerability to addiction. A major challenge to this scientific exploration, however, and one that has probably delayed its maturation, is that the causal connection between mental illness and addiction, which is so obviously a major clinical issue, cannot be readily demonstrated or proven on a clinical level using *human subjects*. It is certainly the case that human-based clinical and epidemiological research has established a clear *association* between mental illness and substance use disorders, and, that substance use (intoxication or withdrawal) can at least temporarily produce or worsen a wide range of psychiatric symptoms. But this evidence does not directly establish, demonstrate, or prove a causal connection *from mental illness to addiction*. In order to most directly show this causality, where mental illness causes addiction vulnerability, an experiment would have to be designed and conducted as follows:

Dual Diagnosis Neuroscience Experiment #1:

> A group of drug naïve healthy subjects are compared to another well-matched group of drug (and treatment) naïve mentally ill subjects, preferably during adolescence or young adulthood (when addictions usually start), in their propensity to acquire addictive disease. Both groups are deliberately given access to, and encouraged to self-administer repeated doses of a highly addictive drug, and the experimental result is to see which group most strongly acquires addiction (which we already know to be an incredibly destructive and life-threatening illness).

Of course in a morally centered, ethically bounded, non-totalitarian society, like we want our own to be, such a study using human subjects cannot occur. On the other hand, it is far more acceptable to our Institutional Review Boards (that evaluate and approve the ethical standards of our medical science), to test the hypothesis that acute intoxication produces non-permanent mental illness like effects, or, even more favorably, therapeutic (e.g., self-medication) effects. Hence, within much of the dual diagnosis scientific literature, which is mostly composed of clinical research, our pursuit of various hypotheses to explain dual diagnosis has largely been ethically constrained to avoid the key causal question of how might mental illness cause, accelerate, or worsen addiction vulnerability.

So now, it becomes clear that understanding causality behind dual diagnosis is actually an important translational scientific domain, where animal modeling is crucial to helping us understand how psychiatric illness relates to addiction illness, complimenting, and filling the gaps of human research. Animal models are not only the only ethical way we can prospectively conduct Dual Diagnosis

Experiment #1, they also can give us unique experimental control (pretty much impossible with human samples) of what drugs we want the subjects to be exposed to, and for how long; what sort of quantifiable objective measures (behaviors) we want to look at to demonstrate addiction vulnerability and severity; and what types or forms of mental illness we want to compare to the healthy subjects. The experimental ability we have to reliably induce experimental forms ('models') of mental illness in laboratory rats for example, is quite important because this circumvents the serious problem we have in prospectively studying mental illnesses in human populations (e.g., like schizophrenia), where only about 1 percent of the population will get the disease, and it is not at all certain who will get it by adulthood. With a reliable animal model of a mental illness you can 'recruit' exactly as many mental ill subjects you need with near 100 percent certainty of which groups actually have the illness. Further, because you have experimental knowledge of what the mental illness symptoms of the animal model are generally like, *it is very straightforward to not only see how the mental illness causes addiction vulnerability, but also, potentially in the same animals, to measure how the acute or chronic drug use can modulate or worsen the mental illness symptoms.* Finally, we'd also like to use animal models to look at disease anatomy and mechanisms in the brain in ways that are not ethically possible in humans.

Although human research had not been conducted to prove the causal link from mental illness to addiction, *there was by the year 2000 a wealth of research from the segregated mental health and addiction research fields that indicated the plausibility of shared anatomy and mechanisms, where brain abnormalities present in mental illness could impact the actions of reinforcing drugs, and by extension, the onset, and severity of addictive disease.* The initial work looking at how mental illness and addiction neuroscience could be integrated to understand how mental illness may cause addiction vulnerability, focused on the prototypical dual diagnosis disorder of schizophrenia (Chambers et al., 2001). This effort in neuroscience-based theory building was subsequently elaborated on and supported by a series of animal studies, allowing us to piece together an anatomical, neurodevelopmental and mechanistic framework for the pathogenesis of dual diagnosis disorders based on the neuroanatomy illustrated in **Figure 2.2**.

The mammalian brain can be understood as being organized, in simple terms, like a computer, where information flows through three main stages, from 1) input systems to; 2) central processing unit to; 3) output systems. These three stages are elaborated in greater detail as follows:

1. **Input:** Regions involved in storing and processing current and past sensory input, experience (memory), and homeostatic information (body systems monitoring) including the hippocampus, amygdala (AMY), hypothalamus, and sensory cortices, etc., convey information to;
2. **CPU:** The brain's 'central processing unit', that is, the prefrontal-cortical (PFC)/ventral striatal/thalamocortical loop system (note the ventral

striatum is also known as the nucleus accumbens (NAC)), where decision-making and motivational computations are performed, which then convey information to; and

3. **Output**: The motor output system (e.g., dorsal striatum, motor cortex/ pyramidal tracts, peripheral muscles etc.), which enact behavior.

At the heart of this circuitry, highlighted in the 'normal' adult condition in **Figure 2.2**, where the higher order 'limbic' input stations (AMY and ventral hippocampus (VHIP)) interface with the central processing stations (PFC/NAC assembly) we can begin to understand how *the primary circuits involved in mental illness are directly connected and overlapping with those involved in addiction*.

As depicted in **Figures 2.3A and 2.3B**, the general neurocircuit pathology that happens in mental illness is a 'neurodevelopmental set-up', where limbic structures within the temporal lobe of the brain, including the VHIP and AMY may be primarily disordered. That is, their structure and function do not develop completely normally, in often quite subtle but functionally (psychiatrically) detectable ways. Thus, some complex combination of often multiple genetic and/or environmental (experiential) etiological factors operate together, from prenatal life up to adolescence, to alter the maturation of temporal-limbic (hippocampus/AMY) networks (**Figure 2.3A**).

Then, as the brain grows through adolescence to early adulthood, its primary neurodevelopmental task is centered on the maturation of the PFC. The PFC must not only refine its internal wiring, but its long-track connectivity with both temporal-limbic circuits (VHIP and AMY), and subcortical motivational circuits (NAC) must undergo structural revision. In this maturational process, we see a host of changes centered in the PFC, including, but not limited to, synaptic pruning of principal pyramidal neurons (with grey matter thinning), refinement and structural fortification of long track fibers (with some white matter thickening), and numerous changes to excitatory (e.g., glutamate), inhibitory (e.g., GABA), and modulatory (e.g., dopamine) transmitter systems. Together, these changes normally allow the PFC to take on an a wide scope of 'executive' functional capabilities, spanning abstract thought, multi-tasking, decision-making, behavioral inhibition, emotional regulation, motor planning, insight awareness, social awareness, and other functions.

Appropriate PFC maturation depends not only on the environmental experiences in childhood and adolescence (neural network architectures are designed to adapt physically and functionally based on experiential input), but also on the structural integrity of temporal-limbic systems (VHIP and AMY) that directly project to the PFC. Thus, in adolescence, the key decision-making, behavioral inhibition, and planning part of the brain (PFC) is *structurally and functionally* maturing in direct connection with, *and as informed by, the inputs of* circuits that govern the contextual memory (VHIP) and emotional systems (AMY) of the brain. So then, if the VHIP or AMY, or both, are already not functioning normally before adolescence, then neurodevelopment the PFC itself becomes impaired, or let us say, is 'derailed' in some way, as adolescence progresses.

Now, with the PFC not developing and functioning normally, sometimes due to environmental and genetic factors that directly alter its maturation, on top of problems arising secondarily from abnormal AMY and VHIP development (**Figure 2.3B**), the overall difference between the mental health status of the young individual, and the population norm, becomes less subtle, clinically detectible, and classifiable. The individual begins to show a greater severity and wider range of thought and impulse control, cognitive, emotional, and/or social performance problems. That is to say, he/she begins showing features of one or more of a combination of adult mental illnesses (consistent with schizophrenia, bipolar disorder, depression, PTSD, and/or personality disorders).

So, here we arrive at the core of the problem in the pathophysiology of dual diagnosis: All of the major brain regions primarily disordered (in various ways) in the context of major mental illness, that is, the PFC, the VHIP, and the AMY—*project directly into the NAC, which is the primary brain site of motivational control for the individual, and a primary site where the pathophysiology of addiction takes place.* This is the crux of the matter: The brain is anatomically designed and hard wired to funnel and integrate information about prior experiences and current circumstances, current and past emotions, and planning narratives (e.g., all from the VHIP, AMY, and PFC) into the NAC (the motivational center of the brain) so that the NAC can most adaptively order, direct, inhibit, select, sculpt, and acquire new behavioral programs, that are directly executed by the motor circuits of the brain. In other words, the fundamental design features of the mammalian brain dictate that the neurocircuitry of mental illness is inseparable from, and is in fact, integral to the circuits of addictive disease. This fact leads naturally to the prediction that in the context of mental illness, the diseases process of addiction happens in a different way, or with a different intensity, than in a healthy brain. So to explore this prediction, we turn our attention to addiction biology.

In terms of the pathology of addiction (**Figure 2.3C**), we know that all the major addictive drugs, including nicotine, cocaine, alcohol, opioids, amphetamines, and cannabinoids, all have at least one key brain effect in common: They cause release of the neurotransmitter dopamine (DA) into the NAC. Now because all these drugs actually have very different (and in some ways even opposing) psychoactive-intoxication profiles, this drug-induced release of DA into the NAC must somehow be encoding something related more to their shared addictive effects, rather than their diverse intoxicating effects. And this is born out of basic research that is trying to characterize what DA is doing naturally in the NAC. DA levels generally increase transiently in the NAC in response to a whole range of normal stimuli or experiences, involving natural rewards such as food, sex, winning games, etc. But, more than that, DA is also released into the NAC in response to novel or surprising events, and aversive or stressful events. So, with all this, DA is best understood not as encoding a specific feeling (e.g., of pleasure, or a specific quality of hedonic intoxication as it is commonly misunderstood as doing), but instead, as helping to orient and facilitate the responsivity of the motivational system (centered in the NAC) to stimuli or contexts that should drive the flow, and sequencing of motor programs in real time, for example on a moment to moment basis, in response to those stimuli or contexts. But that is not all. DA is also a learning signal and facilitator. *DA release happening in the NAC over a longer period of time in response to repeated exposures to different stimuli and contexts, actually effects the wiring and internal connectivity of the neurons in the NAC.* This is a very physical change and is measureable in several different ways: DA release in the NAC changes the activation of NAC neurons, the intracellular machinery of NAC neurons, even the shapes of NAC neurons and the ways they are connected to, or respond to other neurons. *Specifically, DA changes the way NAC neurons respond to inputs from the PFC/VHIP/AMY, which changes how collections of NAC neurons represent motivational information.* These changes in turn alter the way NAC neurons work together to drive the flow, selection, ordering and prioritization of behavioral output programs in downstream motor circuits.

So in addiction, what we have, essentially, *is a pathological growth of the selection and execution of certain motor programs,* specifically those that enact drug-seeking, acquisition, and use. This growth is kind of like a cancer in the sense that as it grows, it robs and destroys normal tissue function around it. But in addiction, what's actually growing is not a tissue mass, rather, it is the wanting, planning, and behavioral programs (actions) devoted to finding and using the drug—all at the expense of motivations and behaviors that normally make up the healthy motivated–behavioral repertoire (like work, taking care of children, etc.).

When we understand that all this wanting, planning, and behavioral action sequencing is actually represented and determined in large part by neuronal firing patterns across NAC neurons, it is easy to begin to understand addiction as a '*neuroinformatic tumor*', where the NAC neuronal network, over time, increasingly expresses firing patterns that sub-serve drug motivation and use, while the firing patterns that represent healthy motivations are suppressed or have a harder time being generated. Of course, as previously mentioned, DA is a key neurotransmitter that operates naturally and normally in the NAC to facilitate plasticity (adaptive changes) in 1) neural network firing patterns, 2) inter-neuronal connectivity, and 3) motivation itself. Keeping in mind that items 1, 2, and 3 in the previous sentence are all pretty much inseparable manifestations of the same thing, we can understand DA as a mediator of motivational learning, behavioral change, and essentially, habit formation within the NAC and its partnering motor structures (dorsal striatum). So, there are all kinds of naturally occurring events, stimuli, and contexts that we are motivationally responding to that through the actions of DA in the NAC and neostriatum, drive short-term and more permanent changes in our behavioral repertoires. The problem with addictive drugs is that they pharmacologically drive a relatively powerful, and quite reliable DA release in the NAC that is closely paired in real time with the action of drug-taking, and whatever other stimuli or experiences that go with it. So now, the very behaviors that got the drug in the brain, end up (via the drug's actions) producing a DA release in the NAC, that causes a change in those NAC neural networks, so that they are now more likely, (*next time, or under similar circumstances*) to drive the same drug-taking behavior again!

So, it happens just like what has adeptly been characterized as a vicious cycle, but in an incremental and progressive way, where the growth of the disease seems to gather momentum over time, worsening, and becoming ever more behaviorally automatic, involuntary, and stamped into habit formation, with repeated doses. More drug-seeking and drug-taking behviors result in even more codes for drug-seeking and drug-taking, to the point where it is compulsive and destructive; to the point where healthy decision-making and the exercise of free will are all seriously degraded.

An important thing to keep in mind, is that this whole disease process *is not voluntary, and is not a choice made by the individual.* The disease—by definition—once underway, happens regardless of the choices and behaviors that the individual *wishes they could make*, and largely despite the damage that the addiction is producing. Often misunderstood as a person voluntarily making bad choices, addiction is actually a brain disease that progressively destroys a person's ability to enact better choices. The question is, how fast, or how many doses of the drug does it take for the individual to become addicted?

In addressing this question of addiction vulnerability, we surmised that a key variable, or rather, neurobiological context, that could determine the rate of acquisition, or severity of addiction, would be the integrity of the connectivity of PFC/VHIP/AMY inputs into the NAC. In other words, we hypothesized that if those connections were not structurally normal, and/or were few in number, and/or not relaying information normally to the NAC (i.e., *in mental illness*), then DA release into the NAC, produced by an addictive drug, would have an *abnormal* reinforcing–motivational effect, to speed up or worsen the acquisition of addictive disease (**Figure 2.3D**).

This new integrated theory of addiction vulnerability in mental illness (sometimes called primary addiction hypothesis) gave us two major advantages: 1) it does not rely on the self-medication dogma (or introduce its conceptual or empirical flaws) to explain how mental illness produces addiction vulnerability; and 2) it is totally and directly testable in the animal model! So, in 2001, we did this experiment (i.e., we executed *Dual Diagnosis Experiment #1*) with the use of a neurodevelopmental animal model of schizophrenia that also allowed us to set up a mental illness and neurocircuit condition, as illustrated in **Figure 2.3B**. First, we 'seeded' mental illness in 7-day-old rat pups, by injecting a tiny amount of neurotoxin into their VHIP. As first characterized by Barbara Lipska, George Jaskiw, and Daniel Weinberger at the NIMH in 1993, this neonatal ventral hippocampal lesion (NVHL) model produces an initial temporal-limbic circuit abnormality in the brains of baby rats that simulates the prenatal effects of genetic and environmental disease ingredients that are thought to underpin human schizophrenia. As these rats mature into adolescence they show a range of mental illness symptoms that map quite well onto human schizophrenia, including problems with working memory, social interaction, self-grooming, and sensory processing deficits. Then, as they go through adolescence they begin to show new onset of abnormal behavioral responses to environmental stimuli (mild stress or novelty) and pharmacological challenges (e.g., with amphetamine), which are all known to be associated with DA release in the NAC. These latter symptoms, because they come on during and after adolescence, and are reducible in the rat model with typical and atypical antipsychotics, are remarkably similar to the positive (e.g., psychotic) symptoms of schizophrenia (and symptoms of 'externalizing' disorders in general), which can also be generated in otherwise healthy people with repeated high doses of amphetamines. In phase with these symptoms, the NVHL model also encompasses a whole variety of brain changes, within, and down-stream from the VHIP, involving the PFC and NAC. These changes, especially those in the PFC, closely resemble those found in brains of people with schizophrenia (and other major mental illnesses), such as abnormal thinning of the cortex, increased neuronal packing densities, loss of dendritic branching around PFC neurons, and a host of other cellular and molecular changes involving systems that support excitatory (glutamatergic) and inhibitory (GABAergic) neurotransmission. On the functional level, PFC neurons and neuronal networks in the NVHL model become increasingly abnormal through adolescence in terms of how they respond to glutamatergic transmission. At the level of the NAC, which, by adulthood is receiving abnormal inputs form the VHIP and PFC in NVHL rats, neurons show abnormal responses to controlled artificial applications of DA, suggesting that the NAC neural network is indeed not able to interpret and respond to pharmacologically provoked DA signaling as a normal brain would.

In executing Dual Diagnosis Neuroscience Experiment #1, all we needed to do was allow young adult NVHL vs. healthy rats to acquire addictive drug use, and see which group acquired the more severe form of addiction. When we did this the first time, we gave the animals access to intravenous hits of cocaine (self-injected by the rats, and by bar pressing). Sure enough, NVHL rats acquired intravenous cocaine use more rapidly than healthy rats, while also developing patterns of intake that were more chaotic and impulsive, putting them at increased risk for lethal overdose compared to healthy rats. After all the rats had acquired cocaine use, we allowed the healthy (non-mentally ill) ones to catch up, so to speak, with the NVHLs in their overall amount of cumulative drug exposure. Then, we allowed all the rats to continue to pursue drug by bar pressing, even as the drug itself was no longer available to them. Now the mentally ill rats persisted in their drug seeking at levels greater than the healthy rats, indicating that the motivational changes that happen in addiction, had happened in a stronger way in the NVHLs. Finally, after both the mentally ill and healthy rats had stopped seeking cocaine (after several days of trying), and had extinguished their drug-seeking (bar pressing) to similar low levels, we caused relapse to drug-seeking in all the rats by giving them low versus high doses of cocaine. Here, again the NVHL rats relapsed to greater levels of bar pressing in an attempt to get cocaine.

So in sum, this initial experiment was the first to demonstrate that the very same brain circuit abnormality that produces a syndrome that captures the developmental, behavioral, pharmacological, and neurobiological features of schizophrenia, also produces an exacerbated course of addictive disease across all of the key stages of addiction (acquisition, maintenance, drug-seeking, and relapse). This result was very interesting in suggesting for the first time that the biology of mental illness and addiction vulnerability may at least under some circumstances be *one and the same*. But, here we only tested this new *integrated neurocircuit theory of dual diagnosis* with respect to the special cases of schizophrenia and cocaine. Certainly this was a great way to start this exploration, because schizophrenia is one of the more severe and frequently recognized dual diagnosis disorders, and cocaine is highly addicting. But as we have discussed earlier in this chapter, the clinical association between mental illness and addiction is much broader than just one mental illness or addictive drug type. Does the same phenomena we showed with NVHL rats, hold true for other addictive drug types and other forms of mental illness?

Answering this question brings us to Dual Diagnosis Neuroscience Experiment #2, which is actually more of a bundle of different, but thematically-related experiments.

Dual Diagnosis Neuroscience Experiment #2:

> Test the degree to which dual diagnosis vulnerability generalizes to different combinations of mental illness and addictions: A) examine if the NVHL-schizophrenia model produces addiction vulnerability to drugs other than cocaine; and B) whether different syndromes of mental illness other than the NVHL-schizophrenia model also produce some degree of addiction vulnerability.

Our own lab and others around the world had by 2012 conducted research consistent with Dual Diagnosis Neuroscience Experiment #2, and this research has shown that addiction vulnerability does generalize to different addictive drug types and different forms of mental illness. For example, it turns out that the NVHL model of schizophrenia causes rats to show addiction vulnerability not only to cocaine but also to nicotine and alcohol, which agrees exactly with our clinical knowledge: People with schizophrenia have much higher rates of addiction (compared to the general population) spanning several different addictive drug types, including nicotine, alcohol, and cocaine. Of note, this is one example of the phenomena of *multifinality* in the pathogenesis of dual diagnosis; one biological context (e.g., the NVHL model) sets the brain up for multiple psychiatric symptoms and even different types of drug addictions.

Again, an important clue to what may be going on in these quite complimentary sets of animal and human findings, is the observation that the link between the mental illness and the substance use disorder vulnerability, does not really seem to be specific to the particular psychoactive/intoxicating profiles of any one additive drug, but rather is general to the addictive properties of these drugs. In other words, since the intoxicating profiles of cocaine, nicotine, and alcohol are all quite different from one another, it is hard to argue that any one of those drug-specific properties could link *all these* drugs to schizophrenia. In contrast, what these drugs do have in common, that is, their shared *addictive* actions (which is not really biologically related to their diverse intoxicating actions), could more parsimoniously link them all to schizophrenia. As we have previously mentioned, however, the intoxicating–psychoactive properties of these different drugs have been variously proposed, according to the self-medication hypothesis, to therapeutically treat symptoms of mental illness. Oppositely, and more consistent with direct empirical evidence and anecdotal clinical observation (e.g., in emergency room settings), these drugs are variously observed to either have no specific beneficial effect in mental illness, or to worsen psychiatric syndromes. With respect to dual diagnosis research using the NVHL model, the findings are indeed consistent with the weight of the empirical clinical evidence, but not self-medication hypotheses, indicating that these drugs variously have no objectively detectible illness-specific beneficial effects, and/or they *worsen the mental illness syndrome*. For example, repeated cocaine exposure in NVHL rats, worsens the positive-like schizophrenia symptoms already present in the NVHL model, analogous to the way chronic cocaine use in people with vulnerability to psychosis (or with full blown schizophrenia) seem to get even more psychotic with more cocaine use. Or, as in recent well-controlled studies of human healthy vs. mentally ill subjects exposed to nicotine, NVHL rats show no differential cognitive benefits from nicotine intoxication compared to mentally healthy rats, while nicotine withdrawal exacerbates schizophrenia-like cognitive symptoms present in NVHL rats. In sum, in the NVHL model, we see that the mental illness generates addiction vulnerability to multiple addictive drug types in a way that does not seem to be specifically linked to their diverse psychoactive properties, whereas their various specific psychoactive effects are more readily linked with, or attributable to generating or exacerbating psychiatric symptoms.

So in a very clear way, animal modeling work following Dual Diagnosis Neuroscience Experiment #2A, that looks at different addictive drugs in one mental illness model, depicts how there is indeed a 'vicious cycle' between the mental illness and addiction where two concurrent, bidirectional, and mutually reinforcing processes are in play:

1.   Mental illness makes addiction to one of several drugs more likely. This causal link is general to multiple addictive drugs, but relatively independent from their unique intoxicating properties.

2. Becoming addicted, produces many intoxication–withdrawal cycles that generally worsen the underlying mental illness. *This causal link is more specific to the unique intoxicating properties of different addictive drugs.*

In this way, the animal modeling provides a fairly complete explanation for the causal linkage between mental illness and addiction, that is bidirectional and logically and empirically coherent (i.e., does not at all need or require a self-medication hypothesis). *Further, this neuroscience begins to shed light on a new way of looking at the tight relationship between mental illness and substance use disorders that demands we make services that can treat both sides of the comorbidity concurrently far more mainstream.*

In a similar vein, an accumulating body of studies that collectively follow Dual Diagnosis Neuroscience Experiment #2B, are also demonstrating that a quite large diversity of different forms of mental illness (i.e., as modeled by different forms and experimental causes of neuropsychiatric illness in a diverse array of animal models) commonly produce some degree of heightened addiction vulnerability. In essence, we are seeing that there is in the pathogenesis of dual diagnosis, an equifinality of many determinants for mental illness that all lead to the same general phenotype of addiction vulnerability. For example, we and others have observed that the olfactory bulbectomy procedure in rats, which produces a syndrome that models multiple features of major depression, also changes the way these rats respond to the motivational and motoric effects of cocaine. Similarly, rats with early developmental damage to the AMY (which generates adult mental illness symptoms like those found in bipolar disorders, or cluster B personality disorders), also show involuntary changes in the way they respond to cocaine, and other reinforcers, consistent with an impulsive, addiction-prone phenotype. Again, the common thread between these models and the NVHL syndrome also, is that in all models, temporal-limbic regions of the brain (i.e., VHIP and AMY) are in some way primarily deranged, which must inevitably produce some type of change in the function of prefrontal-cortical-ventral striatal circuits where motivation and addictions are primarily based (**Figures 2.2 and 2.3**). For this general dynamic to take place, it probably does not even matter that much what sort of initial disease causing factors were involved. A wide range of specific genetic determinants and their combinations, with or without exposure to the neurotoxic effects of childhood abuse, neglect, trauma, or attachment failure, may be in play. All of these classes of factors, which are also recognized to be the foundational ingredients of mental illness, are all known to be causally linked to abnormal development, structure and function of temporal-limbic circuits (which project heavily to the PFC and NAC). This produces the inescapable biological and clinical reality (because motivational circuit function and development depends so much on temporal-limbic circuits) that mental illness and addictions are intimately, physically linked, and in some respects are even unified disease processes. This brings us to the third major type of Dual Diagnosis Neuroscience experiment:

Dual Diagnosis Neuroscience Experiment #3:

> Use biological methods that can define and measure the brain disease processes of mental illness and addictions, to observe where and how these disease processes overlap, interact, and amplify one another.

This area of dual diagnosis research, which is still in its early stages, can build upon Dual Diagnosis Neuroscience Experiments #1 and #2, not only to help us understand mechanistically how mental illness causes addiction vulnerability (in dual diagnosis conditions), but to understand better what addictive disorders and mental illnesses are biological, even as separate entities. This research can then produce an array of new leads about novel illness markers, preventative strategies, and treatment targets that can eventually be implemented clinically to reduce the burden of mental illness and addiction, even as these disorders commonly present in a wide range of different comorbid combinations.

Thus far, mechanisms research focusing on the prototypical dual diagnosis combination of the NVHL-schizophrenia model and cocaine, has shown that the NVHL model even before drug exposure produces a functional and molecular impoverishment of the PFC, especially in regions that project to the NAC (ventral striatum) where motivational control is based, and where cocaine, nicotine, and alcohol all induce DA neurotransmitter release to orient motivation, and where these drugs (by changing local striatal neural network connectivity) change motivation itself. The striatal network and neural activation-altering effects of repeated cocaine exposures that happens in the healthy brain, happen also in the context of the mental illness model. *However, in the mental illness model, these chronic drug effects happen together with and on top of abnormalities in striatal network and functionality due to the neurodevelopmental mental illness itself. Together, these conditions end up producing an amplified, more severe version of not only addictive behavior but biological changes in the habit-forming dorsal striatal area of the brain that underpin the addicted behavior.* By analogy, if the addiction process can be viewed as a chain reaction, like a burning process that is sparked with repeated addictive drug exposure, and involves the 'consumption' of the unburned 'fuel' of normal striatal circuits (and normal motivations), the presence of mental illness operates biologically within those same striatal circuits, like adding oxygen to the striatal 'fuel', to make the 'fire' of addiction burn even more rapidly, aggressively, and energetically. Thus, in one particular experiment using the NVHL model and healthy animals exposed to different histories of cocaine (Chambers et al., 2010), a simple mathematical model was identified that could describe the addiction risk across all the animals. The severity of both the behavioral measure of the addicted phenotype and the level of dorsal striatal network activation (due to one hit of the addictive drug) were found to be a *multiplicative* product of PFC derangement due to the mental illness and the effects of chronic cocaine on trans-striatal activation. In simple algebra:

$$A = MI \times SU$$

Where A is a quantitative measure of addiction severity (measured on behavioral or biological levels); MI is mental illness severity quantified on the level of PFC network dysfunction; and SU is Substance Use effects quantified on the level of changes in trans-striatal activation due to drug history. In a separate study (Chambers et al., 2013), the NVHL model was found to produce a degradation of multiple gene expression in the PFC and NAC, but a pathological growth of gene expression in the dorsal striatum. In contrast, chronic cocaine exposure alone produces a pathological overgrowth of gene expression in both the NAC and the dorsal striatum. So given that *both* the mental illness model and the chronic effects of cocaine produce enduring pathological overgrowth of multiple gene expression in the habit forming *dorsal striatum*, we can begin to understand how these pathologies produces synergistic effects on striatal network function and the burned-in representations of pathological changes in motivated behavior that addiction represents.

Neuroscience of Dual Diagnosis: Future Research

The emerging frontier of integrated neuroscience research on dual diagnosis is expected to build on the empirical foundation, neuroanatomy, and theory outlined in this chapter. These lines of research will elaborate in greater detail the neuroanatomical substrates, neurodevelopmental events, and mechanisms that causally link mental illness and addiction, ultimately providing us with more effective, and parsimonious preventions and decisive treatments. Several of these avenues are briefly described here as areas that basic and clinical neuroscientists and clinicians working in the 2 × 4 Model clinic should stay abreast of to keep track of new advances:

- *Genetics and Neuroimaging:* Implementing these mainstay technologies of psychiatric research in the domain of dual diagnosis research has been gaining steady momentum and has already made important findings. For example, demonstrating the multifinality of dual diagnosis etiology, several genes have already been identified that are implicated in the pathogenesis of *both* mental illness and addiction risk. Also, neuroimaging has suggested the convergent interactive effects of mental illness, addiction risk, and toxicological effects of addictive drugs on the same brain circuits. While suggesting the artifice of our diagnostic schemes that try to separate mental illness and addictive phenotypes, these technologies may eventually be used to inform more comorbidity–combination specific treatment strategies.
- *Glutamatergics:* The key information processing and learning and memory transmitter system of the brain is also important to the function of circuits conjointly involved in mental illness and addiction (e.g., **Figures 2.2, 2.3**). The testing of existing and novel agents that directly or indirectly modulate the glutamatergic system at its many different points (e.g., as with N-Acetyl Cysteine) should continue to be a fruitful area for new advances in dual diagnosis treatment.

- *Adult Neurogenesis:* The death and rebirth (e.g., turnover) of new groups of neurons throughout the lifespan, especially in the hippocampus, is now widely recognized as a special form of plasticity implicated in the pathogenesis and treatment of both mental illness and drug addiction. New treatments that specifically enhance the timing and rate of phases of hippocampal neuronal turnover could parsimoniously facilitate recovery and resilience from mental disorders and several types of addictions.
- *Neuropeptide/Neurohormonal/Neuroregulators:* Beyond the important focus on the endogenous opioid system as an area of pharmacological development for both addiction and several domains of neuropsychiatric illness, other neuropeptide transmitter systems involved in basic homeostatic behavioral control and stress resilience are emerging as interesting candidate systems for dual diagnosis treatment. These include agents that modulate the hypothalamic–pituitary–adrenal (HPA) axis (e.g., corticotropin releasing factor analogues), and transmitters involved in appetite, and sleep regulation (e.g., hypocretin/orexin).
- *New Neuroplastics from Neuroimmunology:* It turns out that much of the cellular and signaling machinery that is critical to host defense in the body (traditionally recognized as the immune system), has a related but quite different role within the hyper-sterile and tightly controlled environment behind the wall of the blood–brain barrier of the central nervous system (CNS): Brain plasticity and response to environmental–experiential psychological challenges. Ongoing research in this area may yield new therapeutic targets or agents that can specifically up or down regulate neuroplastic changes needed in dual diagnosis recovery.
- *Attachment Neuroscience:* A wealth of new basic and clinical neuroscience data is beginning to illuminate how tightly the primary neurocircuitry of dual diagnosis (**Figure 2.2**) is functionally and anatomically overlapping with systems that control social motivation and attachment (and the neurogenic, neurohoromonal, and neuroimmunological systems listed above). The pathophysiology of several forms of mental illness along the trauma spectrum, that also confer addiction vulnerability, involve early forms of attachment disruption, chaos, and failure. In turn, many addicted and dual diagnosis patients seem especially vulnerable to forming pathological attachments to addictive drugs as if the drugs were abusive loved ones. This area of research is particularly exciting because it directly suggests the value of forming and maintaining therapeutic attachments (psychotherapies) in the course of addiction and dual diagnosis recovery, and the biological potential for medications and psychotherapies to work synergistically in some patients. New forms or approaches of psychotherapies for patients and families with dual diagnosis may be developed based on this neuroscience to promote recovery even trans-generationally.
- *Mechanical Interventions:* The term mechanical interventions is used here and elsewhere in this book to designate therapeutic tools that are biologically active in distinction to medications and psychotherapies (which

are also biologically active). Mechanical interventions may include rTMS, ECT, neural stimulators, surgically implanted prosthetic microchips, nanoparticles or biologics that may modulate **Figure 2.2** circuits to parsimoniously prevent or treat addiction and mental illness.

• *Animal Models*: A golden grail of pharmacological research in addiction psychiatry would be to identify effective preventative treatments that could be delivered to risk-stratified youth and young adults that could protect them 1) against addiction even with addictive drug exposure; and 2) the developmental trajectory of mental illness into young adulthood. Potentially such treatments could allow people to avoid the need for intensive psychiatric and addiction treatment in adulthood, much like braces in kids prevent dental disease in adulthood. Animal models of dual diagnosis disorders will be crucial to developing such golden-grail treatments, because they allow precise control and selection of mental illness models, therapeutic drug vs. addictive drug exposures, all at relatively low cost and on rapid developmental time scales (compared to humans).

• *Neural Network Models*: The design and operation of simulated, biologically realistic, programmable neural network models focused on in **Figure 2.2** anatomy holds great potential to understanding motivation as a biological and neurocomputational product of the brain that ultimately selects, sequences, and adapts behavior. This area of research may not only be important to developing new psychotherapeutic, pharmacological, and mechanical treatments for dual diagnosis disorders, but could be critical in unlocking the mysteries of what is required for developing autonomously motivated and behaving, decision-capable, and deep artificial intelligence machines.

Neuroscience of Dual Diagnosis: Chapter Summary and Clinical Implications

The biological and clinical reality we face in behavioral health is that the disease processes of addiction and mental illnesses have a very powerful tendency to gravitate together and coalesce both within individuals and across large clinical populations. This is not a mere co-incidence, or social condition, but is a physical reality and consequence of how our brains are designed; how memory, emotion, decision-making and motivational circuits are developmentally and functionally interactive, and are co-dependent in ultimately driving healthy vs. unhealthy behavioral programs. This is a physical and biomechanical reality that determines that on the whole, mentally ill people are involuntarily more vulnerable to suffering from more aggressive and severe forms of addictive disease compared to people without significant mental illness. The consequences of not fully recognizing this biological reality and failing to align our behavioral health professional training, treatment infrastructures, and health care reimbursement mechanisms to deal with it, have been devastating. The tremendous human, financial, and moral costs incurred by mass incarceration of the mentally ill, the totally ineffective 'war on drugs', the iatrogenic drug epidemic, and the unparalleled toll of illness and death due to untreated addictions itself, should compel us to translate the science outlined in this chapter into a major clinical paradigm shift. This shift should encompass a comprehensive integration of mental health and addiction training, expertise, clinical care, and research. The rest of this book describes the design and operation of the 2 × 4 Model clinic that accomplishes this goal within a given community, and how it may be replicated across a region or nation, to make a reliable, high standard of integrated addiction and mental health care more universally available.

Background References and Further Reading

Berg, S. A., and R. A. Chambers. 2008. "Accentuated behavioral sensitization to nicotine in the neonatal ventral hippocampal lesion model of schizophrenia." *Neuropharmacology 54* (8): 1201–1207.

Berg, S. A., C. L. Czachowski, and R. A. Chambers. 2011. "Alcohol seeking and consumption in the NVHL neurodevelopmental rat model of schizophrenia." *Behavioral Brain Research 218* (2): 346–349.

Berg, S. A., A. M. Sentir, R. L. Bell, E. A. Engleman, and R. A. Chambers. 2014. "Nicotine effects in adolescence and adulthood on cognition and alphabeta-nicotinic receptors in the neonatal ventral hippocampal lesion rat model of schizophrenia." *Psychopharmacology (Berl) 232* (10): 1681–1692. doi: 10.1007/s00213-014-3800-2.

Berg, S. A., A. M. Sentir, B. S. Cooley, E. A. Engleman, and R. A. Chambers. 2014. "Nicotine is more addictive, not more cognitively therapeutic in a neurodevelopmental model of schizophrenia produced by neonatal ventral hippocampal lesions." *Addiction Biology 19* (6): 1020–1031. doi: 10.1111/adb.12082.

Brady, A. M., S. E. McCallum, S. D. Glick, and P. O' Donnell. 2008. "Enhanced methamphetamine self-administration in a neurodevelopmental rat model of schizophrenia." *Pschopharmacology 200* (2): 205–215.

Brady, K. T., and R. Sinha. 2005. "Co-occurring mental and substance use disorders: The neurobiological effects of chronic stress." *American Journal of Psychiatry 162* (8): 1483–1493.

Brewer, J. A., and M. N. Potenza. 2008. "The neurobiology and genetics of impulse control disorders: relationships to drug addictions." *Biochemical Pharmacology 75* (1): 63–75. doi: 10.1016/j.bcp.2007.06.043.

Burkett, J. P., and L. J. Young. 2012. "The behavioral, anatomical and pharmacological parallels between social attachment, love and addiction." *Psychopharmacology (Berl) 224* (1): 1–26. doi: 10.1007/s00213-012-2794-x.

Burns, L. H., L. Annett, A. E. Kelley, B. J. Everitt, and T. W. Robbins. 1996. "Effects of lesions to amygdala, ventral subiculum, medial prefrontal cortex, and nucleus accumbens on the reaction to novelty: Implication for limbic–striatal interactions." *Behavioral Neuroscience 110* (1): 60–73.

Chambers, R. A. 2007. "Animal modeling and neurocircuitry of dual diagnosis." *Journal of Dual Diagnosis 3* (2): 19–29.

Chambers, R. A., R. M. Jones, S. Brown, and J. R. Taylor. 2005. "Natural reward related learning in rats with neonatal ventral hippocampal lesions and prior cocaine exposure." *Psychopharmacology 179* (2): 470–478.

Chambers, R. A., J. K. Krystal, and D. W. Self. 2001. "A neurobiological basis for substance abuse comorbidity in schizophrenia." *Biological Psychiatry 50* (2): 71–83.

Chambers, R. A., and M. N. Potenza. 2003. "Impulse control disorders." In *Encyclopedia of the Neurological Sciences*, edited by M. J. Aminoff and R. B. Daroff, (pp. 642–646). San Diego, CA: Academic Press.

Chambers, R. A., T. J. Sajdyk, S. K. Conroy, J. E. Lafuze, S. D. Fitz, and A. Shekhar. 2007. "Neonatal amygdala lesions: Co-occurring impact on social/fear-related behavior and cocaine sensitization in adult rats." *Behavioral Neuroscience 121* (6): 1316–1327.

Chambers, R. A., and D. W. Self. 2002. "Motivational responses to natural and drug rewards in rats with neonatal ventral hippocampal lesions: An animal model of dual diagnosis schizophrenia." *Neuropsychopharmacology 27* (6): 889–905.

Chambers, R. A., T. Sheehan, and J. R. Taylor. 2004. "Locomotor sensitization to cocaine in rats with olfactory bulbectomy." *Synapse 52* (3): 167–175.

Chambers, R. A., J. R. Taylor, and M. N. Potenza. 2003. "Developmental neurocircuitry of motivation in adolescence: A critical period of addiction vulnerability." *American Journal of Psychiatry 160*: 1041–1052.

Chambers, R. A. 2009. "A nicotine challenge to the self-medication hypothesis in a neurodevelopmental animal model of schizophreina." *Journal of Dual Diagnosis 5* (2): 139–148.

Chambers, R. A. 2013. "Adult hippocampal neurogenesis in the pathogenesis of addiction and dual diagnosis disorders." *Drug and Alcohol Dependence 130* (1–3): 1–12. doi: 10.1016/j.drugalcdep.2012.12.005S0376-8716(12)00481-4 [pii].

Chambers, R. A., J. N. McClintick, A. M. Sentir, S. A. Berg, M. Runyan, K. H. Choi, and H. J. Edenberg. 2013. "Cortical-striatal gene expression in neonatal hippocampal lesion (NVHL)-amplified cocaine sensitization." *Genes, Brain and Behavior 12* (5): 564–575. doi: 10.1111/gbb.12051.

Chambers, R. A., A. M. Sentir, S. K. Conroy, W. A. Truitt, and A. Shekhar. 2010. "Cortical-striatal integration of cocaine history and prefrontal dysfunction in animal modeling of dual diagnosis." *Biological Psychiatry 67* (8): 788–792. doi: S0006-3223(09)01083-X [pii]10.1016/j.biopsych.2009.09.006.

Chou, S. P., R. B. Goldstein, S. M. Smith, B. Huang, W. J. Ruan, H. Zhang, J. Jung, T. D. Saha, R. P. Pickering, and B. F. Grant. 2016. "The epidemiology of DSM-5 nicotine use disorder: Results from the National Epidemiologic Survey on alcohol and related conditions-III." *Journal of Clinical Psychiatry 77*(10): 1404–1412. doi: 10.4088/JCP.15m10114.

Cicchetti, D., and F. A. Rogosch. 1999. "Psychopathology as risk for adolescent substance use disorders: A developmental psychopatholgy perspective." *Journal of Clinical Child Psychology 28* (3): 355–365.

Cicchetti, D., and F. A. Rogosch. 1996. "Equifinality and multifinality in developmental psychopathology." *Development and Psychopathology 8* (4): 597–600.

Compton, W. M., Y. F. Thomas, F. S. Stinson, and B. F. Grant. 2007. "Prevalence, correlates, disability, and comorbidity of DSM-IV drug abuse and dependence in the United States: Results from the National Epidemiologic Survey on alcohol and related conditions." *Archives of General Psychiatry 64* (5): 566–76. doi: 64/5/566 [pii]10. 1001/archpsyc.64.5.566.

DeVito, E. E., S. A. Meda, R. Jiantonio, M. N. Potenza, J. H. Krystal, and G. D. Pearlson. 2013. "Neural correlates of impulsivity in healthy males and females with family histories of alcoholism." *Neuropsychopharmacology 38* (10): 1854–1863.

Dixon, L. 1999. "Dual diagnosis of substance abuse in schizophrenia: Prevalence and Impact on outcomes." *Schizophrenia Research 35* (Suppl 1): S93–100.

Enoch, M. A. 2011. "The role of early life stress as a predictor for alcohol and drug dependence." *Psychopharmacology 214* (1): 17–31.

Grant, B. F., D. S. Hasin, S. P. Chou, F. S. Stinson, and D. A. Dawson. 2004. "Nicotine dependence and psychiatric disorders in the United States: Results from the National Epidemiologic Survey on alcohol and related conditions." *Archives of General Psychiatry 61* (11): 1107–1115.

Grant, B. F., T. D. Saha, W. J. Ruan, R. B. Goldstein, S. P. Chou, J. Jung, H. Zhang, S. M. Smith, R. P. Pickering, B. Huang, and D. S. Hasin. 2016. "Epidemiology of DSM-5 drug use disorder: Results from the National Epidemiologic Survey on alcohol and related conditions-III." *JAMA Psychiatry 73* (1): 39–47. doi: 10.1001/jama psychiatry.2015.21322470680 [pii].

Hartz, S. M., C. N. Pato, H. Medeiros, P. Cavazos-Rehg, J. L. Sobell, J. A. Knowles, L. J. Bierut, M. T. Pato, and Consortium Genomic Psychiatry Cohort. 2014. "Comorbidity of severe psychotic disorders with measures of substance use." *JAMA Psychiatry 71* (3): 248–254.

Jeanblanc, J., K. Balguerie, F. Coune, R. Legastelois, V. Jeanblanc, and M. Naassila. 2015. "Light alcohol intake during adolescence induces alcohol addiction in a neuro-developmental model of schizophrenia." *Addiction Biology 20* (3): 490–499.

Kalivas, P. W., and C. O'Brien. 2008. "Drug addiction as a pathology of staged neuroplasticity." *Neuropsychopharmacology 33* (1): 166–180.

Kessler, R. C. 2004. "The epidemiology of dual diagnosis." *Biological Psychiatry 56* (10): 730–737.

Kosten, T. A., M. J. Miserendino, and P. Kehoe. 2000. "Enhanced acquisition of cocaine self-Administration in adult rats with neonatal isolation stress experience." *Brain Research 875* (1–2): 44–50.

Lembke, A. 2012. "Time to abandon the self-medication hypothesis in patients with psychiatric disorders." *American Journal of Drug and Alcohol Abuse 38* (6): 524–529. doi: 10.3109/00952990.2012.694532.

Lipska, B. K., G. E. Jaskiw, and D. R. Weinberger. 1993. "Postpubertal emergence of hyperresponsiveness to stress and to amphetamine after neonatal excitotoxic hippo-campal damage: A potential animal model of schizophrenia." *Neuropsychopharmacology 9* (1): 67–75.

McLellan, A. T., K. A. Druley, and J. E. Carson. 1978. "Evaluation of substance abuse problems in a psychiatric hospital." *Journal of Clinical Psychiatry 39* (5): 425–430.

McLellan, A. T., D. C. Lewis, C. P. O'Brien, and H. D. Kleber. 2000. "Drug dependence, a chronic medical illness: Implications for treatment, insurance, and outcomes evaluation." *Journal of the American Medical Association 284* (13): 1689–1695. doi: jsc00024 [pii].

Mills, K. L., A. L. Goddings, L. S. Clasen, J. N. Giedd, and S. J. Blakemore. 2014. "The developmental mismatch in structural brain maturation during adolescence." *Developmental Neuroscience 36* (3–4): 147–160. doi: 10.1159/000362328000362328 [pii].

Moffett, M. C., A. Vicentic, M. Kozel, P. Plotsky, D. D. Francis, and M. J. Kuhar. 2007. "Maternal separation alters drug intake patterns in adulthood in rats." *Biochemical Pharmacology 73* (3): 321–330. doi: 10.1016/j.bcp.2006.08.003.

Mokdad, A. H., J. S. Marks, J. S. Stroup, and J. L. Gerberding. 2004. "Actual causes of death in the United States, 2000." *Journal of the American Medical Association 291* (10): 1238–1245.

O'Donnell, P., J. Greene, N. Pabello, B. L. Lewis, and A. A. Grace. 1999. "Modulation of cell firing in the nucleus accumbens." *Annals of the New York Academy of Sciences* *877*: 157–175.

Prochaska, J. J., S. M. Hall, and T. A. Bero. 2008. "Tobacco use among individuals with schizophrenia: What role has the tobacco industry played?" *Schizophrenia Bulletin* *34* (3): 555–567.

Schiffer, B., B. W. Muller, N. Scherbaum, M. Forsting, J. Wiltfang, N. Leygraf, and E. R. Gizewski. 2010. "Impulsivity-related brain volume deficits in schizophrenia-addiction comorbidity." *Brain 133* (10): 3093–3103.

Self, D. W., and E. J. Nestler. 1998. "Relapse to drug-seeking: Neural and molecular mechanisms." *Drug and Alcohol Dependence 51*: 49–60.

Sullivan, M. D., and C. Q. Howe. 2013. "Opioid therapy for chronic pain in the United States: Promises and perils." *Pain 154*: S94–S100.

Tseng, K. Y., R. A. Chambers, and B. K. Lipska. 2009. "The neonatal ventral hippocampal lesion as a heuristic neurodevelopmental model of schizophrenia." *Behavioural Brain Research 204* (2): 295–305. doi: S0166-4328(08)00657-8 [pii]10.1016/j.bbr.2008.11.039.

Van Dam, N. T., K. Rando, M. N. Potenza, K. Tuit, and R. Sinha. 2014. "Childhood maltreatment, altered limbic neurobiology, and substance use relapse severity via trauma-specific reductions in limbic gray matter volume." *JAMA Psychiatry 71* (8): 917–925. doi: 10.1001/jamapsychiatry.2014.680.

Wolf, M. E., S. L. Dahlin, X. T. Hu, C. J. Xue, and K. White. 1995. "Effects of lesions of prefrontal cortex, amygdala, or fornix on behavioral sensitization to amphetamine: Comparison with N-Methyl-D-Aspartate antagonists." *Neuroscience 69* (2): 417–439.

3 The Illness Dimension

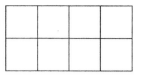

Integrating Equal Focus on Both Mental Illness and Addictions

The 2 × 4 Model clinic follows three fundamental design concepts that guide how the clinicians within the clinic practice and work together to approach and manage the various forms and symptoms of mental illness and substance use disorders (SUDs).

Fundamental Design Concept #1: Merge Mental Health and Addiction Treatment as Equally Important Missions

The first and perhaps most important foundational concept of the 2 × 4 Model design is that the clinic is *fully and overtly committed and capable* of treating mental illness and substance use disorders *with equal levels of prioritization*. It would be misleading to call a 2 × 4 Model clinic either 'a mental health clinic' or an 'addiction treatment program' because it actually cares about and performs both of these missions at the highest level, and, in an integrated way. A mental health clinic that tries to provide some but not most of the key components of addiction care, does not qualify as a 2 × 4 Model clinic because this set up gives more prioritization to mental health care, while short-changing the addiction service provision. Similarly, an addiction treatment service that provides a few mental health treatment measures, but not most that would be found in a standard mental health center, also does not qualify as a 2 × 4 Model clinic, as this set up gives more prioritization to addiction services while short-changing mental health care.

The problem with nonintegrated mental health or addiction care programs (which unfortunately represent the vast majority of behavioral health services in the U.S.), is not that they can't take care of some patients well. Some of their patients can be treated very effectively. The problem is that they are best designed to treat too narrow a band of the behavioral health population in need, particularly those who do not have comorbidities. In the mostly segregated system we now have, the majority of patients who do have mental illness and addiction comorbidities are typically faced with access to a system that only provides one or the other type of care. Or they have to engage in two different treatment centers at the same time, or sequentially, which can be very difficult for the patient and often produces chaotic and wasteful care. At each type of treatment center, they often have a major portion of what is actually ailing them ignored. Worse yet, dual diagnosis patients are sometimes not allowed into treatment by mental health or addiction programs, because the patients are viewed as too different, or too complex from what the treatment system is specialized to treat. A particularly disturbing aspect of this kind of segregated care is that patients are often rejected or transferred out of treatment, or to different treatment systems repeatedly, *like on a referral merry-go round* while never actually receiving any kind of effective treatment for the conditions they have. This reflects a culture present within many behavioral health care centers where the treatments offered tend toward 'one size fits all' diagnostic and treatment approaches that are dictated more by the name of the service, or title of the building, rather than what the individual patient with comorbidities actually has or needs. In this culture, it is common for treatment systems to actually shield themselves of responsibility of taking care of complex patients, or of improving their own capability or expertise, simply by labeling the patient as someone who is 'not best served here', or 'doesn't fit in with what we do.' In this way, treatment centers can actually feel quite smug and confident in their expertise in a specialized area of behavioral health care, even as they ignore or reject large numbers of patients they encounter, precisely because they are *deficient* in expertise. For many patients with dual diagnosis, as illustrated in the following **Case Vignette #2** (information is de-identified and minor details altered to protect involved parties), these conditions can produce catastrophic breakdowns in appropriate longitudinal behavioral health care that can lead to detrimental outcomes.

Case Vignette #2 illustrates two major problems that are pervasive in our current behavioral health system; the 2 × 4 Model clinic aims to remedy these issues by emphasizing a balanced-integration of both mental health and addiction capability and expertise.

Issue #1: Lack of treatment systems for dual diagnosis and the referral merry-go-round. This patient with mental illness and addiction was referred across five different treatment venues, spanning four completely unrelated service systems within a 30 mile radius of one another (primary care, psychiatric hospital, psychiatric ER, mental health outpatient center, and addiction rehab). This chain of referrals was necessitated in part because there was not one venue or professional team in this complex chain that was appropriately capable, or saw itself as being responsible for treating what the patient actually had: Mental illness *and* addiction.

Remedy: The 2 × 4 Model clinic understands that its mission, expertise, and obligation is to treat both the mental illness and addiction in whatever combination of these the patient has, without having to refer the patient to some other service. The buck stops at the 2 × 4 Model clinic. If the patient does need acute hospitalization or supervised withdrawal treatment, the 2 × 4 Model team directs and drives this care for the patient as part of a longitudinal plan using a facility (with beds) that is institutionally linked to the 2 × 4 Model clinic. The patient remains a patient of the 2 × 4 Model clinic before and after

Case Vignette #2

Ms. XY was a 57 year old married architect, who had a serious suicide attempt five years ago and was followed for ongoing treatment of anxiety and depression by her primary care doctor. In recent years, Ms. XY had been receiving an increasing dose regimen of opioids and benzodiazepines for anxiety and chronic pain problems. Unfortunately, however, these medications were (as undetected by the primary care physician who would see the patient in ten minute med checks every three months) producing occupational and family problems and bouts of depression associated with suicidal ideation. For Ms. XY, the suicidal thinking was particularly pronounced when she was in opioid withdrawal. Eventually Ms. XY made a genuine attempt to suicide on a combination of opioids and benzodiazepines. This attempt failed, leading to her admission to a psychiatric inpatient service (which does not provide addiction or detoxification services) where she stayed for one day, until the acute suicidal ideation had cleared and she was discharged to home. Upon a subsequent relapse on pills and then acting on a second suicide attempt within the week, Ms. XY was again evaluated in the psychiatric ER for clearance of her suicidal ideation for a few hours, and then referred to an outpatient behavioral health center that offered 12-step groups and eventually, access to outpatient psychiatrists, but none who had any addiction expertise. After presenting to this program, and because of ongoing bouts of intoxication and suicidal thinking that the 12-step program could not handle, she was referred on to an inpatient addiction rehab center. There, the patient was admitted expressing passive suicidal ideation and acute opioid withdrawal. The rehab center, which does not formally treat mental illness, and only takes voluntary admissions, did not fully evaluate and address the patient's mental illness and suicidal ideation. The next morning, while undergoing an admission exam the patient abruptly walked out of the facility to a local drug store. There, she proceeded to purchase liquor, a knife, and large quantities of over the counter sleep aids that she took to a lockable bathroom at a local hardware store, where she completed suicide.

any needed inpatient stays. Since both the patient's mental illness and addiction are being treated as part of a longitudinal care plan, hospitalizations are more likely to be prevented, or at least better designed to serve the longitudinal outpatient care plan of the 2 × 4 Model team.

Issue # 2: Lack of physician expertise in dual diagnosis and the failure to take longitudinal responsibility for the dual diagnosis patient. This patient with mental illness and addiction was referred across five different treatment venues, where she was seen and evaluated by a primary care doctor, whose prescribing practices put the patient at iatrogenic risk, at least two different psychiatrists, and numerous nurses and therapists who were not able to address this iatrogenic risk. Unfortunately, none of these professionals, and most detrimentally, none of the physicians, who should lead the care and make the key treatment decisions for the patient, had formal training in the diagnosis and treatment of the dual diagnosis condition. Integrated mental health and addiction expertise, if present and appropriately deployed, could have saved the patient's life and generated a sustained recovery.

Remedy: The 2 × 4 Model clinical team is a multidisciplinary team of professionals who are capable and interested in treating both addictions and mental illnesses. This team is led by addiction psychiatrists, who, by definition, are formally trained and board certified to treat both mental illness and addictions. The experience, training and clout of the addiction psychiatrist allows the 2 × 4 Model clinical team to make professional communications that can prevent or stop unhealthy controlled substances being prescribed happening to mentally ill patients from other doctors. The 2 × 4 Model clinic also supports the addiction psychiatrist in providing a new route to recovery for patients via facilitating a doctor to doctor hand off or collaboration that can relieve outside doctors and their addicted patients from the risks of clinical abandonment and hazardous iatrogenic trajectories.

Thus, in the 2 × 4 Model clinic design, where the care of addictions and mental illness are equally prioritized, physicians are trained and equipped to treat both types of disorders in an integrated way, the same team directs the care of the patient and takes longitudinal responsibility for the case, regardless of how that patient's dual diagnosis syndrome may be manifesting in the moment, or how it evolves over time. Any combination or relative proportion of addiction vs. mental illness comorbidity in a given patient can be addressed at a high standard even as the relative proportions of these illness components will evolve. In this way, the 2 × 4 Model is structurally responsive and flexibly adaptive to the *4-quadrant model of dual diagnosis*.

The 4-quadrant model (**Figure 3.1A**), originally introduced by Ries in 1993, has been an influential, and somewhat paradigm-shifting model for community mental health. Consistent with the goals of this book, the 4-quadrant model was originally conceived to help us better grasp the scope of the dual diagnosis spectrum and to be equipped to deal with it in community mental health settings. The 4-quadrant model addresses the reality that while there is a great deal of diagnostic diversity across individual patients who may need treatment by a community mental health center (involving dozens of different types of DSM diagnoses), it may be most helpful to see this population in terms of designing treatment services, in broad strokes, as being composed of two more fundamental components: Mental illness and substance use disorders. So, while acknowledging that mental illnesses and addictions each do occur on a continuum of degree of severity, we can say that either condition, as it may occur in a given patient, is either 1) none to mild or 2) moderate to severe. In this framework it is possible to classify *all* patients seeking behavioral health care onto one 4-quadrant map, where a two degree y-axis component of addiction severity is orthogonal to a two degrees x-axis component of general mental illness severity. The appeal of this simple model is that with it, a given behavioral health treatment system can frame its services to address the entire spectrum of all the behavioral health illnesses it will encounter, but with some ability to specialize four separate treatment teams to each take care of one of the four subgroup quadrants: i) relatively healthy patients (e.g., the worried well); ii) patients with major mental illness but no or mild addictions; iii) patients with major addictions but no or mild mental illness; and iv) 'dual diagnosis patients' with severe cases of both.

Attention to the 4-quadrant model has helped bring both addictions and mental health care into the service portfolios of many behavioral health settings that previously had no addiction treatment at all. Remarkably, the 4-quadrant model has also turned out to be quite translationally important to informing the design of basic neuroscience and clinical research studies on dual diagnosis, like those described in the Chapter 2. In a reverse translation of the 4-quadrant model, studies that aim to understand how the pathophysiologies of mental illness and addictions interact, experimentally create (e.g., in rats) or observationally select (e.g., in humans), four groups of subjects following a 2 × 2 design (presence or absence of mental illness × presence or absence of substance use). This experimental design approach has become a 'gold standard' method in dual diagnosis research, because it allows comparisons between the 4-quadrant groupings on behavioral, clinical, and neurobiological measures, which is crucial to understanding how these disorders are deeply intertwined.

It is interesting to consider that the design of the 4-quadrant model may have actually limited its own success in fostering balanced attention to mental illness and addiction, much like the 'equal but separate' rationale behind racial segregation was not a complete or fully acceptable solution to civil rights. While bringing mental illness and addiction together onto the same map of clinical care, the 4-quadrant model also subdivides this map into four regions that implies a value in segregating patients and treatment teams (or sites) according to mental illness vs. addiction severity. *A major shortcoming to this approach is that patients generally do not exist statically in only one quadrant.* Real world patients actually migrate across a great diversity of time scales (e.g., some within hours, others across years) between these quadrants. This migration may be driven by the developmental evolution or worsening of their psychiatric syndrome; the cyclical or unstable nature of their illness; the happenstance of adverse environmental events (e.g., death of a child); or conversely, clinical improvement in one or both of their mental illness or addiction illness components.

In the face of all this fluidity and migration of real-world patients between the four quadrants of the dual diagnosis map, it actually does not often make sense to design separate treatment services, sites and teams to take care of each of the four quadrants . . . unless, we are willing to destroy the continuity of care and clinical responsibility of one team for each patient, precisely as we see happening in **Case Vignette #2**. The risk and detriment here is actually 2-fold. First, in a system of four equal but segregated quadrants, if patients in quadrants i), ii), or iii), are getting worse (either in their addiction or mental illness components), the system tells the team to just send the patient somewhere else (e.g., to another team who's turf is the destination quadrant), instead of actually holding the team responsible for preventing or treating the worsening condition. Then second, when a team that runs the higher level quadrant gets a patient better, the system would direct that the patient be referred back or out to another, lower level quadrant, thus robbing the successfully treating team of the opportunity to follow that successful, more stable patient over time, keeping that higher-quadrant team overloaded with sicker patients. These dynamics not only destroy continuity of care and relationships between professionals and patients (not to mention professional morale), they also prevent teams from developing a sense of longitudinal clinical responsibility for individual patients and the opportunity to develop collective knowledge about how illnesses evolve and respond to treatment over time. Longitudinal clinical experience with a diverse population of evolving patients is critical for growing team's abilities to recognize certain symptoms earlier, take actions to prevent symptom worsening from either the MI or SUD domain, and to develop an awareness of what works best to get different sets of patients, with different degrees of MI/SUD comorbidity, better and keep them better.

To incorporate the best of what the 4-quadrant model offers, but to circumvent these pitfalls, the 2 × 4 Models goes a step beyond the categorical segregation of the population and assumes more of a continuum approach, where *all* behavioral health patients are understood as being potential or active dual diagnosis patients, *as a matter of degree*. That is to say, every patient will have some degree of mental illness severity and some degree of addiction severity, and each of these two illness components can change over time for a given patient (e.g., like ranging on a scale of severity from 0 to 100) (**Figure 3.1B**). But then, also, the 2 × 4 Model calls for the *capability and expertise of one team at one site* to be able to take clinical responsibility for patients regardless of where they are on their degree of MI or SUD severities, and, regardless of how they may be evolving on these scales (**Figure 3.1C**). So, what we have in the 2 × 4 Model is, in a sense, a transformed 4-Quadrant model, where attention and vigilance to both the mental illness and addiction symptom domains are always maintained and bound up together by the team in all of its clinical operations. Of course, individual patients will have syndromes characterized by differential larger or lesser degrees of MI vs. SUD disorders. But the 2 × 4 Model team is expertly capable of treating this entire diversity, regardless of where the patient is, or moves to on the 4-quadrant map.

This brings us to articulating the second most important foundational concept of the 2 × 4 Model clinic design: *While the clinic is fully committed to, and capable of treating MI and SUDs with equal levels of prioritization for all patients, it is able to flexibly integrate mental health and addiction care according to the needs of individual patients.*

Fundamental Design Concept #2: Flexibly Integrate and Individualize Mental Health and Addiction Treatment

The 2 × 4 Model team will be able to *flexibly* design treatments according to individual treatment needs of different patients with different forms, severities and combinations of dual diagnosis disorders, and it will be all the more experienced and knowledgeable about doing this since it is allowed to have experience with the care of patients from all over the 4-quadrant model map. This design feature means that while the clinic gives equal prioritization to diagnosing and treating both addictions and mental health disorders (made possible because it actually has the expertise and tools to do so—i.e., as in design concept #1); it does not assume that all patients are dually diagnosed in the same way, or to the same degree. Therefore, it does not at all deploy the same set of treatments to everyone, or expect patients to all engage in the same set of treatments.

The clinical power of this design concept can be illuminated with the 'NFL analogy'. Fans of professional American football know that winning teams, that is, those that score a lot of points against their opponents, are very good at *both of* the two fundamental scoring strategies: 1) the running play; and 2) the passing play. Teams that are great at one of these strategies (e.g., having players run with the football down field to score), but not the other (e.g., passing the football in the air to players down field to score), are often labeled as 'one dimensional' and are viewed as relatively easy to defend against. These 'one dimensional' teams are relatively predictable, so defenses can reliably concentrate players in certain locations on the field to more reliably stop the stereotyped scoring strategy. On the other hand, when a scoring offense is excellent at both running and passing, the defense has no reliable way to place defenders on the field that can offer good protection against *both* the running and passing strategies. Moreover, the highly flexible and effective scoring offense, can look at the way the defensive team players are arrayed in front of them before a particular play happens, and decide, based on that 'defensive look', whether they should execute a running or passing play, thereby maximally exploiting the weaknesses in the opposing team's positioning, to gain the most distance toward the goal. Similarly, this is how the 2 × 4 Model clinic flexibly deploys its treatment strategy (offensive scoring plays). Based on the particular diagnostic look of the opponent (whatever particular mental illness/addiction diagnostic combination the patient presents with), the addiction psychiatrist and 2 × 4 Model team 'calls the best play'. Of course, in this analogy, it is not the patient who is the opponent—the patient's illness is the opponent (the diagnosis is the 'defensive look'), and the clinician will 'call in' a mental illness-oriented treatment play (like a running play) or an addiction treatment intervention (like a passing play) depending on what the opponent is showing. With many dual diagnosis patients, the 2 × 4 Model clinician can expect, over the course of months to years (let's call this extended treatment phase 'the game'), to flexibly execute a rich mixture of both running and passing plays, as needed to best remit or 'defeat' the opponent. Alternatively, a patient may present with mostly mental illness, with little or no addiction problem. The defensive look of this patient's illness will then mostly require a strong running game (evidence-based mental health medications and psychotherapies), which the 2 × 4 Model clinic is also *fully* capable of expertly deploying. But sometimes that patient's illness might show evidence of an addiction problem (or vulnerability to addiction) that requires the occasional 'passing play' call (e.g., deployment of an addiction-focused evidence-based medication or psychotherapy). Conversely, we may have the type of patient with relatively little in the way of major mental illness or personality disorder who is addicted to two substances, say nicotine and alcohol. So, for this patient, the 2 × 4 Model team will execute primarily a series of 'passing plays' (addiction treatments), but is always ready with a strong running game if there is new recognition, or onset of a major depressive episode in that patient.

After a while, the addiction psychiatrist and the 2 × 4 Model team become very adept at recognizing differential patterns of 'defensive looks of opponent illnesses' (combinations of dual diagnoses) that may evolve within individual patients (the abstinent alcoholic that becomes depressed), or, that are characteristic across different sets of patients (the patient with schizophrenia that smokes). The knowledge and experience that accumulates from executing and learning when to execute either 'running' or 'passing' plays, provides a level of clinical understanding about the mental illness–addiction spectrum opponent that cannot be acquired if the team refuses, or is unable, to be flexible in executing *both* addiction and mental health treatments. Moreover, the team is much more likely to have an overall losing record (not get as many patients better as it could have) if it is stuck in using only a limited set of passing plays or running plays, even though it can be expected that at least half of the opponent illnesses it will encounter, actually require expertise in both strategies (i.e., integrated dual diagnosis care for dual diagnosis patients).

So in this way, by the 'NFL analogy', the 2 × 4 Model clinic represents a superb offensive scoring machine that can handle a wide range of 'defensive styles' (e.g., dual diagnosis illness combinations). Thus in the 2 × 4 Model design, *one team and one clinic* is expert at treating virtually the entire diagnostic spectrum in behavioral health, including people who are mostly mentally ill without much addiction, those whose illnesses are mostly about addiction, and, those whose syndromes have robust components of both classes of disorders. This is a team that will have a winning record and qualify for the championship playoffs' at the end of the season (e.g., have a high clinical success rate), because it can 'take care' of nearly the full spectrum of its opponents.

In more specific diagnostic terms, the 2 × 4 Model clinic is expertly staffed and equipped to take care of both major MI and SUDs like those listed in the columns in **Figure 3.2.**

The 2 × 4 Model clinic aims to be fully and optimally capable of taking care of patients with a wide range of different *comorbid combinations* of these disorders that, however challenging they are to treat, need to be treated, because they are very real, common, and mainstream in patient populations seeking either MI or SUD care. For example, the 2 × 4 Model clinic expertly treats these types of patients:

- The 28 y.o. female with borderline personality disorder, PTSD, opioid, methamphetamine, and nicotine addictions.
- The 63 y.o. female with OCD, alcoholism and depression.
- The 25 y.o. male vet with alcoholism, opioid, nicotine and marijuana addictions, depression, and PTSD.
- The 47 y.o. male with schizophrenia, nicotine, and marijuana addictions.
- The 30 y.o. female with benzodiazepine and opioid use disorders and antisocial traits.
- The 47 y.o. male with bipolar disorder, narcissistic personality disorder, cocaine, opioid and nicotine addictions.
- The 63 y.o. male with pathological gambling, nicotine and marijuana addictions, social phobia, and depression.
- The 18 y.o. pregnant female with borderline personality disorder, opioid and benzodiazepine use disorders with trichotillomania.
- The 21 y.o. female with major depression and marijuana addiction.
- The 71 y.o. male with narcissistic personality disorder, panic disorder, and alcohol use disorder.
- The 55 y.o. male with schizoaffective disorder with alcohol and cocaine use disorders in remission.
- The 18 y.o. female with bipolar disorder, borderline personality disorder, with opioid and cocaine addictions.
- The 31 y.o. female with schizophrenia and PTSD, with opioid, nicotine and cocaine addictions.
- The 35 y.o. male with antisocial personality disorder, psychotic depression, solvent disorder, alcohol, and nicotine use disorders.
- The 25 y.o. male with opioid, cocaine, methamphetamine, marijuana, and alcohol addictions.
- The 18 y.o. female with bipolar disorder.
- The 28 y.o. male with bipolar disorder, nicotine addiction and alcoholism with antisocial traits.

- The 48. y.o. male with PTSD, nicotine addiction and alcoholism in sustained remission.
- The 32 y.o. male with affective disorder, nicotine, cocaine, and solvent use disorders.
- The 32 y.o. female with borderline personality disorder, depression, and nicotine addiction.
- Etc. . . .

So with this kind of diagnostic diversity in mind, we can begin to estimate, for example, from the list of eleven major mental illnesses (from the MI column) and nine major addictions (the SUDs column) in **Figure 3.2**, how many different diagnostic combinations would be treatable in the 2 × 4 Model clinic as follows:

A. **Permutations of uni-diagnoses.** Sometimes patients only have one mental illness, or just one addiction, but not both, so this would be 11 + 9 = 20 different syndrome types.

B. **Combinations of simple (uni-MI/uni-SUD) dual diagnoses.** When just one of any of the major mental illness types presents with just one of any of the major addictions, we would have a set of 11 × 9 = 99 possible different diagnostic combinations.

C. **Combinations of poly-MI/uni-SUD dual diagnoses.** Often, patients have multiple simultaneous MI diagnoses. Let's say that for the vast majority of patients, this ranges from two to four different MI diagnoses. If a patient has two simultaneous MI diagnoses, that ends up being a comorbid permutation set of 11 × 10 = 110 (not 11 × 11, because a MI cannot be comorbid with itself). But, some mental illnesses can't go together (like schizophrenia and schizoaffective can't be diagnosed together). So, let's take care of this issue mathematically by estimating that if you have a given primary mental illness, it is likely that you will be diagnosed with one of a smaller set of the remaining ten MI's (say from five of ten of the remaining). So with this, it is reasonable to assume that a patient diagnosed with two MIs will have one of up to a total of 11 × 5 = 55 different comorbid combinations. Similarly, if the patient has three different MI diagnoses, we can estimate this would be one combination from a total of 11 × 5 × 3 = 165 possible illness combinations. When a patient has four MI diagnoses we can estimate 11 × 5 × 3 × 2 = 330. This gives us a subtotal of 55 + 165 + 330 = 550 different possible combinations (of two to four MIs) that can present in an individual patient. But now remember, each of these 550 MI comorbid combinations might happen without any SUD, or more commonly, with at least one SUD. Let's say it is just one of the nine comorbid SUDs. That brings us up to a possible range of 550 × 9 = 4,950 different poly-MI-uni-SUD combinations. Adding the 550 different poly-MI combinations without any SUDs, to the 4,950 combinations of poly-MI with one SUD, gives us a total of 5,500 different complex MI-dual diagnosis combinations.

D. **Combinations of poly-SUD/uni-MI dual diagnoses.** Now for the poly-SUD combinatorial space, let's say that as with MI combinations, most patients will have two to four different SUDS simultaneously. Unlike the situation in mental illness, there are no drug-specific types of SUDS that preclude other specific SUD diagnosis. So, if a patient has two SUDs, that's 9 × 8 = 72 possible combinations; if three SUDS, that's 9 × 8 × 7= 504 combinations; if four SUDs, that's 9 × 8 × 7 × 6= 3,024 combinations. Thus for patients who don't have clearly identifiable MI but have two to four different concurrent SUDs, there are 72 + 504 + 3,024= 3,600 possible addiction syndrome combinations. But of course we know that people with multiple addictions very likely also have comorbid MI. So, if it's just one major MI, that's 3,600 × 11 = 39,000 combinations. Summing the 3,600 different poly-SUD combinations that might occur without MI, together with the 39,000 poly-SUD syndromes that occur with just one major MI, gives a total of 42,600 different possible complex SUD dual diagnosis combinations.

E. **Combinations of poly-MI/poly-SUD dual diagnoses.** While realizing that multiple SUD/Multiple MI 'complex dual diagnosis' comorbidity is unfortunately quite common, it is astonishing how many different permutations of this comorbidity are possible. Based on figures estimated in C) above, there are 550 different possible combinations of poly-MI (presentations of two to four MIs) without SUDS, and from D), 3,600 combinations of poly-SUDs (two to four) without MIs. So now, let's estimate how many possible combinations of Poly-MI/Poly SUDs there are. The calculation is simple: 550 × 3,600 = 1,980,000 different possible complex dual diagnosis combinations!

Summing up the overall rough estimate of the total number of different dual diagnosis combinations that may present in behavioral health is given in the table below.

Now, to ponder this quite massive sum further in terms of what it means for integrated dual diagnosis care and behavioral health as a whole, first, let's qualify it. It has to be understood that each of these two million plus combinations of different dual diagnosis syndromes do not happen in the human population with equal frequency. For instance, schizophrenia with nicotine

Syndrome Form	*# Possible Combinations*
A. Uni-diagnoses	20
B. Simple dual diagnoses	99
C. Poly-MI/uni-SUD dual diagnoses	5,500
D. Poly SUD/uni-MI dual diagnoses	42,600
E. Poly- MI/Poly-SUD 'complex' dual diagnoses	1,980,000
Total:	2,028,219

addiction is 5–10 times more common than plain old schizophrenia without nicotine addiction. Many other comorbid combinations (particularly some of the MI combinations) enumerated in this total are rarely diagnosed, because of the way the DSM is designed (and also how nature causes these illnesses to manifest in people). For instance, PTSD and borderline personality disorder can be diagnosed together (and often are), whereas schizophrenia and borderline personality disorder are very rarely diagnosed together (and might often be labeled as schizoaffective). With that said, diagnostic exclusivity does not really happen among the addictive disorders, and we note that the list of eleven major mental illness categories in the MI column in **Figure 3.2** used to make these estimates is actually a quite truncated list of the major illness types that are routinely seen in behavioral health.

So, even if only 10 percent of the 2,028,219 possible comorbid combinations estimated above are clinically frequent in human behavioral health populations (which may be a low-end estimate), we are still talking about a diversity of more than 200,000 different dual diagnosis combinatorial variants, in which patients may have anywhere from one to four MIs, and one to four SUDs (up to eight different diagnoses) simultaneously! This compares to about 20 permutations of uni-diagnosis presentations (in which patients are diagnosed as having only one mental illness or only one SUD; 11 MI + 9 SUDS = 20), representing only about (20/200,000) or 0.01 percent of the range of possible clinical combinations. This illustrates the absurdity of a behavioral health system which, as its mainstream approach, tries to silo treatments, treatment teams, and patients, into different buildings according to specific MI vs. SUD diagnoses, or even subtypes within these categories. Clearly, this analysis, along with the epidemiological findings on dual diagnosis rates reviewed in Chapter 2 (which indicate that comorbid syndromes are much more the rule than the exception), points to the need for our treatment systems (along with our professional training and research efforts) to be flexibly, expertly, and comprehensively capable of directly addressing this diagnostic complexity, more as a rule (rather than an exception), by one team, under one roof. It is far more efficient to design and replicate one clinical model and treatment team that can expertly treat 200, 000 different dual diagnosis combinations, than to build an array of 1000 different types of behavioral health specialty clinics that can each only treat a much more narrow range of 200 permutations clinical diagnostic presentations.

It is interesting to consider that the estimated range of 200,000 or more possible common dual diagnosis combinations is 10 × bigger than the rough number of around 20,000 different genes in the human genome! Again, we are reminded that the classical Mendelian scheme of one gene–one phenotype as an explanation for the etiology and variation of behavioral health syndromes is not workable. Instead, we have to confront the reality that we are faced with much greater biological complexity of multi-finality (one gene can predispose to different phenotypes), equifinality (multiple genes can lead to the same phenotype), multi-gene interactions, and gene-environment interactions. A desire to accept this reality has motivated many psychiatric scientists to question the adequacy of the traditional DSM diagnostic system as a basis for research or clinical care. The R-DoC (Research Domain Criteria) Model originating at the NIMH, proposes that behavioral health illnesses may be better understood, not as specific overarching syndromes, but as collages of all kinds of different symptom sets that can appear in a whole host of many variations. With R-DoCs, it is hoped that different sets or combinations of many genes may be identified (via gene testing/'precision medicine') to code for different combinations of symptoms. Whether this approach (to what some might call a lurch toward phenotypic reductionism in an effort to save the validity of molecular reductionism) catches on and helps us deliver better care, through decreasing, rather than increasing clinical siloes remains to be seen. Nevertheless, the dogma-challenging idea behind R-DoCs, if interpreted on a clinical rather than a research level, is congruent with the idea that we must begin to accept and deal with diagnostic complexity and comorbidities in our behavioral health patients as the norm, rather than the exception. This means that behavioral health clinical teams must begin taking responsibility for much more of the entire set of neurobehavioral symptoms patients actually present with, especially as they span both MI and SUD disorders.

So how is this even possible? If this were easy to do, wouldn't we be doing it already? The answer to the first question is: Yes, it is possible, and actually it is quite straight-forward with the 2 × 4 Model clinic design. Addressing in some greater detail how it is possible, brings us to the third fundamental design concept of the 2 × 4 Model that builds on the first two.

Fundamental Design Concept #3: Embrace the Complexity; Identify and Treat All MI and SUD Illness Targets

In war, military units prefer to find themselves in 'target rich environments' so that they have maximal opportunity to strike successful blows against the enemy. So it is with the 2 × 4 Model clinical team as it comprehensively recognizes, accepts, and confronts the diagnostic complexities that dual diagnosis patients present with. A patient with two or maybe three types, or blends of mental illnesses, concurrent with three different types of drug addiction is a 'target rich environment'. The 2 × 4 Model views this common clinical situation not as something we should avoid or ignore, or refer patients away for, but instead, as an array of problems that we are more likely to address more effectively if we look at them all together as highly inter-related issues. Then, with this diagnostic perspective, the 2 × 4 Model team devises a coherent strategy (i.e., treatment plan), that is attentive to, and takes responsibility for, the whole array of dual diagnosis problems, and is flexible to the emergence of new ones that may present, or old ones that may resolve in the evolution of the patient's treatment.

The 2 × 4 Model clinician embraces this complexity in part, because the more treatment targets there are, the more likely we are to reduce at least one of them! Then, while we are monitoring all their MI and SUD problem areas, and to the extent that most, if not all of their diagnoses are inter-related, the more likely we are going to see multiples of their problem areas improve over the course of treatment.

It is of course completely unrealistic to expect that a patient with a comorbidity of three MI diagnoses and four concurrent addictions is going to enter treatment and then 30 days later emerge completely mentally healthy and drug free. Although not completely impossible, this kind of success would be extremely rare, because unfortunately most of the major mental illnesses and addictions are (like plenty of other medical diseases) of a chronic nature that follow waxing and waning courses over months to years. But, what is quite realistic and common for a patient with three MIs and four SUDS that enters into and stays with a 2 × 4 Model program, is an expectation for there to be a reduction of some of their MI symptoms within a few weeks, and a significant reduction, or cessation of use of one or two of the drugs they are addicted to within the first couple of months. This should be viewed as an excellent and gratifying start for the clinician and the patient. After this start, and as the clinical presentation and treatment plan evolves, the emphasis on treatment will be to consolidate and maintain the gains (improvements) while retargeting (i.e., designing more nuanced or advanced treatments for the more stubborn problem areas). If after a year in care, the patient has four of seven of their major target areas significantly reduced or eliminated, that is a major clinical victory. Although this would not be the kind of victory that should make the team or the patient think that treatment should end completely, it is a level of victory that can significantly improve the overall health, well-being, and longevity of the patient, their functioning as a family member and employee, often in association with greater financial stability, and freedom from the criminal justice system and overutilization of expensive medical care.

What's Old and What's New About the 2 × 4 Model for Integrated Dual Diagnosis Care?

So far this chapter has outlined three fundamental design concepts of the 2 × 4 Model:

1. Merge the mental health and addiction treatment missions as being equally important;
2. Flexibly integrate and individualize mental health and addiction treatment; and
3. Embrace the complexity; identify and treat all MI and SUD treatment targets.

Considering these design concepts, raises the question: If adhering to them could be so important and practical for one clinical team, in one building, why haven't behavioral clinics everywhere already embraced them? A partial set of answers to this question, which is essentially the same as asking why integrated dual diagnosis care still remains largely unavailable, has been provided in Chapter 2. But, returning to this question again here will be very helpful to further explaining the historical and clinical evidence-basis for the 2 × 4 Model, and how the 2 × 4 Model aims to advance from this history and translate from this evidence to the next level of actual clinical implementation.

Ideas about what constitutes integrated dual diagnosis treatment, and descriptions of clinical-service evidence in support of this from behavioral health treatment, are not new. If the 2 × 4 Model stands on the shoulders of giants, then some of the biggest giants are Kenneth Minkoff, Robert Drake, and colleagues, who in the 1990's generated a whole literature and considerable momentum in psychiatry to do more to make integrated dual diagnosis care a more mainstream modality of behavioral health.

As articulated by Minkoff in 2006:

> Two decades of research with a wide variety of populations, from adults with serious and persistent mental illness, to adolescents and families involved with the court system (either criminal justice or child protection) have provided increasing support of the increasing efficacy of integrated treatment programs and interventions, in which appropriately matched strategies for both mental health and substance abuse issues are combined, coordinated, or integrated into the context of a single treatment relationship, treatment team or treatment setting.

As described in a review by Drake of more than two dozen studies conducted by 2003 looking at the clinical evidence base supporting Integrated Dual Diagnosis Treatment, some of the most important and effective aspects of dual diagnosis treatment are:

- "Mental health and substance abuse interventions are combined *at the clinical interface*";
- "The same *clinician (and/or team)* provides appropriate MI/SUD interventions *in a coordinated fashion* and guides the individual toward *learning to manage intertwined illnesses*";
- "The crux of integration is that *the practitioner takes responsibility* for blending the interventions into *one coherent package*";
- "Patients do not need to negotiate with separate clinical directives, teams, programs, or treatment systems";
- "Effective programs *tailor* interventions to the person's stage of recovery"; and
- "Comprehensive services: Individualize services according to needs".

By the early 2000's, having defined some of the key features of integrated dual diagnosis care, and resting on a significant accumulation of services research showing that integrated dual diagnosis approaches provide better efficacies (e.g., compared to segregated approaches), leaders of the Integrated Dual Diagnosis Movement turned to implementation and fidelity research. This transitioned the dual diagnosis field toward *attempting* to get psychiatry and behavioral health at large to more widely adopt integrated dual diagnosis practices, toward measuring the degree that systems had adopted these practices, and toward identifying the many barriers against conversion to a more dual diagnosis capable system.

Unfortunately, despite substantial federal backing by SAMHSA (Substance Abuse Mental Health Services Administration), and the development of a strong and compelling academic literature (and even its own journal: *The Journal of Dual Diagnosis*, pioneered by Peter Buckley), the Dual Diagnosis movement stalled. Certainly, both longstanding cultural issues within behavioral and general health care (see Chapter 2) and the economic crisis beginning in 2008 (which hit behavioral health care, research, and academic psychiatry especially hard) colluded to produce major setbacks for the dual diagnosis movement. But there were also three other major missing pieces, that this book, and the 2 × 4 Model aims to help provide, to re-energize the integrated dual diagnosis movement.

First, as we have already covered in Chapter 2, there is the neuroscientific argument, that had previously not been fully characterized or translated. The emerging body of basic science showing that mental illness and addictions are intimately related, and in some ways even unite neurobiological and developmental diseases processes, adds new urgency to the need to integrate clinical expertise and care for these disorders. Moreover, this new subfield of psychiatric neuroscience calls into question why dual diagnosis should only be a concern of SAMHSA (a federal behavioral health services improvement organization) and not a concern of NIDA, NIAAA and NIMH, which are the major federal granting organizations that fund basic and clinical neuroscience research on the causes and treatments of behavioral health disorders. In other words, the participation that is needed to advance integrated dual diagnosis treatment at our core research and academic medical institutions, had still not quite formed the critical mass needed to drive profound change. Now, to the extent that psychiatric neuroscience has provided a new understanding about how addiction and mental illness are deeply interconnected, this neuroscience provides a foundation upon which clinical practice must stand. The integrative neuroscience of dual diagnosis (described in Chapter 2) is a foundation on which the three fundamental design features of the 2 × 4 Model, (described in this Chapter) stands.

Second, there is the need to increase the development and utilization of an expertly trained physician work force in addiction psychiatry as leaders of integrated dual diagnosis services. While the dual diagnosis movement has been rightly focused on methods of evoking systems and cultural change (i.e., to support the integration of MI and SUD care), at the level of services delivery, it has overlooked the need to include and pursue an emphasis on the role and training of the physician leaders in these services. We took notice of this issue in 2007 in Indiana when the state was considering a range of integrated dual diagnosis fidelity instruments for measuring dual diagnosis treatment capability among its psychiatric hospitals and community mental health centers. These instruments, including the Comorbidity Program Audit and Self-Survey for Behavioral health Services (COMPASS), the Integrated Dual Diagnosis Treatment (IDDT) Fidelity Scale, and the Dual Diagnosis Capability in Addiction Treatment (DDCAT), each offered various perspectives on whether a given system was dual diagnosis capable. However, they were all fairly agnostic and insensitive to determining how, and whether or not physicians that worked in the clinical systems being examined, were trained, motivated, or being utilized to be involved in integrated dual diagnosis care. This issue came up because in many settings in Indiana that scored reasonably well in dual diagnosis capability on one or more of these measures, service line administrators would admit that the fidelity ratings generally over-estimated actual dual diagnosis capability because the psychiatrists and other physicians that worked in these systems were 'just not on board'. Among all the professional staff, the physicians seemed to be the least accepting or knowledgeable about how to take care of both mental illness and addictions. So, to quantify this issue directly, we designed the DDPAT (Dual Diagnosis-Physician Infrastructure Assessment Tool) and deployed it across all of Indiana's long term state mental health hospitals and community mental health centers. The DDPAT revealed to us that state wide, among 215 physicians (including 194 psychiatrists) working in behavioral health centers, *where majorities* of patients had dual diagnosis conditions, only three physicians were formally trained (in residencies and fellowships) to treat both mental illness and addiction, and were ABMS certified in addiction psychiatry! When including a larger pool of physicians who were either ABMS certified in addiction psychiatry or ASAM (American Society of Addiction Medicine) certified (this represented only 17 individuals state wide), only a minority of seven of these doctors were actually being utilized by the systems they worked in, to treat both mental illness and addictions! Clearly, there was a mismatch between how psychiatrists were being trained and used, and the intent of these systems to actually become dual diagnosis capable. The lesson here seemed to be that we can certainly attempt to integrate mental health and addiction *services*, but if you don't have a psychiatric physician work force who themselves, as professionals, are *individually professionally integrated* (in terms of their interests and expertise), you end up with very little real integration of treatment.

Addressing this issue, the 2 × 4 Model explicitly calls for all of its professionals, *especially the physicians*, to be cross trained, motivated, and institutionally supported to treat both mental illness and addictions at a high level of expertise. The importance of physician leadership and expertise in the success and vitality of a well-functioning 2 × 4 Model clinic cannot be underestimated, because addiction psychiatrists are the only professionals that exist that have the formal training, expertise, and professional clout needed in the performance of all the treatment planning dimensions of the 2 × 4 Model: 1) Diagnostics; 2) Psychotherapeutics; 3) Medications; and 4) Communications. Hence the addiction psychiatrist has an indispensable clinical and leadership role in the 2 × 4 Model of seeing the big picture both for individual patients, and the clinic's patient population and mission as a whole that is needed for balancing the treatment focus between MIs and SUDs, and directing efforts along each of the four treatment strategy dimensions of the integrated care model. In essence, the 2 × 4 Model assumes that the integrated dual diagnosis movement, cannot ultimately be completed or effective without a physician workforce to go with it and lead it. The 2 × 4 Model design and operational description as provided in this book is a job description for cross-trained professionals, and especially the *addiction psychiatrists* that are needed to staff and lead 2 × 4 Model programs (more on this in Chapters 9 and 10). The 2 × 4 Model thus formally weds addiction psychiatry and integrated dual diagnosis care in a way that has previously not been an emphasis or explicit goal of the integrated dual diagnosis movement.

The third missing piece of the integrated dual diagnosis movement the 2 × 4 Model (and this book) aims to provide, is the exposition and deployment of a relatively simple structural model that embodies both the conceptual and tangible/concrete elements of what integrated dual diagnosis care should be, and what its scientific rationale is. The simplicity and flexibility of this model is designed to help psychiatrists and other clinical professionals better understand integrated dual diagnosis care, its capability of treating the entire spectrum of MI and addiction patients, and how it can be more universally implemented and verifiable from both inside and outside the professional clinical community. That is to say, the 2 × 4 Model aims to frame and formalize integrated dual diagnosis care in the clearest terms, so that it can be brought out of its origins as a niche area of psychiatry, and generalized to a much broader clinical application and larger community of professionals. This 2 × 4 Model design and operations manual can thus serve several purposes: As a professional textbook for general psychiatrists and addiction psychiatrists, a clinic design manual for health service administrators, a work in applied translational neuroscience, a guidebook for optimizing professional teaching and training contexts that seek to integrate mental illness and addiction care, and a guidebook for dual diagnosis fidelity, that should of interest to government and insurance company stakeholders. The 2 × 4 Model aims to encapsulate what integrated dual diagnosis care is, and how it should be designed, implemented, and staffed for the broadest possible behavioral health and public health impact. Toward these ends, Chapter 11 will describe more in depth how the 2 × 4 Model clinic can serve as a natural, ideal training home for addiction psychiatrists and other cross-trained (MI/SUD) professionals; Chapter 12 discusses how the 2 × 4 Model can be replicated and expanded as a more standard and universally present clinical model in behavioral health.

Background References and Further Reading

Barnett, J. H., U. Werners, S. M. Secher, K. E. Hill, R. Brazil, K. Masson, D. E. Pernet, J. B. Kirkbride, G. K. Murray, E. T. Bullmore, and P. B. Jones. 2007. "Substance use in a population-based clinic sample of people with first-episode psychosis." *British Journal of Psychiatry* 190 (6): 515–520.

Carra, G., C. Crocamo, P. Borrelli, I. Popa, A. Ornaghi, C Montomoli, and M. Clerici. 2015. "Correlates of dependence and treatment for substance use among people with comorbid severe mental and substance use disorders: Findings from the 'psychiatric and addictive dual disorder in Italy (PADDI)' study." *Comprehensive Psychiatry 58*: 152–159. doi: 10.1016/j.comppsych.2014.11.021.

Caton, C. L., A. Gralnick, S. Bender, and R. Simon. 1989. "Young chronic patients and substance abuse." *Hospital & Community Psychiatry 40* (10): 1037–1040.

Chambers, R. A., and M. N. Potenza. 2001. "Schizophrenia and pathological gambling (Letter)." *American Journal of Psychiatry 158* (3): 497–498.

Chambers, R. A., M. C. Connor, C. J. Boggs, and G. F. Parker. 2010. "The dual diagnosis physician-infrastructure assessment tool: Examining physician attributes and dual diagnosis capacity." *Psychiatric Services 61* (2): 184–188. doi: 61/2/184 [pii] 10.1176/appi.ps.61.2.184.

Conway, K. P., R. J. Kane, S. A. Ball, J. C. Poling, and B. J. Rounsaville. 2003. "Personality, substance of choice, and polysubstance involvement among substance dependent patients." *Drug & Alcohol Dependence 71* (1): 65–75.

Drake, R. E., S. M. Essock, A. Shaner, K. B. Carey, K. Minkoff, L. Kola, D. Lynde, F. C. Osher, R. E. Clark, and L. Rickards. 2001. "Implimenting dual diagnosis services for clients with severe mental illnesses." *Psychiatric Services 52* (4): 469–476.

Drake, R. E., and M. A. Wallach. 2000. "Dual diagnosis: 15 years of progress." *Psychiatric Services 51* (9): 1126–1129.

Drake, R. E., K. T. Mueser, M. F. Brunette, and G. J. McHugo. 2004. "A review of treatments for people with severe mental illnesses and co-occurring substance use disorders." *Psychiatric Rehabilitation Journal 27* (4): 360–374.

Erickson, C. A., and R. A. Chambers. 2006. "Male adolescence: Neurodevelopment and behavioral impulsivity." In *Textbook of Men's Mental Health*, edited by J. Grant, and M. N. Potenza. Washington, DC: American Psychiatric Publishing.

Grant, J. E., L. Levine, D. Kim, and M. N. Potenza. 2005. "Impulse control disorders in adult psychiatric inpatients." *American Journal Psychiatry 162* (11): 2184–2188. doi: 10.1176/appi.ajp.162.11.2184.

Hulvershorn, L. A., C. A. Erickson, and R. A. Chambers. 2010. "Impact of childhood mental health problems." In *Young Adult Mental Health* edited by J. E. Grant and M. N. Potenza, (pp. x, 448) Oxford, NY: Oxford University Press.

Insel, T. R. 2014. "The NIMH research domain criteria (RDoC) project: Precision medicine for psychiatry." *American Journal of Psychiatry 171* (4): 395–397. doi: 10.1176/appi.ajp.2014.140201381853442 [pii].

Kalman, D., S. B. Morissette, and T. P. George. 2005. "Co-morbidity of smoking in patients with psychiatric and substance use disorders." *American Journal on Addictions 14* (2): 106–123.

McGovern, M. P., A. L. Matzkin, and J. Giard. 2007. "Assessing the dual diagnosis capability of addiction treatment services: The dual diagnosis capability in addiction treatment (DDCAT) index." *Journal of Dual Diagnosis 3* (2): 111–123.

Minkoff, K. 2001. "Best practices: Developing standards of care for individuals with co-occurring psychiatric and substance use disorders." *Psychiatric Services 52* (5): 597–599.

Minkoff, K., and C. A. Cline. 2006. "Dual diagonsis capability: Moving from concept to implimentation." *Journal of Dual Diagnosis 2* (2): 121–134.

Minkoff, K., and R. E. Drake, Eds. 1991. *Dual Diagnosis of Serious Mental Illness and Substance Disoder.* San Francisco, CA: Jossey-Bass.

Mueser, K. T., D. L. Noordsky, R. E. Drake, and L. B. Fox. 2003. *Integrated Treatment for Dual Disorders: A Guide to Effective Practice.* New York: Guilford Press.

Petrakis, I. L., R. Rosenheck, and R. Desai. 2011. "Substance use comorbidity among veterans with posttraumatic stress disorder and other psychiatric illness." *American Journal on Addictions 20* (3): 185–189.

Ries, R. K. 1993. "The dually diagnosed patient with psychotic symptoms." *Journal of Addictive Diseases 12* (3): 103–122. doi: 10.1300/J069v12n03_09.

Schulte, S. J., P. S. Meier, J. Stirling, and M. Berry. 2010. "Unrecognized dual diagnosis-a risk factor for dropout of addiction treatment." *Mental Health and Substance Use 3* (2): 94–109.

Strain, E. C., R. K. Brooner, and G. E. Bigelow. 1991. "Clustering of multiple substance use and psychiatric diagnoses in opiate addicts." *Drug & Alcohol Dependence 27* (2): 127–134.

Szerman, N., J. Martinez-Raga, L. Peris, C. Roncero, I. Basurte, P. Vega, P. Ruiz, and M. Casas. 2013. "Rethinking dual disorders/pathology." *Addictive Disorders & Their Treatment 12* (1): 1-10. doi: 10.1097/ADT.0b013e31826e7b6a.

Ziedonis, D. M. 2004. "Integrated treatment of co-occurring mental illness and addiction: Clinical intervention, program, and system perspectives." *CNS Spectrums 9* (12): 892–904.

4 The Treatment Dimension

Vertical Binding of Diagnostics, Psychotherapies, Medications, and Communications

Vertical Binding of Components in the 2 × 4 Model

In Chapter 3, we discussed the core design feature of the 2 × 4 Model in terms of allotting equal focus on both MI and addictions, and being able to integrate this focus across and within individual patients. We can call this *equal and integrated* focus on the diagnostic dimension the *vertical binding* in the 2 × 4 Model. This chapter will now begin to stretch the 2 × 4 Model out across its treatment dimension and introduce how this *vertical binding* should be carried out across each of the four components of the Treatment Dimension (Diagnostics, Psychotherapies, Pharmacotherapies, and Communications) (**Figure 4.1**). This means that for each of these four components, the 2 × 4 Model clinic is appropriately equipped, staffed, and capable of integrating key evidence-based tools and techniques that have traditionally belonged, sometimes too exclusively, to either the MI or SUD treatment fields. For instance, in the Diagnostics component, core diagnostic tools and techniques that are essential in either mental health care or addictionology must *both* be available and routinely used in the 2 × 4 Model clinic.

Chapters 5, 6, 7, and 8 will get into specific detail about the tools and techniques that should be used in each of the four components of the Treatment Dimension, with respect to MI and addiction care, and how they are *vertically bound* in the 2 × 4 Model. The current chapter will set up this detailing by considering general principals of the vertical binding, namely, how we need to merge expertise, tools, and cultures appropriately from the MI and addiction fields. In this process we will want to keep and bind the elements that are most important and effective for the treatment mission, and modify or even discard others that are unnecessary or even detrimental to the integrated mission.

Dogmas, Traditions, and Hang-Ups We Need to Let Go for the Sake of Vertical Binding

From either the MI or the addiction treatment side, the 2 × 4 Model should keep and integrate the best elements and discard the worst. The best/desirable elements include tools, clinical attitudes, approaches, and cultural philosophies that have been traditionally held onto in either the MI or addiction treatment fields (but not both), which should be preserved and strengthened in the 2 × 4 Model, while sacrificing (deemphasizing or discarding) other elements that are at least somewhat in conflict with the desirables. The presence of opposing elements, if unresolved and unreduced, can act as real hang-ups and barriers to dual diagnosis integration, and can produce conflict on the team, as we will cover more in depth in Chapter 10. We now discuss the *top ten* common major hang-ups to integration as they present from either the mental health or addiction treatment side (or both), and how they need to be addressed, reduced, or resolved in the 2 × 4 Model, sometimes by favoring the more beneficial or crucial element from one side over the other.

Hang-Ups from the Mental Health Field Side

#1 Professional and Patient Stigma against Addicted Patients

A lack of familiarity on the mental health care side with addiction neuroscience, diagnosis, and treatment, has created situations where addictions are viewed as being something different from mental illness, like, being viewed as not quite legitimate brain conditions or illnesses that are on par with mental illness. This kind of thinking is akin to what society as a whole has done in terms of stigmatizing addiction as something other than a biomedical problem, which inevitably pushes it into being viewed as belonging to the categories of criminal or religious problems. This kind of dynamic then lends itself to a sort of prejudice and segregationist thinking, sometimes shared among professionals and patients alike, where there is a tendency to want to keep addictions swept under the rug, or, to keep addicted patients 'out of our clinic'. This unfortunate dynamic in some ways is even more disturbing, and quite a bit more hypocritical (when it happens in mental health settings), than what society as a whole does in contributing to the stigma of addiction. Of all groups that one would think would be most sensitive to stigma, would be mental health professionals and their patients, who have a long history of dealing with, and suffering from stigma. Of course there are forgivable reasons for why the MI side might stigmatize the addiction side. Sometimes, we make ourselves feel better in dealing with the difficult problems we have by saying, "*well, at least I'm not dealing with the really bad problems they have.*" In this kind of inverse of 'the grass is greener on the other side' thinking, there is a premium placed on keeping the patients with the *other* diagnoses away from the ones *we prefer*. Another powerful form of stigma is one that can be very personal and based on a traumatic experience from the past. I'll never forget getting feedback from one of our psychiatry residents, after an addictions course I taught, where he told me that he really hoped to avoid seeing or treating addictions in any of his patients, because he was abused by his dad when his dad was drunk, and he felt like he could not get over this counter-transference in seeing patients with addictions.

However understandable these stigmatizing tendencies are, the 2 × 4 Model approach recognizes the truth that mental illness and addiction are simply too comingled and biologically inter-related brain illnesses, for segregationist thinking to be at all clinically helpful. Certainly, achieving a deeper under-standing of the neuroscience of addiction and dual diagnosis (see Chapter 2) among mental health professionals will be important to replacing stigmatized views of addiction with a biomedical disease-model understanding. This scien-tific understanding on the part of professionals, perhaps in combination with some utilization of the Golden Rule, will likely shed off on mentally ill patients who may also judge patients with addictions. For mental health professionals who may be profoundly traumatized by their own personal experiences with addictions in themselves or others, there should be a strategy undertaken to either overcome the counter-transference or to seek another profession. Formal training and supervision in addiction psychiatry, can go a long way in helping physicians learn to understand and overcome stigmatizing tendencies or problematic counter-transferences.

#2 No Drug Testing; Avoiding Probing Too Far (in Interviews) into Substance Use

The fact is, drug testing, and engaging in frank, open, and comfortable con-versations about past or ongoing drug use are key and indispensable to addiction and dual diagnosis treatment. Not looking for and assessing addictions using these approaches rules out any legitimate claim that a behavioral health clinic may have that it can competently address substance use disorders as brain-illness comorbidities that are endemic and often lethal in mentally ill people everywhere. Common reasons that MI treatment centers cite for not conducting routine UDS (urine drug screening) include: i) they claim to have no logistical support for testing, or that testing is too costly; ii) fear of disrupting the therapeutic alliance between patients and treatment professionals; and iii) fear of UDS testing results being used against patients. The first issue (logistics of drug testing) is just something that has to be overcome by the treatment team and administrative leadership. When done appropriately, drug testing can be done quite efficiently and cost-effectively (i.e., compared to the routine costs of testing in other areas of medicine). Not having routine drug testing in an addiction or dual diagnosis clinic in the U.S. would be as incompetent and inexcusable as an Emergency Room not having an EKG machine.

The second and third issues (fear of drug testing disrupting therapeutic alliance and tests being used against patients) are actually quite related concerns that are rooted again, in the unfortunately common (and false) view of drug testing as being all about detecting crime and sin in order to leverage punish-ment. Of course, this is how these tests have been and will likely continue to be widely used by the criminal justice system, schools, or employers, to justify incarceration or exclude people from work, or other activities (e.g., *to catch and punish*). But in the health care setting, especially in addiction and dual diagnosis treatment, this testing *should never be used for punitive purposes.* Drug testing (and also verbal inquiry about drug use) in the 2 × 4 Model clinic should be used frequently and always and only to help patients via facilitating proper diagnosis and treatment strategies involving both medications and psychotherapies. This is no different from how all other diagnostic tests are used in the rest of legitimate medical care, and as a core value of sound medical ethics, to benefit the care of the patient, not to deprive or punish them. The important point here is that the treatment team members and the patients all need to understand that there is no need to fear that drug testing could interfere with the therapeutic alliance, or that it could be used against patients when the treatment team is committed to using this testing for medical purposes only, and are vigilant in protecting the integrity of this 'treatment only' application of UDS testing. When this is done correctly, we have found that *drug testing actually enhances the therapeutic alliance, and de-stigmatizes addiction by* reinforcing in the minds of patients that they are suffering from a brain-based biomedical disease process, that should be assessed with regular testing of body fluids, or other biological substrates just like almost all other medical diseases. But again, for this to work, the patients and the clinical team have to ensure that drug testing results gathered in the clinic are not handed over to *any* third parties (e.g., probation or other criminal justice agencies), with the exception of the very rare circumstance of there being a direct court order (i.e., a subpoena from a judge), which is also the same standard for disclosing medical data to the courts, as in the rest of medicine. Thus, the 2 × 4 Model embraces the emphasis on drug testing more commonly valued on the addiction treatment side, and calls for the reduction and elimination of attitudes and concerns against it on the MI care side.

#3 Over-Interpretation of Patient's Substance Use as 'Self-Medication'

As discussed in Chapter 2, many mental health treatment professionals, including psychiatrists, have long adhered to the traditional view that mentally ill patients use addictive drugs so often primarily because these drugs have some therapeutic efficacy in mental illness. This is a view that is echoed between professionals and patients, between patients and professionals, and between professionals, students, and trainees in the field. It is so prevalent in clinical parlance that 'self-medication' has nearly become synonymous with 'dual diagnosis'. However, as we have previously outlined (Chapter 2), the evidence that self-medication is the best explanation for dual diagnosis is quite poor, while recent neuroscience suggests that dual diagnosis is better understood as one disease leading to another. Unfortunately, adherence to the self-medication hypothesis (which views drug use as medicine-taking) has contributed to a mental health treatment culture that generally has not fully acknowledged or embraced responsibility for recognizing and treating the co-occurring drug use as addiction—a disease process that, along with the mental illness, requires evidence-based therapies.

Although the self-medication hypothesis is commonly used by many patients with SUDs, and it would seem to deflect stigma associated with an addiction diagnosis, it is well-recognized in the addiction field that patients with addiction characteristically use all kinds of drug use rationalizations to justify their continued drug use (to themselves and others) that are not objective, accurate, or logical. In fact, a goal of Motivational Enhancement Therapy (MET) as a key evidenced-based psychotherapeutic modality for addiction that should be used often in the 2 × 4 Model clinic, is to help patients achieve an accurate appraisal and accounting of the negative vs. positive aspects of continued drug use. When done well, this process often leads patients to questioning and ultimately dismissing many of their previously held drug use rationalizations, including the typically quite false idea that the drug use they are/were engaged in was just an act of medicine-taking, rather than being harmful. While decisions about how and when to challenge 'self-medicating' drug use rationalizations do have to be considered carefully by clinicians, it is important that 2 × 4 Model team members are acting together to 'not drink the cool-aid of self-medication', by ignoring addictions or reinforcing drug use rationalizations in the minds of addicted and mentally ill patients. It should also be considered that labeling drug use in mentally ill patients as being self-medication also does not ultimately serve to effectively combat the stigma of addiction diagnoses in these patients. Denial of addiction by treatment professionals is arguably a reaction to stigma that actually keeps the illness stigmatized. Embracing addiction as a disease that should be diagnosed and treated, is arguably the only way to medically de-stigmatize it. The 2 × 4 Model clinic supports the view and language (favored from the addiction treatment side) that compulsive, harmful drug use is an illness, and that 'putting lipstick on a pig' by rationalizing harmful drug use as 'self-medication' is not generally neuroscientifically or clinically accurate, or beneficial to treatment and patient outcomes.

#4 Attitudes that Recognizing and Treating Substance Use is 'Not my Job'

This common attitude, often reinforced by the training biases (toward the mental health side) of clinicians, the particulars of clinical funding mechanisms, and sometimes even the name of the clinic, can cause otherwise excellent behavioral health clinicians to not accept responsibility for diagnosing and/or treating addiction. Sometimes, the ongoing, untreated substance abuse can even be useful to mental health professionals or treatment teams (but not for patients) as an excuse or handy explanation for why their patients aren't getting better, which takes blame for treatment failure away from the treatment team. Like, "the reason Mr. J. is not getting over his depression is not because my psycho-therapy or meds are not working but because of his drinking . . . but, hey we can't do anything about that because we don't treat that!" Of course the absurdity and irony of this scenario is that alcoholism is actually a well-known cause of treatment refractory depression, insomnia (and many other psychiatric symptoms) that is itself, actually treatment responsive, if you are actually willing to treat it according to the evidence base. So, a mental health clinic that specializes in the treatment of depression, but not in co-occurring substance use disorders, is actually *less capable and less expert* in treating a broader array of depressive illnesses. In the 2 × 4 Model clinic, it is the job of all team members to try to recognize and be aware of all the signs and symptoms of both mental illness and addictions, in whatever combination they may occur, and to contribute to a treatment plan that addresses both illness domains.

Hang-Ups from the Addiction Field Side

#5 *Professional and Patient Stigma against the Mentally Ill*

The still widely held misunderstanding (or clinical approach in mainstream behavioral health) that addicted and mentally ill patients are mostly mutually exclusive patient populations has caused addiction professionals and patients to view their work in recovery as something different than what happens in mental health care, or to view the difficulties of mentally ill people as being different from what addicted patients face. Sometimes we see attitudes held by both addiction professionals and addicted patients that having mental illness is a form of stupidity or retardation. For some people, as hard as it may be to live with the criminalized or sin-related stigma of addiction, at least it's not as bad as being understood as being 'mentally defective' or 'incompetent', as in mental illness. So again, this kind of 'I am better than them' prejudice and prosegregation thinking (that can be just as intense and hypocritical as the same dynamic that plays out from the mental health side toward the addictive side) can seduce treatment systems into believing that the waiting rooms and therapeutic groups for addicted vs. mentally ill patients should be kept separate. In the 2 × 4 Model clinic, the clinical team members work with each other and all their patients, to combat stigma and prejudice against both mental illness and addiction, and to encourage integration of services and patients as needed to improve clinical outcomes.

#6 *Professional and Patient Focus on Certain Types of Addictions but Not Others*

In a dynamic that is rather similar to the selective stigma against mental illness that might happen in an addiction treatment center, it is often commonplace to see addiction treatment centers focus on some types of addiction but not others, even when the other addictions that are present (but are being ignored) are causing just as much if not more harm. Typical contexts and scenarios that fit this dynamic are, for example, the for-profit methadone clinic that *only* accepts cash for the treatment, *only,* of opioid addiction, using *only* one treatment— methadone. In some instances, clinicians and patients can both get carried away with focusing on certain addictions based on which drugs are legal vs. illegal, under the false assumption that DEA scheduling, and the 'war on drugs' were actually the scientific and medical gold-standards that should be used to determine which drugs or addictions are actually more dangerous or severe, and thus deserving of therapeutic focus. For example, we see that nicotine addiction, although representing one of the most severe and prevalent forms of all addictions, and one that produces the greatest amounts of premature illness and death in the U.S. (and many parts of the world), is ironically the addiction that is most highly prevalent and most often ignored in the addiction treatment setting. So, while nicotine addiction ranks among the worst of all addictions, tobacco and nicotine addiction is perfectly legal; even as revenue from tobacco sales (either via campaign donations or taxes) is channeled to support political campaigns or state governments that are vigorously emphasizing the war on drugs—the criminal prosecution of drug trade and use—because some set of drugs, *other than nicotine*, are highly addictive and dangerous. The 2 × 4 Model clinical approach to addictions proactively seeks to resist biases introduced from unscientifically informed and inconsistent government or political stances on drugs of abuse, also does not want to actively support or work as an agent in the 'war on drugs' (i.e., understood to mean the criminalization of addictive disease). Accordingly, all additions that a patient may have, including those involving both the legal and illegal substances (or even nonsubstance addictions like pathological gambling), are fair game for treatment, and should be prioritized as such according to their clinical severities, the totality of harm they are causing, and their responsiveness to various treatment attempts.

A similar sort of drug-type bias, that turns out to be a quite common pitfall for many addiction treatment centers, is highly relevant to the contemporary iatrogenic prescription drug epidemic. This is the incorrect assumption that certain drugs, when they are legally prescribed by doctors, should automatically not be viewed as contributing to active addictive disease, and should not be viewed as potential targets of addiction treatment. Reliance on this false assumption has led many a patient, who is actively ill or perpetually at risk from dying from addictive drugs, being prescribed these drugs by doctors, even as they sit through, and 'graduate' with flying colors from an addiction treatment curriculum. Of course, this issue is quite complex given the number of very real clinical indications that addictive drugs (i.e., spanning opioids, stimulants, benzodiazepines, and cannabinoids) may be prescribed for, and the solid evidence base that exists for the proper use of these drugs for some of these indications. To top it off, we even use some addictive drugs (methadone, buprenorphine, and nicotine) in the treatment of addictive disease, based on the best evidence. At the same time there are brands of addiction treatment centers that operate at the other extreme of inattention to the evidence base, where absolutely no medications, or only a limited set are allowed for the treatment of addiction. In addressing these complexities, the 2 × 4 Model clinic strives to adhere as closely as possible to the clinical–scientific evidence base on the utility and harms caused by addictive drugs, and assumes that these drugs can be, and are often used and prescribed both incorrectly or harmfully vs.

optimally, by doctors depending on circumstances, how they are used, and the skill, knowledge, and training of the physician. Again, the 2 × 4 Model clinic strives to avoid rigid, over-arching policies about addictive drug pharmacy in its patients, whether that be on the one hand a tendency to ignore outside iatrogenic prescribing to its patients, or oppositely, to never allow patients to be on prescribed controlled substances for addictions or other indications. The 2 × 4 Model clinic relies on the individualization of care, as guided by an expert understanding of the evidence base, and clinical decision-making of the addiction psychiatrist and their colleagues on the treatment team. In the 2 × 4 Model clinic, an emphasis on evidence-based medication management of addiction disease is important (not instead of psychotherapy, but along with it), just as medication management of mental illness has long been understood on the mental health side, as an important approach to treatment along with psychotherapy.

#7 Interpreting Patient Non-Compliance as Deliberate Resistance or Disinterest

Addiction treatment based in the tradition of 12-step group therapy places a premium on patient's regular attendance to group sessions that may occur 1–3 times a week for many weeks to months. This level of treatment, while certainly beneficial to many patients, is not best for all, and is not feasible for all. This pace and intensity of treatment participation is also not customary in main-stream mental health care. Clinicians 'born and raised' in the addiction treatment tradition sometimes tend to view group therapy as the only real treatment or the only treatment that works, in which attendance is the only, or most important measure of recovery. But this absolutist idealization of 12-step groups is not well supported by the evidence base. Many real world patients who need addiction and dual diagnosis services face a wide range of problems that can make regular participation in groups a challenge or even poorly effective. Contextual/situational problems include lack of access to, or inability to afford transportation and co-pays, lack of child care coverage, and an inability to sacrifice employment. Homelessness may be a barrier. Mental illness itself is often a barrier. Patients with various forms of social anxiety or paranoia and negative symptoms (e.g., in schizophrenia) may rarely feel comfortable in groups. Other patients with poorly controlled illness traits or impulsivity symptoms (e.g., anti-social or manic symptoms) may be too disruptive in groups.

As is widely understood on the mental health side, the 2 × 4 Model clinic understands that like any real treatment, the efficacy of group therapy is not unlimited and not guaranteed; it actually does have side effects and for some patients with certain forms of mental illness and comorbid addiction, it is contraindicated. Regardless of the cause for limited compliance with attendance, the addiction treatment culture has a tendency to over-interpret poor attendance as a failing in the patient that can elicit a response to want to punish the patient or get rid of them (via closing charts or discharge). Patients can get labeled as having a lack of desire to get better, as being lazy, or as having a form of pathological ambivalence and self-manipulation, where the addicted person tries to 'have their cake and eat it too', by being in addiction treatment on paper but not in person. While the latter hypothesis should always be considered in the poorly compliant patient, and may be in play to some extent, the former factors must also be given consideration. In addition, it must also be considered that the discussion content of the group, the dynamic in the group, or even the professional leadership of the group may also be a problem, especially for persons with certain forms of mental illness. So, with all this in mind, although the 2 × 4 Model clinic does emphasize group therapy as one highly effective and important therapeutic tool, it does not view it as a cure-all tool that is mandatory for all patients, or one that should be dosed at a 'one-size fits all' duration or frequency. And, while group attendance is a measure of compliance in treatment, it is not the only measure of compliance, and it is not even the only, or best measure of progress in recovery.

Even in the ambivalent, precontemplative patient, who is *at present* poorly compliant with groups or other appointments, it should be the goal of treatment to move them forward, with attempts to engage them into care. On the addiction treatment side it is often said that "good clinicians should be aware not to work harder than their own patients in promoting recovery." The 2 × 4 Model rejects absolutist adherence to this view as it understands that the brain disease of addiction, especially in the context of mental illness, causes biological failures in motivation and good decision-making. Sometimes the clinician actually does have to do more than the patient, to work harder than the patient is doing, to set the stage for progress, or to evoke significant change. As in the mental health field, the 2 × 4 Model understands and is prepared for the fact that patients with addictions can require significant case management, forced hospitalizations (sometimes against their immediate wishes by commitment), or on-site outreach as in the act-team model.

#8 Tendency to Want to Fire Patients Who Relapse, or, Are in Some Way Poorly Compliant

As mentioned previously, poor or inconsistent compliance or relapses can cause the addiction treatment team to want to somehow punish or get rid of the patient. Up to a point, this tendency to push away poorly responding or compliant patients has some utility, because it provides a bit of a triaging function to orient team effort and work on patients that might be the most likely to benefit. However, this tendency, especially when expressed in its more overbearing forms, can be rooted in religious or criminal justice-based judgment that has influenced, or contaminated, the addiction treatment culture, creating motives to achieve purity via the enforcement of 'zero tolerance' policies. Eliminating challenging patients is also is a way for a treatment center to avoid taking care of sick and *comorbid* patients while being able to report to their payers falsely elevated success rates (focusing on those *who meet their narrow and sometimes arbitrary definitions of completed treatment).* By the standards of the medical model, these tendencies—to get rid of sick or comorbid patients—as practiced by some addiction treatment programs, can actually represent real fraud, or at best, a serious violation of medical ethics. In mainstream health care, abandonment of the sick is a legal and financial liability and an ethical violation, and should be viewed as abandonment of the obligation of the treatment team to find ways to improve its own services. From the mental health side, the training of psychiatrists and psychotherapists routinely explores the way in which patients who offer resistance, or who are treatment refractory, can elicit a counter-transference in the therapist that makes them want to abandon the patient. Part of this counter-transference is normal in that for many professionals who put a lot of stake in their own effort and clinical skills, it is painful to experience failure or an inability to get the patient better. But, in the 2 × 4 Model, patients are not discharged because they are sick, or complicated with dual diagnosis comorbidities, or are relapsing, or are challenging to treat. This does not mean that there are not some conditions where discharge is the best or only option (see Chapter 10), or where clinical efforts need to be refocused on more responsive patients or treatment strategies. Merely, this means that the professional responsibility and objective of the 2 × 4 Model clinic should be maintained to persevere in the longitudinal treatment of dual diagnosis for all patients regardless of their illness severity and comorbidity, and to role model and elicit this persistence in even the most ill and treatment refractory patients.

General Hang-Ups (from Both the Mental Health and Addiction Treatment Sides)

#9 Assumption that MI or Addiction Has to Be Treated Sequentially or in a Certain Order

From the mental health side, the conventional wisdom (or mythology) has often been professed that you have to treat the addiction first and then, when that's done, start on the mental health care. Although based on some truth (e.g., it's harder to treat schizophrenia in someone who is using methamphetamine daily), this idea has often been overused to inappropriately delay mental health care, or, to send dual diagnosis patients elsewhere for treatment (e.g., to split their care). By the same token, an addiction treatment center might determine that the comorbid mental illness 'is not under well-enough control' for the addiction treatment they provide (which often includes treatments that do not tolerate mental illness symptoms, or involves professional staff that have little to no mental health training). The 2 × 4 Model clinic rejects these tendencies to treat mental illness vs. addiction illnesses in rigid, segregated sequences, and allows treatment plans to be flexibly designed so that any number of possible integrated strategies could be pursued based on the diagnoses and circumstances of the individual treatment. Addiction and/or mental health treatment interventions can be pursued entirely, partially, sequentially, or simultaneously.

An overall emphasis on the addiction component may come first, or an emphasis on mental illness may come first, or both can happen at the same time. Since the 2 × 4 Model clinic is well equipped to handle any of these approaches, and the clinical team is experienced with all these options, the treatment strategy is not constrained by the clinical short comings or limited focus of the clinic itself (typically on only mental illness or addiction).

#10 Failure to Recognize that MI Treatments Impact Those for Addiction and Vice-Versa

As mentioned in Chapter 2, there is a widely prevalent misunderstanding (actual or apparent) within both the mental health and addiction communities, that *treatments* for addiction have no bearing on the effects of treatment of mental illness. This false notion applies in terms of psychotherapies and medications, sometimes making clinicians and treatment services behave like they actually believe patients have two different brains, one that holds the addiction and one that holds the mental illness. It is not entirely clear why treatment services could adhere to such an obviously false understanding, other than being dutifully compliant with the mainstream culture of behavioral health care (and funding streams) that widely accept and in many ways propagate the segregation of mental health and addiction treatment services. The 2 × 4 Model rejects the view that it is OK or acceptable as the standard of care for patients with mental illness and addiction comorbidity to get their services in two different systems, by two different sets of clinicians or teams (i.e., divided according to MI vs. SUD treatment). Split care for MI and addiction treatment, even if offered to patients by separate systems that are in some degree of communication, is understood by the 2 × 4 Model as generally substandard, and something that should be avoided and discarded by treatment systems that are striving to improve and build behavioral health services.

Now for Specifics: Elements and Binding of MI and Addiction Treatment Components

Chapters 5–8 will now describe the key elements that should be included in the diagnostics, psychotherapies, medications, and communication components of the treatment dimension of the 2 × 4 Model. The elements within each of these components need to be vertically bound together or integrated so that patients can be examined for, and treated for their dual diagnosis conditions in whatever combinations they may present with. To some extent, the ordering of the vertical components as they are presented in this design manual (and in the 2 × 4 Model grid from left to right), beginning with diagnostics and ending with communications, does represent how team services are temporally deployed to patients in the early stages of entry into care. Generally, as in the rest of medicine, diagnostic workups are started first followed by treatments (introductions to therapists and group therapies, the addiction psychiatrist and medications). Then, as the patient's case begins to evolve, the physician leader and team members will make professional communications about their patient's status, progress, and care that are designed to clear the way for, and elicit support for the patient's recovery from the outside world. At the same time though, diagnostics are still recurrently used to track treatment trajectories. Thus, as the case progresses beyond initial evaluation, the treatment components will be returned to, surveyed, and engaged recurrently and concurrently as needed for the care of the individual patient. This *horizontal binding of the treatment components* of the 2 × 4 Model will be discussed in more detail in Chapter 10.

Background References and Further Reading

Chambers, R. A. 2010. "Dazed and confused by self-medication." *The American Journal of Psychiatry 167* (5): 600; author reply 600–1. doi: 167/5/600 [pii] 10.1176/appi. ajp.2010.10010099.

Chambers, R. A., and M. S. Greene. 2016. "Physician understanding and treatment of addiction: Have 'pseudo addiction' and 'self-medication' led us astray?" *Journal of Addiction and Dependence 2* (3): 1–4.

Drake, R. E., and K. T. Mueser. 2002. "Managing comorbid severe mental illness and substance abuse." In *Comorbidity of Substance Use and Psychiatric Disoders*, edited by F. Moggi. Seattle, WA: Huber Press.

Lembke, A. 2012. "Time to abandon the self-medication hypothesis in patients with psychiatric disorders." *The American Journal of Drug and Alcohol Abuse 38* (6): 524–529. doi: 10.3109/00952990.2012.694532.

Lopez-Quintero, C., J. Perez de los Cobos, D. Hasin, M. Okuda, S. Wang, B. F. Grant, and C. Blanco. 2011. "Probability and predictors of transition from first use to dependence on nicotine, alcohol, cannabis, and cocaine: Results of the National Epidemiologic Survey on alcohol and related conditions (NESARC)." *Drug Alcohol Depend 115* (1–2): 120–130. doi: 10.1016/j.drugalcdep.2010.11.004.

Mangrum, L. F., R. T. Spence, and M. Lopez. 2006. "Integrated versus parallel treatment of co-occurring psychiatric and substance use disorders." *Journal of Substance Abuse Treatment 30* (1): 79–84.

McLellan, A. T., and K. Meyers. 2004. "Contemporary addiction: A review of systems for adults and adolescents." *Biological Psychiatry 56* (10): 764–770.

Moos, R. H. 2005. "Iatrogenic effects of psychosocial interventions for substance use disorders: Prevalence, predictors, prevention." *Addiction 100* (5): 595–604.

Substance Abuse and Mental Health Services Administration (SAMHSA). 2009. *Integrated Treatment for Co-Occurring Disoders: The Evidence*, edited by Center for Mental Health Services. Rockville, MD: U.S. Department of Health and Human Services.

Szerman, N., and L. Peris. 2014. "Personality disorders and addiction disorders." In *Textbook of Addiction Treatment International Perspective*, edited by N. el-Guebaly, G. Carra, and M. Galanter, (pp. 2063–2083). Milan, Italy: Springer-Verlag Italia.

Torrey, W. C., R. E. Drake, M. Cohen, L. B. Fox, D. Lynde, P. Gorman, and P. Wyzik. 2002. "The challenge of implementing and sustaining integrated dual disorders treatment programs." *Community Mental Health Journal 38* (6): 507–521.

Van Boekel, L. C., E. P. Brouwers, J. Van Weeghel, and H. F. Garretsen. 2013. "Stigma among health professionals towards patients with substance use disorders and its consequences for healthcare delivery: Systematic review." *Drug & Alcohol Dependence* *131* (1–2): 23–35.

Weiss, R. D., and H. S. Connery. 2011. *Integrated Group Therapy for Bipolar Disoder and Substance Abuse.* 1st ed. New York: Guilford Press.

Willenbring, M. L. 2001. "Psychiatric care management for chronic addictive disorders: Conceptual framework." *The American Journal on Addictions 10* (3): 242–248.

Williams, J. M., and D. Ziedonis. 2004. "Addressing among individuals with a mental illness or an addiction." *Addictive Behaviors 29* (6): 1067–1083.

5 Diagnostics

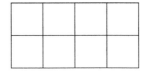

Elements and Integration of Diagnostics for MI and SUDS

This chapter will describe the essential observational elements—the approaches and tools for diagnostics that are used in the 2 × 4 Model clinic. The key themes here are 1) the need for a multiplicity of diagnostic perspectives (tools); and 2) the need to maintain routine and repeated use of these tools. The clinic should not rely on just one way to look at patients because they and their illnesses are too complex to be grasped from just one angle. Patients need to be examined in many ways, with the use of several tools, in addition to the clinical psychiatric examination. This chapter will outline what those tools and approaches are that are *required* for the 2 × 4 Model, and another set that are more elective (i.e., very helpful but not absolutely required). The emphasis on *maintaining routine and repeated use* of the diagnostic elements is in place to point out that if a given diagnostic tool is used quite rarely, like once or twice a year, then that really means it is not being used. For example, a clinic that says it *can* use UDS, but does so less than five times a year (total, over the entire census of patients), does not really maintain routine and repeated use of UDS. This clinic would not qualify as a 2 × 4 Model program. The routine and repeated use of testing is also meant to imply that patients need to be examined and tested repeatedly over time, so that illness evolution can be observed for updating, individualizing, and refining the treatment strategy. Patients in treatment should and will change over time; these trajectories need to be tracked across many temporal data points within and across different patients to assess outcomes, guide care, and adjust treatment programing.

Required & Routine Diagnostic Elements in the 2 × 4 Model Clinic

The 2 × 4 Model clinic binds together the most essential and routinely used measures from the mental health and addiction treatment traditions to form a *Required & Routine Kit of Diagnostic Tools* (**Figure 5.1**).

The six categories of tools listed on the right side of **Figure 5.1** are essential in the 2 × 4 Model clinic. Many of these diagnostics may be ordered, used, or collected, by several different members of the treatment team independently, whereas the addiction psychiatry physician has ultimate authority to order or collect any of these lines of data (as needed). The observations are tracked by, and made accessible to the team via charting in the Electronic Medical Record and supporting data bases.

In contrast to the Required & Routine Diagnostics in **Figure 5.1**, the following elements need to be available for frequent or occasional use by the 2 × 4 Model clinic, but not necessarily on site:

Accessible On or Off Site for Frequent or Occasional Use

1. TB testing (i.e., PPD skin testing)
2. Neuroimaging
3. Neuropsychological Testing
4. EKG
5. Full Physical Examination

Gene testing is rising in popularity in psychiatry, but has not yet (as of the printing of this edition) met the muster of scientific rigor to justify routine use, and should only be used in the context of exploratory research.

The Six Categories of Required & Routine Diagnostics: A Detailed Tour

1. Addiction Psychiatry/Dual Diagnosis Clinical Interview, Exam and Evaluation

The Addiction Psychiatry/Dual Diagnosis (AP/DD) evaluation retains its importance as the cornerstone and gold standard of the diagnostic assessment in the 2 × 4 Model clinic. Readers should look to general text books for more complete and detailed descriptions of the standard psychiatric examination or methods in addiction history taking, but it should be understood here that the AP/DD evaluation seeks to bind the ingredients from both of these traditions in the most efficient and informative way. The AP/DD evaluation may be thought of as an augmented or advanced form of the standard psychiatric evaluation that in skilled hands, is the best way to understand patients with potential or actual dual diagnoses. Some of the key features and recommendations for this exam are listed as follows:

• Time allotment: The initial evaluation should be at least an hour, but it can be broken into two segments, for example, of 30 minutes each. Standardized return visits should typically happen in shorter blocks in 10– 60 minutes, averaging near 30 minutes including charting time. Most of the time with the patient should be spent with the psychiatrist looking and interacting with the patient squarely, not typing and computer gazing.

- HPI (History of present illness): The goal of the HPI is to summarize the illness saga that led them to treatment, framing why they are in front of you and what they want. This is a story, *a history of the illness and how it has evolved in the individual and their interactions with their environment*. It is not a Review of Symptoms, although ROS data can definitely be peppered in or summarized at the end (which will also satisfy billing requirements). A guiding approach to constructing the narrative is, for patients with dual diagnosis (i.e., most behavioral health patients), to weave the disease history of the MI and SUDs together like the way the two strands of DNA intertwine to make the double helix. Remember, the scientific assumption of the HPI of the AP/DD evaluation (see neuroscience in Chapter 2), is that the MI and the addiction(s) are more like two components of one syndrome, not two unrelated disorders. Accordingly, it is good to take every opportunity in the HPI to describe how one illness component has emerged, surged, evolved, or remitted in relation to the other. This is the first place in the evaluation where the *Fundamental Design Concept #1 of the 2 × 4 Model, to merge the mental health and addiction treatment missions as being equally important* (see Chapter 3), *is represented in the work-up.*
- For the AP/DD evaluation, Past Psychiatry HX of the traditional psychiatric work up is broken up into two components, SUD HX and PSY HX: This action does the opposite of what the HPI is doing, by purposely segregating the psychiatric history from the SUD history, so the evaluator can think about them separately for the sake of thoroughness, and to protect against one component of the dual diagnosis illness from inaccurately overshadowing the other. Important details about either SUDs or MI not included in the HPI are put into the PSY or SUD HX sections. These sections could also include ROS data from the illness components (e.g., being more check-list like) so that all the key bases are tagged for each illness domain. Most important in PSY HX, are detailing of self-injurious behavioral, history of suicidal thinking and attempts, psychiatric hospitalizations, illness symptom history, and mental health medication history. In the SUD HX, it is important to cover all the major drugs, including alcohol, opioids (prescribed and illicit), benzodiazepines (prescribed and illicit), stimulants (prescribed and illicit), cocaine, cannabinoids, and of course nicotine. Nicotine is just as crucial to cover as any of the other addictive drugs (remember, nicotine kills more people in the U.S., more than any other addiction, and it is just as addictive as cocaine or opioids); it is important for the clinician to try hard not to forget it. Whether the patient does or does not use nicotine (and how they do it) should always be documented because this information will have important prognostic, treatment, and economic implications for the patient. For all the other drugs that are identified as being part of the patient's active substance use disorder set, there should be an accounting of the life-pattern: Age when

use started; escalation in use (dose and route); sustained gaps in use (and why); and approximate time and date of last use. Obviously, the latter information could be crucial for immediate treatment planning in terms of detoxification/withdrawal treatment (DWT) programming. Second, it is important to gather information pertaining to the medical, psychiatric, occupational, educational, social–familial, and legal consequences of use. The economy of the patient's use (e.g., weekly costs of use, methods used to support the addiction) is also valuable to understand. Finally, understanding the patient's past experiences in treatment can be important. It can be astonishing to learn how so few patients have been able to get access to adequate behavioral health or integrated dual diagnosis treatment services over their lifetimes, despite the severity and durations of their illnesses.

- Social HX: Aside from the HPI and MSE (Mental State Exam), this is most important part of the AP/DD evaluation, because this is where the clinician will find a huge amount of information pertaining to the patient's treatment prognosis, resilience, barriers to care, and life story as a human being. This has major implications for treatment strategy and expectations about the pace of care and recovery. The quality of information culled in this section is what often separates the rookies from the seasoned clinicians. If medical school and the first 2 years of psychiatric residency are about recognizing *the disease in the person*, the Social HX section when done well, is where senior residents and addiction psychiatrists excel in finding the *person with the disease*. Important topics in this section include life-story-geography (where the patient is from, what their original family was like), educational history, number and ages of children, number of parents involved in making these children, marital/relationship history, sexual orientation, work history, legal history, where they currently live (how far from the clinic/transportation options), who they live with (do any of them use drugs and what kind), income sources, health insurance status, legal history with details on current status of criminal charges, obligations, any punitive measures being leveraged by the Criminal Justice System against them, current or past child protective services cases, what they like to do for fun, and exercise/sports history.

- MSE: The mental status exam for addiction psychiatry is the same as the standard psychiatric mental status exam but with a little more content or enhanced points of focus. Chief among these are: 1) Appearance section; look for and document physical/somatic signs of drug use (e.g., needle track marks, cigarette stains on fingers); 2) Behavior section; document evidence for intoxication or withdrawal; 3) Affect section; document irritability that could be part of drug-seeking behavior; 4) Thought Content; document evidence for drug seeking (e.g., drug use rationalizations, attempts by the patient to get the doctor to prescribe addictive drugs), assess motivation level of the patient for recovery, that is, estimate patients stage of change (see Chapter 6), current and recent craving levels for one or more substances, brief review of major current triggers; 5) Judgment/ Insight/Cognition; comment on their level of impulsivity, awareness of illness, degree of intellectual or cognitive impairment (by brief objective testing) that may be drug history or MI related.

- Assessment Summary/Diagnosis/Plan: Again, this concluding section of the evaluation would be the same as in the standard psychiatric work up including its use of DSM diagnostic language. Although DSM-5 eliminates the Axial (I, II, III, IV, and V) system, the addiction psychiatry assessment for the 2 × 4 Model system still prefers parts of it. In particular, the medical summary (Axis III) is important to note and update. This is a place to track the medical illnesses that have resulted from addictions, or, could worsen addictions (pain syndromes, dental problems, infections, and hypertension), or, could interact with medications the addiction psychiatrist might want to prescribe. Medications being prescribed by other doctors and the names and contacts of primary care doctors that are taking care of the patient are handy to include here too. The stressor set (formally Axis IV) is a place where ongoing criminal, legal, child protective services case data and contacts, financial and insurance problems, and other barriers to recovery may be noted and updated. Together, these Axis III and IV sections create targets for action interventions in the treatment plan that will be discussed in more detail in Chapter 8 (Communications). Chapters 6 and 7 also describe the other key parts of the dual diagnosis treatment plan (psychotherapies and medications) in considerable detail.

As a final brief note on the AP/DD evaluation, it is worth reiterating the recommendation that a patient's nicotine use status be put into the diagnostic section even if they do not currently use any form of nicotine (e.g., either make a diagnosis of 'tobacco use disorder' or say 'does not use nicotine'). We have found that this notation is helpful not only as a reminder that the clinician has screened this crucial clinical attribute, but also because nicotine use status has so many implications for overall prognosis and treatment planning (see Chapter 7).

2. Objective Drug Testing

Addictions are unique across the spectrum of mental illnesses in that these disorders allow us to directly measure their activity—aside from the clinical interview—through objective testing of biologics from the body. There is no other category of psychiatric disorder that provides clinicians with this level of observational power to compliment subjective reporting and objective observation of behavioral and cognitive symptoms that may emerge in the interview. Accordingly, the 2 × 4 Model clinic views drug testing as an essential diagnostic modality second only in importance to the clinical interview. Key components and recommendations for objective drug testing are considered below.

- Frequency of testing: Testing should be *random and fairly frequent* for patients with active addictions that are primary targets of the treatment plan. Randomness of testing of course is important to maintain the element of surprise in safeguarding against tampering. When patients offer their urines for testing, it is useful to occasionally accept that offer and other times say 'it is not necessary today'. Notably, when the frequency of testing becomes too high, for example, like a frequency of once a week or more over a sustained period of time, the testing actually loses its randomness. Again, the proper frequency of testing should be determined by the clinical situation, not based on some kind of cook-book algorithm (that often becomes non-random). Some cases (e.g., patients who are struggling with relapse while on buprenorphine) will be best managed by testing, at least for a while, happening more than once a week. Other patients (e.g., those known to be in sustained recovery from all target substances, who are not being prescribed any controlled substances) can be checked once a year. In general, there is a middle group of patients that will get tested about once every one or two months, whereas patients being prescribed controlled substances as part of their treatment should get testing about once a month or more. If it's once a month though, it is important to still try to make it random. Doing it like clockwork every 28 days is not random. Use clinical judgment to tailor the rate and instances of testing to the situation so that it will optimally give data that will be important to informing the clinical treatment plan.

- Diversity of Testing: The 2 × 4 Model clinic should also have capabilities for testing the same drug in multiple ways, and for testing a number of different drugs in same way. So for example, ETOH (alcohol) can be tested three different ways in the clinic: 1) by breathalyzer, 2) by urine testing and 3) blood draws. Then within some of these modalities, it is helpful to have more than one type of measure for ETOH. For instance, urine testing can (and should) provide a detection of both raw ETOH levels and ETG (ethylglucoronide: A longer-lived direct metabolite of ETOH in the body). Testing for drugs via portals other than urine and blood (e.g., hair, saliva, and breath carbon monoxide monitoring (to detect recent smoking)) can be useful as long as the clinic understands the strengths and weakness of these tests.

The basic drug testing panel collected for 'send outs' for chromatography/quantification testing, should contain around 10–20 drug target-molecules that are tested for. A number of opioids including, but not necessarily limited to buprenorphine, methadone, morphine/codeine, and hydrocodone should be on the panel. Tests for ETG, ETOH, cocaine, amphetamines, benzodiazepines, and THC (tetrahydrocannabinol) should also be included. On top of these there should be flexibility to order tests for other opioids, specific benzodiazepines, synthetic stimulants and cannabinoids, and metabolites of buprenorphine and nicotine (cotinine). Testing for therapeutic agents that are being prescribed can also be very helpful to confirm compliance and/or authenticity of the urine sample.

- Speed vs. Cost vs. Accuracy vs. Scope of Testing: Architects routinely tell their clients that any major building project involves resolving the balance between low cost, quality, and speed of construction. You can't realistically have it all. The same is true for urine drug testing in terms of Speed (of results reporting), Cost, Accuracy, and Scope (number of different drugs tested for per sample). The 2 × 4 Model clinic needs to have options, so that it can resolve this balance on a case by case basis or for different clinical contexts. The clinic should be able to conduct both 'bedside' screening urine tests (e.g., dip cups that use rapid antibody detection methods) that give results within 5 minutes of urination, and the more definitive 'gold standard' tests that require 3–10 days, that use more sophisticated chromatography machines in labs off site. In general, the rapid tests are less expensive but instant. They are less flexible (can't add tests for drugs you may want) and are less accurate than the 'send outs', but are not susceptible to destruction by leaks in transit. The send out tests are technically far superior by providing high accuracy of results (including requested drug levels) with more extensive content and flexibility. Sometimes it is best to only order the rapid tests and other times (i.e., more frequently) the team should rely on the send outs. Sometimes both should be ordered on the spot (e.g., test the urine with the rapid, then send the sample out for the chromatography/quantification). This option of dual testing can be valuable for several reasons, one of which is it gives the team a sense of the accuracy of their rapid testing. A point of warning is that the clinic needs to be vigilant as to costs. Some companies that manage send outs can charge $200–$300 per test (while providing a base drug panel), which is actually too extensive. Such charges are unnecessary and might even be viewed as price gouging on patients or insurance companies that are paying for care. If a clinic is taking care of 300 patients, and on average that census is tested with send outs 10 times a year, and each test costs $250, that is a total annual budget of $2,500 per patient or $750,000 year. This would be an unreasonable and unnecessary expense level. Some drug testing companies like to do their own collections on the clinic's behalf (e.g., as if to free up the clinical staff for other responsibilities). The 2 × 4 Model design does not encourage this approach as the employees from the outside agency are not part of the treatment team (i.e., there could be confidentiality issues among other things), and *the act of ordering and collecting tests is itself a meaningful clinical intervention that has implications for the rest of the treatment planning efforts including other diagnostics, psychotherapies, pharmacology, and even professional communications.* The 2 × 4 Model team has to have the flexibility to order and collect tests whenever it is a good time to do so, regardless of who on the team is around. Accordingly, all the major staff, psychiatrists, nurses, therapists, case managers, and their students should be able to collect tests fairly independently (albeit with appropriate supervision from senior team leaders).

- Observed Urine Collections: Some patients will attempt to deceive and manipulate their urine drug test results because minimization and denial is a part of their illness, and society has long indoctrinated them into thinking that addiction is a criminal and sinful behavior that should be hidden. Accordingly, the 2 × 4 Model clinic has to engage in measures to counteract this behavior. The first thing that should be done is to ensure patients (and really act on this claim) that their drug testing results will be used to help them as a tool to direct treatment and not to hurt, judge, or punish them (see below section on reporting of drug testing). Another measure is the direct observation of urine collection. This has to be understood as an invasive procedure and not one that is without risks or downsides. Like drug testing in general, it should be done with a mixture of randomness and directedness, like when clinical suspicion is high for faking urines. Remember, many patients seeking help in the 2 × 4 Model clinic have suffered considerable sexual abuse and exploitation, and this has often led to or been intertwined with their addictive disease (e.g., in prostitution). All efforts must therefore be taken to prevent any sort of enactment or simulation of these dynamics in the clinic; same–gender monitoring is important and the psychiatrist (the professional who may be prescribing controlled substances to the patient, and discussing sexual intimacy and behavior with patients) should not do observed collections.

- Reporting of Drug Testing to Outside Agencies: As previously mentioned, it is crucial that the treatment team and patients understand that drug testing in the 2 × 4 Model clinic is being used for treatment purposes only and not to catch and punish the patient according to the non-treatment focused agendas of outside agencies. It is therefore important that drug testing results not be released to the criminal justice system under any circumstances (e.g., regardless of the whether the results are 'good' or 'bad'), unless the clinic has been issued a specific court order (is compelled to provide the information by a specific a subpoena, or in court testimony). This recommendation is not intended to provide cover for patients who are evading the criminal justice system. Rather it is to preserve the boundary between psychiatric care and punishment which is of paramount importance. The criminal justice system is of course welcome to test their subject as they see fit outside of the 2 × 4 Model clinic, according to the parameters of the legal case and as following the rules of the 'legal chain of custody' that surrounds their testing. At the same time, the 2 × 4 Model clinic is not set up to conduct testing under the legal chain of custody (which usually is required for the courts or law enforcement to use the results to make decisions about the legal status of their subject). And, the criminal justice system is not professionally trained, qualified, or experienced on a biomedical level to understand the clinical context of testing that is occurring in the 2 × 4 Model clinic, or to directly interpret the results of drug testing that is ordered in the 2 × 4 Model clinic. Further discussion of appropriate boundary management and communication between the 2 × 4 Model clinic and the criminal justice system pertaining to clinical test results and related issues is provided in Chapter 8.

3. PDMP Data

The advent and expanded clinical use of Prescription Drug Monitoring Program (PDMP) databases has been one of the most significant advances in addiction prevention, diagnosis, and treatment in the past decade. These internet-based data portals allow pharmacists and physicians to gain immediate access to fairly complete and updated controlled substance prescribing and dispensation patterns to patients. In most states, all outpatient retail pharmacies are required by law to report to the PDMP database most (or all) DEA scheduled substance dispensations to all patients within days of the dispensa- tion. Although originally intended to function as law enforcement tools, PDMPs have found much broader and impactful utility as clinical tools. These platforms have played a significant role in opening the eyes of physicians and other medical professionals to the depth and scope of the iatrogenic prescription drug epidemic. PDMPs typically provide a wealth of actionable data on the exposure of mentally-ill/addicted patients to addictive drugs that have been prescribed to them. This information usually includes types of drugs (e.g., generic names and formulations of opioids, stimulants, benzodiazepines), doses and quantities, when the prescriptions were written, when they were dispensed, name and address of prescribers and pharmacies where the drugs were dispensed, and how they were paid for (e.g., with commercial insurance, Medicaid or self-pay).

A growing research literature is characterizing the clinical utility of PDMP assessment in the prevention, diagnosis, and treatment of addictions. In our own 2 × 4 Model clinic, we have shown that PDMP data can be independent from the clinical exam, predict and corroborate certain types of mental illness (e.g., personality disorders) and addiction diagnoses. We have also shown that repeated queries of the PDMP database, during treatment can help measure addiction treatment outcomes on an individual and population level.

In the 2 × 4 Model clinic, PDMP data should be queried (covering at least the year prior to the intake) for every new patient evaluation. The PDMP should also be re-checked periodically as indicated by the clinical context. Situations that might prompt a PDMP check might include: a) patient reports a new prescription for a controlled substance from a prescriber outside the clinic; b) patient is being placed on a new pharmacological treatment for opioid addic- tion; c) patient has entered a relapse phase. PDMP data inquiry should be documented in summary form in the clinical chart. An optimally informative and efficient way to couch this data would be to document the number of prescribers, pharmacies, and the numbers and types of controlled substances prescribed in the last year. More detailed information on the date, types, quantities, and prescribers responsible for the most recent prescriptions, may provide important actionable data for treatment planning and communications (see Chapter 8).

4. Treatment Encounter Tracking

The EMR (Electronic Medical Record) should readily allow for the tracking of the numbers, frequencies, and types of clinical service encounters that the patient is engaging in on site as well as the rates of cancellations and 'no shows'. The types of service encounters of interest include; dates and numbers of 1:1 psychotherapy appointments, meetings with the psychiatrists, nursing visits including for outpatient DWT (Detox/withdrawal Treatment) appointments, group therapy sessions, family therapy sessions, case management meetings, etc.

Treatment encounter tracking is helpful not only in understanding the patient's diagnosis and prognosis but in terms of assessing clinical outcomes. All of this is important to updating and sculpting the patient's treatment plan in real time as cases evolve. Obviously, attendance is *an* indicator of level of engagement and commitment to treatment, which can help assess the patient's stage of change in recovery. It also is an important measure of how well they are doing clinically. Of course, patients not showing up for treatment are more difficult to monitor, are more likely to be using, and/or in an active illness phase. At the same time, the 2 × 4 Model team must be careful not to over-interpret attendance levels to appointments in general (or certain types of appointments in particular) as always reflecting a patient who is not interested in getting better, or who is too sick to treat. This data is always important to pay attention to, but how it is to be interpreted and acted upon should nearly always be individualized on a case by case basis, and as part of an effort to increase the patient's engagement in care and the efficacy of care. Integrated dual diagnosis treatment is a two-way street, a partnership between the patient and the treatment team. For every ambivalent or psychiatrically ill patient that is not engaging in the recommended level of care, there are also shortfalls, barriers, inadequacies, and failures in the proper provision of care on the treatment side. Sometimes it is a problem within the clinic (e.g., an ineffective doctor or therapist), or outside of the clinic (e.g., when too many patients have insurance plans that actually block or do not adequately support care). And of course there are the other externals, like problems in transportation, legal obligations, or other work or family obligations that can compete with treatment time. Treatment encounter tracking should be used as a starting point to understand which of these many barriers may be operating independently or together to slow progress for the patient.

Sometimes, it is clear that patients are progressing well clinically despite showing a relatively minimal rate of participation in certain types of appointments. In these situations, tracking can be used appropriately to downgrade the emphasis on these types of services. Thinking of different types of service encounters as if they were medications can help in this planning. If a patient is not benefiting or is not compliant with specific medication that is being prescribed (but is showing progress elsewhere), then the practitioner is medically justified in stopping that treatment and moving onto other approaches. At the other extreme is the patient who is recommended to have a high frequency of weekly groups, psychotherapy sessions, and perhaps even doctor or nursing appointments, who is actually compliant with all of this—while still maintaining a highly level of poly-drug use and frequent intoxication. In this scenario, which illustrates how level of engagement and clinical outcomes are not necessarily always the same, there would also be a need to reexamine and reformulate the treatment plan. As discussed more in Chapter 10, the 2 × 4 Model clinic understands and accepts that different patients will progress at different rates, and will benefit most optimally by individualized mixtures and frequencies of service encounters. Treatment encounter tracking is one important way to discover and therapeutically optimize the best and most realistic service mix for a given patient.

Treatment encounter tracking can also be examined to help assess the efficacy and degree of involvement of different types of service encounters for groups of patients. This information can in turn assist the clinic in assessing the adequacies or timing of specific types of service provisions and logistics. It is a way to monitor not only the activity of individual patients, but their flow through specific service channels and professional hands allowing for determination of specific problem areas, bottlenecks, and service resource allocation imbalances.

5. Clinical Rating Scales

Rating scales and other methods that quantify levels or degrees of symptomatology have long been a staple of western medicine. In recent decades, rating scales have become increasingly used not only as research tools (e.g., to measure efficacy of anti-psychotics), but as clinical assessment tools. The 2 × 4 Model incorporates the use of several types of rating scales as important diagnostic tools with respect to the caveats that: 1) they should be used to compliment the clinical exam and evaluation (not to replace it); and 2) that they are fallible and susceptible to inaccuracies (like any other diagnostic approach in medicine), especially when they incorporate subjective information. The following rating scales are recommended as a foundation of quantitative assessments that are particularly useful in 2 × 4 Model treatment planning.

- Folstein MMSE: The Folstein Mini-Mental Status Exam has served well throughout medicine as a general screening tool for dementia. This 30 point scale (30 = no cognitive deficit detected) can quantify degree of severity of the cognitive problem, provide some indication of the domain (or even anatomy) of the cognitive problem. It is a performance test and not a subjective self-rating, so it is relatively objective. The scale does not identify the cause of the underlying cognitive problem, but can be very useful to measure cognitive function generally due to a wide range of causes that may be found in the dual diagnosis treatment population. This information can be useful for treatment planning including case management and professional communications. It is repeatable but relatively insensitive to minor cognitive problems.

- COWS: The Clinical Opiate Withdrawal Scale, is a rapid rating tool that quantifies the severity of opioid withdrawal. It is a multi-item scale that uses a combination of objective observations and self-reports, with a max score of 49 (severe withdrawal). The scale is a good adjunct to the vital sign data in assessing withdrawal and is rapidly repeatable, being sensitive to changes in symptoms on the order of minutes (e.g., with office dosing of buprenorphine). It is a handy way for the clinician to keep in mind the many features of opioid withdrawal. The major drawback of the scale is it lacks specificity; positive scores can be obtained by other conditions (e.g., flu or alcohol withdrawal).

- CIWA: The Clinical Institute Withdrawal Assessment for Alcohol scale rapidly assess alcohol withdrawal. It is a multi-item scale with a max of 35 (severe withdrawal) that has essentially the same strengths and weaknesses as the COWS. It is an important compliment to the vital signs in diagnosing and gauging treatment response for the potentially life threatening condition of alcohol withdrawal.

- ACES: The Adverse Childhood Experiences Scale is a 10 point scale that quantifies a person's childhood history of exposure to several forms of abuse, neglect, and household dysfunction that are strongly linked to abuse and neglect. It is very rapid to administer and is a great way to orient other diagnostic work and treatment planning. Child abuse and trauma is a major root cause of adult mental illness, addiction, general medical disease, and early death in the U.S., and may ultimately be the largest public health challenge that we do the least about. The 2 × 4 Model clinic should consider itself to be a front line preventative and treatment center for families that have suffered with childhood abuse and neglect. Because many forms of dual diagnosis disorders are both the cause and effect of childhood abuse and neglect, treatment of dual diagnosis conditions in adults becomes a primary approach to breaking the trans-generational cycle of childhood abuse, neglect, and domestic violence in families. The ACES should be performed routinely on all new patients in the clinic with results charted in the EMR. Theoretically, the results should not change over time for an adult (and so the scale does not have re-test utility). The scale is susceptible to involuntary selective recall or other purposeful agendas patient's may have to cover or exaggerate their exposure to abuse and neglect.

- SOGS: The South Oaks Gambling Screen is a quantification of self-reported symptoms and behaviors that are useful for documenting pathological gambling (PG) diagnoses and illness severity. It has a maximum score of 20 (severe PG). PG, as one of the more common 'non-chemical' or 'behavioral addictions', is quite similar to drug addictions, and is often comorbid with them. But we lack an objective assay (e.g., like a UDS) to detect illness activity as we have for drug addictions. The SOGS and other gambling rating scales can makes up for this gap to some extent and help confirm a diagnosis for a condition that can be quite elusive. The SOGS can be repeated for assessing treatment response, if questions are modified to reflect illness activity over a defined time span.

- Miscellaneous: Of course, other than the aforementioned 5 rating scales that are recommended for routine use in the 2 × 4 Model clinic, additional scales can be added for research, clinical, or administrative purposes. For example, rating scales that measure history or styles of social and emotional attachments in patients, such as the Experiences in Close Relationships-Relationship Structure Questionnaire (ECR-RS) may provide important clues as to their form of dual diagnosis and prognosis in care. Scales that quantify life-history of head injuries indicative of Traumatic Brain Injury such as the Ohio State University TBI Identification Method (OSU-TBI-ID) may also be helpful. The caution here is to avoid doing too many rating scales on patients or allowing scales to substitute for gold-standard clinical interviewing and psychotherapies. Scales that do not direct or inform treatment, or that do not do so enough to warrant the time it takes to do them, should probably not be used.

6. Medical Assessments

The 2 × 4 Model clinic is not designed or intended to be a venture in primary care or internal medicine, although it could be equipped to accommodate a primary care doctor embedded within it. It should have rudimentary capabilities for medical diagnostics needed for the psychiatrists and the nursing team to make referrals to primary care and other specialists. Psychiatric physician and nursing staff in the 2 × 4 Model clinic should only rarely engage in primary care work; shortages of psychiatric physicians and addiction-trained psychiatrists are even worse than shortages of primary care doctors. And, it is important for physicians to operate as much as possible with their own zones of training and expertise. With that said, the physicians and nurses of the 2 × 4 Model clinic need to be able to screen for basic medical problems, especially those that are commonly associated with, or are caused by addictions. Diagnosis and treatment of intoxication, withdrawal syndromes, determination of blood levels, and medical safety of psychotropic meds that patients may be prescribed in the clinic should be routine. Accordingly, the clinic should be equipped with a medical exam room (with bathrooms for UDS testing), scales for weight and height measures, reliable instruments for vital sign assessments, equipment for blood drawing and storage, and rapid pregnancy tests.

Taken together, the diagnostic tool box of the 2 × 4 Model clinic should represent a means to collect a multicomponent data stream that provides insights not only about the patient's diagnosis but how the patient's illness is evolving over time. This data stream, formed by the repeated collection of many data over time, is crucial for helping the addiction psychiatrist and the team understand what is and what is not working in the treatment, so that clinical decision-making can be made part of well-informed treatment strategy changes. This data stream, when compiled over groups of patients can also inform larger strategies and logistics needed to address strengths and weaknesses in overall diagnostics, staffing, and treatment programming (see Chapters 10 and 11). For these purposes, the use of EMRs and auxiliary database software platforms (e.g., Microsoft Excel) stored on shared drives, and accessible to multiple team members, are regarded as indispensable to the diagnostics of the 2 × 4 Model clinic. The diagnostic tool box together with the electronic data stream that it informs in the EMR, can thus be used in 2 × 4 Model clinic not only for clinical purposes but for professional training, program quality improvement, and research (Chapter 11).

Background References and Further Reading

Carroll, K. M., and B. J. Rounsaville. 2002. "On beyond urine: Clinically useful assessment instruments in the treatment of drug dependence." *Behaviour Research & Therapy 40* (11): 1329–1344.

Corrigan, J. D., and J. Bogner. 2007. "Initial reliability and validity of the Ohio State University TBI identification method." *Journal of Head Trauma Rehabilitation 22* (6): 318–329.

Crum, R. M., J. C. Anthony, S. S. Bassett, and M. F. Folstein. 1993. "Population-based norms for the mini-mental state examination by age and educational level." *The Journal of the American Medical Association 269* (18): 2386–2391.

Felitti, V. J., R. F. Anda, D. Nordenberg, D. F. Williamson, A. M. Spitz, V. Edwards, M. P. Koss, and J. S. Marks. 1998. "Relationship of childhood abuse and household dysfunction to many of the leading causes of death in adults. The Adverse Childhood Experiences (ACE) Study." *American Journal of Preventive Medicine 14* (4): 245–258.

Fraley, R. C., M. E. Heffernan, A. M. Vicary, and C. C. Brumbaugh. 2011. "The experiences in close relationships-relationship structures questionnaire: A method for assessing attachment orientations across relationships." *Psychological Assessment 23* (3): 615–625.

Hackman, D. T., M. S. Greene, T. J. Fernandes, A. M. Brown, E. R. Wright, and R. A. Chambers. 2014. "Prescription drug monitoring program inquiry in psychiatric assessment: Detection of high rates of opioid prescribing to a dual diagnosis population." *The Journal of Clinical Psychiatry 75* (7): 750–756. doi: 10.4088/JCP.14m09020.

Kalapatapu, R. K., and R. A. Chambers. 2009. "Novel objective biomarkers of alcohol use: Potential diagnostic and treatment management tools in dual diagnosis care." *Journal of Dual Diagnosis 5* (1): 5–82. doi: 10.1080/15504260802628684.

Kleber, H. D., R. D. Weiss, R. F. Anton, T. P. George, S. F. Greenfield, T. R. Kosten, C. P. O'Brien, B. J. Rounsaville, D. M. Ziedonis, G. Hennessy, and H. S. Connery. 2006. *"Practice Guidleine for the Treatment of Patients with Substance Use Disorders"*, edited by APA Steering Committee on Practice Guidlines. Washington, DC: American Psychiatric Association.

Lehman, A. F., C. P. Myers, and E. Corty. 1989. "Assessment and classification of patients with psychiatric and substance abuse syndromes." *Hospital & Community Psychiatry 40* (10): 1019–1025.

Lesieur, H. R., and S. B. Blume. 1987. "The South Oaks Gambling Screen (SOGS): A new instrument for the identification of pathological gamblers." *The American Journal of Psychiatry 144* (9): 1184–1188. doi: 10.1176/ajp.144.9.1184.

McLellan, A. T., L. Luborsky, G. E. Woody, C. P. O'Brien, and K. A. Druley. 1983. "Predicting response to alcohol and drug abuse treatments. Role of psychiatric severity." *Archives of General Psychiatry 40* (6): 620–625.

Moeller, K. E., K. C. Lee, and J. C. Kissack. 2008. "Urine drug screening: Practical guide for clinicians." *Mayo Clinic Proceedings 83* (1): 6–76. doi: 10.4065/83.1.66 S0025-6196(11)61120-8 [pii].

Mordal, J., B. Holm, J. Morland, and J. G. Bramness. 2010. "Recent substance intake among patients admitted to acute psychiatric wards: Physician's assessment and on-site urine testing compared with comprehensive laboratory analyses." *Journal of Clinical Psychopharmacology 30* (4): 455–459.

Sullivan, J. T., K. Sykora, J. Schneiderman, C. A. Naranjo, and E. M. Sellers. 1989. "Assessment of alcohol withdrawal: The R Clinical Institute Withdrawal Assessment for Alcohol scale (CIWA-Ar)." *The British Journal of Addiction 84* (11): 1353–1357.

Wesson, D. R., and W. Ling. 2003. "The Clinical Opiate Withdrawal Scale (COWS)." *Journal of Psychoactive Drugs 35* (2): 253–259. doi: 10.1080/02791072.2003. 10400007.

6 Psychotherapeutics

Psychotherapeutics for Both MI and SUDS

The core concepts of psychotherapeutics in the 2 × 4 Model clinic are:

1. Vertical binding of psychotherapies. Maintain a clinical focus on both MI and SUD illnesses, and the integration of psychotherapeutic approaches for each of these, as called for based on the patient's individualized dual diagnostic assessment (i.e., the balance of their MI vs. addiction quality and severity and stage of change).
2. Multiplicity of psychotherapy approaches. Utilization of multiple styles and forms of evidence-based psychotherapies, including both individual and group psychotherapies.

Toward Vertical Binding of Psychotherapies in the 2 × 4 Model

The primary goals of treatment are to help patients achieve sustained reductions or elimination of psychiatric illness symptoms and addictive drug use. As discussed in Chapter 2, the mental illness and addiction pathologies are often co-occurring, biologically inter-related and to a major extent mutually reinforcing. Therefore, treatment aims not only to reduce both MI and SUD symptoms but to break up the capacity of these diseases to be connected with and reinforce one another (**Figure 10.3**). In essence, the underlying MI is an agent that facilitates the continuation and worsening of addiction, and vice versa, the uncontrolled SUD pours fuel on the fire of the MI. The 2 × 4 Model aims to free patients from both the tyranny of psychiatric symptoms and the slavery of drug addiction.

This view of addiction treatment—as the liberation of an individual from a kind of slavery—is a useful model for understanding how psychotherapies should work in the 2 × 4 Model, as anchored on the neuroscientific and clinical evidence base in the addiction field, and integrated with mental health recovery.

Biologically and phenomenologically, addiction is a progressive brain disease that gets incrementally worse with every dose of the addictive drug that reaches the brain. How big each incremental change is depends on the individual; their age, gender, severity and form of underlying mental illness, and how severe their current addiction illness is, etc. Nevertheless, the disease is progressive and it happens physically, biologically, in the brain, as a process involving many regions, but most centrally in the ventral striatum (also known as the (NAC)). As described in Chapter 2, the NAC is a key information processing network that maintains, processes, and adapts the neural codes that govern *motivation*.

It is helpful to think of motivation as more than just the 'desire' or 'energy' that compels us to do certain things. We can understand motivation as a library of neural codes (i.e., neuronal firing activity patterns distributed across a large population of NAC neurons) that helps the brain call up, select, organize, and sequence motor programs that are primarily represented in the *dorsal striatum*, and are behaviorally acted out by the primary motor system (striatum/motor cortex/spinal motor neurons/muscles). In this view, motivation is like the brain's software that helps it link one behavior program to the next, in the 'best' possible sequence. If you list all the discrete motor programs one executes in a single day, the thousands of different behaviors that we can literally see people perform—these are actually strung together in the sequence that they occur, by neural activity that we can't see, but is happening in the brain. This neural activity is represented in large part in the NAC, and is the biophysical medium of motivation. Now, how this 'motivation' software performs, that is to say, what the neural codes (firing pattern representations) are, how complex they are, how many of them can be stored by the NAC, how fast they can be re-written or adapted to new situations, how well they can actually control the selection and sequencing of motor program, etc.—*all this depends on the integrity of the hardware*. In turn, the hardware is the population of neurons in the NAC, and their connectivity with each other and other parts of the brain that are impacted by mental illness (e.g., neurons in the PFC, hippocampus, AMY (see **Figure 2.2**)). Accordingly, the health and functionality of the motivational software and hardware of the NAC is connected with and dependent on, the health and integrity of the broader limbic areas of the brain where decision-making, emotion, cognition, and social interactions are represented. In alignment with this biological and anatomical reality, the 2 × 4 Model calls for the integration (vertical binding) and individualization of key evidence-based psychotherapies from both the MI and SUD treatment fields (**Figure 6.1**). The following sections provide an overview of the goals, content, and structural organization of this psychotherapy integration which aims to liberate the individual patient in the 2 × 4 Model clinic from the tyranny of mental illness and the slavery of drug addiction.

Addiction As a Neurobiological Civil War within the Individual's Motivation Circuits

In a normal brain that is not suffering with addiction (or MI), the NAC hardware that controls motivational processing is healthy and structurally intact. The person has good decision-making and can orient and sequence their behaviors toward goals (occupational, educational, familial, etc.) that are beneficial to them and their family or community. Their healthy 'motivational–behavioral repertoire'—which is like a rich library of neural codes that are the software for motivation and behavioral output—is supported by healthy hardware, that is, the NAC-based neural network. When functioning in a normal way, in a healthy brain, the complex decision-making and motivational capacity of the individual vividly reflects the *faculty of free will*.

As the addiction process begins to progress with repeated drug taking, the faculty of free will begins to diminish. There is actually a loss of free will, like what happens to an individual when they are becoming enslaved. In this way, the disease process of addiction represents a pathological, involuntary erosion of free will, which is very different from how addiction is often misunderstood as being a voluntary choice of a free will that is intact, but bad, wrong, or sinful and deserving of punishment.

The loss of the faculty of free will in addiction, viewed in terms of the software of motivational programming, can be understood as a loss of diversity and/or flexibility in the neural codes represented in the NAC. In addiction the individual has reached a state where too often, and under too many circumstances, they are motivated to seek out and use the drug(s) and act on these motivations through their behavior. They seek drugs and use them, even when 'part of them' doesn't want to, even when they know it's hurting them or others they love, and when it is no longer fun. They may still have many of the healthy, nondrug taking motivations (and neural codes) stored in the NAC, but many of them are being suppressed from expression by the disease. In some very real, biophysical sense, the healthy motivations are becoming computationally dominated by the drug-seeking and drug-taking motivations and neural codes. Worse still, many of the healthy motivations and their neural codes are becoming overwritten, isolated, forgotten, or destroyed by the addiction-oriented motivations.

When we realize that both the healthy and the addiction-related motivations are both stored in, sculpted in, and executed within the same territory of the brain—the hardware of the NAC neural network—we can see and feel the experience of having the disease of addiction as being a lot like a civil war! To extend this analogy to the American Civil War (1861–1865), it is very much like you have one country (one brain network) that is in conflict with itself, that is being torn apart by two sets of motivations: One set that is healthy, that yearns to survive as a whole, intact and free; the other set that is diseased, devoted to preserving the *slavery of addiction*, even at the expense of the whole. Of course it's not literally true that the NAC becomes physically divided into two anatomically separate regions where healthy vs. drug motivations are stored. Rather, it's more likely that the repeated hits of the addictive drug(s) have physically altered (sickened) the NAC territory in a more distributed anatomical pattern, so that the battle between drug use vs. healthy motivation is happening in a fairly distributed space, more like a guerrilla civil war, where there is no clear anatomical 'front line' in the NAC. Nevertheless, it is a battle for territory and control, a battle for both the hardware and the software of motivation.

As the addictive disease worsens, before treatment begins, there is a pathological progression of changes that underpin the growth and influence of motivations that serve drug-seeking and taking. The disease gains territory both biophysically—in terms of the extent of pathological biological changes within the NAC neural network that the drug exposure is causing, and on the neuroinformatic level—in terms of how the neural firing pattern representations that underpin the motivation to seek and use drugs begin to dominate the behavioral selection and sequencing functions of the NAC. In this way, the disease can also be likened to a cancer, or to a parasite growing from within, that is fueled for growth by an external agent, the ongoing intake of the addictive drug(s). But again, this pathological growth is not just located in any old organ system. It is happening in the very center of the brain's architecture that is responsible for supporting both the faculty of free will and the will to survive (i.e., the motivations that support the survival of the individual and his species). So, as the disease progresses, as the *enemy gains power in the brain*, it begins to not only erode the free will of the individual, but it takes on the motivation to survive itself, regardless of the consequences for the host. It is often in this phase that the individual becomes aware that a battle for survival has begun. A battle between survival of the addiction, which thus far has been gaining strength vs. survival of the individual and their free will, their healthy motivations, which are losing. It is often at this point that the individual recognizes they are not equipped to fight this enemy alone, and they begin to seek help.

Intervening in the Civil War of Addiction: Reconnaissance on the Stage of Change

This view of addiction as a civil war happening within the individual fits nicely with a well-known aspect of addiction phenomenology that is readily observable across most patients with the disease. They are to some extent ambivalent about their recovery. Said another way, there is to some degree for all these patients, some 'part of them' that wants to continue using, or to go back to using. But they also carry another part of them that wants to stop using or stay clear from using.

Considering where patients are in this 'motivational civil war', is an important task in the psychotherapeutic assessment of addiction. The brilliant contribution of Prochaska and DiClemente, known as the Stages of Change (also called the Transtheoretical Model), gave us a very clinically useful way to estimate and describe where patients are in their own civil war against addiction (or other forms of motivational ambivalence). Patients may be understood as existing in or progressing though the following:

	Stage	Clinical Characteristics
1.	Pre-contemplation	Addiction progressing; patient not in treatment
2.	Contemplation	Patient awareness of the internal battle for survival
3.	Preparation	Looking for help and strategies to fight the addiction
4.	Action	Internal war is on! Recruit outside help and fight!
5.	Maintenance	Momentum is on the side of recovery; enemy retreating
6.	Relapse*	Surprise attack! The enemy is back; return to action!

* Note that later formulations of the stages have redefined relapse as external to the stages, as it represents a regression instead of progression.

Of course, understanding addiction is not as simple as memorizing these 6 stages and expecting that every individual will progress through them in orderly fashion, in this exact sequence, and with predictable time allotments at each stage. Patients can be in stages that are best characterized as being blends of these stages. Sometimes, they seem to skip stages, or we inaccurately estimate which stage they are in. Or, they can be in multiple stages at the same time in the context of poly-addictions, with roughly one stage being accurate to each drug they are addicted too. For example, the man who is sober from alcohol but still smokes, is in Maintenance with respect to alcohol but Pre-contemplative with respect to nicotine. Often, when patients get to stage 6, they can rebound to any of the preceding stages; sometimes they appear to oscillate among the stages 4, 5, and 6.

In any event, we do try to clinically estimate a patient's current stage of change for each drug they are addicted to, because it has major implications for treatment planning both in terms of psychotherapeutics and medication management. In general, the goal is to appropriately match the team's therapeutic resources and efforts (which are always precious) to the patient's ability to accept and respond to those resources and efforts. The 2 × 4 Model clinic provides both individual and/or group therapies for patients, and the focus of these therapies should definitely attend to where patients are in their Stages of Change. These approaches also borrow core principals from the 12-steps, which are complimentary to the Stages of Change Model. When boiled down to its fundamentals with religious allusions extracted out, the 12-steps, as utilized in the 2 × 4 Model clinic, can be reformulated as three principal components.

Returning to the civil war analogy, we can view the 2 × 4 Model clinical intervention as being like a liberating army that aims to restore the wholeness and unity of the individual's healthy motivational function (faculty of free will/healthy survival motivations), while abolishing the slavery of addiction. Of course a better equipped army is more likely to succeed against the enemy, and so the 2 × 4 Model thrives on bringing a wide array of weapons to the fight from both the psychotherapeutic and pharmacological arsenals. These tools and approaches are then selected, combined and timed based not only on the patient's addiction and MI diagnoses, but on their Stage of Change.

BOX 6.1 2 × 4 Model Version of 12-Steps: Three Principal Components Corresponding to Stages of Change

1. Recognizing there is a disease that impairs free will, requiring external help.

    (Pre-contemplation/Contemplation)

2. Acknowledging and acting on the need to repair damage caused by the disease.

    (Preparation/Action)

3. Role modeling and supporting others seeking addiction recovery and mental health.

    (Maintenance/Relapse Prevention)

Stage of Change, Psychotherapies, and Vertical Binding

In the 2 × 4 Model, which embraces patients with a diversity of different combinations of MI and addictions, clinicians have the opportunity, and responsibility really, to note that both the progression of an individual's addictive disease, and their ability to fight it and respond to different treatments, does depend considerably on the type and severity of co-occurring MI they have. In other words, how individual patients progress through the Stages of Change, is influenced to some extent by the co-occurring MI. Similarly, the choice of psychotherapeutic treatments should be made based on both MI diagnosis and the Stage of Change (which is also influenced by the MI).

A basic understanding of how the co-occurring MI can influence a patient's progression through the Stages of Change can be arrived at by merging our understanding of how MI biologically exacerbates and accelerates addictive disease (Chapter 2) with the Neurobiological Civil War analogy developed in this chapter. Recall from Chapter 2 that the presence of MI biologically allows for a more rapid progression of addictive disease in part because even before exposure to addictive drugs, the NAC network is not healthy and/or is biologically more susceptible to the pathogenic effects of addictive drugs. This relative lack of NAC network health is caused by one or more of a number of many possible primary developmental abnormalities (of genetic and/or experiential causes) happening in other parts of the brain, that project into the NAC, including the PFC, hippocampus and/or AMY (see **Figure 2.2**). It really does not matter whether the actual neurodevelopmental problem was induced by an environmental experience or genetic factors, or both, because all of the above have biological implications and can change the development, function, and structural integrity of motivational neural networks. So, if the VHIP is not normal and/or the AMY is not normal, and/or the PFC is not normal, it can be inevitable that the NAC will also be altered because all of these frontal-temporal-limbic regions project directly to it.

So now, in the brain with MI, we are talking about a NAC network that is already, in some way, more limited in how it can store, manage, adapt, and implement motivational programs that select and sequence behavior. The normally healthy *faculty of free will* is impacted in some way at baseline by the mental illness (either chronically or episodically depending on the type and pattern of mental illness), so that the individual is more likely to enact on faulty decision-making, or to rely on a more limited, stereotyped, or chaotic set of emotional or cognitive patterns, to drive the selection and sequencing of behavior. For some patients the motivational abnormality is relatively chronic and stable (e.g., schizophrenia, PTSD) while for others it can be quite episodic and/or unstable (e.g., bipolar, borderline personality disorder). Across many of these mental illnesses, the *motivation to survive* is also often chronically or episodically compromised to some extent, as evidenced by the high prevalence of suicidal thinking and completed acts in these conditions. Under these circumstances we are talking about a brain, and a NAC network, that is especially vulnerable to the aggressive effects of addictive drugs to rapidly take and occupy 'motivational space'. By further compromising the functional and anatomical integrity of an already compromised NAC network, addictive drugs are more rapidly able to elevate drug-seeking and taking as a prime directive at the expense of natural motivations in the brain with MI.

Motivational Enhancement Therapy and Dual Diagnosis

So in the context of MI, the NAC is ripe for the motivational system civil war induced by addictive drugs.

The addiction can progress quite rapidly, and, because the MI may produce problems with insight and judgment anyway, the patient is even more prone to staying stuck in the Pre-contemplation stage, where they are not fully aware of the conflict within, even as the damage of addiction accumulates. But with persistent but gentle psychotherapeutic support, as provided in the course of Motivational Enhancement Therapy (MET), the patient and clinician can nonjudgmentally explore the pros and cons of continued drug use, and question the assumptions and rationalizations the patient may have (that are often quite pathological) that he/she uses to justify ongoing substance use. Once the patient is 'escorted' from *Contemplation to Action*, the addiction psychiatrist is aware that as a rule of thumb, the more mentally ill the patient is, the harder it might be to: a) recover accurate self-reporting information on ongoing drug use; b) achieve quick and easy remission of a use pattern with just one form of treatment; and c) maintain patients in a stable pattern of remission that is relapse free. Much of this can be attributable to the fact that MI brains on average are biologically vulnerable to more severe forms of addiction than healthy brains, and so these addictions can be seen as more treatment refractory. The clinician can therefore expect that patients with MI may sometimes be harder to get into *Maintenance*, and depending some on the quality of MI, are more likely to vacillate between epochs of *Maintenance and Relapse*.

Again the civil war analogy comes in handy for understanding what MET is trying to do, and how the technique that goes with it, motivational interviewing, best serves the goals of MET. In MET, we see the patient in conflict, in a motivational civil war. Inside, they have the healthy motivation and the diseased motivation. In MET, we are aiming to join with them on the healthy side and help them strengthen the healthy motivation. We are providing *therapy* to *enhance* their healthy *motivation*. (They don't call it Motivational Enhancement Therapy for nothing!) It is almost as if we clinicians are a foreign power providing military aid to one side of a nation (the patient) in civil war, while the drug(s) represents a competing power, providing the enemy side with aid in the civil war. But it is even better to think of the experience of MET from within the therapeutic relationship as being a bit more involved than simply one entity giving aid to the other. A more compelling analogy for a more powerful alliance is that the patient (that is, the healthy side of their motivation) and the clinician (and the treatment team) are engaged in an active partnership to weaken and vanquish the enemy. Both the patient and the treatment team members are active allies in the fight and both are invested in recovery. Both have skin in the game, and both may be called upon at the same or different times to help grow or take back healthy motivational 'territory', to progress through the Stages of Change and to achieve partial or full recovery.

In this civil war analogy, we can readily understand the value of a core principal in motivational interviewing that is necessary for MET to work. This is the nonjudgmental style of interviewing and the attention needed to maintain a nonpunitive stance both in terms of the manner of the therapeutic relationship and the treatment decisions that are being made for the patients. A big reason that the punitive/judgmental stance is so ineffective and even potentially harmful is that the patient cannot simply take that kind of attitude from the clinician and direct it only at the part of them that is sick, where the diseased motivation resides. What happens when a punitive dynamic is used in treatment is that the whole patient, both the healthy and the sick parts, absorbs the negative attitude, energy, or action by the clinician—which indiscriminately wounds even the healthy part of the patient—like collateral damage. This runs the risk of alienating the patient, and their healthy motivation from the clinician and the clinical team—potentially driving them further into the arms of the addiction. It is generally not motivating for a patient to feel like a bad person or like a failure, especially if they are reading this impression from the clinical team. And in fact, it can drive relapse in the patient when the painful feelings of defeat become a great excuse to use. The 'harm amplification' of the criminal justice/punitive approach to addiction, is not only an anti-harm reduction approach to care, but it is an anti-motivational enhancement approach, as it risks indiscriminating damage to the whole patient (and the capacity for their healthy motivations to grow), even as it is trying to attack the unhealthy-disease motivations.

Cognitive-Behavioral Therapy and Dual Diagnosis

The professional framework that any member of the 2 × 4 Model clinical team should be operating under for conducting their relationships with patients should be psychodynamically informed with attention to maintaining appropriate boundaries and noting transference and counter-transference phenomena. Working on this foundation, motivational interviewing techniques and MET should be applied to assess where patients are in their Stage of Change, and how they should be treated to facilitate therapeutic progress through the stages. Cognitive-Behavioral Therapy (CBT) and its variants, widely used for the treatment of a range of mental illnesses, including depression and personality disorders, are also an important approach that members of the team should also be using in conjunction with motivational interviewing and MET.

As applied in the treatment of dual diagnosis and addictions, CBT in the *Pre-contemplative to Action* Stages of Change, is helpful for growing patient's abilities to see and work against the cognitive and motivational fallacies operating within them that are supporting (i.e., rationalizing) their ongoing drug use. For example, it is common for dual diagnosis patients to claim that they cannot attend recommended therapy sessions or nursing appointments because of their work schedules. Certainly, there may be some kind of a time conflict between work and treatment, and the patients are genuinely in need of financial resources. However, if the issue of their employment is examined more broadly over a longer time scale, it is readily apparent for many patients that: a) active, untreated addiction has been, and remains, the actual threat to their ability to work; and b) their preoccupation with keeping employment, especially when at the expense of attending treatment, often reflects motivation that is contaminated by a pathological desire to maintain resources to buy substances. In this way, the patient is demonstrating a pathological cognitive and motivational pattern, caused by addictive disease and often exacerbated by the underlying mental illness, where they are framing the causal events surrounding their addiction in a way that is almost exactly opposite to reality. This kind of addiction-based 'reality reversal' can almost seem psychotic in its proportions. Thus, while their addiction-thinking can frame their participation in treatment as the enemy of their gainful employment, the reality is that it is their addiction that is destroying their ability to work, and they are not going to be able to get better from their addiction (eventually work in stable employment) without treatment. Fortunately, unlike true schizophrenia-range delusions, this kind of 'reality-reversal' thinking is relatively addressable via psychotherapeutic (e.g., CBT approaches) when persistently applied. One of the most incisive CBT-oriented statements that could be used in response to the "but I gotta go to work" rationalization, perhaps delivered with a friendly smile, is "Yeah, but it's hard to work when you are strung out or dead, right?"

Another example of addiction-related 'reality reversal' is the patient who relapses onto opioids at the funeral of their sister who just died from an opioid overdose: "It was just too much for me being there at the wake, seeing my sister in the casket like that wishing I could have been there to save her . . . and everyone crying . . . and then passing out pills . . . I just couldn't resist using at that point . . ." Again, a CBT approach could be used at this juncture, to challenge this cognition, by exploring whether the patient really believes the deceased sister would really want the patient to join her, and how the drug use at the wake is dissonant with the tragedy. And of course, one of the most common fallacies that has long been a pitfall for many clinicians, is the idea—commonly espoused by dual diagnosis patients (and sometimes clinicians)—that the addictive drug use merely represents an appropriate, rational, and justifiable act of medicine taking for the neuropsychiatric symptoms. As described in Chapter 2, CBT-informed psychotherapy should be utilized carefully by 2 × 4 Model clinicians to challenge self-medication hypothesis-based drug use rationalization, and to help patients understand more generally that the ongoing drug use is not part of the cure, but more of the disease.

In the *Action, Maintenance and Relapse* stages, CBT provides a potent therapeutic approach or workspace for the patient and clinician to identify and manage triggers and craving episodes, and to analyze and dissect the chain of events that led to the latest relapse. Again, an empathic, motivational interviewing approach is a good foundation upon which the CBT does its job. The therapist works to make sure that the patient is not feeling defensive, shameful, judged, or stigmatized by their experiences, cognitions, and pathological motivations that are caused by the addiction. Then, the patient is more able to 'show the monster', that is, to let the addiction come out and show, the patient and the therapist alike, how it operates. Conversations about trigger sets can help the patient discern which relapse triggers have to be either confronted or avoided in early recovery. Discussions about what to do during 'craving storms' can provide patients with strategies to distract themselves from or tolerate (e.g., via mindfulness) the feelings of drug-longing until they have passed over. Relapse 'dissections' are opportunities to understand the sometimes complicated and partially unconscious chain of events (experiences and decisions) that led to the latest relapse. Again using the NFL analogy, CBT applied to relapse dissections with patients should be approached a lot like game film reviews, where coaches and players get together to watch detailed footage of their latest team loss to figure out what, where, and when the problems happened. As with the motivational interviewing approach, the goal is not to make the patient feel bad about what went wrong, which could make a player (patient) feel incompetent and want to give up, but to equip the patient with a better understanding of where they can improve, so that they can act on their capacity to improve when the next trigger challenge is encountered.

Multiplicity of Psychotherapeutic Modalities

The 2 × 4 Model clinic puts a premium on offering a diversity of psychotherapies, and views the provision of both individual and group psychotherapies as being essential. This is not to say that it requires that every patient do intensive individual psychotherapy or that every patient should do groups, or that every patient should do both of these. Such rigid algorithmic requirements are typical of cook-book, mill like programs that are not good at individualizing treatment, and often end up kicking sick patients out. Instead, the 2 × 4 Model concept is that both individual and group psychotherapies are being done in the clinic in high volumes, so that the team therapists each carry substantial caseloads of individual and group patients, and, substantial proportions of patients making up the clinic census are being cared for at any one time in any of the three possible configurations: 1) individual only; 2) group only; 3) individual and group. In some cases, it is also perfectly acceptable for patients to be in more than one psychotherapy at the same time and/or more than one group therapy simultaneously. This therapeutic redundancy (when done with appropriate professional guarding against splitting) allows a beneficial effect of getting more professional eyes from the same team onto patients, which is usually more beneficial than not for the care of especially sick patients, and can aid treatment team members in terms of load sharing. *In general—and contrary to the view of some professionals outside of the addiction field—addiction and dual diagnosis care is an incredibly rich arena for psychotherapeutic interventions, and for the integration of those approaches with psychopharmacologies* (see Chapter 10).

The reader should note that this emphasis on delivering eclectic individual and group psychotherapies, reflects how the 2 × 4 Model clinic operates, even within the psychotherapeutic dimension, as a team effort. In essence, this approach will for many patients provide not only the 'corrective parenting' that 1:1 psychotherapies are thought to provide, but to some extent a 'corrective multi-parenting/family experience.' This can give many patients the best chance to form not just one, but multiple enduring therapeutic attachments with 2 × 4 Model team professionals. In turn, the strength and number of these therapeutic attachments can be crucial determinants for the long-term persistence, prognosis, and resilience patients with mental illness and addictions need to get better. Multiple positive relationships represent multiple lifelines to positive recovery. A caveat to this principle is that lack of communication or splitting between therapists and/or between the physician-therapist/psychopharmacologist and the other team therapists can be clinically detrimental. For this reason (and see Chapters 9 and 10), the 2 × 4 Model clinic strives to offer *all* the psychotherapies (and psychopharmocologies) the patient needs, as provided under one roof, by one treatment team. Thus, the sharing of patients between the 2 × 4 Model clinic and another treatment systems (such that different professional psychotherapies are split, or where the provision of medication management and psychotherapies are split) are not encouraged. Insofar as peer support programs, such as AA, NA, or club houses, are not professional treatment services, patients may be encouraged to attend these outside of the 2 × 4 Model clinic.

As suggested in prior chapters, a major purpose of the psychotherapeutic flexibility and eclecticism of the 2 × 4 Model clinic, and in particular, the provisioning of both individual and group therapies, is that individual patients will have a diversity of different dual diagnosis conditions, with differential responsivities, benefits vs. side effects, of being in group vs. individual therapies. For example, while group therapies for patients with florid mania or paranoid psychoses are often relatively contraindicated, patients with depression and PTSD may fare well in groups. While some patients excel in groups and serve as powerful and inspiring role models, other patients only hide out in them, or doze off ('present in body only') and/or can be disruptive. Individual psychotherapies can then be used to augment or serve in place of group therapies.

The tactical approach and theoretical foundation for conducting (leading) both individual and group therapies in the 2 × 4 Model clinic should include elements of motivational interviewing, MET, and CBT approaches as described above. This foundation is then best garnished with a range of possible psychotherapeutic approaches, that borrow from psychodynamic, interpersonal therapies, objection relations, attachment theories, and standard supportive/educational approaches, as informed by the patient composition, group size, the proximal treatment goals of the therapy, and to some extent, the interests and skill sets of the clinician. It is perhaps easier for clinicians to realize that all of these psychotherapeutic styles are applicable to some degree in both individual and group psychotherapies when it is understood that individual therapy is really a special case of group therapies (albeit the former is composed of only two members, with 50 percent being professional staff). However, confidentiality safeguards (involving individual patient disclosures) have to be more closely watched in group compared to individual therapies.

In keeping with the vertical binding goals of the 2 × 4 Model, individual and group therapies should both flexibly attend to addressing both MI and SUD diagnostic targets in whatever proportion they may be represented in patients (or groups of patients). This may mean that the therapist implements an eclectic approach that skillfully intercalates both a traditional MI-focused therapy (e.g., dialectical behavioral therapy (DBT) for borderline personality) and a SUD-school approach (e.g., that uses the core elements from the traditional 12-steps). Alternatively, the more well-formalized dual diagnosis therapies, such as the trauma-informed Seeking Safety therapy may be implemented to address both PTSD and substance use disorders.

Individual Psychotherapies in the 2 × 4 Model Clinic

It is not common for dual diagnosis patients to get too much psychotherapy, or for the clinic to be in a position where it can afford to offer too much.

The effort of every clinical team member that contacts the patient can be important on a psychotherapeutic level and should be viewed as such. Obviously, this includes the psychiatrists. The best dual diagnosis care that an addiction psychiatrist (or any physician) can provide, and the approach that the 2 × 4 Model encourages the psychiatrists to routinely adopt, is one in which the doctor is working in both psychotherapeutic and psychopharmacologically-informed domains. Thus, when a patient is seeing both the addiction psychiatrist and a team therapist concurrently, it can be understood (and in fact, is a perfectly acceptable and desirable situation) that the patient is seeing two different therapists simultaneously in the 2 × 4 Model clinic (one being the psychiatrist, as the minor therapist, and the other being the psychologist or social worker as the major therapist). The crucial role of the addiction psychiatrist and the nature of his or her interactions and collaborations with other 2 × 4 Model team members will be elaborated further in Chapter 9, but suffice to say here that psychiatrists working in the 2 × 4 Model clinic should not be viewed—either by themselves or other team members—as just 'script writing machines' or 'prescribers'). Rather, they are treatment directors, team leaders, and experts in integrating psychotherapeutic and medication interventions.

Patients in the 2 × 4 Model clinic will often be cared for by their psychiatrist and their primary clinician, both of whom are interacting with the patient on a psychotherapeutic level, most typically with the clinician engaging more fully in a dedicated 1:1 psychotherapy. However, it could be the psychiatrist who is primarily engaging in the 1:1 psychotherapy (with medication management), or, the patient may not require much engagement in a 1:1 psychotherapy by anyone. Regardless of who is engaging the patient psychotherapeutically, the following techniques and themes are important to employ and maintain awareness.

Important Themes for Individual Therapies

1. Maintain an eclectic psychotherapeutic tool box. A motivational interviewing/MET foundation, with a second layer of CBT approaches, should be garnished with psychodynamic, interpersonal, and supportive psychotherapeutic approaches.

2. Always monitor transference and counter-transference dynamics and act wisely within them. A common projection of patients with addiction is that the clinician (and especially the psychiatrist, who can prescribe controlled substances) is either a cop or a drug dealer, since these two role archetypes are primarily what they have previously experienced and become used to in their prior interactions with authority figures surrounding drug use. Since the addiction psychiatrist and the other clinicians are neither of these, it is important that they not fall into playing these roles even when the patient could be attempting (via projective identification) to have the clinicians act in these roles.

In counter-transference, one of the most important and challenging jobs of the clinician is to not show disappointment, judgment, disgust, or otherwise demeaning attitudes to patients (projecting criminality, badness, or sub-humanness onto them) when their diseases get the best of them, when they seem to be failing and perpetually relapsing. A tragic mistake is to be angry with a patient who drops out of care for some time and then returns weeks or months later to get help, only to be greeted by a scowling face, and a conversation that seeks to judge them for 'screwing up'. It is important to remember that after relapses and long absences from the clinic, the patient is in front of you again because they want help. They want to get better, and there is something they see in the team and their relationship with it that they know is part of the solution. If they didn't feel that way, they would not have come back. Have a celebratory attitude that they have returned, not a condemning one, because their return is a victory, however minor it may seem. The importance of this stance is very high given that so many dual diagnosis patients are in great therapeutic need for stable, enduring, healthy relationships—not only as a corrective approach to what may have been their past psycho-social traumas, but as a measure to help the patient learn to build and maintain healthy relationships while they attempt to break their pathological attachment to alcohol, nicotine, and other drugs of abuse.

3. Monitor boundaries. Many dual diagnosis patients, in relation to their co-occurring personality disorders, (or the past psycho-social traumas that contributed them), are vulnerable to, or can engender (via projective identification), boundary violations on the part of the clinician. Of course, there are many contexts where seasoned clinicians can make important therapeutic interventions that are in the boundary zone, and, too rigid attention to boundaries can compromise the ability of the team to provide individualized care, or to deploy exceptional measures that a patient may truly need. In general, problems with working on the boundaries are avoided if there is good communication on the treatment team and good consensus about the treatment plan (e.g., no secrets are being kept between clinicians about a patient; more than one set of eyes are on the patient regularly). Typical problems and challenges that can arise could include certain patients being seen too much (consuming too much in the way of clinical resources needed for other cases); instances where significant clinical actions are being taken without being charted (e.g., for a 'VIP' patient); improper monitoring and professionalism in an eroticized transference; and with over-medicalizing the care (e.g. getting sucked into doing internal medicine instead of psychiatry). Many patients, either because they cannot get access to adequate primary care, or because they are trying to avoid dealing with their addiction and mental illness, can attempt to manipulate the psychiatrist (i.e., via projective identification) into acting as an internist or ER physician. While it is the job for the psychiatrist to be competent in

identifying the need for nonpsychiatric medical interventions that don't directly relate to their addictions or mental illness (or treatment), it is not the job for the psychiatrist in the 2 × 4 Model to manage these conditions and be a primary care doc; a referral to the right medical expertise is needed. Full physical examination, especially involving private areas, is best left for outside medical professionals who are not engaging the patient in intensive psychiatric and psychotherapeutic care, and potentially prescribing them controlled substances. Similarly, observed urine drug testing and depot injections of medications into gluteal regions should be done by nursing team members.

4. Keep in mind and work on the patient's *Time Event Horizon*. Many dual diagnosis patients, and also those with MI or addiction only, have a common world view and style of thinking where only events that are relatively close up in time seem to matter, and drive their decision-making and behavior. This blindness to the 'long-term view' impairs healthy action planning and goal directed behavior. Understanding this phenomenon is a very interesting and active area of neuroscience research that likely relates to the function of prefrontal cortical-temporal limbic networks, and the combined impact of genetic, environmental–experiential, and drug toxicological forces on these circuits. A key behavioral marker of addiction vulnerability, described in both humans and animals that relates to the *Foreshortened Time Event Horizon*, is the *discounting of delayed rewards*, where the value of perceived or actual rewards diminishes at an abnormally accelerated rate as the access to that reward is put off further into the future. Clinicians should assess via therapeutic interactions and regular observations the degree to which this cognitive style is characteristic of their patients, and how it affects their progress on the Stages of Change. Care should be taken by clinicians to avoid colluding with this cognitive style (e.g., as another example of projective identification by patients—when they want psychiatrists to prescribe them controlled substances immediately, before the team or the patient is actually ready). Clinical awareness of a foreshortened time event horizon can provide clinicians with important opportunities to provide supportive and insight-oriented psychotherapeutic interventions, as well as the need for implementing other approaches into the treatment plan (e.g., like contingency management).

5. Monitor and adeptly address resistance to treatment. Pathological ambivalence about recovery involving some degree of addiction-related motivation (remember the enemy in the patient's motivational 'civil war') is present in nearly all addicted and dual diagnosis patients to some extent, effecting their movement through the Stages of Change. Resistance to recovery and change can manifest in a million different ways both direct and indirect. Monitoring and assisting the patient with this resistance is key, and done well using MET and CBT approaches, again, while making all attempts to withhold negative attitudes and punitive projections back onto the patients.

Group Psychotherapies

As previously mentioned, the 2 × 4 Model clinic should offer both individual and group psychotherapies to patients with the expectation that some patients will do either one or both of these at any one time, but without the absolute requirement that all patients have to do either or both. And, just as psychotherapies in the 2 × 4 Model clinic should be eclectic (and evidence based), the group therapies offerings should be diverse and eclectic, both in terms of focus and patient composition. Larger 2 × 4 Model programs, with larger clinical staffs, will be able to have a larger number and diversity of groups, but even minimally sized programs for example, with one therapist leading groups, can host multiple groups a week. Again, eclecticism across groups is a key value for individualizing care that may be enacted with the following parameters to consider for diversifying groups in the 2 × 4 Model.

Parameters of Diversity to Consider in Group Schedule Design

1. Specific groups for patients in specific Stages of Change. For example, there may be different groups for Contemplative vs. Action vs. Maintenance/ Relapse prevention stages.
2. Gender or age specific groups.
3. Groups that focus on more on specific forms of psychiatric comorbidities (e.g., schizophrenia vs. borderline vs. PTSD comorbidities).
4. Groups that meet on different days or times of day (to accommodate patients with different work or childcare responsibilities).
5. Groups that focus on specific life challenges in the context of dual diagnosis recovery (e.g., parenting and healthy attachment formation).

A 2 × 4 Model clinic should provide at least three of these diverse group options. In the design of the group schedule, some important considerations would be the duration and frequency of groups (generally one to three hours per group, meetings from once a month to three times a week), the minimum and maximum capacities allowed, and polices on allowing late patients into the groups. In general, the clinical team members and administrators should be well trained enough to design and run the group program offerings based on the clinic population and resources of the clinic (and, as based on the clinical evidence), without too many arbitrary requirements imposed by an external agency.

Some things that should be minimized or avoided in the 2 × 4 Model clinic group programming are as follows.

Things to Avoid in 2 × 4 Model Clinic Group Therapy

1. Language or conceptualizations that the group therapy is either a 'class' or a punishment. Although group therapy (or any psychotherapy including

individuals) is to some extent educational, and the biological changes that therapies should evoke involve neural learning mechanisms; group therapy is not education. It is not a class or a school. Patients should not be thought of as 'graduating' from a class when they 'complete' an arbitrary number of therapy sessions or having served a sentence as evidenced by a diploma or certificate of compliance. Group therapy is a health care treatment. Period. Its duration, focus, and intensity for an individual patient is determined by the recommendations of the treatment team, as informed by the evidence base, and the motivation, capability, and diagnostic needs of the patient. Outside agencies and especially those organizations that are not professionally trained or designed to provide behavioral health care have no basis for arbitrarily determining what a patient or set of patients should receive for group therapies in the 2 × 4 Model clinic. Group therapies are treatments for recovery, and measures of treatment compliance, but participation in them should not be looked at as direct, definitive measures of recovery or health. Generally speaking, views that patients need to complete an arbitrary set of group (or individual) therapy sessions as evidence for recovery, or evidence for 'appropriate' participation in treatment, are not evidenced-based and do not necessarily correlate with actual recovery or clinical status of the patient.

2. Avoid allowing group therapy to substitute for clinical care that should happen in 1:1 private clinical sessions (e.g., with individual therapist, nurse, or psychiatrist). While patients in groups will routinely disclose personal information, experiences, and feelings, the group leader should help members avoid disclosing clinical information in groups that is best left for, and protected by, the confidentiality of individual clinical appointments. In even more clear terms, group therapies should not be used to make individual diagnostic assessments or treatment planning decisions for individual patients in front of other patients. This is not to say that the behavior of a patient in the group cannot be used to inform, say, the psychiatrist in making a clinical diagnosis, as communicated outside the group setting. This can be a good thing. Rather, the idea is that the group setting should not be used to conduct individual clinical care, or to directly elicit clinical information from patients that might otherwise be protected by rules of confidentiality in clinical care. Groups are primarily treatment forums, not places for evaluating individual patients.

3. Avoid advocacy or anchoring of a group on a particular religious perspective or belief. Patients in need of group treatment will represent a broad spectrum of religious or nonreligious beliefs and denominations. Care should be taken to avoid alienating any one patient based on specific advocacy of any of these beliefs, including the direct or indirect equation of having the active disease of addiction as being without God, or in a state of sin, or being morally corrupt. While applying the three core components from the traditional 12-steps are important in group and individual therapies in the 2 × 4 Model clinic (e.g., i) recognizing there is a disease that impairs

free will, requiring external help; ii) Acknowledging and acting on the need to repair damage caused by the disease; iii) role modeling and supporting others seeking addiction recovery and mental health) the group leader should try to steer clear of using religious language to frame addictive disease or recovery. Patients are of course welcome (and can be encouraged) to practice religion as they see fit outside of the clinic (or to attend more religious AA/NA groups on the outside) and to express and conduct themselves according to their religion as they want inside the group. It's just that the clinical teams, group leaders, and the focus of the treatment should not be dependent on, espouse or promote, any kind of religious perspective, acknowledgement, characterization, or denial of the existence of God.

4. Avoid having groups being too drug-specific in focus. Having some groups focus on alcohol only, while others focus on opioid addiction, for example, can encourage clicks and cross-illness stigma between different groups of patients. There is enough similarity between addiction syndromes involving different drug types such that on the level of group therapy, the work of recovery is essentially the same. The fact that many, if not most patients, are also multi-addicted makes the design and composition of groups according to drug type impractical and of limited utility. The design of different groups according to co-occurring mental illness focus is more useful and practical given that these illnesses do produce certain cognitive and social patterns that may be better addressed in like-collections of patients.

5. Don't be too rigid in the use of out-of-the-box group-curriculums. There are several group therapy kits available for professionally-run addiction and dual diagnosis clinics. These kits provide a schedule of content including discussion topics, educational materials, handouts, etc. and also procedural and technique tips for professional group leaders. These kits can be very helpful for providing content structure and goal sets for the groups and their clinical leaders (especially the less experienced ones), and may also be evidence based (e.g., have efficacy demonstrated in clinical studies). Using these kits and adhering to them closely may be particularly desirable if they are being used as part of a research study, like as an active control treatment for patients randomized in a placebo controlled pharmacological trial of a new addiction medication. On the other hand, groups that are too rigidly run can have adverse effects on patient's experience, making them feel bored, unheard, and making the group experience feel too much like school. An important challenge that must be met for the running of any group by the clinician leader is achieving the optimal balance of attention to process vs. content in the group, and deciding on when and how it is constructive to discuss group process in the group as opposed to sticking only with content. There should be some flexibility in allowing the group to at times divert off the content focus, if it seems constructive to the group or the overall mission of the clinic. Seasoned groups leaders will know when and how it is a good idea to deviate from the schedules provided in group kits.

Part of the point of avoiding too rigid a stance with the running of groups in the 2 × 4 Model clinic is about encouraging creativity with group content and design. Experimentalism in group formats can be quite intellectually stimulating and engaging for clinical team members and patients alike, which can increase participation and ultimately efficacy. Bringing guests into groups (e.g., well-recovered patients who can serve as role models), having food served, or watching and discussing movies, inviting in family members and children into groups, can all be helpful ways to energize groups. Specialty groups that take on a particular patient demographic or aspect of dual diagnosis recovery (e.g., the dual diagnosis groups for expectant moms) can be great experiences for clinicians and patients.

Contingency Management

Contingency Management (CM) is a solidly evidence-based intervention where patients are presented with material rewards as they progress in addiction recovery. The rewards may or may not be delivered on a probabilistic schedule, but are typically anchored to a concrete event, achievement, or milestone in recovery. The evidence is clear that this positive reinforcement approach to motivational enhancement works to enhance success rates, compliance, and maintenance in recovery. The major downside of the approach is that it does require some form of financing that typically cannot be derived from insurance revenues for the clinic. This means the clinic's CM budget (unfortunately like so many evidence based approaches in behavioral health) typically comes from either grants or philanthropy support. Another issue is that many dual diagnosis patients in the clinic may be extremely impoverished, lacking basic necessities of transportation, food, housing insurance coverage, etc. and so it can be hard for the clinic to rationalize maintaining a CM budget when the money could be used for these types of necessities. On the other hand, there may be specific niches in the clinic where CM approaches make great sense, even in the face of these realities, like for use to enhance smoking cessation (gift card option for every breath CO test that is negative), or to support depot naltrexone injections (e.g., gift card for each injection or a bigger prize for reaching six injections).

Studies have shown that per patient, the material costs of CM can be surprisingly minimal, even while remaining clinically effective across a broad socioeconomic spectrum and diversity of dual diagnosis patients. The efficacy of CM is well known in the clinical research world. CM is actually a routine staple of clinical research where patients are paid to participate in assessments, brain scans, blood tests, pharmacological trials, etc. Unfortunately, although we know CM works, the effects that CM has on the outcomes of clinical trials are not well understood in a systematic way. There may be some clinical trials where the CM component boosts the placebo effect in the placebo arm, and others where it amplifies the efficacy of the experimental agent more specifically. The treatment of addiction disease may be particularly influenced by CM approaches since is it known that the neurobiology of economically-driven intuition, motivation, and behavior is seated in some of the same core circuits that involve addiction. Because so much treatment trial research is accompanied by CM, while actual clinical care is often not, it may be argued that treatment programs that do not incorporate CM are not following the bulk of the evidence base!

One important way the 2 × 4 Model clinic can systematically utilize and implement a CM-informed clinical strategy without providing patients with direct material rewards, is to help patients overcome various barriers, punishments, and financial penalties that they unfortunately often experience while trying to succeed in treatment. This often involves the work happening in professional communications (Chapter 8), where the psychiatrist and clinical team members understand that they can have a significant impact on advocating for an array of resources including appropriate insurance, housing or food-stamp support, for patients showing effort, and progress in recovery.

Family Therapies

Mental illnesses, addictions, and dual diagnosis disorders typically are family affairs where one or more family members of the patient are also sick and may or may not be in treatment. Furthermore, the principal causative elements of dual diagnosis disorders (genetics, traumatic abuse, and neglect) flow through families and across generations. Family members may be contributing to the patient's illness, or the patient's illness may be putting family members at risk. At the same time, the family system may be an important source of recovery strength and motivational enhancement for the patient. Accordingly, contact with family member collaterals (in person or by phone) is encouraged in the 2 × 4 Model clinic with due attention to normal safeguards to patient confidentiality. Family members almost always provide extremely relevant clinical information and can often be the team's only window into what the patient is doing outside the clinic. Allowing family members (parents, spouses, and children) into appointments with the addiction psychiatrist, when not over used, can provide important information not only about the patient's diagnosis but also their attachment style and functionality that could not otherwise be observed.

Family Sessions oriented more toward treatment should also be available in the 2 × 4 Model clinic. These sessions can be run by the psychiatrist or other therapy staff. Typically, if the goal is to conduct a series of dedicated family therapy sessions (e.g., with the patient and a spouse), a clinic therapist would piggy-back that series onto the patient's other treatment plan interventions.

Experiential Therapies

As previously mentioned, successful recovery from addiction and dual diagnosis disorders must involve some degree of *neuroplasticity*—changes in brain circuitry are required to produce changes in mental experience and behavior. Growth out of pathological patterns of motivated behavior will require change and growth of new connectivity between neurons that support motivated behavior. At the same time, adaptation to new, healthier environments will also require neuroadaptive change. These themes from translational neuroscience can be understood and expressed to patients with the plant analogy. For the tree (their brains) to grow, which is necessary for their recovery, they need exposure to not one but several elements at the same time. This often includes sun (psychotherapies), water (medications) and nutritive soil (new experiences). It is up to the addiction psychiatrist and the 2 × 4 Model team to deliver the best combinations and balance of these elements, with psychotherapies and medications being directly provided in the clinic. But a host of experiential approaches and therapies, many of which are evidence based, should also be discussed, supported, and/or prescribed to patients in an individualized way, including any one or more of the following:

1. Exercise-based therapies (especially sustained cardiovascular);
2. Participation in recreational sports;
3. Travel experiences;
4. Gaming/cognitive exercises;
5. Educational pursuits;
6. Participation in the arts (visual/musical/theatrical);
7. New job pursuits/volunteering;
8. Moving;
9. Ending unhealthy relationships;
10. Acquiring new healthy relationships; and
11. Participation in religion.

Consideration and support for many of these options may enter the psychiatric and psychotherapeutic session content for individual patients and may even extend to onsite provisioning of support. For example, a group in the clinic dedicated to exercise-enhanced recovery may focus its members on training for a walk, mini-marathon, or triathlon event.

Background References and Further Reading

Alcoholics Anonymous World Services. (2001). *Alcoholics Anonymous: The Story of How Many Thousands of Men and Women Have Recovered from Alcoholism.* 4th ed. New York: Alcoholics Anonymous World Services.

Bickel, W. K., M. L. Miller, R. Yi, B. P. Kowal, D. M. Lindquist, and J. A. Pitcock. 2007. "Behavioral and neuroeconomics of drug addiction: Competing neural systems and temporal discounting processes." *Drug and Alcohol Dependence 90* (Suppl 1): S85–S91.

Carroll, K. M., and B. J. Rounsaville. 2007. "A perfect platform: Combining contingency management with medications for drug abuse." *American Journal of Drug and Alcohol Abuse 33* (3): 343–365. doi: 779736811 [pii] 10.1080/00952990701301319.

Carroll, K. M., B. J. Rounsaville, and F. H. Gawin. 1991. "A comparative trial of psychotherapies for ambulatory cocaine abusers: Relapse prevention and interpersonal psychotherapy." *American Journal of Drug and Alcohol Abuse 17* (3): 229–247.

Chambers, R. A., W. K. Bickel, and M. N. Potenza. 2007. "A scale-free systems theroy of motivation and addiction." *Neuroscience and Biobehavioral Reviews 31* (7): 1017–1045.

Fletcher, K., J. Nutton, and D. Brend. 2015. "Attachment, a matter of substance: The potential of attachement theory in the treatment of addictions." *Clinical Social Work Journal 43* (1): 109–117.

Flores, P. J. 2001. "Addiction as an attachment disorder: Implications for group therapy." *International Journal of Group Psychotherapy 51* (1): 63–81.

Ilgen, M. A., J. McKellar, R. Moos, and J. W. Finney. 2006. "Therapeutic alliance and the relationship between motivation and treatment outcomes in patients with alcohol use disorder." *Journal of Substance Abuse Treatment 31* (2): 157–162.

Johnson, B. 2010. "The psychoanalysis of a man with heroin dependence: Implications for neurobiological theories of attachment and drug craving." *Neuropsychoanalysis 12* (2): 207–215.

Martino, S., K. Carroll, D. Kostas, J. Perkins, and B. Rounsaville. 2002. "Dual diagnosis motivational interviewing: A modification of motivational interviewing for substance-abusing patients with psychotic disorders." *Journal of Substance Abuse Treatment 23* (4): 297–308.

Meier, P. S., M. C. Donmall, P. McElduff, C. Barrowclough, and R. F. Heller. 2006. "The role of the early therapeutic alliance in predicting drug treatment dropout." *Drug & Alcohol Dependence 83* (1): 57–64.

Miller, W. R., and S. Rollnick. 2002. *Motivational Interviewing: Preparing People for Change.* New York: Guilford Press.

Miller, W. R., A. Zweben, C. C. DiClemente, and R. G. Rychtarik. 1994. *Motivational Enhancement Therapy Manual.* Washington, DC: National Institute on Alcohol Abuse and Alcoholism, Project MATCH Monograph Series.

Mills, K. L., M. Teesson, S. E. Back, K. T. Brady, A. L. Baker, S. Hopwood, C. Sannibale, E. L. Barrett, S. Merz, J. Rosenfeld, and P. L. Ewer. 2012. "Integrated exposure-based therapy for co-occurring posttraumatic stress disorder and substance dependence: A randomized controlled trial." The *Journal of the American Medical Association 308* (7): 690–699.

Moos, R. H. 2007. "Theory-based active ingredients of effective treatments for substance use disorders." *Drug & Alcohol Dependence 88* (2–3): 109–121.

Moos, R. H. 2008. "Active ingredients of substance use-focused self-help groups." *Addiction 103*(3): 387–396. doi: 10.1111/j.1360-0443.2007.02111.xADD2111 [pii].

Mueser, K. T., R. E. Drake, S. Sigmon, and Brunetter M. F. 2005. "Psychosocial interventions for adults with severe mental illnesses and co-occurring substance use disoders: A review of specific interventions." *Journal of Dual Diagnosis 1* (2): 57–82.

Najavits, L. M. 2001. "Helping 'difficult' patients." *Psychotherapy Research 11* (2): 131–152.

Prochaska, J. O., and C. C. DiClemente. 2005. "The transtheoretical approach". In *Handbook of Psychotherapy Integration*, edited by J. C. Norcross and M. R. Goldfried. New York: Oxford University Press.

Prochaska, J. O., and C. C. DiClemente. 1984. *The Transtheoretical Approach: Crossing Traditional Boundaries of Therapy.* New York: Dow Jones-Irwin.

Robinson, T. E., and K. C. Berridge. 1993. "The neural basis of drug craving: An incentive-sensitization theory of addiction." *Brain Research. Brain* Research Reviews *18* (3): 247–291.

Velasquez, M. M. 2016. *Group Treatment for Substance Abuse: A Stages-of-Change Therapy Manual.* 2nd ed. New York: Guilford Press.

Watkins, T. R., A. Lewellen, and M. C. Barrett. 2000. *Dual Diagnosis: An Integrated Approach to Treatment.* 1st ed. London: SAGE Publications.

Weiss, R. D., M. L. Griffin, J. S. Potter, D. R. Dodd, J. A. Dreifuss, H. S. Connery, and K. M. Carroll. 2014. "Who benefits from additional drug counseling among prescription opioid-dependent patients receiving buprenorphine-naloxone and standard medical management?" *Drug & Alcohol Dependence 140*: 118–122.

Yonkers, K. A., A. Forray, H. B. Howell, N. Gotman, T. Kershaw, B. J. Rounsaville, and K. M. Carroll. 2012. "Motivational enhancement therapy coupled with cognitive behavioral therapy versus brief advice: A randomized trial for treatment of hazardous substance use in pregnancy and after delivery." *General Hospital Psychiatry 34* (5): 439–449. doi: 10.1016/j.genhosppsych.2012.06.002 S0163-8343(12)00178-8 [pii].

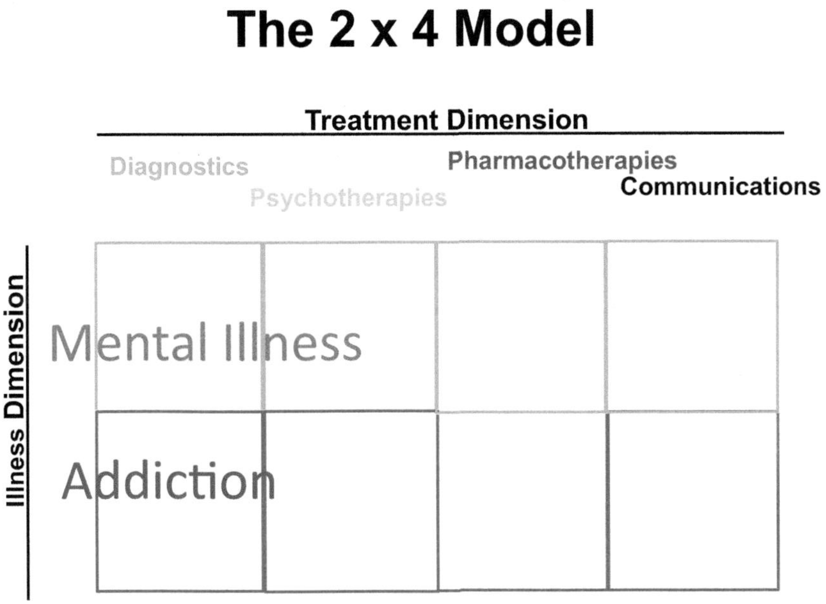

The 2 x 4 Model

Treatment Dimension

Diagnostics   **Pharmacotherapies**

Psychotherapies   **Communications**

Illness Dimension

Mental Illness			
Addiction			

Figure 1.1 The 2 × 4 Model

Figure 2.1 Segregation of Mental Health from Addiction Services

A) Epidemiological evidence characterizing patients in need of behavioral health care is not appropriately addressed by **B)** the behavioral health system built against this evidence, which is largely split along mental health vs. addiction treatment professional workforces and infrastructures, and falsely assumes that addictions and mental illnesses occur in separate populations and separate brains.

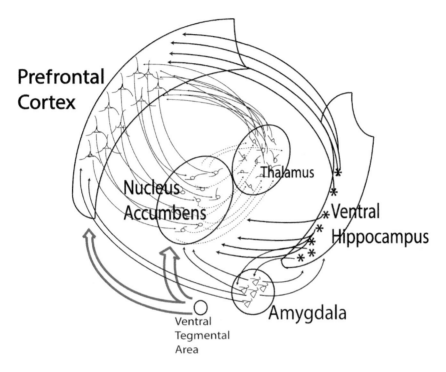

Figure 2.2 Integrated Neurocircuitry of Mental Illness and Addiction: The Interfacing and Motivation, Emotional, and Cognitive Neural Networks

Neural networks primarily responsible for decision-making (prefrontal cortex), emotion (amygdala) and multimodal memory storage and recall (ventral hippocampus), all send direct projections of glutamate bearing axons (thin black arrows)) that converge into the primary motivational center of the brain (nucleus accumbens). This direct interfacing of the major emotional and cognitive systems of the brain (that are abnormal in multiple forms of mental illness) with the nucleus accumbens, where the dopamine-mediated neuroplastic effects of addictive drugs (red open arrows) alter motivational programming, is responsible for the fundamental biological linkage between mental illnesses and addictive disease.

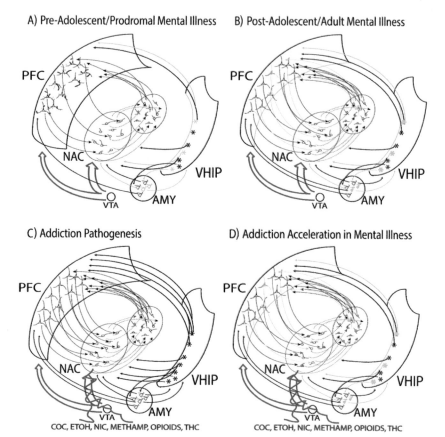

A) Pre-Adolescent/Prodromal Mental Illness

PFC

NAC

VHIP

VTA

AMY

B) Post-Adolescent/Adult Mental Illness

PFC

NAC

VHIP

VTA

AMY

C) Addiction Pathogenesis

PFC

NAC

VHIP

VTA

AMY

COC, ETOH, NIC, METHAMP, OPIOIDS, THC

D) Addiction Acceleration in Mental Illness

PFC

NAC

VHIP

VTA

AMY

COC, ETOH, NIC, METHAMP, OPIOIDS, THC

Figure 2.3 Enhanced Acquisition, Progression, and Severity of Addiction Disease in the Context of Mental Illness

A) Pre-Adolescent/Prodromal Mental Illness. Genetic factors and environmental experiences (e.g., childhood trauma) impact the form and function of temporal–limbic neurons and network connectivity, spanning AMY and VHIP regions symbolized by blue neurons and axonal projections. **B) Post-Adolescent/Adult Mental Illness.** By adulthood many forms of major mental illness that produce addiction vulnerability (e.g., schizophrenia, personality disorders, post-traumatic stress spectrum disorders, unipolar and bipolar illness) show broader prefrontal cortical and temporal–limbic (AMY/VHIP) involvement, symbolized by blue neurons and axo-dendritic structures spanning all these regions. The anatomical spreading of illness involvement may differ in scope and mechanism across different types of mental illness, but probably involves different degrees of i) disturbances in peri-adolescent synaptic pruning of local dendritic arborizations in the PFC (symbolized by decreased dendritic complexity of pyramidal neurons and cortical thinning); ii) dysregulation of hippocampal neurogenesis (puffy blue hippocampal neurons); iii) worsening alterations in local AMY neuronal physiology (puffy blue AMY neurons); and iv) alterations in the formation of long range axo-dendritic connectivity between PFC/AMY/VHIP, not to mention a host of finer irregularities involving key neurotransmitter and neurohormonal systems. In any case, a disturbance of PFC/AMY/VHIP network structures and function are expected to have convergent, down steam effects on NAC network form and function, and the motivational information the NAC network represents. Since all of these structures directly project into the NAC, then motivational control, learning and memory are dependent on all these structures; a greater scope and severity of PFC/AMY/VHIP involvement in the mental illness (i.e. more severe mental illness) generally produces greater disturbances in motivated behavior. **C) Addiction Pathogenesis.** Repeated use of additive drugs (symbolized by red zig zag in the VTA (Ventral Tegmental Area)-Dopamine pathways into the NAC, produces a host of neuroplastic effects impacting the shape, connectivity, and information processing of NAC neurons (symbolized by red colorization of some NAC cell bodies, dendrites and axonal (GABAergic) projections to downstream pallidal and thalamic structures). These NAC network changes, represent changes in the encoded motivational repertoire such that motivations to seek out and use addictive drug(s), are involuntarily promoted, or become increasingly dominant at the expense of normal motivations that drive healthy social, occupational, and neurovegetative behaviors. **D) Addiction Acceleration in Mental Illness.** In the context of an underlying mental illness, especially in the adolescent neurodevelopmental phase (as the mental illness is progressing from **A** to **B**), the biological, disease causing impact of addictive drugs on the NAC-based neural network (shown as a milder form in **C**) is more severe and happens with greater temporal speed (acceleration of diseases process) in **D**. Thus, fewer doses of the addictive drug are needed to entrain a greater contribution of the NAC network (and associated downstream dorsal striatal structures required for habit formation) into driving drug-seeking and taking behavior, at the expense of an already impoverished and dysfunctional motivational–behavioral repertoire. Thus, the motivational network vulnerability caused by mental illness (blue structures), amplifies and accelerates the NAC network impact of addictive drugs (red structures) that drives a relatively greater proportion of motivational encoding of addictive over healthy behavior.

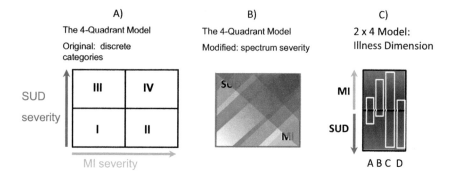

Figure 3.1 4-Quadrant Model and its Adaptation to the 2 × 4 Model

A) The Original 4-Quadrant Model: Discrete Categories. **B)** The Modified 4-Quadrant Model: Spectrum of Severity. **C)** 2 × 4 Model Adaption: Severity of MI and SUD in Individual Patients. A: patient with mild MI/mild SUD; B: patient with major MI/mild SUD; C: patient with major MI/major SUD; D: patient with mild MD/major SUD.

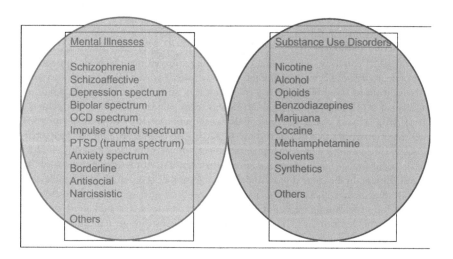

Figure 3.2 Major Forms of Mental Illness and Substance Use Disorders Seen in the 2 × 4 Model Clinic in Various Comorbid Combinations

A great diversity of comorbid combinations of these conditions are routinely encountered in behavioral health patients seeking care.

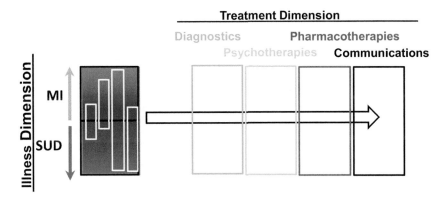

Figure 4.1 Stretching Out the Illness Dimension Across the Four Components of the Treatment Dimension in the 2 × 4 Model

Four different patients with differential degrees of mental illness and addiction severity (white rectangles) treated in the 2 × 4 Model clinic will have individualized treatment plans, as determined by differential deployments of diagnostics, psychotherapies, pharmacotherapies, and professional communications.

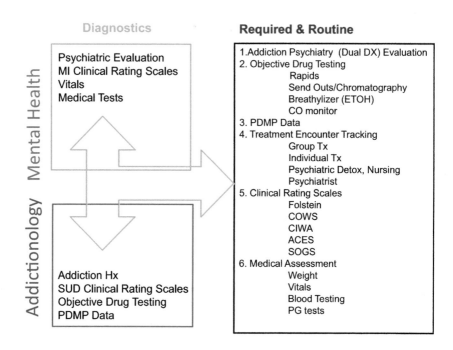

Figure 5.1 Diagnostic Tools and Approaches in the 2 × 4 Model

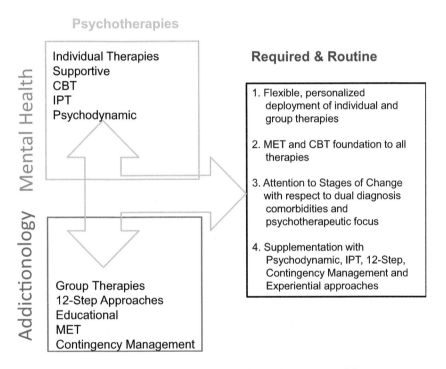

Figure 6.1 Psychotherapeutic Tools and Approaches in the 2 × 4 Model

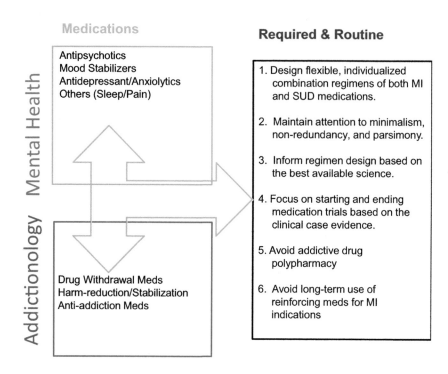

Medications

Antipsychotics
Mood Stabilizers
Antidepressant/Anxiolytics
Others (Sleep/Pain)

Drug Withdrawal Meds
Harm-reduction/Stabilization
Anti-addiction Meds

Mental Health

Addictionology

Required & Routine

1. Design flexible, individualized combination regimens of both MI and SUD medications.

2. Maintain attention to minimalism, non-redundancy, and parsimony.

3. Inform regimen design based on the best available science.

4. Focus on starting and ending medication trials based on the clinical case evidence.

5. Avoid addictive drug polypharmacy

6. Avoid long-term use of reinforcing meds for MI indications

Figure 7.1 Medication Tools and Approaches in the 2 × 4 Model

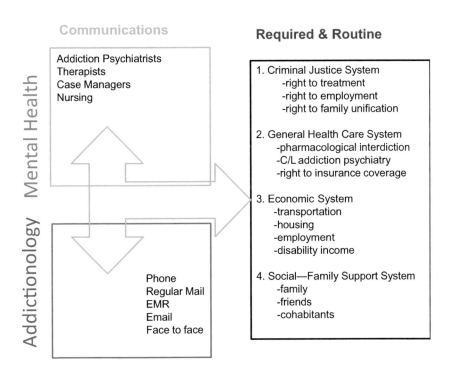

Figure 8.1 Communication Approaches in the 2 × 4 Model

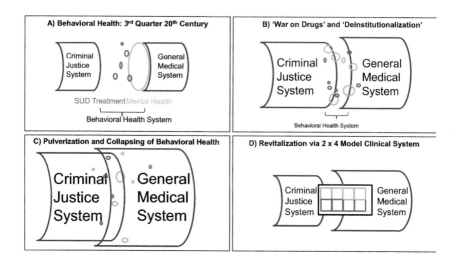

Figure 8.2 Historical Fragmentation and Future Rebuilding of Integrated Dual Diagnosis Care at the Interface of Criminal Justice and the Health Care System

A) By 1975, behavioral health was still composed of a relatively strong infrastructure and professional workforce, although addictionology and mental health were largely unintegrated. **B)** With progression of the 'war on drugs' and 'deinstitutionalization', more mentally ill/addicted people became criminalized and behavioral health became more fragmented, loosing infrastructure, workforce, and funding. **C)** These trends outpaced advances in neuroscience and psychopharmacology, contributing to overgrowth of the mass incarceration industry and the nonbehavioral health focused medical–industrial complex. Unsustainable growth of the social and economic costs of mass incarceration and highly interventional medical care aimed at illnesses and injuries resulting from untreated addictions and mental illness, became an auto-reinforcing dynamic, driving further degradation, and fragmentation of behavioral health. **D)** Implementing widespread integration of mental health and addiction treatment through building a 2 × 4 Model clinical system could significantly strengthen the clinical effectiveness, reach, and efficiency of behavioral health. 2 × 4 Model system communications and collaborations with criminal justice and non-behavioral health care systems, will create much greater cost and mission effectiveness of those systems, allowing their economies to be appropriately sized to sustainable levels, while generating a higher level of public health and well-being.

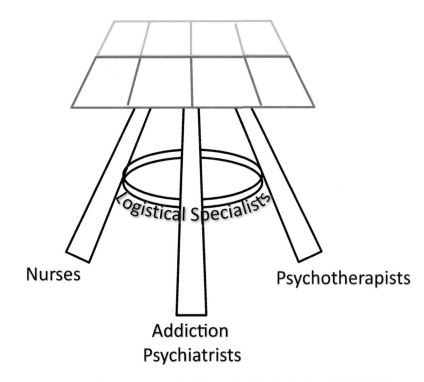

Figure 9.1 The Three Legged Stool of Clinical Staffing in the 2 × 4 Model Clinic

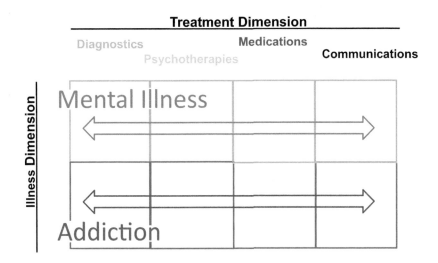

Figure 10.1 The 2 × 4 Model: Horizontal Binding

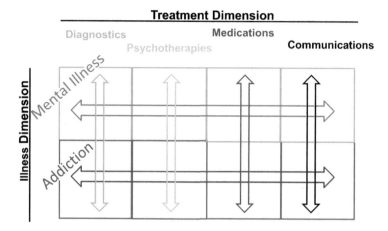

Figure 10.2 The 2 × 4 Model: Two Dimensional (Vertical and Horizontal Binding)

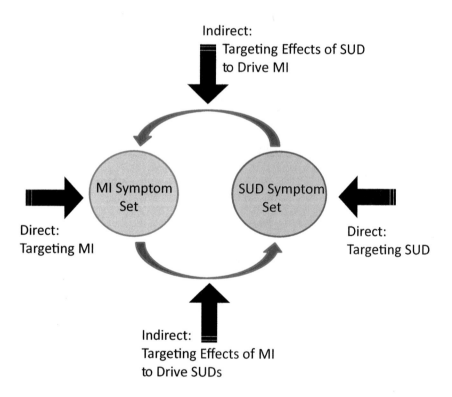

Figure 10.3 Points of Attack in 2 × 4 Model Treatment

The 2 x 4 Model & Addiction Psychiatry ACGME Milestones

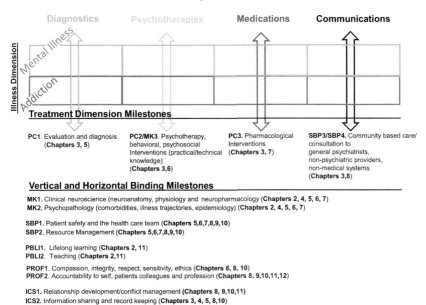

PC1. Evaluation and diagnosis **(Chapters 3, 5)**

PC2/MK3. Psychotherapy, behavioral, psychosocial Interventions (practical/technical knowledge) **(Chapters 3,6)**

PC3. Pharmacological Interventions **(Chapters 3, 7)**

SBP3/SBP4. Community based care/ consultation to general psychiatrists, non-psychiatric providers, non-medical systems **(Chapters 3,8)**

Vertical and Horizontal Binding Milestones

MK1. Clinical neuroscience (neuroanatomy, physiology and neuropharmacology **(Chapters 2, 4, 5, 6, 7)**
MK2. Psychopathology (comorbidities, illness trajectories, epidemiology) **(Chapters 2, 4, 5, 6, 7)**

SBP1. Patient safety and the health care team **(Chapters 5,6,7,8,9,10)**
SBP2. Resource Management **(Chapters 5,6,7,8,9,10)**

PBLI1. Lifelong learning **(Chapters 2, 11)**
PBLI2. Teaching **(Chapters 2,11)**

PROF1. Compassion, integrity, respect, sensitivity, ethics **(Chapters 6, 8, 10)**
PROF2. Accountability to self, patients colleagues and profession **(Chapters 8, 9,10,11,12)**

ICS1. Relationship development/conflict management **(Chapters 8, 9,10,11)**
ICS2. Information sharing and record keeping **(Chapters 3, 4, 5, 8,10)**

Figure 11.1 The 2 × 4 Model and Addiction Psychiatry ACGME Milestones

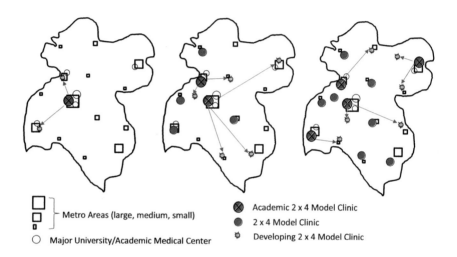

Metro Areas (large, medium, small)

○ Major University/Academic Medical Center

⊗ Academic 2 x 4 Model Clinic

● 2 x 4 Model Clinic

✸ Developing 2 x 4 Model Clinic

Figure 12.1 Guided Replication and Geographical Spread of a System of 2 × 4 Model
Clinics Across a Region or State over Several Years

Academic 2 × 4 Model clinics founded in university towns could provide training, support
and fidelity monitoring to developing 2 × 4 Model clinics in proximity. These developing
clinics would be started in existing community mental health centers, addiction treatment programs, or psychiatric hospital and rehab centers that want to become fully dual
diagnosis capable and expand into longitudinal outpatient missions according to the
2 × 4 Model design.

7 Medications

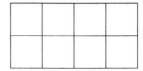

The design, implementation, and management of medication regimens for patients in the 2 × 4 Model clinic is a responsibility of the addiction psychiatrist and other professionals with prescribing privileges the addiction psychiatrist may be supervising. As will be developed in this and later chapters, a key principal of prescribing in the 2 × 4 Model program is attention to both vertical and horizontal binding of pharmacotherapies. In terms of vertical binding, this means emphasizing the need to deploy medications that address both MI and SUD indications (at equal levels of prioritization) and to design *these integrated* regimens in ways that address the differential needs of individual patients. In parallel to the 2 × 4 Model requirement that the psychotherapeutic component of treatment (Chapter 6) should encompass and routinely use an eclectic toolbox of evidence-based psychotherapies, so should the 2 × 4 Model clinic psychiatrists be routinely prescribing a wide range of evidence-based medications according to individual patient's needs. This pharmacological eclecticism is needed not only to ensure that a comprehensive variety of dual diagnosis patients (e.g., with different combinations of mental illness(s) and addiction(s)) are appropriately treated in the clinic, but to ensure that *multiple* pharmacological tools are available as much as possible for use for any one indication, should attempts with an initial or front line treatment fail. There is no perfect treatment for any one type of mental illness or addiction for every patient, and therefore, it is not really appropriate for the clinic to offer only one type of treatment for a given illness category when multiple evidence-based treatments are available. Clinics that only offer one type of medication treatment for a given indication (when others are available) run the danger of becoming 'pill mill' like, where care lacks sufficient individualization, and the emphasis of the program is more on delivering certain treatment products for the sake of business efficiency, rather than actually getting clinical results.

The horizontal binding of medication therapies (discussed in greater detail in Chapter 10) refers to the need to maintain awareness and clinical decision-making about medication choices with respect to what is happening in the other components of the treatment dimension, namely, the Diagnostics and Psychotherapeutic dimensions. In this way, changes in medication regimens are being driven by what is happening with changes in the patient's clinical data trajectories, and, those changes are being optimally integrated with, responsive to, or interactive with, what's happening in the psychotherapies. For this to happen well, the addiction psychiatrist should not only be on top of the patient's clinical data stream. He should also be in close communication with the other psychotherapeutic staff about the patient's status, while also maintaining a basic psychotherapeutic stance and awareness in the room with the patient while performing psychopharmacology.

The emphasis on both vertical binding (integration of MI and SUD focus) and horizontal binding (integration of psychotherapies and medication management) in the 2 × 4 Model clinic allows the medication regimen design and monitoring to be responsive to the patient's clinical needs in a way that is comprehensive and self-sufficient within the walls of the 2 × 4 Model clinic. This is in keeping with the overarching goal of the 2 × 4 Model design *to provide expert integrated mental health and addiction care, by one treatment team, under one roof.* For maintaining the integrity of this capability, it is important that the addiction psychiatrists and the treatment team avoid splitting psychopharmacology regimens with outside physicians (e.g., where some medications are prescribed by the addiction psychiatrist inside the 2 × 4 Model clinic, and other psychotropic meds are prescribed by a family physician, internist, or another psychiatrist across town). Splitting pharmacological care in this way is a set up for producing irrational polypharmacy, conflicting pharmacological strategies, poor communications between prescribers, and creating uncertainty about what is going on with the patient (in terms of the interactions between meds, understanding side effects, etc.), or who really is directing psychiatric care. Thus, as described in more detail below and in Chapters 8 and 10, pharmacotherapy regimens in the 2 × 4 Model clinic are also relevant to the communications component of the treatment dimension, for example, when the addiction psychiatrist makes a doctor-to-doctor communication with an outside prescriber asking him to stop prescribing benzodiazepines and stimulants to their patient with opioid addiction.

Core Tactics to Prescribing in the 2 × 4 Model Clinic

Here, we discuss in some greater detail six key tactics that should be used to enact appropriate, vertical binding (integration) of MI and SUD medication regimens, and to ensure that this binding is optimally science-based, safe, and effective (**Figure 7.1**). The reader should understand that this section (and book) is not intended, and does not serve as a comprehensive or authoritative review of psychopharmacology for the addiction or mental health fields. There are many excellent reviews and textbooks available (some listed at the end of this chapter) that should be consulted for this kind of in depth knowledge, and of course, reading this book cannot serve as a substitute for residency training in psychiatry and/or fellowship training in addiction psychiatry. Instead, this chapter is intended to instruct the reader who is already advanced via formal training and supervised clinical experience in these areas, to optimally *integrate*

MI and SUD pharmacology. This work involves not only the judicious use and timing of agents to target MI syndromes and symptoms, but the deployment of SUD illness treatments at various stages of the recovery process, spanning drug withdrawal, harm-reduction/stabilization, and anti-addiction phases.

1. Design Flexible, Personalized Combination Regimens of Both MI and SUD Medications

In general, the evidence base for the medication treatment of addictions, especially those involving nicotine, alcohol, and opioids, is now well-established, and on par with the treatment of major mental illness (e.g. schizophrenia, bipolar, and depression). Accordingly, as with the standard of care in the medication management of mental illness, it is no longer acceptable to not offer and/or to not provide these treatments for addiction, when the patient has the appropriate clinical indication and is wanting to pursue the treatment. What this means for the 2 × 4 Model clinic is that patients with dual diagnosis comorbidities (who make up about half or even the majority of all patients), should routinely be on combination medication regimens that target both MI and SUDS. On the other hand, those patients with little to no MI symptoms or history, but who have active addiction or are in early recovery, would predominantly be on SUD meds. Then, those patients with active or recent MI symptoms but with SUDS in full sustained remission, may often be on MI meds only. Thus, equal focus and attention to both addiction and mental illness in the 2 × 4 Model clinic should compel an appropriate balance and weighting of MI vs. SUD meds, based on what individual patients have, and not on the biases of the prescriber, or the name of the clinic (e.g., in favor or against MI vs. SUD diagnosis or treatment), or over-valued (and often false) notions that treating the MI alone should take care of the SUD, or, that MI symptoms in patients with addictions are always a result of acute intoxication or withdrawal. Awareness of the fact that patients with comorbid addictions and mental illness often show quite rapid evolution of symptoms, and that revision of clinical diagnoses is often necessary (based on changes in substance use patterns), points to the need for pharmacological regimens of dual diagnosis patients to be temporally flexible. And again, individualization of dual diagnosis medication regimens should also sometimes entail the use of switching between different pharmacological options for a given specific psychiatric or addiction diagnosis. Thus, just as we should not treat all bipolar patients with lithium only (never using valproate or carbamazepine), we should not treat all patients with alcohol addiction with disulfiram only (never using naltrexone or acamprosate).

2. Maintain Attention to Minimalism, Non-redundancy, and Parsimony

A danger with aggressive targeting of a range of different symptoms or comorbid MI/addiction syndromes a patient may have is to overload them with too many medications. The expert dual diagnosis pharmacologist keeps in mind that increasing the number of medications a patient is on, increases risk and incidence of one or more of a host of problems:

- Potential for multiple unusual side effects.
- Inability to discern side effects from underlying illness symptoms.
- Stepping further away from the evidence base (prescribing blind to efficacy data).
- Unnecessarily escalating the cost of care.
- Noncompliance.
- Diversion/waste of medications.

A few simple rules of thumb can be followed to avoid these problems of 'irrational polypharmacy'. Adhering to these guidelines can help the prescriber keep a good balance between SUD and MI meds in the same regimen so that too many meds targeting one illness category do not 'crowd out' the meds for another illness category:

- Avoid the use of off label (non-FDA approved) medications, or medications for which the evidence base is sparse for an indication, when there is an FDA approved med for that indication, or a medication for which the evidence base is more solid. For example, if a patient has an anxiety disorder, don't have them on gabapentin (not FDA approved, poor evidence for anxiety), but not a SSRI (selective serotonin reuptake inhibitor). Also avoid, if possible, heaping one med (with poor evidence base) on top of another (that does have a strong evidence base (e.g., an SSRI for anxiety)) just because the latter agent may not be performing at an ideal level, or just because the patient wants it.
- Avoid the use of two agents for a given indication, especially when those two agents have similar mechanisms of action. There are shades of grey in this rule of thumb. For example, for a patient who needs antipsychotic treatment, it is best (based on the evidence base) to chronically have them on one antipsychotic, and only one at a time. But, if they must be on two based on their poor clinical response to monotherapy, avoid the use of two atypical neuroleptics or two typical neuroleptics (e.g., better to use one of each). Similarly, having a patient on fluoxetine and sertraline long-term is absurd, while fluoxetine with bupropion is justifiable. For 2 × 4 Model patients who need short term benzodiazepines, having them placed on two benzodiazepines at the same time is close to indefensible and not supported by the evidence base. Essentially, the idea is to have patients on one med for an indication (and not two), unless they are treatment refractory to either med alone, and those two meds have significantly different mechanisms of action.
- Avoid allowing patients to dictate the pharmacological treatment paradigms they want, and the drift toward polypharmacy. Patients in the 2 × 4 Model clinic are not qualified to dictate to the addiction psychiatrist what meds

they should be on. Unfortunately, many patients in the U.S. have been conditioned by the business and marketing arms of the Medical–Industrial complex to believe that health care is principally a market of products that doctors and other health care providers are sales clerks for. Hence, good care can often be understood by many 'consumers' as being a state of affairs where doctors should give them what they want (regardless of why they want it), as informed by 'direct to consumer' commercial marketing. Patients with addictions are especially susceptible to this dynamic because they often already have impaired judgment and insight about why they are taking certain meds or drugs, and what those drugs are actually doing to them. Further, the addicted patient is often very familiar and comfortable with the dealer–customer relationship model that exemplifies the context of illicit drug dealing, or legal purchasing of cigarettes or alcohol, for example, at the convenience store. Addicted patients often, whether consciously or unconsciously, project these types of dealer–customer relationships onto their prescribing physicians, who in turn can be susceptible to fulfilling the projection (enacting a form of projective identification), because they want to please their patient, or earn their business. Alternatively, many patients with mental illness harbor the feeling that medications are symbols of being cared about by the prescriber, where more meds and higher doses of them can be construed as evidence of greater care, or appreciation of the patient's suffering. The addiction psychiatrist must be aware of and gently resist these forms of projective identification, through maintaining an appropriate psychodynamic stance while also leaning back on their knowledge of the pharmacological evidence base.

Ultimately, it is helpful for the addiction psychiatrist to remember, and for the doctor and patient to discuss together, the truth that every treatment decision regarding what medication the patient takes, has to be a unanimous decision of *both the physician and the patient*. Usually there is agreement, but sometimes there is not. When there is agreement, based on the knowledge of the doctor, their assessment of the patient, and the patient's consent, the med goes on. When there is not agreement, the med does not happen. But this disagreement, and lack of action on a specific medication, need not at all jeopardize the entire collaborative–therapeutic relationship, or the treatment strategy as a whole. When the physician is working with an eclectic therapeutic tool kit that includes multiple medication options for any one MI or SUD indication, and a range of psychotherapeutic techniques, the physician has considerable leverage and flexibility in medication treatment while maintaining a minimalistic approach. Along these lines it can be quite helpful for the addiction psychiatrist to explain to patients the value of selecting certain medications because of their potentially parsimonious utility (e.g., bupropion for both depression and nicotine addiction), or the benefit of not changing or adding too many medications at any one time. In general, a clinical case that is heading toward too much polypharmacy (e.g., five or more medications for

MI indications) should alert the addiction psychiatrist to the possibility that there could be a significant personality disorder-based dynamic in play (that encourages, but does not really respond to polypharmacy), and that there is not enough psychotherapeutic treatment happening in the case.

3. Inform Medication Regimen Design Based on the Best Available Science

In the tradition of modern western medicine, adherence to evidence-based prescribing practices seems like it should go without saying. Unfortunately it does not, especially in behavioral health and addiction care, where particularly serious shortages of expert physician training and workforce, and deficits in appropriate insurance coverage persist. On top of this, the modern era of commercialization of medical care has allowed corporate marketing of medications, diagnostic tests, procedures, and treatment centers to partially obscure or overshadow the best evidence base, or at least outpace the evidence base in the interest of profits.

In this context, it is important that the addiction psychiatrist remains in touch with the evidence base via regular contact with the peer-reviewed literature, participation in CME (Continuing Medical Education) symposia, affiliation with academic medical centers, or through direct participation in education and research as a faculty member. But being in touch with the evidence base is often not enough. Sometimes the evidence base in a certain area is woefully deficient or off the mark and in need of revision. It too can be influenced by novelties, fads, and fashions that may ultimately not pan out despite the highest initial endorsements of academic leaders. And, some areas of the literature are riddled with conflict, uncertainty, ambiguity, and mixed opinions. Certainly, the area of dual diagnosis treatment and pharmacology remains a frontier and so it is important that psychiatrists in the 2 × 4 Model clinic develop a sense of the *best* of the evidence base, while assuming that evidence base is not infallible or up to revision (acquiring this sensibility and awareness is an important part of what formal addiction psychiatry fellowship training should accomplish). This means that 2 × 4 Model psychiatrists should be familiar with (and/or able to determine in a quick literature search) where the weight of the evidence is for particular medication treatments; whether a treatment is FDA approved (and for what indications); whether its use for an indication is supported by one or more double-blind placebo controlled trials (DBPCTs); what the outcome measures were in the trials (Self-report? Urine drug screens? Hospitalization rates?); the durations of the trials; what the comparison arms were in the trial; what sort of psychotherapies were included in the trial arms; what sorts of patient groups were included or excluded in the trials. Unfortunately, for behavioral health care and dual diagnosis treatment in particular, the issue of diagnostic exclusions in clinical research is particularly problematic because patients with dual diagnosis comorbidities are often excluded (or not accurately reported on) in trials.

In general, for medication regimen design in the 2 × 4 Model clinic, the following points should be considered as a way to adhere to the best of the evidence base:

- If a given MI or SUD target disorder has a single FDA-indicated medication, then use it, unless the patient cannot tolerate it or it has proven ineffective.
- If a given MI or SUD target disorder has multiple FDA-indicated medication treatments, then use the best one. The best one is determined by head-to-head trial studies (if available), reviews of the pharmacological literature (looking at several meds for an indication), the amount and history of the clinical evidence (e.g., how many DBPCTs; how many years have people been using the drug), knowledge of side effect and risk-benefit profiles for a medication in the patient's history, and cost considerations.
- If the first one selected as best is not adequately effective or causes unacceptable side effects, then go to the next best FDA approved medication. If the list of FDA approved meds for an indication is exhausted, then try combinations of FDA approved meds before going 'off label'.
- When a given indication has FDA approved meds and none of them show efficacy or tolerability, only go 'off label' as a last resort. Before taking this last resort consider the following possibilities: The psychiatric diagnosis is incorrect or insufficient; there is substance abuse that is ongoing and undetected; the patient is non-compliant.
- If a given indication does not have an FDA approved medication treatment (e.g., borderline personality disorder, cannabis use disorder, and cocaine use disorder) then use medication for which the evidence base is strongest. Strength of the evidence base can be assessed (similar to the second point listed above) roughly by the number of published studies that are DBPCTs vs. 'open label' case controlled, or cross-over design trials vs. uncontrolled case series. Single case reports are generally not adequate for assessing efficacy. Attention to the basic science literature, which usually suggests a neuroscientific rational and mechanism of action for a given medication treatment, can also be considered viable evidence as long as there is also compelling clinical trial evidence, especially DBPCT data. N-Acetyl Cysteine in the context of cannabis addiction is one such example. A word of caution about the FDA approval of meds for a given indication, is that while FDA approval is a reliable marker of efficacy for a given condition, lack of FDA approval is not necessarily a reliable marker for lack of efficacy. The FDA system of approval does suffer from the fact that drug companies wishing to gain FDA approval must pay the FDA for their evaluation of the drug, and the three extremely expensive DBPCT studies that need to be positive for FDA approval. This process can cost pharmaceutical companies past $1Billion, especially for agents with relatively novel mechanisms. Thus, agents that may have genuine clinical efficacies for treating addictions

but are not patentable (giving pharmaceutical companies exclusive profit protections), may not earn FDA approvals.

- Avoid the use of a medication for a given indication if it is not FDA approved and there are no DBPCTs to support its use. Anecdotal experience with a given agent in a given indication is generally never enough to justify its regular use in treatment, especially for the treatment of addiction where there is considerable desperation for new treatments and proportional potential for fraud. If the addiction psychiatrist is convinced that a given medication treatment is effective, but it is not FDA approved and no DBPCT (or other compelling clinical trial data) exists for its use, then that agent should be tried in the context of a well-designed DBPCT as approved and monitored by an Institutional Review Board.

4. Focus on Starting and Ending Medication Trials Based on the Clinical Case Evidence

The growing availability and diversity of medications for ever more illness indications, along with 'direct-to-consumer' marketing, has produced unprecedented growth in the numbers of different types of medications patients may be prescribed for medical and psychiatric purposes, often simultaneously, by many different physicians who do not consult with one another. Many physicians feel pressure from various sources that they should prescribe as many medications as they can, to address as many symptoms as they can find in the shortest amount of time, for a given patient. As the time that physicians, including psychiatrists, have been allotted to spend with each patient has atrophied over recent decades in order to meet 'productivity' quotas, there has also been an increasing reliance on the mere act of prescribing medications. Mass prescribing seems to make up for the lack of connection between doctors and patients, so that pills can symbolize and encapsulate the message that the "doctor is doing something for me even though I only see him for 8 minutes and the whole time he is looking at a computer screen". In parallel, the health care market has created a sense and expectation in many patients that more medications are equivalent to more and better care.

The bottom line is that these medical cultural trends have led to many patients being prescribed extremely complex and often deleterious medication regimens. Within psychiatry, several problems specific to behavioral health care have conspired to create 'irrational polypharmacy regimens' that can have a host of negative consequences like those listed in point two. Lack of sufficient numbers of psychiatrists in the medical workforce has forced many physicians, that is, those in primary care, who have no formal psychiatric training, to take on the responsibility of taking care of mentally ill patients. In the absence of residency training in psychiatry and psychopharmacology, and in the absence of working relationships with psychiatric consultants or therapists, these prescribers tend to rely predominantly on pharmaceutical marketing advice (i.e., information from drug reps), which does not often promote the principal of "less is more" when it comes to prescribing psychiatric medications. Within behavioral health, where many psychiatrists are unfortunately literally discouraged by billing systems or service models from performing psychotherapies in conjunction with medication management, there also tends to be an overemphasis on solving all problems with more pills in lieu of adequate provision of psychotherapy. A final major contributor to irrational polypharmacy within psychiatry is a consequence of the fragmented nature of behavioral health care. Short term/ acute crisis inpatient units often still function in a way that is disconnected from long-term longitudinal outpatient care services, or even worse, are operating in contexts where there are no adequate long-term outpatient services. This sets up a situation where it is routine for inpatient physicians to be starting psychoactive medication regimens that can be quite complex and involve relatively high doses, without any intent or ability (because of where they are practicing) to take responsibility for monitoring the long-term efficacies of those regimens.

For dual diagnosis patients, the problem of 'irrational polypharmacy' is particularly common and significant, for a number of reasons that ultimately relate to the phenomenology of addictions, and the lack of preparedness, interest, or support that most psychiatrists have in treating these conditions. For example, ongoing substance use in psychiatric patients can often go undetected and untreated by psychiatrists who for whatever reason are not able to address addictive disorders. In turn, this substance use often exacerbates the patient's psychiatric syndrome and degree of occupational and social dysfunction, while also making psychiatric medications even less effective. This then, is a set up for the non-addiction focused psychiatrist to resort to irrational polypharmacy, targeting the treatment refractory psychiatric syndrome, often involving atypical dosing of meds, complex drug combinations, off-label utilization, and generally, major deviations from the evidence base. Add to this the fact that patients with addictions, including dual diagnosis patients, have a brain disease that compels them to compulsively seek out, accumulate, and put substances in their bodies, often via an oral route, often involving pharmaceutical agents. In many cases this involves pathological manipulation of physicians by patients, to prescribe either uncontrolled or controlled agents, either of which may have street value, and can be used by patients to barter for other addictive drugs. All these conditions together create a perfect storm where addicted/dual diagnosis patients are particularly likely to be over loaded with too many, or inappropriately selected psychoactive medication regimens.

To address this iatrogenic hazard in dual diagnosis patients, addiction psychiatrists in the 2 × 4 Model clinic should not only strive to maintain non-redundancy and parsimony in their own pharmacological regimens (as in point two above) but they should be willing and able to *frequently* engage in tapering and ending psychotropic medication regimens. Efforts to end inappropriate, ineffective or harmful medication regimens should hold just as high a priority in the work as starting medications or escalating doses. Assumptions that patients should be kept on a psychotropic medication just because they have been on it for so long should never be made. The clinician should be on the lookout for clinical evidence that a diagnosis may not be correct, that the indication for treatment with that specific med is unclear, or that the patient may be worsened or pathologically dependent on that med. As a rule of thumb, the addiction psychiatrist can expect that a third to half of the medication-related discussions and decisions that are made in the 2 × 4 Model clinic will be to reduce and eliminate unnecessary or harmful psychotropic medications.

Increasing comfort with taking mentally ill, addicted, and dual diagnosis patients off of medications is gained with increasing experience in doing it enough to notice that patients actually often do get better in the long run when you 'de-complicate' their psychotropic regimens. In general, 2 × 4 Model physicians should avoid starting a psychotropic medication, whether it be for treating a substance use disorder or a mental health condition, unless he/she plans on monitoring the long range outcome for him/herself, and has an exit strategy (including capability and willingness) for taking the patient off the med if needed. This "don't start something you don't plan to manage or finish" principal when it comes to psychopharmacology, allows the 2 × 4 Model doctor to accumulate a much deeper experiential knowledge base about the long-term utility of different treatment regimens for different kinds of dual diagnosis patients. And, because the core design and operational goals of the 2 × 4 Model clinic include the provision of long-term integrated mental health and addiction care, 2 × 4 Model clinic physicians are supported by the treatment system itself in adhering to this guiding principal.

Of course, maintaining appropriate willingness and action in taking patients off of psychotropic regimens includes being open to stopping meds that others outside the 2 × 4 Model clinic have started, as well as questioning and reversing what oneself has started as the unfolding case evidence may suggest. The key to deciding when it's time to end a medication trial is in paying close attention to the clinical outcomes data and clinical trajectories emanating from the patient. This data is collected longitudinally from ongoing diagnostics, addiction psychiatry evaluations, and input from the therapists in the clinic who are seeing the patient's behavior evolve both in groups and individual therapies. This horizontal binding of psychopharmacology with the other treatment components of the 2 × 4 Model (described in more detail in Chapter 10), allows the addiction psychiatrist to not only tailor the optimal integrated dual diagnosis medication regiment to each individual patient, but to be able to best modify the regimen as the patient's syndrome evolves over time. To do this well, the psychiatrist must develop a sense of what sort of evidence is needed to evaluate the efficacy of a given medication for a given patient, and what sorts of signs in that evidence stream is indicative of treatment failure. Ultimately, if the weight of the case evidence says the medication is not working, or is producing more harm than benefit, it is the obligation of the doctor to take the patient off the med. However, in doing this, it is important to keep in mind that while treatments may fail, patients do not (rather, sicknesses may remain treatment refractory, but sick people seeking treatment are not failures). Accordingly, it is not appropriate to fire or discharge the patient from the 2 × 4 Model clinic because a specific treatment has failed, while they are still sick, and are treatment seeking. Instead, when a treatment has failed, it is time to end that treatment, and generate and execute a new treatment strategy that may or may not include alternative medications. In this way, the 2 × 4 Model physician avoids making the provision of a specific treatment into a precondition for being in the clinic. While helping the clinic avoid the 'pill mill' trap of making the termination of a specific medication treatment equal to terminating the patient from the clinic entirely, this approach also gives the addiction psychiatrist even more room and comfort to objectively evaluate and stop a specific medication regimen when it is time to do so, without being fearful that it could mean throwing the patient entirely out of care. The focus on starting and ending medication trials, based on the clinical case evidence, is made possible by, and necessitates the long-term mission of the 2 × 4 Model clinic, and its emphasis on having multiple treatment tools to deploy from both its psychotherapeutic and pharmacological tool kits.

5. Avoid Addictive Drug Polypharmacy

There are three major groups of FDA approved prescription drugs that are controlled substances and carry substantial risk of misuse, addiction, psychiatric complications, and overdose. These are: 1) stimulants (STIM); 2) the sedative-hypnotics (a.k.a., 'benzoids', including barbiturates, classic benzodiazepines, and atypical benzodiazepines (BZD)); and 3) the opioids (OP). All of these drugs carry legitimate, evidence-based indications, and can be used appropriately in outpatient primary health care and psychiatry. The key question for the addiction psychiatrist is: Under what conditions do the prescription of these drugs become inappropriate, too high a risk, or harmful to the patient? In answering this question the prescriber should carefully evaluate the issues of durations and combinations.

In general, the longer a patient is taking an addictive drug, regardless of who is providing access to that drug (e.g., a doctor vs. an illicit drug dealer), and regardless of what reason or purpose the patient may initially have to take that drug, the more likely the drug will carry risk of addiction and other adverse consequences. So, if possible, always keep the durations of medication treatment with addictive drugs as short as possible, especially in the case of benzoids, regardless of the indication. This guideline is not as feasible (or desirable) in the treatment of certain chronic neuropsychiatric conditions where stimulants or opioids are indicated (e.g., methadone for long-term opioid addiction maintenance treatment, or modafinil for narcolepsy). However, in these latter contexts, the prescriber can at least, as a rule of thumb, almost always avoid prescribing combinations of two or more major groups of addictive drugs chronically.

As a matter of course, the addiction psychiatrist in the 2 × 4 Model program should strive to avoid prescribing cross-group combinations of addictive prescription drugs (e.g., STIM + BZD, STIM + OP, BZD + OP, or STIM + BZD + OP) long-term, and to closely scrutinize, advise against, and/or interdict other doctors who are prescribing such combinations to the patient from outside the 2 × 4 Model clinic (see Chapter 8). The basis for this guide point is 3-fold. First, there is very little empirical evidence to justify any of these drug combinations for any indication long-term. Second, the weight of the evidence, especially with respect to long-term OP + BZD combinations, actually does suggest that the risks and harms of such combinations, including the production of iatrogenic illness and premature death, are significant. Third, chronic cross-groups controlled drug combinations when found in patients, regardless of whether they are resulting from procurement from illicit dealing vs. physicians carrying DEA registrations, are a very strong indicator of the patient having multiple addictions.

Among the different types of controlled prescription combinations, the ones involving benzoids and opioids (e.g., BZD + OP, or STIM + BZD + OP) are the most dangerous due to the high risk of lethal overdose and other related adverse events. We are easily reminded of the degree and scope of this risk, by recent epidemiological data characterizing the modern prescription drug epidemic: By 2008, Americans were more likely to die from a prescription drug overdose, often involving OP or OP + BZD combinations, than from car accidents or suicide. At the same time, rates of overdoses resulting from prescribed OP or OP+ BZD combinations resulting in ER admissions or deaths had far outpaced rates of overdoses on drugs sold to patients by illicit drug dealers. Nevertheless, there are three main clinical contexts where OP + BZD combinations are acceptable, involving acceptable risk/benefit ratios:

1. In hospital (medical or psychiatric) settings where the cardiopulmonary status of patients is relatively closely monitored, where they do not have access to alcohol or other street drugs, and where health care professionals, not patients themselves, are administering the addictive drugs.
2. In hospice (where the goal is comfort care in course of the dying process).
3. In DWT programs (inpatient or outpatient, staffed by well-trained addiction treatment professionals).

Notice that what is common among all these contexts, is both the temporary/limited timeline for the drug combinations, and the relatively high level of risk-reduction intrinsic to these contexts, related to the high level of focused, professional monitoring (Contexts #1 and #3), or the context where a lethal event or an addictive outcome is not really a serious adverse outcome in an actively dying patient (Context #2). Context #3, involving DWT programing, essentially reduces to Context #1 when happening in an inpatient setting. However, Context #3 may also happen in the outpatient setting, and indeed should be a normal component of the 2 × 4 Model clinic (see DWT later in this chapter and Chapter 10). Under these outpatient circumstances, it is important that a) patients be monitored face to face frequently (every 1 to 3 days) by subjective and objective measures performed by nursing and physician team members; b) that scripts for controlled substances (e.g., BZDs) given in the course of DWT only be given for similarly short runs (every 1 to 3 days) in phase with return monitoring appointments; and c) that the overall trajectory of withdrawal treatment programing involves tapering of BZD doses to a clear endpoint at which time the BZD dosing goes to zero.

Controlled substance combinations involving stimulants, but not involving OP + BZD combinations, for example, STIM + BZD, or STIM + OP, are much less dangerous than OP + BZD combinations in terms of risk of acute lethal overdose. However, these combinations still carry other significant longer-term risks such as generating or contributing to iatrogenic addiction, psychiatric worsening, or diversion via illicit gifting, bartering, or dealing. The 2 × 4 Model psychiatrist should remember that as of yet there is no clear evidence base or sufficient number of controlled trials of STIM + BZD or STIM + OP combinations for any indication, and no such combination is FDA approved for any indication. Moreover, these combinations involve contradictory pharmacological effects (e.g., as 'uppers' and 'downers'), and are similar to illicit drug combinations known as 'speed balls', which can be highly intoxicating and reinforcing. Many well-intentioned psychiatrists and primary care doctors alike are susceptible to the pitfall of pursuing an array of specific symptoms in a single patient with pharmacologically contradictory combinations of controlled substances, even as the target symptoms for one drug may really represent the side effects of another. For example, many physicians fall into the trap of treating patients who are having daytime sedation, or are having trouble with memory and concentration with stimulants (while they are also being prescribed opioids or benzoids), under the guise of treating narcolepsy, or attention deficit disorder.

Under these circumstances, controlled substance polypharmacy can itself generate complex neuropsychiatric pictures that can greatly complicate and worsen the underlying 'natural' psychiatric syndrome, potentially rendering the patient even more dependent and at risk for decline, due to chronic controlled substance prescribing.

6. Avoid Long-Term or PRN Use of Reinforcing Meds for Mental Illness Indications

Many physicians, and unfortunately, psychiatrists in particular, can also fall into the trap of attempting to treat mood instability (e.g., as in the context of natural bipolar disorder or borderline personality disorder) with combinations of 'uppers' and 'downers', under the non-evidenced-based (and often false) assumption that the downers will somehow precisely chop down the undesirable highs of the underlying illness, while the stimulants will somehow precisely pull up the depressive low states. In reality, it is rarely if ever possible for patients with mood instability to accurately balance and control their own mood states with the mixed use of 'uppers' and 'downers'. Moreover, the Janus-like effects of both of these drug classes each entail acute withdrawal states that work oppositely from their initial acute intoxicating effects: STIMs become sedative-like in their withdrawal, and BZDs and OPs become stimulating in their withdrawal. Given this complexity, it is not generally possible for patients or their prescribers to be able to differentiate underlying mental illness-based mood states from the interactive or distinct intoxicating or withdrawal effects of the prescribed 'uppers' and 'downers'. A greater degree of clinical uncertainty and pathological chaos can thus ensue in mentally ill patients taking controlled substance polypharmacy, leading to even more escalation in psychiatric instability, and of course, let's not forget, liability to onset, or worsening of iatrogenic addiction. Given that the biological vulnerability to addiction is even greater in mentally ill brains (Chapter 2) than for healthy brains, single or multi-drug controlled substance prescribing carries especially high risk for mentally ill people and should be avoided. In explaining this to patients, to help them understand why they should not expect to be placed on multiple addictive drug prescriptions in the 2 × 4 Model clinic for mental health indications, the Trampoline Analogy (as if presented to a patient, Ms. R) can be very helpful:

The Trampoline Analogy

Imagine, Ms. R., that the mood instability you experience with your psychiatric illness is like you being a 3-year-old child on a trampoline with a big teenager, who weighs a 100 more pounds than you do, who you cannot see or predict very well—because he is such a fast jumper. If you, the 3 year old, were on the trampoline by yourself you could manage the ups and downs of jumping by yourself, and even learn to control it, to be safe, and have some fun in the process. But you are not alone, and there is this wild and wooly teenager you cannot see well—your mood disorder—who is jumping up and down somewhere on the trampoline. If he's near you and jumping, your own jumps may get dampened, or, your jumps may get amplified far higher than you intended, and so you get knocked down a lot, maybe even hurt, and it's hard to learn how to jump in the best way. Now imagine, under these circumstance, if we introduced a stimulant and/or a depressant (benzoid or opioid) into the mix, in an effort to get your illness under control. This would be like inviting a couple more teenagers, also weighing a 100 more pounds than you do, who you also cannot see that well, or precisely control that well, onto the trampoline. They are going to be jumping too, and when they do they are going to make the illness even harder to see and predict. Sometimes the jumps of the teenager representing your mood disorder and the jumping of the teenagers representing the stimulants and/or depressants are in opposite phase so that they cancel out, and you could feel more stable, for a moment. But other times they jump with the kind of timing relevant to each other, such that the wave form they create together is additive and of much higher power and amplitude than what even the illness by itself could have done. Now there is even more instability, more chaos, more risk of injury, and more risk of you being thrown and battered. And you will think, mistakenly, that you have to invite even more, or even bigger wild and wooly teenagers on board, which inevitably ends up really hurting you or knocking you off the trampoline altogether.

In this analogy, it's easier to see the importance of getting rid of, and avoiding those other wild and wooly teenagers (the addictive 'uppers' and 'downers' that are making things worse on the trampoline), and instead work on strategies that will make you bigger, stronger, and wiser in comparison to that wild teenager who is your mental illness. Antidepressants that are not addictive, can give you weight and help you grow bigger on that trampoline so you are not knocked around by that illness as much; mood stabilizers can help us change the bouncyness of the trampoline, so that we can better control how high or low you go; psychotherapy will give you much better vision and resiliency to see where that wild and wooly teenager mood disorder is on the trampoline, and how he is jumping at the moment, so you can know how to best make your own jumps.

In addition to avoiding prescribing combinations of addictive drugs, and minimizing the use of long-term prescriptions of addictive drugs, the 2 × 4 Model clinic physician should avoid the use of 'PRN' regimens of STIMs and BZDs or OPs, that is, where, with the PRN order, the doctor actually formally instructs the patient that they should self-administer the addictive medication, whenever they feel like it. Writing PRN scripts for controlled substances on an outpatient basis is a very common mistake that many fine physicians with the best intentions can get caught up in. They do it because they want to empower patients to take responsibility for their own care, knowing that they cannot be at their patient's side every day. Doctors know it makes patients feel good for them to delegate to them the sense of control that comes with deciding when to take a med. Also, much of the medical training culture (i.e., where medical students and residents get trained) is still inpatient based, and involves a great deal of useful PRN-ing of med regimens. However, the PRN-ing of meds that happens in the inpatient setting has been inappropriately exported to the much less professionally monitored outpatient world, in hopes that it could be as useful, even though the outpatient world it a totally different ball game.

When the doctor orders a PRN regimen in the inpatient setting, the dosing decision is still always accompanied by professional medical supervision, usually by the nursing team, and often with the use of objective measures (e.g., vital signs) to inform the dosing decision. And it is the nursing team that controls the overall supply and dosing, not the patient. The nurses track the overall amount taken by the patient so it is usually known with 100 percent certainty how much the patient has taken per day and whether or not the trend of use is up or down. Finally, the relatively high-controlled setting of the inpatient unit generally means that patients do not have access to other addictive, recreational, or diverted drugs that could be used to make the PRN regimen dangerous. All these safeguards are thrown out the window when doctors write PRN regimens of controlled substances on an outpatient basis.

In the context of outpatient mental health and addiction treatment, multiple unnecessary risks and adverse consequences can result from PRN prescribing. First it delegates to a mentally ill patient (who may lack insight, and can suffer from significant impulsivity and impairments in decision-making) the professional responsibility of knowing when they should take these drugs, even as they are not equipped with the medical knowledge and objective point of view of the prescribing physician. Second, it sends the message to the patient, that the doctor isn't really concerned with how much, or when, a patient takes an addictive substance, even the ones she is prescribing; with PRNs of controlled substances, the doctor is simulating too closely the types of commercial exchanges and dynamics that surround illicit drug dealing. Third, and in relation to this dynamic, the PRN-ing of controlled substances to mentally ill patients may actually encourage the acquisition of addictive patterns of drug self-administration that patients (and their prescribing physicians) can pathologically mislabel and rationalize as 'self-medication' (e.g., 'pill-popping' of symptoms underpinning addiction). Fourth, outpatient PRN-ing invites even more chaos and uncertainty in patients whose lives are often incredibly chaotic and uncertain. The physician, by writing PRNs, has now made it all but impossible to know how much or when the patient is taking their meds; how they may be interfering with recovery or generating psychiatric symptoms; how they may or may not be diverting, or ingesting these meds concurrent with the psychotherapeutic services of the clinic. For all these reasons, 2 × 4 Model clinic prescribers should avoid the use of PRN instructions of controlled substances including OPs, BZDs, and STIMs, and only sparingly resort to it using nonaddictive medications. In addition, the 2 × 4 Model doc should proactively advise against and interdict this kind of prescribing that could be happening to their patients involving outside physicians, via proactive communications (Chapter 8).

So in sum, the addiction psychiatrist working in the 2 × 4 Model clinic should avoid chronic addictive drug polypharmacy and the use of addictive substances chronically and/or on a PRN basis for mental health indications. Several important nuances, caveats, and exceptions are now important to consider with respect to these principals.

- The use of opioid maintenance therapies: Buprenorphine and methadone are themselves addictive opioid medications that can be used effectively and therapeutically on a long-term basis for opioid addiction. This is well supported by an extensive and long-standing clinical evidence base that supports these meds for long-term harm reduction. Long-term use of these medications for opioid addiction may be indicated, safe, and optimal for certain patients. However, the addition of other reinforcing, controlled substances to these meds (e.g., benzodiazepine, other opioid, stimulants, cannabinoids) should not happen.
- The use of nicotine replacement therapies (NRTs): Nicotine is an addictive drug that, like methadone/buprenorphine, can be used effectively as a withdrawal therapy, maintenance therapy, or 'stepping stone therapy' in the treatment of a type of addiction (i.e., tobacco use disorder). These

applications are reasonably well supported by the evidence base, but most importantly, nicotine is not associated with increased risk of dangerous or lethal intoxications and overdoses when taken in combinations with other addictive drugs. Therefore, the use of NRTs (and varenicline, which has some nicotine-like properties and can be somewhat reinforcing) is generally well-justified regardless of the presence of other chronic addictive drug regimens (e.g., like methadone or buprenorphine).

- Cases involving a question of adult ADHD: Diagnoses of attention deficit disorder (ADD)/attention deficit hyperactivity disorder (ADHD) in adults, and its treatment with STIMs, have gained popularity and greater acceptance in psychiatry, but nevertheless remain controversial. In the experience of this author and in clinical populations that have, or are seeking treatment for addiction and dual diagnosis, a diagnosis of ADD or ADHD warranting a STIM prescription in an adult is rarely appropriate, because the cognitive symptoms that fulfill the ADD/ADHD diagnostic criteria are typically readily explainable by 1) the use of 'recreational' drugs, e.g., cannabis and or ETOH; 2) the use of controlled prescription drugs (most commonly OPs and BZDs); and 3) the presence of mental illnesses that are well known to generate ADD/ADHD range cognitive styles and symptoms, including schizophrenia, major depression, bipolar disorder, PTSD, borderline personality disorder, and others. Accordingly, it is advisable that the 2 × 4 Model clinician should avoid the use of STIM medications altogether, especially if the patient is being prescribed, or is under clinical suspicion of using another mind-altering addictive substances. If neither of these concerns are present (which will be exceedingly rare in an addiction/dual diagnosis clinical context) it may be OK to prescribe a scheduled STIM medication, but only as a monotherapy (when it is certain that the patient is using no other addictive drugs) and there is little to no chance that another major psychiatric disorder does not better explain the ADD symptoms.
- Cases involving patients who are using cannabis: Marijuana use is the most common form of substance use after alcohol and nicotine in many parts of Europe and the Western hemisphere, and it is very common in dual diagnosis patient populations (e.g., may be found in 20–60 percent of patients). The good news is, despite the legal sanctions that still exist against marijuana sale and use in many places, the serious short and long-term health risks of cannabinoids in adults are actually less than for heavy tobacco or alcohol use. Although cannabinoids can synergize with alcohol intoxication to produce acute nausea and vertigo ('the spins'), and cannabinoids can drive short-term psychotic reactions, it is essentially impossible to suffer a lethal overdose on pure cannabinoids. Further, combining marijuana with OPs and/or BZDs does not significantly amplify the acute overdose risks of either OPs or BZDs. The bad news is that cannabinoids can produce a range of psychotic, cognitive, and mood symptoms while people are using them, and these drugs are definitely addictive (albeit less so than nicotine, opioids, and amphetamines). While cannabinoid-induced psychiatric symptoms are typically mild and transient

(after cessation of use) they nevertheless can (and usually do) complicate diagnosis and treatment of mental health and/or addictive disorders, especially in dual diagnosis patients.

Based on these issues, it is generally recommended that 2 × 4 Model physicians should avoid prescriptions of medical marijuana or pharmaceutical grade THC (e.g., dronabinol) for all non-terminally ill dual diagnosis patients, and those who are on opioid therapies for opioid addiction. This also means being proactive in interdicting doctors who may also be legally prescribing THC to the dual diagnosis patient (see Chapter 8). Of course, many dual diagnosis patients may present with drug use rationalizations for why they need marijuana for physical and/or psychiatric indications. But, the clinician should remember that the evidence base, and FDA approval for the use of THC for physical symptoms is quite well circumscribed (i.e., to dronabinol, for nausea and vomiting in the context of cancer chemotherapy, and for anorexia in the context of HIV). Moreover, both of these types of symptoms are treatable with other noncontrolled, non-reinforcing agents. Finally, despite ongoing research efforts, a convincing demonstration of the efficacy, or net positive risk–benefit ratio of THC treatment for any type of psychiatric condition, has, as of the writing of this edition (2017) not been established.

On the other hand, it is not necessarily the correct or best strategy for the addiction psychiatrist to withhold treatments for other addictions or mental health conditions, because the patient has an active cannabinoid use disorder (e.g., as supplied by illicit sources). For example, since there is no evidence that buprenorphine and methadone can effectively treat cannabinoid addiction, and since cannabinoids do not substantially raise the risk of lethal overdose on these drugs, it is not necessarily always the best plan, or even reasonable, to stop buprenorphine or methadone treatments because the patient is smoking pot. Instead, efforts should be made to assess, address, and treat the Marijuana use as its own problem (e.g., via psychotherapeutics or other pharmacological measures). If, over a long period of evaluation and therapeutic effort, the patient is not showing great progress with either their opioid or marijuana addictions (e.g., while on buprenorphine), and/or if there is a reasonable clinical suspicion that the patient could be diverting their opioid replacement therapy to pay for their marijuana supply, then the psychiatrist may then be well justified to taper off the opioid replacement treatment and go with a non-controlled substance alternative for opioid addiction (e.g., naltrexone). Sometimes the process of tapering off the opioid maintenance treatment can serve to successfully leverage the patient's motivation against the cannabinoid addiction. Other times, it leads to a different and more effective strategy in treating the opioid addiction. Regardless, with this kind of leveraging, the clinician should not threaten to kick the patient out of treatment altogether. The goal is to find a strategy that works for sick patients, and avoid those that don't.

- Cases involving patients who are using cocaine/amphetamines: As with cannabinoids, patients with multiple addictions will also often present with addictions to cocaine, methamphetamines, amphetamines, or other stimulants including a variety of STIMs indicated for ADD, narcolepsy, restless leg syndrome, etc. Again, these patients may be presenting a strong self-medication like rationalization for using these drugs, but the 2 × 4 Model clinician should avoid 'pouring gas on the fire' of dual diagnosis (exacerbating mood and psychotic syndromes and addiction) by prescribing these drugs, and they should interdict other doctors who may be doing so. At the same time, these drug are not known to greatly increase the risk of lethal overdoses on OPs (or buprenorphine), nor does buprenorphine treat addiction to these stimulant drugs. Therefore, as with comorbid cannabinoid use disorders, addictive patterns of psychostimulant use are not necessarily deal breakers for prescribing opioid replacement therapies for concurrent opioid addiction. Efforts should be made to treat all the addictions a patient has, and to monitor long-term progress with respect to each drug; if strategies are not working then change them.

In sum, for patients with complex addictions presenting to the 2 × 4 Model clinic, who's illnesses involve OPs, STIMS, BZDs, and/or THC, the best guidelines to follow with respect to prescribing controlled substance are: 1) do not stray away from what is FDA approved, indicated, and well supported by the evidence base; and 2) if you have to use a controlled substance for any reason, keep it to just one.

Written Guidelines for Prescribing Drugs in the 2 × 4 Model Clinic

Written guidelines can serve as an important reference source and benchmark for prescribing practices followed in the 2 × 4 Model clinic. In the practice of good integrated dual diagnosis treatment, there will be a healthy tension between the value of individualizing care vs. standardizing care, or, said another way, flexibility vs. algorithm. As discussed in prior chapters, the 2 × 4 Model program places high value on clinical flexibility and individualization of treatment plans, given the diversity of care approaches that different types of dual diagnosis patients, and demographic groups, will need. At the same time, there is an evidence base and cultural norms of efficient and safe practice that necessarily put limits on freedom of practice, especially when it comes to managing and using controlled (e.g., reinforcing) prescription drugs. Written guidelines should not be used to dictate rules of prescribing practices so that there is no need for clinical decision-making; rather, guidelines can be immensely helpful to ensure that all prescribers are making decisions about prescriptions, within the same, and generally accepted parameter space. Guidelines can also represent a helpful treatment planning structure for physicians and nurses, and their respective trainees to follow, that facilitate more efficient and clear interactions in team-level coordination of care. Guidelines are particularly useful at key transition points in the pharmacological treatment of dual diagnosis disorders, such as when starting or finishing DWT, or when starting long-term therapies, for example, involving buprenorphine.

Generally, prescribing guidelines should be reviewed and agreed upon by all members of the 2 × 4 Model team that prescribe medications, with copies presented to new comers including residents, fellows, and new attending staff during orientation. They should be based on the known clinical–scientific evidence, safety considerations, and the training and clinical experience of the team leaders (e.g., the addiction psychiatrists and nursing staff). They are of course, amenable to revision and updates over time, according to changes in clinical conditions or the evidence base, etc., but they should change relatively slowly and carefully over time. They should be written in a way that conveys a sensibility of whether a particular guideline or limit being expressed is more of a soft or a hard limit, that is, being something that can happen sometimes, given certain circumstances, vs. something that should happen extremely rarely or almost never.

Sometimes clinicians get into the habit of relying on clinic guidelines (sometimes relabeled as 'policies') as a justification for not bending to a patient's request for a particular medication or treatment strategy. This can feel useful especially for clinicians who have real trouble with managing what it feels like to disappoint or anger patients, and to take on the role of the 'bad guy'. Like, "I'd like to do such and such for you but it's against our clinic policy". In the 2 × 4 Model program, it is recommended that clinicians try to steer clear from using or referring to guidelines in this particular way with patients. First of all, 'policies' are more in line with what political or governmental organizations or commercial businesses use to conduct their affairs. In contrast, the 2 × 4 Model program is a health care entity that uses the biomedical evidence base, training, and clinical experience of individual practitioners to inform clinical decisions, on behalf of the welfare and health of the patient. 'Policies' can imply other motives, not necessarily in the interest of the patient. And, the practitioner who leans on 'policies' as a reason to not do something the patient wants, may inadvertently be both undermining the good, evidence-based motives in the guidelines (e.g., by regarding them as arbitrary), and artificially separating their own clinical judgments from them (e.g., by suggesting that the prescriber has to do it a certain way regardless of what she really thinks). So with this in mind, if the prescriber is making a decision that follows a particular 2 × 4 Model clinic guideline and this decision is different from, or in conflict with what the patient wants, the prescriber should explain the rationale(s) for the decision (that may often be the rationale(s) for the guideline in general), while avoiding an arbitrary statement of "it's against our clinic's rules or policies". It's really about the clinician making the best decision for the patient and owning that decision.

The remainder of this chapter will present a number of guidelines for pharmacological practice in the 2 × 4 Model clinic that were developed and applied with good success in our own 2 × 4 Model prototype. These guidelines are recommended for adoption, and as needed, for careful modification in other 2 × 4 Model programs.

BOX 7.1 Guidelines for Prescribing Stimulants

The prescribing of controlled stimulants (e.g., modafinil, amphetamine, methylphenidate, etc.) for adult patients for any indication in the 2 × 4 Model clinic should be rare and considered only a treatment of last resort, and limited to a clear FDA approved target indication, according to the following rules:

1. Patients presenting for treatment of adult ADHD, or, who claim to have this diagnosis while requesting stimulants, should not be assessed at face value as having this diagnosis either according to their own self-appraisal or as a professional referral. Such patients must undergo a full dual diagnosis evaluation to determine whether the patient a) meets clinical criteria for ADHD; b) has one or more other mental health disorders that could independently account for ADHD symptoms or disturbances in cognition and attention; and/or c) has one or more substance use disorders that may either account for the ADHD symptoms and/or could be manifesting as drug seeking behavior focused on stimulants.

2. Controlled psychostimulants for ADHD should not be started when the patient has a psychiatric disorder or addiction that better accounts for ADHD symptomatology.

3. Controlled psychostimulants for any indication should not be started when the patient is also being prescribed buprenorphine, benzodiazepines, or other controlled substances, for the treatment of concurrent substance withdrawal or dependence of any kind. Continuation of maintenance psychostimulants should also be questioned, considered as hazards, and usually tapered in the course of DWT from opioids, benzoids, or alcohol, since the later syndromes typically encompass hyper-sympathomimetic states that psychostimulants are well known to exacerbate.

4. Patients discovered to be treated with controlled stimulants (i.e., from an outside physician) who are being prepared for, or are being treated with other controlled substances in the clinic should be a) subject to a doctor to doctor communication to discuss the cessation of the controlled stimulant prescription; and/or b) be tapered off of the controlled stimulant according to a predetermined schedule agreed upon by the practitioner and patient.

5. Patients with substance use diagnoses other than nicotine dependence should generally not be prescribed a controlled psychostimulant for an ADHD diagnosis (or other neuropsychiatric indications for stimulants) even when uncomplicated by other psychiatric comorbidities. In these cases, ADHD treatment strategies that do not involve controlled substances (e.g., atomoxetine/bupropion) should be employed.

BOX 7.2 Guidelines for Prescribing Benzoids

The prescribing of controlled benzoids including barbiturates, typical benzodiazepines (e.g., lorazepam), or atypical benzodiazepines (e.g., zolpidem, pregabalin), should be monitored closely for the treatment of substance withdrawal. Benzoid prescribing should otherwise be limited as treatments of last resort for other FDA indications, and for as short-as-possible courses according to the following guidelines:

1. Patients presenting for treatment of anxiety, insomnia, or seizure disorder, or who claim to have one or more of these diagnoses while requesting benzoids, should not be assessed at face value as having these diagnosis either according to their own self-appraisal or as a professional referral. Such patients must undergo a full dual diagnosis evaluation to determine whether the patient a) meets diagnostic criteria for anxiety, insomnia, or related indication; b) has one or more other mental health disorders that could independently account for anxiety, insomnia, or seizure disorder symptoms; and/or c) has one or more substance use disorder(s) that may either account for the anxiety, insomnia, or seizure disorder symptoms and/or could be manifesting as drug seeking behavior that is focused on acquisition of benzoids.

2. Benzoids for anxiety, insomnia, or seizure disorder should not be started when the patient has another psychiatric disorder, or addiction that better accounts for anxiety, insomnia, or seizure disorder symptomatology, *except for* when treating substance withdrawal.

3. Benzoids for any indication should not be started or maintained (i.e., without tapering) when the patient is also being prescribed buprenorphine or methadone, or other benzoids (for the treatment of substance withdrawal).

4. Patients discovered to be treated with controlled benzoids (i.e., from an outside physician) who are being prepared for, or are being treated with other controlled substances in the clinic should be subject to a doctor to doctor communication to plan the tapering and cessation of the benzoid.

5. In cases of anxiety or insomnia that are uncomplicated by the presence of other psychiatric or substance use disorders that better account for anxiety or insomnia, patients may be treated with a short course of a benzoid that will be tapered over days to months as agreed upon by the physician and patient.

6. Treatment of a chronic seizure disorder with a benzoid should occur in consultation with a neurologist, and as a last resort after treatment failures involving adequate trials of non-controlled anti-seizure medications.

BOX 7.3 **Guidelines for Prescribing Opioids**

The prescribing of controlled opioids (i.e., natural or synthetic agents that are partial or full agonists at the μ opiate receptor) as FDA indicated for the treatment of opioid use disorders should be done carefully, monitored closely, and used exclusively for the treatment of opioid withdrawal syndromes and/or opioid addiction after a full initial dual diagnosis evaluation by the psychiatrist.

1. Opioid medications should not be prescribed in the 2 × 4 Model clinic for any indication other than for FDA approved applications for short–term opiate withdrawal or long–term maintenance treatments for opioid addiction (Opioid Use Disorder in DSM-5). Other opioids (e.g., hydrocodone, oxycodone, morphine, and codeine) used for other FDA approved indications (e.g., for pain), that do not have an opioid addiction-related indication, should not be prescribed in the 2 × 4 Model clinic. Methadone and buprenorphine should also not be prescribed in the 2 × 4 Model clinic to target any type of pain or any other target symptom when there is not a primary opioid addiction diagnosis.

2. Buprenorphine and methadone (for 2 × 4 Model programs that incorporate government-regulated methadone maintenance programing) are the only two types of opioids that should be prescribed in the 2 × 4 Model clinic.

3. Patients with pain syndromes should be treated via the use of non-opioid, noncontrolled pharmacological strategies and/or other psychotherapeutic or experiential/rehabilitative methods. If a patient is already on buprenorphine (or methadone) for the indication of an opioid use disorder and has a clear somatic source, injury, or surgery-related source of pain, then the dose of buprenorphine (or methadone) can adjusted temporarily to assist in the control of the pain, as long as dosing limits normally observed for the treatment of addiction with those drugs are not exceeded.

4. Patients with acute or chronic pain syndromes (due to somatic disease, injury, or surgical causes) that may require opioids (other than with dose adjustments of buprenorphine/methadone in patients already on these meds for opioid addiction) should be referred for diagnostic workup and treatment of that pain by an outside specialist who can conduct a complete medical, neurological, and/or surgical examination and history taking of the patient.

5. Patients receiving *any type* of opioid medications *for any indication* outside of the 2 × 4 Model clinic must have that medication tapered off and stopped in order to be started and/or maintained on buprenorphine/ methadone in the 2 × 4 Model clinic.

Pharmacotherapies and Staging of Recovery in the 2 × 4 Model Clinic

As will be discussed more in Chapter 10, the 2 × 4 Model clinic operates two outpatient service lines simultaneously that are in interaction with one another in terms of patient flow, treatment planning, and shared nursing and physician staffing. These are 1) the shorter-term DWT service; and 2) the Longitudinal Integrated Dual Diagnosis Treatment (LIDDT) service. Many patients entering the clinic for the first time will start with the DWT service and then transition to the LIDDT service. Other patients already engaged in LIDDT can have the DWT service added on for a while as needed. Both of these services can overlap and are complimentary to one another. The main difference is their focus: DWT is about getting patients safely (and as comfortably as possible) off of alcohol and/or other drugs, and to prepare and motivate them for long-term treatment. LIDDT is about long-term treatment of addiction and mental illness. The following sections will overview pharmacotherapy principals and guidelines for DWT and LIDDT.

Pharmacotherapies in Detoxification/Withdrawal Treatment (DWT)

In the DWT service, the primary pharmacological goal is to achieve cessation of substance use with as few medical and psychiatric complications as possible. In this process, the term 'detoxification' treatment is a bit misleading, because the treatments themselves are not serving to actively remove the drugs or their metabolites (i.e., the 'toxins'). This work is being done by the body, mostly the liver and kidneys, automatically. Instead, what we are actually doing is addressing the homeostatic biological changes that have happened in the brain, as a result of drugs and/or alcohol being on board for a long while. These homeostatic changes actually represent neurobiological adaptations to the presence of the drug(s) that are intended to make the brain perform as normally as possible with that drug on board. The trouble is, this kind of tolerance, when unopposed by the presence of the drug (as drug levels are lowering via metabolism or elimination) can become very uncomfortable, medically dangerous, and even lethal. But while the brain can certainly adapt to the absence of the drug just as it adapted to its presence, it needs time to do this comfortably. Pharmacotherapies in the DWT service are designed to stretch out the withdrawal process to a more comfortable and safer pace (e.g., to give the neuroadaptations of the withdrawal process more time to catch up with the sober state), and/or to relieve specific symptoms that happen in the course of withdrawal.

There are some generalities and specifics that are important to review in the work of the DWT service. The first is that DWT is not a treatment for addiction; rather, it is an important first step that leads to addiction treatment. Second, there are different levels of discomfort, medical, and psychiatric risk that accompany different drugs and different patients in withdrawal. It is up to the psychiatrists and nurses to discern these nuances, with a general understanding that the level of medical danger, from greatest to least, goes from alcohol withdrawal, to benzoid, and then to opioid withdrawal. Conversely, the subjective experience of pain and suffering that goes with these withdrawal syndromes can often follow the opposite pattern from opioid withdrawal to benzoid to alcohol. Of course, virtually all addictive substances, including nicotine, THC, cocaine, and amphetamines produce withdrawal syndromes, but these syndromes are typically and subjectively mild, are not medically dangerous, and so do not require rigorous treatment offered in DWT programing. Third, while each drug type and individual use pattern produces qualitatively different withdrawal syndromes and durations, the rule of thumb for alcohol, benzoid, and opioid withdrawal is that they all create an excitatory state in the brain that is acutely dangerous and/or uncomfortable for on the order of 1–3 weeks. Therefore, a well-designed and monitored DWT pharmacotherapy regimen can, for patients that actually stop using the target substance completely, get most patients safely through withdrawal in 1–2 weeks.

In the pharmacology of withdrawal treatment, there are essentially three main clinical contexts: the 1) OP patient; 2) the ETOH/BZD patient; and 3) mixed/polysubstance cases (i.e., involving some combination of 1 or 2. In Context 2, ETOH and BZD are grouped together because the brain conditions and pharmacological approaches of these two situations are so similar. For the OP patient, the psychiatrist considers a clonidine taper to be the core of the therapy, accompanied by various other adjunct medications to address upset stomach, nausea, diarrhea, pain, and insomnia. Although BZDs can help some symptoms of opioid withdrawal, the risk–benefit ratio of these meds in the outpatient setting for opioid withdrawal is not generally considered favorable, unless of course the patient has comorbid BZD dependence as well. Part of the purpose of clonidine is to help avoid having to use another controlled substance, a BZD, in the OP patient, which is important considering that BZD + OP combinations can be lethal. On the other hand, if one has to use BZDs in the OP patient, because of needing to address polysubstance withdrawal, there probably is little utility in using clonidine as well. Methadone or buprenorphine tapers are sometimes used for OP withdrawal and this is acceptable under many circumstances, especially if patients have already been in long-term treatment on these meds, and are transitioning off them for whatever reason. However, for the patient initiating opioid addiction treatment, coming off of street and/or iatrogenic sources of opioids, there is not much utility in using intermediary opioids, primarily because it just 'kicks the can' of opioid withdrawal down the road. Yes, an opioid taper may ease the symptoms of withdrawal on a day to day basis, but it also prolongs the whole process of detoxification, and to some extent, the suffering. Going through opioid withdrawal is never pleasant no matter how it's done—hard and fast vs. easier, but prolonged—and one approach is not necessarily medically safer than the other. At some point of any detox regimen or taper, the team and the patient still have to confront the unavoidable challenge of total abstinence, and how you get there does not necessarily have much impact on the patient's success at this transition point, or what happens much later in long-term treatment. So, the patient does not really gain a lot from using prolonged DWTs using opioids on an outpatient basis, while the risk of diversion, relapse, or complex overdoses (involving the prescribed meds) is greater when these meds are used, and are greater for every day the withdrawal treatment is prolonged. In general, these concerns are much less for long-term patients who are well known to the clinic and have been in maintenance treatment for some time (e.g., with buprenorphine and methadone) and are not being tapered.

For the patient with ETOH or BZD use disorders needing DWT pharmacotherapy, the core treatment remains a BZD taper. Some centers still use barbiturates for this purpose but because these drugs provide no real advantage over BZDs, and are not as safe, barbiturates are not recommended in the 2 × 4 Model clinic. In general, the choice of BZD to use can vary between clinics based on team experience and familiarity with a given drug, and of course characteristics of metabolism and pharmacokinetics can help determine which type is best to use in a given situation. Longer as opposed to shorter acting BZDs are preferred to allow smoother withdrawal experiences and to avoid rebound withdrawal, for example, as can commonly happen with short acting alprazolam (and for which reason, we do not recommend alprazolam for use in the 2 × 4 Model clinic). In our own 2 × 4 Model program, we like to use chlordiazepoxide for ETOH withdrawal and clonazepam for BZD withdrawal as our front line agents, varying off of these under specific circumstances. Gabapentin can be used as a CNS calming agent and anti-seizure med to assist in withdrawal treatment when the risk-benefit profiles of BZDs are deemed unacceptable on the outpatient basis. For treatment of either ETOH or BZD withdrawal, it is recommended that BZD tapering proceed from the initial dose, more aggressively initially, and becoming more incremental over time as the dose nears zero. Aiming to approximate a hyperbolic decay curve in this way can optimize the risk–benefits of the tapering regimen and give the patient a better sense of readiness toward the end of the taper. Of course, it is important for the DWT team to monitor the patient's clinical withdrawal data (vitals, COWS/CIWA, UDS results, and clinical exam), and alter the taper accordingly to optimize treatment as necessary over the course of the taper, while being careful to not allow the taper to experience inappropriate delays, halts or reversals in progression. Patients with mixed use disorders involving OPs and BZDs and/or ETOH, should be considered as being in a particularly dangerous situation, and managed very carefully in the outpatient DWT service. Many of these types of polysubstance patients are sicker and more likely to overdose, divert, relapse, or not follow instructions of the taper, or, they may be particularly adept at manipulating the team into deviating inappropriately from the taper. Often the best decision for these patients is to go inpatient. But if the outpatient approach is deemed appropriate (e.g., a relatively stable long-term methadone patient who needs to come off a benzoid) it is recommended that the clinic follow a locked-in, invariable, scheduled taper that is presented to the patient at the start. The clinical decision-making regarding the regimen is then mostly focused on deciding on the starting dose, which then subsequently proceeds to zero on an automatic schedule. The duration of the taper depends on how 'high on the slide' (e.g., the starting dose) the psychiatrist chose to begin with. Subsequent decision-making depends on repeated clinical assessments of the patients, to determine if they are adequately and safely tolerating the taper. If they are not, the plan should change to an inpatient detox or some other approach, rather than merely delaying or altering the locked-in tapering regimen. The following sets of guidelines are recommended for DWT pharmacotherapy in the 2 × 4 Model clinic.

BOX 7.4 General Guidelines for DWT Service

1. Use clinical presentation (subjective/objective data) as primary guide in medication tapering decisions.

2. Maintain clinical suspicion that patients will under-report recent use, types of drugs used, or ongoing use in the course of DWT.

3. Outpatient detox is not an option in all cases. Conditions that may indicate the need for an inpatient, supervised (i.e., in a professionally staffed facility) detox include one or more of the following:

a. Severe medical co-morbidity and instability;
b. Severe poly-drug co-morbidity;
c. Severe psychiatric comorbidity;
d. Unstable, or lack of housing, or house-mates actively using; and
e. Recent record of treatment failure in outpatient detox.

4. Do not prescribe medications as 'PRN' as determined by the patient (i.e., do not delegate clinical decision-making to the patient; do not promote or introduce random variability into medication instructions or use).

5. Remember priority levels in treatment of substance use withdrawal:

a. ETOH withdrawal is by far the most potentially lethal condition.
b. Opiate withdrawal is very uncomfortable, but very rarely lethal when uncomplicated.
c. Successful DWT has almost no impact on the long-term success of addiction treatment—*the most important function of DWT is its use in preparing and engaging the patient for their long-term addiction treatment.*

---

continued

BOX 7.4 General Guidelines for DWT Service—*continued*

6. If the patient is receiving substances they are in DWT for from a local practitioner, make attempts to inform this prescriber of the clinical situation, if not already accomplished with the referral.

7. Key communications should be made with patients:

a. A successful detox is not an end to itself, just a first step.
b. A successful detox reduces but does not eliminate discomfort.
c. Compliance with medications and instructions are critically important to successful DWT.

8. 'Eyes on' contact between prescriber and patient: Any patient receiving any controlled substance in the course of detoxification, should be at least briefly assessed by the prescribing provider, with that encounter (with brief MSE) documented in the chart by the prescriber and/or team member (e.g., nursing notes).

9. Limits to DWT using BZDs. Precautions and standards should be adopted to protect patients from repeatedly undergoing unsuccessful outpatient detoxifications, in which the benefits of DWT treatment are inadequate and BZD dispensations may actually be contributing to drug use disorders and/or diversion. The following guidelines are recommended:

a. Patients presenting for two consecutive detoxes requiring BZDs (for treatment of either ETOH or BZD withdrawal) within 90 days, and/or more than three BZD detoxes per year, should be re-valuated as not appropriate for, or being treatment unresponsive to outpatient detoxification using BZDs.
b. Patients approaching, or at these limits, should be informed and considered for alternative treatment strategies using noncontrolled medicines, or inpatient/supervised detoxification options.

BOX 7.5 **Guide for Alcohol DWT**

Assessments

Day 1

1. Pertinent clinical history (gathered primarily by nursing team)
   - recent and past alcohol history;
   - recent and past SUD history (including nicotine);
   - psychiatric History;
   - medical history; and
   - medications.

2. Treatment goals/commitment to recovery education/assessment to determine if higher level of care is needed.

3. CIWA

4. Vital signs

5. ETOH breathalyzer

6. General Urine Drug Screen (cocaine/amphetamine/BZD/THC/OP/ETG)

7. PDMP data check

8. Optional: Blood draw for LFTs (Liver Function Tests), CBC (Complete Blood Count), psychiatric medication levels, pregnancy test

Day 2+

1. Assess treatment compliance/abstinence/symptoms

2. CIWA

3. Vital signs

4. ETOH breathalyzer/UDS as needed.

Treatment

Day 1

1. Discuss and determine long-term treatment goals for alcohol dependence
   - schedule intake for treatment group/individual therapy; and
   - schedule addiction psychiatrist appointment for med management.

2. Treatment of alcohol withdrawal:

   General BZD Taper: (Chlordiazepoxide) (half life=6–30 hrs) (dose equivalence: Lorazepam 1mg=25 mg chlordiazepoxide)

continued

BOX 7.5 **Guide for Alcohol DWT**—*continued*

Start   50 mg PO (per oral) QID (4 times a day) (e.g., CIWA >20)

      <u>or</u>

      50 mg PO TID (3 times a day) (e.g., CIWA 16–20)

      <u>or</u>

      50 mg PO BID (twice a day) (e.g., CIWA 9–15)

      <u>or</u>

      25 mg PO BID (e.g., CIWA <9)

In cases of significant liver impairment:

(Oxazepam) (half life=5–10 hrs) (dose equivalence: lorazepam 1mg= 15 mg oxazepam)

Start   30 mg PO QID

      <u>or</u>

      30 mg PO TID

      <u>or</u>

      30 mg PO BID

3. Vitamin replenishment (optional):

      MVI (multivitamin) 1 tab QD (once a day) × 14 days

      folate 1mg QD × 3 days

      thiamine 100 mg QD × 3 days (thiamine 100 mg IM (intramuscular))

4. Consider gabapentin as adjunct instead of BZD if risk–benefit analysis of BZD is a concern.

Days 2–21:

1. Patient to return every 1–3 days in week one, two times/week in week two.

2. Aim for up to 0–25 percent reduction in BZD dose/day to compete taper in 7–21 days.

3. As taper proceeds, weigh the BZD dosing toward evening to facilitate sleep architecture.

BOX 7.6 **Guide for Opioid DWT**

Assessments

Day 1

1. Pertinent clinical history (gathered primarily by nursing team)

   - recent and past alcohol history;
   - recent and past SUD history (including nicotine);
   - psychiatric History;
   - medical history; and
   - medications.

2. Treatment goals/commitment to recovery education/assessment

3. COWS

4. Vital signs

5. ETOH breathalyzer

6. General Urine Drug Screen (cocaine/amphetamine/BZD/THC/OP (morphine, codeine)) +/– specific opioid panel

As needed (methadone/buprenorphine/oxycodone/hydrocodone).

7. PDMP data check

8. Optional: Blood draw for LFTs, CBC, psychiatric medication levels, pregnancy test

Days 2+

1. Assess treatment compliance/abstinence/symptoms

2. COWS

3. Vital signs

4. Repeat UDS as needed

continued

BOX 7.6 Guide for Opioid DWT—*continued*

Treatment (7–14 days)

Day 1

1. Discuss and determine long-term treatment aims for opioid addiction

   • schedule intake for treatment group/individual therapy; and
   • schedule med management (e.g., buprenorphine/methadone/ naltrexone, other).

2. Treatment of opiate withdrawal: clonidine

If indicated, give 0.05 mg PO test dose, re-assess in 1–2 hrs, expect 10 mm drop in SBP (systolic blood pressure) (want SBP>110)

Start from 0.1 mg QD to 0.1 mg TID.

Adjunct meds:

ibuprophen (headache, musculoskeletal pain) 600 mg TID.

loperimide (diarrhea) 4 mg BID

compazine (nausea) 5–10 mg BID or (phenergan 25 mg)

hydroxyzine (for sleep) 50–100 mg HS (at bedtime)

MVI one tab PO QD 14 days

Days 2–21

1. Patient to return every 1–3 days in week one, two times/week in week two.

2. Taper clonidine over 5–21 days depending on opioid history and clinical course.

3. Continue adjunct meds 5 to 21 days depending on clinical course.

BOX 7.7 Guide for Benzoid DWT

Assessments

Day 1

1. Pertinent clinical history (nursing staff assessment)

   - recent and past alcohol history;
   - recent and past SUD history (including nicotine);
   - psychiatric History;
   - medical history;
   - medications; and
   - determine current amount and source(s) of BZD.

2. Treatment goals/commitment to recovery education/assessment

3. CIWA

4. Vital signs

5. ETOH breathalyzer

6. General Urine Drug Screen (cocaine/amphetamine/BZD/THC/OP).

7. PDMP data check

8. Optional: Blood draw for LFTs, CBC, psychiatric medication levels, pregnancy testing

Days 2+

1. Assess treatment compliance/abstinence
2. CIWA
3. Vital Signs
4. Repeat UDS as needed

Treatment Course

1. Course: For uncomplicated BZD detox allow from 7 days to up to 6 months for a completed taper (prolonged). For BZD detox in setting of *ongoing opiate maintenance treatment or pregnancy*: plan to complete detoxification in 2–4 weeks (short).

2. Decision: Keep patient on current BZD (if it's long acting) (clonazepam) (**Dose equivalence: Lorazepam 1mg=0.25 mg clonazepam**) or switch patient from current short acting (alprazolam, lorazepam) to long acting (clonazepam)

3. Taper dosing in Q2 week to Q4 week intervals (by 25 percent of dose) (prolonged) or 25 percent decrease every 2–3 days.

4. As taper proceeds, weigh dosing of medication to evening to address insomnia.

BOX 7.8 **Guidelines for Polysubstance DWT**

BZD + OPs:

- Follow BZD withdrawal guidelines;
- No clonidine;
- Use adjunct meds for opiate withdrawal;
- If aim is to detox only from BZDs, go to Box 7.9; and
- Consider inpatient DWT.

BZD + ETOH:

- Follow ETOH withdrawal guidelines; and
- Consider inpatient DWT.

ETOH + OPs:

- ETOH withdrawal regimen (BZD with adjuncts for ETOH and OP withdrawal);
- No clonidine;
- Consider Guidelines for BZD DWT During Opioid Maintenance; and
- Consider inpatient DWT.

ETOH + OPs + BZD:

- Strongly consider inpatient DWT;
- ETOH withdrawal regimen (BZD with adjuncts for ETOH and OP withdrawal); and
- No clonidine.

BOX 7.9 Guidelines for Benzoid DWT During Opioid Maintenance

Patients receiving opioid maintenance therapy (methadone or buprenorphine) and requiring DWT from BZDs should be treated according to a locked-in tapering schedule.

clonazepam (mg) (dose equivalence: Lorazepam 1mg=0.25 mg clonazepam)

Starting Dose Level	Total Daily Dose	Days to Complete
2 mg TID	6 mg/day × 3 days	24
2 mg BID	4 mg/day × 3 days	21
1mg QAM, 2 mg QPM	3 mg/day × 3 days	18
1mg BID	2 mg/day × 3 days	15
0.5 mg QAM, 1 mg QPM	1.5 mg/day × 3 days	12
0.5 mg BID	1mg × 3 days	9
0.5 mg Q Bedtime	0.5mg × 6 days	6

Rules of the protocol

1. Patient receiving opioid maintenance therapy at an independent facility (other than the 2 × 4 Model clinic or closely affiliated healthcare facilities) that need/request detoxification from benzoids should not be accepted into the 2 × 4 Model DWT outpatient detoxification program while still engaged in treatment elsewhere. Patients should be informed that split care is clinically hazardous; that patients must seek referrals associated with the independent facility, or they may transfer their behavioral health care comprehensively to the 2 × 4 Model clinic.

2. Based on initial clinical data, the psychiatrist starts the patient at any of the above doses as the starting dose. Once on that starting dose, the regimen is automatic and non-negotiable with the patient.

3. The clonazepam 2 mg TID (equivalent to 24 mg/day lorazepam) is the maximum dose allowable by the protocol for outpatient detox, and should be chosen carefully only for patients expected to have high tolerance. Patients who *seem to require more than this dose should be considered as inappropriate for outpatient DWT and should be treated on an inpatient basis.*

4. Patients are evaluated and monitored, and scripts are dispensed in face to face appointments every 3–4 days.

Patients who in clinical evaluation (interview, exam, vitals, and CIWA) show they are not adequately tolerating, or are not stable on the taper, should be admitted for inpatient/supervised DWT.

5. Patients are presented with the protocol in verbal or paper copy in advance of starting the regimen.

Pharmacotherapies in Long-Term Integrated Dual Diagnosis Treatment (LIDDT)

As previously mentioned, this design and operations manual for the 2 × 4 Model clinic is not intended to serve as a core textbook of pharmacology for mental illness or addiction care. A comprehensive treatment of these topics should be ascertained from other sources (see references for this chapter) and there is no substitute for residency training in psychiatry and fellowships in addiction for gaining practical experience with conducting good psychopharmacology in these fields. With that said, it is within the scope of this book and chapter to talk about how psychiatric and addiction psychopharmacologies can be integrated and conducted to optimize the mission of LIDDT.

Expert dual diagnosis care by a physician requires a foundation of psychiatric knowledge and training in the general pharmacology of mental disorders. Upon this foundation, we need a second level of knowledge and training in the pharmacological treatment of addictive disorders. This is logical and consistent with the flow of professional training toward becoming an addiction psychiatrist: First, in four years of general adult psychiatry training and, second, in a year of addiction psychiatry fellowship training. Since 100 percent of psychiatrists do the first level of training, but, unfortunately, less than 5 percent do the second, we will consider the pharmacological treatment of MI only briefly and go into the pharmacological management of addictions more in depth.

Pharmacotherapies and Clinical Pearls for MI in the 2 × 4 Model Clinic

The following provides a brief tour of medication categories or types that are important and widely used in the 2 × 4 Model clinic, along with a description of some relevant clinical pearls.

Antipsychotics

These drugs are a mainstay in the 2 × 4 Model program, given the relatively high frequencies of schizophrenia and bipolar spectrum disorders that are found in association with drug addictions. They are also helpful for augmentation strategies in severe or treatment refractory major depression with and without psychosis. These medications should be selected carefully according to their side effect profiles (metabolic and EPS-related), with attention to the fact that some of the side effects (e.g., sedation) can be used advantageously to assist with sleep cycle control without having to resort to benzoids. Generally, the preference is for *atypical* over *typical* neuroleptics due to the more favorable side effect profiles of the former in terms of motor side effects, and their apparent ability to better augment treatments for mood disorders. There is not good evidence that either typicals or atypicals can directly treat addictions. However, clozapine, which may stand apart from all other neuroleptics in terms of its efficacy for schizophrenia and mood stability, may also have some unique anti-addiction properties related to its modulation of the noradrenergic system. The heavy direct dopamine receptor blocking effects of many typical neuroleptics, and their hepatic metabolism (that can impact the metabolism of used substances), may complicate the course and treatment of many addictions including those involving nicotine, amphetamines and cocaine. Atypicals also provide more of a serotonin 5-HT2A receptor blocking effect, which could be significant toward minimizing the severity of psychotic experiences some dual diagnosis patients may have when dabbling in the use of LSD, mushrooms, and related hallucinogenics. The use of long-acting *injectable neuroleptics* is also important in the 2 × 4 Model clinic because dual diagnosis is so often associated with patients being treatment refractory, frequently missing oral doses of medications, and/or having a complex differential diagnosis with respect to the causal components of their psychosis. For example, is Mr. J still psychotic and homeless because he is doing crack cocaine, or because he's not taking his oral anti-psychotic, or because he has treatment refractory schizophrenia, or because of more than one, or all of these things? One way to tease this out is to be sure the med is getting in him with an injectable neuroleptic. Another advantage of injectable neuroleptics, whether they are a typicals or atypicals, is they do their work with flatter, more stable blood levels. This means that the dopamine receptor blockade they provide is more steady, which likely creates a more steady homeostatic response in the brain in terms of dopamine release (e.g., neuroleptic blockade of striatal dopamine receptors is known to increase mesolimbic dopamine release as a compensation). These more steady conditions, may at least theoretically not contribute as much (as oral typical neuroleptics would) to the chaos in dopamine neurotransmission that is being caused by addictive drug use.

Mood Stabilizers

The classic mood stabilizers, *lithium, valproate,* and *carbamazepine* are very important to dual diagnosis treatment and should be frequently tried in the 2 × 4 Model clinic given the ubiquity of mood instability in the dual diagnosis population and the relatively high frequencies of bipolar spectrum disorders that are found in addicted patients. A key aspect of this group of drugs, especially in regards to lithium and valproate, is their capacity to address *impulsivity,* which is a core symptom domain that links addiction and mental illness, both behaviorally and biologically (e.g., involving abnormal PFC function). More than for any other drug, the literature supports the value of lithium for limiting and preventing impulsive suicidality, which is a major killer of dual diagnosis patients. Likewise, impulsive aggression directed toward others may be relatively well curtailed by lithium and the anti-epileptic mood stabilizers compared to other classes of medications, and these drugs can produce these effects without the short-term risk of exacerbating suicidal thinking that has been associated with starting SSRIs.

History of traumatic brain injury (TBI) is another problem that is common for dual diagnosis patients, in which multiple causal linkages could be in play that connect these disorders. Given that various levels of TBI can produce CNS irritability and structural changes associated with seizures and impulsivity, anti-epileptics that may have mood and/or impulse control benefits (*valproate, carbamazepine*, and *lamotrigine*), may be good choices.

Topiramate, also discussed more in depth later under anti-addiction treatments, is another anti-epileptic for which there is evidence for mood stabilization properties (e.g., for bipolar disorder) despite lack of FDA approval for this indication. The potential value of this agent for affective control and for treating several types of addictions, make it potentially classifiable as a Parsimonious Dual Diagnosis Agent (PDDA; an agent proven by multiple placebo-controlled trials and FDA approved for the treatment of both a mental illness and an addiction). At present, only *bupropion* enjoys that distinction.

Gabapentin has been widely used and over-marketed by its manufacturer (earning them a multi-hundred million dollar U.S. false marketing lawsuit), for the treatment of anxiety and bipolar disorders. Given this history, and the lack of good data supporting its use for these indications, gabapentin is not recommended for these in the 2 × 4 Model clinic. However, the agent is an anti-epileptic and so may have utility on the context of TBI or epilepsy co-morbid with dual diagnoses. Moreover, it has proven efficacy and FDA indications, for various neuropathic pain syndromes that the addiction psychiatrist can utilize, particularly on behalf of avoiding addictive opioids or benzoids, like pregabalin (which is more reinforcing, but indicated for similar conditions as gabapentin). Finally, the evidence base is actually much better for gabapentin in the context of alcohol withdrawal and the early stages of recovery from this addiction, than it is for its other psychiatric uses; the CNS calming and anti-epileptic effects of the agent may be helpful not only in protecting against delerium tremens, but also insomnia and craving that lingers through extended withdrawal.

Antidepressants/Anxiolytics

The SSRI's (e.g., fluoxetine, sertraline) are mainstays of antidepressant treatment in general psychiatry. Due to their excellent tolerability, safety profiles, and efficacy for a range of disorders frequently encountered in the dual diagnosis clinic, including various forms of depression, PTSD, anxiety, and OCD syndromes, they should be frequently used in the 2 × 4 Model program. Generally, they should be used as front line agents for anxiety disorders, and as such, are important tools for helping the psychiatrist avoid long-term use of benzoids. The stress resilience offered by SSRI's can also come in handy during the course of recovery when patients are having to confront, in a sober state, the totality of the damage the addiction(s) have caused.

The SNRI's (serotonin-norepinephrine reuptake inhibitors) (e.g., duloxetine) are also effective antidepressants with good safety profiles. Duloxetine in particular is evidence based and FDA approved for pain syndromes (fibromyalgia, neuropathic pain) which are common in dual diagnosis patients, especially those with opioid addictions. As such, it is a helpful tool for comorbid pain and depressive disorders, when opioids need to be avoided. The NRIs (norepinephrine reuptake inhibitor) *atomoxetine* also has SNRI like properties (e.g., likely useful as an antidepressant/anxiolytic), but is effective and indicated for ADHD, allowing it to serve as an important tool for avoiding stimulants in dual diagnosis patients with mood and prominent ADHD symptoms.

The old TCAs (tricyclic agents) (e.g., amitriptaline, clomipramine desipramine) are inexpensive and solidly effective antidepressants that have lost their luster due to inferior overdose risk and other side effect profiles in comparison to the SSRI/SNRIs. However they still have their somewhat unique roles and evidence bases (e.g., amitriptyline for chronic pain or insomnia; clomipramine for OCD, desipramine may have some efficacy to support recovery from psychostimulants, in the absence of FDA indications for these addictions).

The 'atypical antidepressants' include mirtazapine, trazodone, buspirone, and bupropion. Mirtazepine and trazedone, while not as popular as SSRIs for straight-up anxiety and depression (and maybe not as effective), are very good for treating insomnia and supporting proper sleep architecture, while avoiding the dependence and cognitive risks of benzoids. Buspirone is well known as the non-benzoid anxiolytic, but has the reputation of being a high-priced placebo, although some patients do show and claim major benefits with it.

Bupropion is a gem of an agent for the 2 × 4 Model clinic as up to present time it enjoys unique status as the first PDDA with FDA approval. It is an excellent antidepressant that carries activity that influences dopamine and cholinergic systems, which likely relates to its capacity to treat nicotine addiction. This activity also likely gives this drug some other benefits such as lack of sexual side effects (which may be the biggest problem with SSRIs), potential to support appetite suppression and weight loss, and some potential for off-label indications for other addictions (e.g., psychostimulants) and ADHD-range symptoms. The main drawbacks of this drug are its seizure potential (at high doses/with eating disorders) and its potential to cause agitation, insomnia, or even hypomania in vulnerable individuals, especially those with depressions that have strong anxiety components, or that may be better understood as bipolar spectrum conditions.

Miscellaneous Agents

Non-benzoid agents for various components of anxiety disorders are important for use in the 2 × 4 Model clinic. The following agents have a reasonably well-developed evidence base to justify their use in several contexts: *Propranolol* can be helpful for benign essential tremor, acute performance anxiety (e.g., public speaking), and for nightmares. *Prazosin* has a quite good evidence base (despite lack of FDA approval) for nightmares related to PTSD. The anticholinergic/antihistamine *hydroxyzine* can be a useful acute anxiolytic and sedative, that avoids benzoids.

Pharmacotherapies, Guidelines, and Clinical Pearls for Addiction Treatment in the 2 × 4 Model Clinic

Having covered DWT, we now move on to the two other categories of pharmacotherapies for SUDs in the 2 × 4 Model clinic that happen in the course of the LIDDT. These are the 1) harm-reduction/stabilization strategies; and 2) anti-addiction strategies. Both of these evidence-based approaches provide effective long-term treatments that stabilize addiction and dual diagnosis patients by reducing the medical, psychiatric, social, and occupational harm that ongoing substance use generates. In general, it is easier for patients and clinicians to enter into and accomplish the goals of harm-reduction/stabilization strategies. But only the *anti-addiction* treatments are actually able to facilitate the highest level of harm-reduction and stabilization, by generating sustained remissions and cures in terms of total cessation of drug use. A helpful explanation for this distinction that most patients and health care providers can readily understand is the Monster Analogy.

The Monster Analogy of Addiction Treatment in the 2 × 4 Model Clinic

Imagine that the addiction is like a wild animal, or a monster, that is loose inside your house. It is tearing everything up, eating things, destroying things, defecating all over your belongings, and hurting you and the people you love. Harm-reduction/stabilization strategies aim to cage this monster, to put it in one place and keep it there where it cannot do nearly as much harm. You still feed it, but as little as possible to keep it alive. But often, this is much easier than killing it completely, and for some people killing the beast is just not possible, no matter how much the person wishes it so. And yet, keeping the monster alive means that on occasion it can reach out between the bars and claw at you, someone, or something in the house. There is the risk that it could even escape altogether, eventually killing you.

But most of the time the cage (harm-reduction/stabilization) is better than nothing. In many cases it is even a way to starve and weaken the monster in preparation for slaying it, which only anti-addiction treatments can provide. But, slaying the monster with anti-addiction treatment in the short-term can be much harder (and sometimes riskier to do), but in the long-term it is the best chance to permanently eliminate the beast and make sure it cannot hurt or kill you ever again. Then again, we can always fall back on harm-reduction/ stabilization should the anti-addiction treatments fail initially. Knowing we can cage the monster again, should we miss on killing it, should help us not be afraid to keep trying.

Accordingly, during the initial evaluation phase, and periodically through the course of treatment, most patients should be considered as candidates for harm-reduction/stabilization or anti-addiction, depending on the situation and type of addiction(s) they have. It should also be taken for granted that patients can be switched between these strategies over time, as needed to achieve the best outcome, often via trial and error, through sustained longitudinal effort.

Harm-Reduction/Stabilization Agents

Buprenorphine for the treatment of opioid use disorders is formulated with or without naloxone and is available as a sublingual or implantable agent. As the bulk of research and clinical experience with buprenorophine has been with the sublingual form ('strips/films' or 'tabs'), the focus of this book will be on the sublingual form. Buprenorphine was developed to be used in 'office based' opioid addiction treatment, as an alternative to methadone maintenance treatment programs. The 'office based' concept meant that it could be used by psychiatrists or primary care doctors for opioid addiction outside of the highly government regulated opioid maintenance programs that have had such limited reach because of the low numbers of treatment slots (compared to the population in need), and the degree to which they largely operate outside of mainstream health care and appropriate health insurance coverage (e.g., as 'cash' only programs). The hope, then, was that buprenorphine could facilitate the integration of opioid addiction treatment into psychiatry and primary care.

This potential for buprenorphine to serve as a key pharmacological tool for this integration has unfortunately been only partially realized. The eight hours of training necessary to gain the DEA waiver to prescribe this drug (for addiction) does not suffice or substitute for formal training and certification in addictions treatment, nor does it 'create' an expert treatment team of nurses and therapists that the physician needs to surround him/herself with to optimize the use of this med. This problem is typically less severe for psychiatrists who often do work on behavioral health teams, who have at least some formal training in addiction diagnosis and treatment, and who have been trained in both the pharmacological and psychotherapeutic management of behavioral brain disorders. Still, many psychiatrists without addiction fellowship training have been reluctant to treat opioid addiction, and the total lack of training and team support in addictions has been as major barrier for the far more plentiful supply of primary care doctors.

In many respects, the design of the 2 × 4 Model is an ideal context in which buprenorphine treatment of opioid addiction can take place in terms of its goals of being integrated with other addictions and mental health care, as provided by the most highly trained physicians to do this job (e.g., addiction psychiatrists). The following evidence-based rules and guidelines governing buprenorphine prescribing are recommended in the 2 × 4 Model clinic.

BOX 7.10 **Guidelines for Buprenorphine Treatment of Opioid Addiction**

1. Prescription of benzoids and buprenorphine simultaneously should not happen on an outpatient basis, outside of short-term DWT that require benzodiazepines. Prior to buprenorphine induction, patients taking both benzoids and opiates (including buprenorphine or methadone) from outside sources, should successfully complete detoxification from benzoids prior to buprenorphine induction. Patients discovered to have developed benzoid use after induction on suboxone should be treated in protocols for benzodiazepine detoxification or be considered not an appropriate candidate for continued buprenorphine treatment until the benzoid use is stopped. Simultaneous or concurrent prescriptions of buprenorphine and benzoids other than those called for in the protocol for benzodiazepine detoxification for opiate maintenance patients, should not occur.

2. *The maximum daily dose of buprenorphine should generally not exceed 16 mg QDay (once-a-day).* Patients needing treatment with buprenorphine after being prescribed higher doses from outside physicians or clinics (e.g., 24 + mg QDay) should be informed that they will be started at <16 mg QDay. Patients at doses <16 mg QDay may be titrated up to the maximum allowable dose of 16 mg QDay. The rationale for this ceiling that may be discussed with patients is a) for most patients, the clinical benefits of buprenorphine can be optimized at <16 mg QDay (e.g., as low as 4 mg QDay); b) for most patients, the pharmacological efficacy and receptor occupancy of buprenorphine reaches asymptotic levels at about 12–16 mg QDay; c) prescriptions of doses >16 mg QDay are associated with diversion; d) the cost–benefit ratio of prescriptions for doses >16 mg QDay is unfavorable to the goal of providing affordable access to the medication for the largest number of patients who need treatment.

3. Dispensation of prescriptions for buprenorphine requires concurrent face to face contact, dual diagnosis exam, and clinical evaluation with the prescribing physician typically every four weeks, and more rarely at a maximum spacing of every six weeks. Telephone call-ins or other verbal orders made by the physician to make up for missed appointments, lost prescriptions, or missing pills should not happen. Patients may not receive buprenorphine from physicians outside of the 2 × 4 Model program. The physician may temporarily delegate another physician or behavioral health professional in the 2 × 4 Model clinic (nurse, therapist) to provide buprenorphine scripts as long as those encounters are face to face interviews, and a clinical exam by an addiction psychiatrist still happens at least every 4–6 weeks.

continued

BOX 7.10 **Guidelines for Buprenorphine Treatment of Opioid Addiction**—*continued*

Delegates can be appointed, for example, when the psychiatrist goes on leave from the clinic, or when unstable patients require more frequent observation and shorter runs of scripts, or, to encourage greater compliance with group or individual therapy.

4. Prescriptions for new supplies of buprenorphine should not be made prior to the originally planned terminal date of the last prescription (that is calculated by the amount prescribed and instructions for dosing). This rule stands despite any request by the patient to the contrary, as rationalized by lost or stolen doses, or doses taken (intentionally or unintentionally) at higher doses or rates than prescribed.

5. Refills for buprenorphine allowing new supplies without clinical evaluation every 4–6 weeks are not issued.

6. Patients are advised that the medication should be taken at a frequency of once-a-day, and that it may be taken effectively every other day. Patients are to be advised that multi-daily dosing is not clinically necessary and may adversely reinforce pill taking habits that support addiction pathology. Patients who do take the medication in split daily doses should be encouraged to work toward once-a-day dosing via ongoing MET and CBT psychotherapeutic treatment approaches.

In the 2 × 4 Model clinic, the decision to treat opioid use disorder with buprenorphine should be made carefully after thorough clinical evaluation by the addiction psychiatrist (Chapter 5), after consideration of other treatment options, and as contextualized by the strategies being considered for other addictions and mental illness(s) the patient is likely suffering with. In particular, there should be consideration and discussion of the approximate duration and goals of treatment (i.e., whether it is intended as a bridge to an anti-addiction medication treatment). In general, the evaluation and preparation for *induction* on buprenorphine should take anywhere from 1–4 weeks after the initial dual diagnosis evaluation by the addiction psychiatrist. The clinician should keep in mind that although a timely initiation of treatment is generally desirable (and may need to happen as fast as within 48 hours, for example, for the special case of the pregnant patient), the imperative to start opioid maintenance treatment in patients actively using opioids is almost never a medical emergency. For example, if a patient has been using opioids for many years, it makes little sense to short-change a thorough evaluation, and to improperly prepare a patient for initial dosing (that is best done when a patient is in a state of opioid withdrawal), all to deliver buprenorphine 40 minutes after meeting the psychiatrist for the first time. Sometimes drug-seeking (and relief-seeking) patients will try to manipulate an immediate script: "if you don't give it to me, you will be responsible for my arrest . . . you will be responsible for my relapse . . . you will be responsible for my overdose" etc. It is often helpful for the dual diagnosis psychiatrist to keep in mind that diverted prescription opioids, including black market supplies of buprenorphine, are unfortunately becoming ubiquitous, as a byproduct of poor training and clinical care in the prescribing of these drugs.

Typically, buprenorphine induction, which should happen in a programmatic and clinically monitored way in the clinic, involving both nursing and physician staffing, should be prepared for and planned *days to weeks in advance.* The chief among several reasons for this approach is that patients should undergo some degree of programmatic DWT before induction to give the buprenorphine the best chance of effectively 'hooking'. If the patient has recently been intoxicated on other opioids, and/or if there are high levels of other opioids on board at the time of induction, and the patient is not in withdrawal, there is a good chance that the buprenorphine will have little effect, or even cause the patient to go into acute opioid withdrawal. This type of experience (which is possible given the high affinity/partial agonist properties of the drug) can undermine the credibility of the medication in the mind of this patient, causing them to continue to use other opioids concurrent with the buprenorphine, (which further undermines its efficacy and sets up treatment failure), eventually leading the patient to believe the drug has little value, other than to serve as a opioid of last resort that can be sold on the street for better things. Preparing and planning for induction is also important for ensuring other prerequisites, including establishing that the patient has proper insurance coverage for the treatment, ability to actually get to the clinic regularly, etc. Conversely, not writing for buprenorphine on day one carries the advantage of sending a powerful signal to the patient that buprenorphine is part of treatment, and not a product of a retail or drug dealing service where customers conduct their exchanges instantly 'on demand'. In addiction psychiatry, there is a partnership and therapeutic relationship between the doctor and patients, but it is the expertise, experience, and clinical evaluation of the psychiatrist that should primarily drive the clinical decision-making and tempo of treatment, not the need of the patient (or rather, the pathological motivation) that is part of the addiction disease, which often causes the patient to project onto the psychiatrist the role of customer service clerk or drug dealer. The following guidelines detail the components of diagnosis, treatment planning and patient education that should be in place leading up to buprenorphine induction (see **Box 7.11**).

Once the preparations for buprenorphine induction have been made and an induction date has been set, the patient is instructed on a course of DWT leading up to the induction day. On this day, the patient will be administered his first dose of buprenorphine in the clinic, under direct supervision and observation

BOX 7.11 Guide for Preparing for Buprenorphine Induction

Diagnostic Requirements

1. *Full clinical dual diagnosis evaluation by the psychiatrist,* including clinical diagnosis of opiate dependence with thorough consideration of other treatment options (methadone program, naltrexone, psychotherapies), and initial planning of long-term treatment trajectory.

2. *UDS collected* (general panel + specific opioids requested).

3. PDMP data collected and documented (for a year prior to induction).

Initial Treatment Planning

1. *Interdiction of iatrogenic or other opioid prescribing* by outside prescriber(s) if found on PDMP or reported by the patient or collateral informant. Communication with outside prescriber must be verbal and documented in the chart. A formal release of information (ROI) is necessary if the patient is seen by a prescriber outside of the clinical system that hosts the 2 × 4 Model clinic. If the patient cannot be convinced to cooperate with ROI or communication with outside prescribers who are providing opioids, induction on buprenorphine should be delayed until the appropriate ROI is made.

2. *Financial planning clarified:* Insurance status and method of payment for treatment is settled prior to induction. The patient has seen the insurance advisor (if one is available in the clinic). Insurance coverage of treatment is strongly advised. Patients must understand the total cost of treatment will include the potential for medication co-pays and co-pays for groups and individual psychotherapy.

3. *Confirm reduction of insurance barriers:* Prior authorizations and other barriers set up by insurance companies to avoid supporting medication treatments for opioid addiction have been circumvented or overcome by the psychiatrist and/or treatment staff.

4. *Transportation and time commitment planning clarified:* Patient to understand the transportation requirements and expectations to attend a schedule of appointments at the 2 × 4 Model clinic for medication management, group and individual therapies, and ongoing diagnostic testing.

5. Completion of the necessary clinic orientations, therapist evaluations, medical screenings, and intake procedures for becoming a regular patient in the clinic.

of the nursing and/or physician team. It is up to the psychiatrist (in partnership with the patient) to consider the extent to which the DWT phase leading up to the induction day should involve coverage with DWT meds (see 2 × 4 Model guide for opioid DWT). In general, the goal is for the patient to reach a state of mild to moderate opioid withdrawal, which typically occurs 1–5 days out from the last opioid use (depending on the patient, the type of opioid being used, and the prior pattern of use). The aim of this planning is to have the patient abstinent long enough for the buprenorphine to 'hook' (without pharmacological interference from other opioids) and yet not have the DWT phase so long that the patient is bound to relapse when they definitely should not (e.g., just before induction day).

As per the 2 × 4 Model Guidelines for Buprenorphine Induction, the induction day involves a process of assessment and patient education before, during, and after the observed first dosing. Collecting this information and conducting induction in this programmatic way provides additional diagnostic and prognostic information (e.g., can the patient follow treatment instructions? Was the patient able to enter and adhere to controlled opioid withdrawal on their own? Did objective measures of withdrawal measured before dosing improve (suggesting a good 'hook') or worsen (suggesting interference with opioids on board) after dosing?) Additionally, the supervised dosing of induction is an excellent time to make sure the medication is being used correctly, and for discussing expectations, goals, limitations, and instructions for treatment.

Programmed induction days do require planning, scheduling of physician and nursing team time, and clinical attention to the patient that typically exceeds what happens in regular follow-up appointments. This resource allocation is appropriate and constructive given that the proper initiation and maintenance of buprenorphine treatment should not be embarked on trivially or without commitment to the long-term plan. The deliberate nature of the induction day and the careful clinical evaluation and planning of the addiction psychiatrist leading up to it are protective against the slippery slope of the clinic taking on attributes of the 'pill mill' where quantity of care, economic advantage (for the treatment system), and high-volume delivery of opioids becomes more important than quality of care and patient well-being. With that said, there are some patients and situations that may not need an induction day. If a patient is well known to the clinic and has already started on buprenorphine on an induction day in the clinic within the last year or so, but has had some time off the medication (for whatever reason), it can be reasonable to restart that patient back on the med unsupervised (sometimes termed a 'home induction'). Also, if the patient has been on buprenorphine via a referring legitimate clinical entity that the 2 × 4 Model clinic has good lines of communication with, and has received a transfer of care from, then a continuation of treatment without a formal induction day becomes an option. But as a rule of thumb, new patients without recent formal experience in physician directed buprenorphine treatment should not be started via unsupervised home inductions.

BOX 7.12 Guidelines for Buprenorphine Induction

1. *The induction day is normally planned and agreed upon by patient and psychiatrist days to weeks in advance.* Buprenorphine should generally not be induced on the same day the patient arrives in the clinic for the first time, or on the same day the patient is first evaluated by the psychiatrist. Pregnant or extreme high acuity patients may be considered as an exception to this prolonged planning phase.

2. *Patients should be directed to attempt 3–7 days of complete abstinence from opioids of any kind prior to induction,* with the expectation of entering mild to moderate withdrawal. Medications for DWT may or may not be used in the lead up to the induction day.

3. On induction day:

- Patients should arrive with financial resources and/or co-pays adequate to acquire a 7 day script of buprenorphine. They should have insurance coverage for the treatment.
- *Patients undergo a dosing pre-check* (managed by the nursing team) that will document the following:

  - time/date/type/quantity of last opioid use
  - COWS
  - Vital sign checks: BP, pulse
  - UDS recently collected on record, rapid UDS is optional.

- After pre-check the patient is given a script for seven days supply of buprenorphine with instructions to return to the clinic with the medication after it is procured at the pharmacy. *The patient should not take any of the medication prior to supervised dosing — the team should inspect the dispensation to ensure this has happened.*
- After returning with the medication, the patient should undergo a supervised dosing (with psychiatrist and/or nursing team observing and interacting) in which the patient is given the med with instructions on how to use it correctly. The subsequent 10–15 minutes of time, during which the medication is being absorbed, should be used to discuss clinical expectations and rules of ongoing buprenorphine therapy (see 2 × 4 Model education and care measures for buprenorphine treatment).
- Post-check: From 20 min to 1 hour after dosing, patients should undergo: A second round of COWS and vital sign collections, with the pre- and post-check data documented in the EMR.

4. After induction day patients are seen in follow-up appointments with increasingly lengthening intervals, to establish a pattern of Q4–5 week return visits. (e.g., return in one week, then two weeks, and then four weeks).

Around or during induction on buprenorphine, the team should be educating the patient about the expectations, goals, limitations, and boundaries of buprenorphine treatment. The following education and care measures should be discussed with the patient, and may also be provided in hard copy format as a supplement to the verbal communication (see **Box 7.13**).

Methadone maintenance has served as a mainstay of harm-reduction/ stabilization treatment for opioid addiction for many decades, and there is a wealth of well-replicated clinical trial evidence that, like buprenorphine, it is effective in reducing dangerous opioid use. Evidence that methadone treatment reduces the medical, psychiatric, social, financial, and legal risks of uncontrolled opioid addiction is even deeper and older than with buprenorphine.

A brief overview of the pharmacological science, as well as policy and cultural histories of methadone and buprenorphine, is important for understanding how these two treatment options should be differentially, and most optimally made available with regard to the 2 × 4 Model clinic. The key pharmacological difference between methadone and buprenorphine, is that there is no ceiling effect with methadone. The positive aspect of this double edged sword is that the dose of methadone can be pushed higher and higher to achieve opioid agonism effects beyond what buprenorphine can provide, so that potentially, patients with more severe forms of addiction can be covered more effectively than what the ceiling of buprenorphine provides. On the other hand, the absence of a dose ceiling-effect with methadone means that patients can much more readily be pushed into a lethal overdose. This fundamental difference between the meds has major implications for how they are implemented clinically. Methadone maintenance is a treatment that is incredibly tightly regulated by federal and state laws, arguably more so than any other domain of treatment in behavioral health or health care in general. This 'treatment by regulation' is in place to keep the treatment as safe and effective as possible (e.g., to prevent overdoses), and also to avoid diversion. But, it is also a residuum of a history of tremendous social and governmental stigma against opioid addiction and its treatment, as reflected by the great irony that while governments are so involved in regulating methadone maintenance and determining how it is delivered, they also tend to be proactive in making sure the treatment is limited in availability and not well covered by public insurance programs. Interestingly, however, governments and insurance companies have generally not stood in the way, and in fact have well supported the use of methadone for pain indications as a quite unregulated domain of primary care, even though it has been in this format where methadone has contributed significantly to iatrogenic overdoses and addictions.

The tight level of government regulation and control of methadone maintenance treatment for opioid addiction has produced some other interesting effects on the *culture and manner* of methadone treatment that also has pros and cons. Methadone maintenance is a relatively regimented, inflexible, and nonindividualized modality of care where medical decision-making is quite minimized, because the format of care does not call for it. Patients persist in

BOX 7.13 Education and Care Measures for Buprenorphine Treatment

1. Treatment goals for suboxone maintenance therapy: Patients are informed that they will be monitored for success over time with respect to these goals, and that lack of progress can signify treatment failure and need for change to an alternate therapeutic modality:

- Cessation of episodes of opioid-induced intoxication and withdrawal.
- Cessation of illegal activities of financing, procuring, and use of opioids and other addictive drugs.
- Cessation of all use of opioids (other than buprenorphine prescribed).
- Financial, occupational, social, medical, and psychiatric gains observed from cessation of illicit opioid use.
- Preparation or action to initiate more definitive recovery-oriented therapies for opioid addiction and/or other non-opioid addictions the patient is suffering with.

2. Familiarity with the pharmacological actions and expectations of buprenorphine: Action as a long acting high affinity potent partial agonist at the μ-opiate receptor:

- Significantly blocks other opioids; may cause withdrawal if taken after other opioids.
- Potent at low doses, but provides diminishing returns at higher doses; relatively safe in overdose.

3. Has a maximal binding level and efficacy around 16 mg a day for most patients: Strips or tablets must be absorbed across oral mucosa; potential for release of naloxone (if present in the formulation) if the medication is crushed and injected.

4. Participation in treatment: Patient understands that attendance and participation in individual and/or group psychotherapies, performed by one or more members of the treatment team as part of an individualized treatment plan, is an important and expected component of their treatment. Various levels of participation in psychotherapies are recommended by the team as determined by:

- Planned goals and durations of buprenorphine treatment and transition to other treatments.
- Occupational hours or child care obligations.
- Financial and/or transportation obligations.
- Presence of co-morbid medical or psychiatric conditions that would impact participation or efficacy of psychotherapeutic modalities.

care, or are ejected out of it, based largely on how well they follow the rules and continue to be able to afford the rigorous time, and often financial sacrifices, that entail this type of treatment. The highly regimented, non-individualized style of care that methadone maintenance treatment follows allows these clinics to efficiently treat a high volume of patients, with an industrial scalelike efficiency, where cultural adherence to the rules of care can go pretty far in substituting for a lack of physician expertise or training in addictions (although there are some methadone programs that are fortunate to be equipped with highly trained addiction psychiatrists, who can conduct more individualized care). This level efficiency and rule-based treatment can be a good thing for regions where there is great unmet demand for opioid treatment and little professional expertise. Moreover, the rules and requirements that patients must follow to be in this care, can be quite helpful for certain patients who are relatively uncomplicated by other mental illnesses and addictions, and respond well to the structural supports, concrete limits, and routines that these programs provide. Perhaps the most important of these rules and routines is the mode of methadone dispensations, that is, the way patients in the early stages of treatment, must actually show up at the clinic daily to receive doses of *liquid methadone medication directly in the mouth.* Only after many weeks and months of observation in care, where they have proven themselves to be reliable participants, and have shown themselves to be responsive to treatment (via UDS), do patients advance to the privilege of being allowed to take home multiple doses of the medication, without having to show up to the clinic every day. This degree of treatment participation and supervision of medication dosing is uniquely rigorous in comparison to virtually any other type of outpatient treatment in psychiatry or general health care.

For many patients, this regulated culture of methadone maintenance treatment works quite well, and operates as a very effective and reliable format to prevent both overdoses and diversion. But for other patients, it does not work well. Many patients with opioid addiction have comorbid mental illnesses and other addictions that methadone programs are too narrow in focus to recognize or treat. Many patients simply cannot afford the out of pocket cash payments that these programs often require (ranging from $280 to $500/month) in regions and states where they remain excluded from insurance coverage. Many patients cannot realistically meet the transportation, time demands, and rigors of showing up every morning, often before the sun comes up, often many miles from their homes or places of work, to stand in a line in the cold for 30 minutes, to get a medication, every day.

Buprenorphine was introduced after 2000, as an alternative for opioid maintenance treatment that would expand access to treatment and overcome many of the *pharmacological and cultural* downsides that methadone maintenance treatment entails. Hence, the absence of restrictive regulation surrounding buprenorphine treatment (and the relatively broad based insurance coverage support it has) meant that it could readily and ideally be done in a way that is fully integrated into comprehensive addiction and mental health treatment as in the 2 × 4 Model program. Buprenorphine treatment could thus allow opioid addiction to be treated by the team not as if it is the only thing that the patient has, but as one item on a problem list of many brain-based comorbidities that need to be treated. Of course, the relative lack of regulation surrounding buprenorphine treatment, while allowing it to be done in a much more flexible and individualized way, and as part of a much more comprehensive behavioral health treatment program, also requires *more* expertise and attention of the prescribing physician, not less than what methadone maintenance entails. Outside of the highly regulated structure and rules of the methadone clinic, the physician untrained in behavioral health and addictions has a much more difficult job, and could quickly get overwhelmed or into trouble trying to treat significant numbers of mentally ill addicted patients. This eventuality was unfortunately not well considered as buprenorphine was originally rolled out to all doctors, most with no behavioral health care training, only requiring them to have an active DEA registration and completing a day of training, to become an opioid addiction treatment specialist. Since 2000, many excellent physicians who acquired the buprenorphine DEA waiver realized they were out of their field of expertise or interest set, and did not have adequate professional team support for treating these patients. So they backed out. Others, who were not so conscientious, and were more profit-motivated, have taken up buprenorphine delivery in large quantities, for both addiction and pain indications (although the latter indication is not FDA approved or subject to DEA waiver rules) in highly efficient, quantity focused, cash-only practices. While ironically recapitulating the high-throughput, cash-only treatment model that methadone programs were troubled with, and that buprenorphine was intended to serve as an alternative to, these types of cash-only practices have led to significant levels of illicit diversion of buprenorphine, that methadone maintenance programs do not produce, on par with what has happened with other opioids prescribed for pain indications that generated the iatrogenic opioid addiction epidemic. Recognition of this emerging problem has led some to call for a more complete return to rule-based care, regulation, and control of buprenorphine treatment, in high-throughput treatment clinics, where doctors don't really have to know their patients, following a cultural model that is much more consistent with methadone maintenance.

The 2 × 4 Model rejects this rearward-facing solution and instead provides a treatment system design, formally trained professional expertise, and team approach that seeks to optimize the potential for buprenorphine treatment, which it was originally envisioned to have, as an alternative to methadone. At the same time, the 2 × 4 Model recognizes that methadone maintenance programing offers a unique therapeutic format that is well suited for *certain* patients (e.g., those who are not suffering from other complex addiction and mental illness; those who need tighter control and supervision of their dosing; those who need a higher level of opioid receptor agonism than what buprenorphine can provide; those who might benefit psychosocially from the daily routine of dosing in the methadone clinic). The 2 × 4 Model program thus views methadone maintenance as having an important role to play, as an alternative to buprenorphine treatment and other evidence-based approaches in the continuum of opioid addiction care. If anything, the major blemish that remains to be corrected with methadone maintenance programs is the fact that far too often, their services are not covered by health insurance, forcing them to exist in, and be identified with, a high quantity/low quality, for profit, cash-only market, which only reinforces the stigma and doubt that many in the community have about the benefits of this care.

With these considerations in mind it is recommended that the 2 × 4 Model clinic should operate as a home base for buprenorphine-based opioid maintenance treatment, so that this form of opioid maintenance treatment is fully enveloped and integrated in 2 × 4 Model programing. At the same time, the 2 × 4 Model program can be *tightly linked* to a well-functioning methadone maintenance program. In this set up, the methadone treatment program is not enveloped within the 2 × 4 Model clinic because that would change the culture of methadone treatment (and the uniquely beneficial effects of that treatment culture). But by being *tightly linked*, the 2 × 4 Model program and the methadone program a) are only a short distance apart; b) are in close communication; and c) share frequent consultative efforts and clinical collaborations. In essence, this concept is one where the methadone clinic operates like a satellite to the 2 × 4 Model program, where patients can be transferred and shared between the programs (depending on their clinical needs), and where the clinical staffing and psychiatric physicians may even be shared. Certainly, an arrangement like this works best if (and it is highly recommended that) both the 2 × 4 Model program and the methadone program are owned and operated by the same clinical organization, ideally a non-profit community mental health center, or academic medical center.

NRT (with gum, patches, lozenges, sprays, etc.) actually represents another important modality of harm-reduction and stabilization, but for nicotine addiction which remains among all addictions, the leading cause of premature illness and death. NRT is often marketed as a primary approach to nicotine cessation. However, this application is actually not particularly effective, in parallel to the way tapers of methadone or buprenorphine do not actually often contribute much to long-term abstinence from opioids. But because smoking or chewing tobacco is so harmful to so many tissues and organs, there is certainly a role for long-term conversion to NRT as a substitute that is far safer, again in parallel to long-term maintenance of opioid addiction with methadone. In this long-term harm-reduction application, the nicotine patch is probably not as effective for most people as would be the gum, because the patch does not well replicate the pharmacokinetics of smoking or chewing tobacco well enough to replicate the drug taking that happens with tobacco use. So while the patch can certainly help people cut back their smoking and/or reduce or eliminate nicotine withdrawal on a short term basis (e.g., like on a hospital unit), the gum is better for long-term maintenance because it better satiates the craving that happens with nicotine addiction. At the end of the day though, totally stopping nicotine use is very challenging for the addicted patient regardless of what path (cold turkey vs slow taper of nicotine patches) the person took to stop. So, it is highly recommended that anti-addiction therapies for nicotine addiction (see below) be viewed as the primary tools for patients who are attempting to totally remit the disease, however they arrive at their actual nicotine quit date.

As a final word on harm-reduction/stabilization strategies, many clinicians rightly long for a strategy for stimulant addiction (e.g., involving cocaine and/or amphetamines) that could follow this approach, for example, using 'softer', long acting stimulants, (e.g., modafinil). This approach has certainly been tried and studied to some degree. It is conceivable that for some patients who have been diagnosed with ADHD and have addiction vulnerability, psychostimulant treatment may be enacting some form of harm-reduction maintenance function as with methadone for opioid addiction. However, the evidence for the utility of this approach is not particularly good, so that 'stimulant maintenance treatment' has not made it past either being highly controversial, or to the threshold of gaining FDA approval. Limited acceptance of 'stimulant maintenance treatment' seems to be rooted in at least three problems: 1) Prescribing a stimulant in a patient with stimulant addiction does not seem to greatly reduce the overall level of stimulants they may use. While methadone or buprenorphine can often completely knock out other opioid use, prescribed stimulants do not clearly, as effectively, do the same. It is not clear why this should be although some have hypothesized that substitution/main-tenance therapy works better for CNS depressants because these drugs tend to shut down behavior (and binging) with continued use in a given episode. In contrast, the simulating motoric and motivational effects of stimulants can actually charge more use, as access to the drug increases, so that the limiting factor is not passing out but merely running out of drug. Because of this, stimulant substitution therapy can often be more like pouring gas on the fire. 2) Part of what is being done with opioid maintenance treatment is reducing the risk of opioid overdose (and episodes of withdrawal). But while stimulants can certainly produce lethal overdoses (e.g., via stroke, heat exhaustion, myocardial infarction, etc.) and withdrawal syndromes, these risks (and degrees of severity) are nowhere near what opioids entail. So in essence, the harm that can be reduced by therapeutically substituting street stimulants with doctor-prescribed stimulants is not really there in terms of curbing overdoses or cyclical episodes of intoxication and withdrawal. Finally, 3) the risk of diversion or improper use of psychostimulants, when prescribed as a substitution therapy may be even higher than with the methadone or buprenorphine in the context of opioid addiction. This is because both of these opioid maintenance treatments (unlike the stimulants) have their own anti-diversion/misuse strategies built in (e.g., daily supervised liquid dosing, or in the case of buprenorphine, partial opioid receptor agonism and formulations with an opioid blocker). A major problem with many of the psychostimulants is that they can be readily chemically converted to methamphetamine for illicit sale and this can be a very lucrative black market business. An adult patient diagnosed with addiction and seeking psychostimulants is probably much more likely to divert and misuse stimulants in this way than is a 10-year-old boy who is being evaluated for ADHD. For these reasons, and as previously discussed in prior sections of this chapter, the 2 × 4 Model clinic does not advocate for or utilize psychostimulant substitution strategies, preferring instead to attempt anti-addiction strategies for psychostimulant addiction.

Anti-Addiction Agents

In distinction to the harm-reduction/stabilization agents, the anti-addiction agents are definable by the following three characteristics: They are 1) minimally to nonaddictive; 2) they do not rely on the exact same pharmacological mechanism of action as the addictive target drug (i.e., they are not merely pharmacological substitutes for the addictive drug); and 3) they aim to facilitate full-sustained cessation of use of the drug (and its substitutes), for example, qualifying as a state of remission or 'a cure' of the disease. In general, these drugs attempt to interfere with brain processes that are intrinsic to supporting the addiction (e.g., craving, propensity for trigger-induced relapses, and extended binges), rather than merely interfering with the acute intoxicating or withdrawal effects of a given addictive drug. These anti-addiction agents are the pharmacological compliments of motivational enhancement therapy and should be used in conjunction with anti-addiction psychotherapies. Presently, there are five FDA approved pharmacological agents for addiction that meet this description, with at least two others that have a substantial and still growing evidence base that puts them within reach of FDA approval. These are briefly covered in this section. This list is expected to grow in the coming years as addiction treatment neuroscience and pharmacology are high public health priority fields and remain as relatively untapped and fertile frontiers for discovery.

Bupropion, as previously mentioned, holds the undisputed title of being the first PDDA. It is effective and FDA approved for both a mental illness (depression) and a type of addiction (to nicotine). This profile makes it a frequently employed tool in the 2 × 4 Model clinic. Bupropion also has attractive features of not causing sexual side effects or weight gain, and can even support modest weight loss. This medication, although not addictive or performing as a stimulant, does have some subtle stimulant-like aspects, giving some patients a feeling of increased energy and focus. For this reason, this medication may be a good choice for patients with addiction and mood disorders that involve prominent lethargy. Bupropion may also be a good off-label choice for an ADHD indication, especially when it is important to avoid stimulants. Some evidence suggests bupropion may also have utility in psychostimulant addiction (cocaine/amphetamine) as an off-label application, which is all the more justifiable since these addictions still do not yet have FDA approved medication treatments. The major downsides with bupropion are agitation, and potential for provoking mixed-mania range symptoms, especially in patients with bipolar spectrum illness that are not protected adequately with mood stabilizers. Of course the well-known seizure risk of bupropion in eating disordered and/or anorexic patients should also be considered.

Varenicline is arguably the most effective single anti-nicotine addiction medication treatment that has been developed and FDA approved thus far. Its major downside in comparison to bupropion is that it is not also an antidepressant, and, it has, deservedly or not, earned a reputation for actually provoking mood symptoms and suicidal thinking. However, there is considerable evidence that these mental illness-like side effects, observed almost exclusively in the post-FDA approval phase of clinical utilization could largely be an artifact of how the original effectiveness studies were done. As per the usual pharmacological research approach for either mental illness or addiction medication development, which continues to ignore the evidence base pointing to the biological, clinical, and epidemiological connection between mental illness and addiction, investigators typically go to considerable lengths to exclude patients with dual diagnosis comorbidities in order to obtain 'scientifically well controlled' and 'pure' clinical samples. The pivotal trials with varenicline that led to FDA approval thus involved treatment groups in which mental illnesses of various forms had been largely excluded (or under-reported). Unfortunately, this approach did not attend to the clinical reality that approximately half of U.S. smokers have some form of mental illness (and/or other major addictions) in which suicidality is not uncommon. So, when varenicline started being prescribed to smokers in general, it was inevitable that it would become associated with mental illness symptoms. Recent clinical trial evidence that is inclusive of dual diagnosis patients, suggests that varenicline is safe and effective for mentally ill patients in psychiatric care, and that the medication probably is not a major risk for causing depression or suicidal thinking as once thought.

The choice to go with varenicline vs. bupropion, which are both effective anti-craving medications, is a clinical decision that must be made by the psychiatrist based on evaluation of many clinical variables including consideration of what happened with past strategies to help the patient stop using nicotine. The 2 × 4 Model physician must keep in mind that nicotine addiction is one of the most severe, most common, and certainly, the most deadly of all forms of addiction that exist, in terms of its total public health impact. Nicotine addiction not only damages and kills more people than any other type of addiction, but it sickens and kills more people than *any other* disease causing agent or disease process in the U.S! And, because nicotine addiction is so highly concentrated in patients with mental illness (and in patients with other addictions), it is producing this carnage with especially high intensity in patient populations seeking care in psychiatry and integrated dual diagnosis care. Accordingly, nicotine addiction treatment should be viewed as a top priority of the 2 × 4 Model program. The treatment of nicotine addiction, with both pharmacological and psychotherapeutic modalities should be pervasive throughout all the services and expertise sets of the professionals that the 2 × 4 Model program is equipped with. Finally, as is routine in the treatment of other deadly diseases like cancer, the treatment of nicotine addiction in the 2 × 4 Model program should be as aggressive as the patient can tolerate, and persistent. 2 × 4 Model program psychiatrists who are trying to remit nicotine addiction should not hold back on changing up treatments (e.g., going from bupropion to varenicline, or vice versa) or implementing overlapping concurrent treatments, even to the point of using bupropion, varenicline, and NRT simultaneously with psychotherapy and contingency management if this is what it takes to help the patient stop purchasing and using tobacco. With that said, the patient does need to be ready and motivated to stop to some extent for even the most aggressive approaches to work, and they should not be endlessly treated with medication regimens, regardless of lack of treatment response. The Boulder-Stuck-in-the-Field Analogy can be a helpful narrative for illustrating a treatment philosophy that clinicians and patients can collaborate on to maintain persistence of effort for nicotine and other stubborn addictions.

The Boulder-Stuck-in-the-Field Analogy

In general, the approach of the addiction psychiatrist should be to understand that nicotine addiction, in many patients seeking care in the 2 × 4 Model clinic, is like a boulder that is stuck in the ground that needs to come out, so that the field can be used productively for cultivation. The boulder stubbornly resists coming out, and we cannot really see how big it really is or what its contours are underground. But we are prepared to use several tools, shovels, chains, and picks, sometimes one at a time, sometimes all at once, to get that boulder to budge. Sometimes if we are lucky it comes out pretty quickly, and we just roll it off the field. Other times we try hard and make little progress, and so we are exhausted and have to rest for some time. But eventually we come back to it, after we have rested and taken care of other priorities. And we try again, refreshed, pulling here, digging there; little by little, we dislodge the rock, never quitting as long as we own this field or until it comes out.

Ultimately, it should be understood between the psychiatrist and the patient, that if the long-term goal of nicotine addiction treatment is sustained (and hopefully permanent) cessation of nicotine use, then treatment with the anti-addiction medications must eventually occur without any form of concurrent nicotine use (via smoking, chewing, vaping, or NRT). The continuation of significant nicotine use, after 'quit dates' and after the optimal doses of varenicline and/or bupropion have been achieved likely sabotages the long-term value of these drugs to help the patient achieve total remission. These drugs are primarily designed for and proven as agents that work during abstinence, not for patients that continue to use nicotine regularly. NRT is best suited to reducing nicotine intake from tobacco (from patients who are not ready and willing to stop nicotine), or to bridging to varenicline and/or bupropion. Whereas the anti-addiction agents bupropion and varenicline are best reserved for patients trying hard to achieve total cessation.

A final note on varenicline is that, although it may not have efficacy for mental illness, it may have anti-addiction efficacy beyond nicotine. Mounting evidence suggests it has some efficacy for alcohol addiction as well and so this med may be a particularly good choice for patients with both nicotine and alcohol addictions.

Disulfiram, for alcohol addiction, is the oldest anti-addiction medication, being around for many decades. It is also probably one of the least effective because it tries to work, much like our criminal-justice system, on the defective principal that you can punish addiction out of the individual. Unfortunately, patients taking disulfiram who decide to drink simply need to stop taking it for a day or so to be able to drink and not get sick from the acetaldehyde build-up that disulfiram causes when people drink. Some patients have such severe forms of alcohol addiction that getting sick on disulfiram while drinking, does not even stop the compulsion. In recent years a breath of fresh air and hope for disulfiram has nevertheless emerged from both basic neuroscience and clinical channels suggesting that disulfiram has efficacy for treating psycho-stimulant addiction in terms of reducing craving and relapses, likely via activity on central dopamine neurotransmission (that has nothing really to do with its aldehyde dehydrogenase inhibiting activity). Given that cocaine and ampheta-mine addictions still don't have FDA approved medication indications, this evi-dence is strong enough to make disulfiram a front line consideration for these addictions, and may even be relevant to its efficacy in alcohol addiction, albeit in a way that was not previously well understood. Thus patients with both cocaine and alcohol addiction may be particularly good candidates for disul-firam therapy. However, the subtle dopamine stimulatory actions of disulfiram, do make it liable to risk for psychiatric side effects in the psychotic and manic spectrum, and so it should be used carefully in certain contexts. Of note, the potential for disulfiram to work for more than one addiction is an important theme that is relevant to other anti-addiction agents including naltrexone (alcohol and opioids), and as already mentioned, varenicline.

Acamprosate is an evidence-based, FDA approved treatment for alcohol addiction that by our best understanding, works via glutamatergic modulation in cortical-striatal circuits to blunt craving and relapse in patients attempting to maintain enduring sobriety. The clinical trial data shows that it can both decrease frequency of relapses and decrease the size (number of drinks and duration) of relapses. A major advantage of this medication in the context of alcoholism (relative to naltrexone) is that it does not engage or stress the liver; it is a very simple molecule that is discarded unchanged in urine and feces. Its disadvantage is that it has been tested and recommended for efficacy with frequent, high dosing intervals, such that patients need to take 2 × 333 mg tabs, 3 times a day (2 grams/day), necessary for getting the molecule across the blood–brain barrier. This may be a lot of effort for many patients, making incomplete compliance all the more likely, but for some who can do it, this dosing may encourage more constant daily attention and focus that is conducive to maintaining sobriety.

Naltrexone oral is a key treatment for both alcohol and opioid addiction that likely has efficacy for some other 'behavioral' addictions also, like pathological gambling. For alcoholism, many experts and some data suggest that oral naltrexone is overall superior to acamprosate, for reducing craving, relapse frequencies, and binging durations. However, unlike acamprosate, naltrexone is burdened by the potential for liver toxicity that is so often a concern in severe alcohol addiction anyway. For patients on opioid maintenance therapy for opioid addiction (methadone or buprenorphine) with alcoholism, naltrexone is also not an option.

Long-acting injectable naltrexone is a significant step up from the oral medication both in terms of efficacy and side effect profile. For the indications of both alcohol and opioid addiction, this medication arguably represents the most important advance in addiction pharmacology in the last decade. The chief advantages of long-acting injectable naltrexone are 1) the treatment team is assured of a month of compliance once the injection is in; 2) the patient does not have to remember to take daily doses; 3) the patient cannot turn the medication off or stop it with psychiatric or drug relapse episodes; 4) the pharmacokinetic properties of the injectable (relative to the oral med) creates lower stable levels of drug which reduces risk of liver toxicity. The general down sides of the injectable are a) its cost (which precludes its use for the uninsured unless philanthropy is involved, and makes it more likely that health insurance companies will try to block its use); b) the anxiety that goes with, and risk of large needle trauma to the gluteal region; c) the inability to reverse it, once it's in, which is problematic when patients actually need short term opioid medication coverage for acute pain as in trauma or postsurgical contexts.

For patients with opioid addiction, long acting injectable naltrexone is probably the best medication that has been developed thus far for giving patients the greatest chance of effecting a cure and/or putting their disease in long-term remission. The catch however, is that opioid addicted patients have to be willing and ready to do it. They have to be willing to bear the intensified short-term discomfort that accompanies the withdrawal phase before (and often after) they take the injection. They also need to be able to accept that the med will largely block the pharmacology of an opioid relapse.

In general, patients with opioid addiction should at initial evaluation be considered as potential candidates for methadone, buprenorphine, or injectable naltrexone. The addiction psychiatrist and the patient will then determine together, based on a range of clinical and individualized contextual variables, which med will be started first, and what the timeline and longer range goals of staying on that med should be. In this process, there is some estimation of whether a patient is most likely to succeed, at the highest possible level, with short- or long-term, harm-reduction/stabilization treatment (methadone/buprenorphine) that eventually leads to injectable naltrexone. Some patients will go to naltrexone right away after DWT and with no opioid maintenance therapy, while some will go to harm-reduction treatment for the rest of their life. Regardless, patients should not be permanently pigeonholed as being assigned one of these treatments and having to stay there. It is the job of the 2 × 4 Model team and the patient to monitor the success levels of the current regimen and treatment plan, and to always be vigilant about readiness and opportunities to change the pharmacological treatment, if it could get the patient closer to better health and/or a more complete recovery. Sometimes it can take months or even years for the team to settle on the best long-term plan, or to help the patient reach full remission as effected by injectable naltrexone. The 2 × 4 Model holds that the best and most acceptable standard of care for opioid addiction treatment, is one where the treatment team is able to commit to the long-term care of the patient from the very start and is able to flexibly deploy a range of pharmacological and psychotherapeutic treatments depending on what will benefit the patient the most. The 2 × 4 Model design, while incorporating the use of buprenorphine and naltrexone into integrated dual diagnosis care, and operating in a tight relationship with a methadone maintenance program, makes this standard of care imminently possible.

Topiramate is an anticonvulsant/antimigraine drug that in parallel to bupropion, may also represent a bonafide, PDDA, given the reasonably strong evidence that it has efficacy as both a mood stabilizer and an anti-addiction medication. However, the drug still lacks FDA indications for psychiatric or addiction indications. The mechanism of action of the drug is quite complex and incompletely understood but seems to modulate both glutamatergic and GABAergic neurotransmission with activities involving calcium channels (transmitter release) and sodium channels (action potential propagation). The anti-addiction properties of the drug may extend to alcohol and psychostimulant addiction, and possibly behavioral addictions such as compulsive eating, where it does have FDA approved efficacy, as a component of weight loss medication.

N-acetyl Cysteine (N-AC) long used for the treatment of acetaminophen-overdoses and acute COPD exacerbations, has more recently been discovered to be centrally active as a pro-drug for both glutathione and cysteine, which respectively appear to convey antioxidant (anti-neurotoxic) and glutamatergic modulatory effects. N-AC is particularly intriguing because much of the evidence and enthusiasm for it as an anti-addiction drug has emerged from the basic science side, making it an all-too-rare example of how preclinical neuroscience can successfully translate to addiction pharmacology. The anti-addiction efficacy of N-AC, although still not FDA approved, has been most broadly demonstrated in animal models, reducing relapse activity to cocaine, amphetamine, and nicotine, potentially with a special efficacy in animals that are both addicted and mentally ill, suggesting it could be a PDDA. In humans, the strongest anti-addiction evidence is a bit more circumscribed to cannabis dependence, where it has shown efficacy in a rigorous double-blind placebo controlled trial. Clinical data suggesting it could also have utility in schizophrenia (which has symptomatology similar to THC intoxication) also support its potential as a PDDA.

A number of miscellaneous agents of importance to the 2 × 4 Model clinic are worth mentioning briefly here. Of course 2 × 4 Model clinics should be equipped with life-saving doses of naloxone in case patients are brought in, or enter a state of opioid overdose on the clinics campus. Although still an experimental and anecdotal application, naloxone could also be applied for testing or inducing acute withdrawal states, for example, in preparation for transitioning to naltrexone therapy. Clonidine although long used as a standard for opioid DWT, may also have some benefit for blunting stress-induced craving in opioid and other addictions. As such, it might have utility as an adjunct to opioid maintenance treatment, to help keep doses low, or for assisting naltrexone in relapse prevention. As previously mentioned, gabapentin, while falling out of favor as a psychiatric medication, has gained empirical support as a DWT treatment and potentially an anti-addiction medication, at least in the early stages of cessation recovery from alcohol and opioid addiction. Further studies are needed to bring these possibilities to the threshold of FDA approval. Finally, there is a science-based rational for the use of THC, (e.g. in medication form) to facilitate the transition of patients from opioid maintainance (e.g. buprenorphine) to long-acting injectable naltrexone, potentially as used in supervised inpatient setting. However, a solid clinical evidence base is still needed (and not yet available) to support this approach.

Background References and Further Reading

Brady, K. T., and J. M. Roberts. 1995. "The pharmacotherapy of dual diagnosis." *Psychiatric Annals 25* (6): 344–352. doi: 10.3928/0048-5713-19950601-06.

Brady, K. T., H. Myrick, and S. McElroy. 1998. "The relationship between substance use disorders, impulse control disorders, and pathological aggression." *American Journal on Addictions 7* (3): 221–230.

Brown, R. M., Y. M. Kupchik, and P. W. Kalivas. 2013. "The story of glutamate in drug addiction and of N-acetyl cysteine as a potential pharmacotherapy." *The Journal of the American Medical Association Psychiatry 70* (9): 895–897.

Carroll, K. M., L. R. Fenton, S. A. Ball, C. Nich, T. L. Frankforter, J. Shi, and B. J. Rounsaville. 2004. "Efficacy of disulfiram and cognitive behavior therapy in cocaine-dependent outpatients: A randomized placebo-controlled trial." *Archives of General Psychiatry 61* (3): 264–272. doi: 10.1001/archpsyc.61.3.26461/3/264 [pii].

Fullerton, C. A., M. Kim, C. P. Thomas, D. R. Lyman, L. B. Montejano, R. H. Dougherty, A. S. Daniels, S. S. Ghose, and M. E. Delphin-Rittmon. 2014. "Medication-assisted treatment with methadone: Assessing the evidence." *Psychiatric Services 65* (2): 146–157.

Grant, J. E., S. W. Kim, and B. K. Hartman. 2008. "A double-blind, placebo-controlled study of the opiate antagonist naltrexone in the treatment of pathological gambling urges." *Journal of Clinical Psychiatry 69* (5): 783–789.

Grant, J. E., S. W. Kim, and B. L. Odlaug. 2007. "N-acetyl cysteine, a glutamate-modulating agent, in the treatment of pathological gambling: A pilot study." *Biological Psychiatry 62* (6): 652–657.

Grant, J. E., R. A. Chambers, and M. N. Potenza. 2004. "Adolescent problem gambling: Neurodevelopment and pharmacological treatment." In *Gambling Problems in Youth:*

Theoretical and Applied Perspective, edited by J. Derevensky and R. Gupta, (pp. 81–98). New York: Kluwer.

Grau-Lopez, L., C. Roncero, C. Daigre, L. Miquel, C. Barral, B. Gonzalvo, F. Collazos, and M. Casas. 2014. "Observational study on medications prescribed to dual-diagnosis outpatients." *Journal of Addiction Medicine 8* (2): 84 89.

Gray, K. M., M. J. Carpenter, N. L. Baker, S. M. DeSantis, E. Kryway, K. J. Hartwell, A. L. McRae-Clark, and K. T. Brady. 2012. "A double-blind randomized controlled trial of N-acetyl cysteine in cannabis-dependent adolescents." *The American Journal of Psychiatry 169* (8): 805–812. doi: 10.1176/appi.ajp.2012.12010055118421 7 [pii].

Green, A. I., D. L. Noordsy, M. F. Brunette, and C. O'Keefe. 2008. "Substance abuse and schizophrenia: Pharmaco-therapeutic intervention." *Journal of Substance Abuse Treatment 34* (1): 61–71.

Herman, B. H, J. Frankenheim, R. Z. Litten, P. H. Sheridan, F. F. Weight, and S. R. Zukin, Eds. 2002. *Glutamate and Addiction, Contemporary Clinical Neuroscience.* New York: Humana Press.

Johnson, B. A., N. Ait-Daoud, C. L. Bowden, C. C. DiClemente, J. D. Roache, K. Lawson, M. A. Javors, and J. Z. Ma. 2003. "Oral topiramate for treatment of alcohol dependence: A randomised controlled trial." *Lancet 361* (9370): 1677–1685.

Johnson, B. A., N. Ait-Daoud, X. Q. Wang, J. K. Penberthy, M. A. Javors, C. Seneviratne, and L. Liu. 2013. "Topiramate for the treatment of cocaine addiction: A randomized clinical trial." *The Journal of the American Medical Association Psychiatry 70* (12): 1338–1346.

Kosten, T. R., and P. G. O'Connor. 2003. "Management of drug and alcohol withdrawal." *New England Journal of Medicine 348* (18): 1786–1795.

Kreek, M. J., K. S. LaForge, and E. Butelman. 2002. "Pharmacotherapy of addictions." *Nature Reviews Drug Discovery 1* (9): 710–726. doi: 10.1038/nrd897nrd897 [pii].

Letmaier, M., D. Schreinzer, R. Wolf, and S. Kasper. 2001. "Topiramate as a mood stabilizer." *International Clinical Psychopharmacology 16* (5): 295–298.

Levounis, P., E. Zerbo, and R. Agarwal, Eds. 2016. *Pocket Guide to Addiction Assessment and Treatment.* Arlington, VA: American Psychiatric Association Publishing.

Litten, R. Z., M. L. Ryan, J. B. Fertig, D. E. Falk, B. Johnson, K. E. Dunn, A. I. Green, H. M. Pettinati, D. A. Ciraulo, O. Sarid-Segal, K. Kampman, M. F. Brunette, E. C. Strain, N. A. Tiouririne, J. Ransom, C. Scott, R. Stout, and Ncig Study Group. 2013. "A double-blind, placebo-controlled trial assessing the efficacy of varenicline tartrate for alcohol dependence." *Journal of Addiction Medicine 7* (4): 277–286.

Lobmaier, P., M. Gossop, H. Waal, and J. Bramness. 2010. "The pharmacological treatment of opioid addiction—a clinical perspective." *European Journal of Clinical Pharmacology 66* (6): 537–545.

Ma, J. Z., N. Ait-Daoud, and B. A. Johnson. 2006. "Topiramate reduces the harm of excessive drinking: Implications for public health and primary care." *Addiction 101* (11): 1561–1568.

Myrick, H., R. Malcolm, P. K. Randall, E. Boyle, R. F. Anton, H. C. Becker, and C. L. Randall. 2009. "A double-blind trial of gabapentin versus lorazepam in the treatment of alcohol withdrawal." *Alcoholism: Clinical & Experimental Research 33* (9): 1582–1588.

O'Brien, C. P. 1997. "A range of research-based pharmaco therapies for addiction." *Science 278* (5335): 66–70.

Potenza, M. N., M. Sofuoglu, K. M. Carroll, and B. J. Rounsaville. 2011. "Neuroscience of behavioral and pharmacological treatments for addictions." *Neuron* 69 (4): 695–712. doi: 10.1016/j.neuron.2011.02.009S0896-6273(11)00106-1 [pii].

Prochaska, J. J., S. Das, and K. C. Young-Wolff. 2017. "Smoking, mental illness, and public health." *Annual Review of Public Health 38*: 165–185. doi: 10.1146/annurev-publhealth-031816-044618.

Rounsaville, B. J., R. Weiss, and K. Carroll. 1999. "Options for managing psychotropic medications in drug-abusing patients participating in behavioral therapies clinical trials." *American Journal on Addiction 8* (3): 178–189.

Rubio, G., I. Martinez-Gras, and J. Manzanares. 2009. "Modulation of impulsivity by topiramate: Implications for the treatment of alcohol dependence." *Journal of Clinical Psychopharmacology 29* (6): 584–589.

Schatzberg, A. F., and C. B. Nemeroff. 2004. *Textbook of Psychopharmacology*. 3rd ed. Washington, DC: American Psychiatric Publishing.

Strain, E. C., and M. L. Stitzer. 2006. *The Treatment of Opioid Dependence*. Baltimore, MD: Johns Hopkins University Press.

Williams, J., R. Anthenelli, C. D. Morris, J. Treadow, J. R. Thompson, C. Yunis, and T. George. 2012. "A randomized, double-blind, placebo-controlled study evaluating the safety and efficacy of varenicline for smoking cessation in patients with schizophrenia or schizoaffective disorder." *Journal of Clinical Psychiatry 73* (5): 654–660. doi: 10.4088/JCP.11m07522.

8 Communications

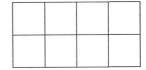

It is simply not enough for the addiction psychiatrist and the 2 × 4 Model team to limit their efforts to achieve mental health and addiction recovery to within the confines of the clinic walls. Unfortunately, the disease processes that exist within patient's brains are intensively related to, and worsened by many forces active outside the clinic, in the communities, cultures, and conditions patients live in. Inpatient stays can temporarily shelter patients from these detrimental forces, but the goal of the 2 × 4 Model clinic as an outpatient program is to generate long-term recovery outside of hospitals and 'rehabs', facilitating improvement as patients live, work, and relate to others in the community. *Therefore, the 2 × 4 Model team must act not just to temporarily shelter patients from the outside world (e.g., by occasional hospitalization), but by actively exerting positive force through communications, back into the outside world, so that it too can be changed to support, rather than hinder or destroy patient recovery.*

This chapter describes communications as the fourth component of the treatment dimension in the 2 × 4 Model design. Professional communications about 2 × 4 Model patients will often encompass a consideration and summary of the diagnostic and psychotherapeutic work, and medication modalities of care that patients receive. Thus, through this summarization, communications are *horizontally bound* with the other components of the 2 × 4 Model on the treatment planning dimension. Certainly, communications should be viewed as facilitating the other treatment components and as representing a real treatment intervention in its own right. It is possible for adverse external conditions to seriously limit or completely negate the impact of some or even all the medications and psychotherapies the clinic may deploy for a given patient. When this dynamic happens, it is just as much the responsibility of the team to try to deflect, interdict, or positively modulate those external forces as it is to make the right diagnoses, and select and provide the right treatments within the clinic. In this way, the addiction psychiatrist and the 2 × 4 Model program should view itself not only as representing a new type of integrative psychiatric clinic, but as an advocacy and educational center, and hub of consultation-liason work, in active communication with many other types of outside professionals and groups.

Leading External Threats to Integrated Dual Diagnosis Recovery

Categorization of the types of external forces and social conditions that inhibit recovery and keep patients stuck in destructive mental illness and addiction disease trajectories, enables a discussion of communication strategies and templates that 2 × 4 Model clinicians can use to alleviate them. As with psychotherapies and medication approaches, it cannot be realistically expected that any one, or even a series of communications made on behalf of a patient, will be guaranteed to be massively effective in changing the clinical picture. However, like these traditional psychiatric interventions, well-selected and well-executed communications to the outside world can sometimes be real game changers. Even if they only produce incremental improvements by themselves, well-done communications can still boost the effects of the meds and psychotherapies to allow patients to gain momentum into full-on recovery. The efficacies of diagnostic evaluations, psychotherapies, and medications require patient compliance, which ultimately depends on teamwork and trust of patients in the therapeutic relationship. Showing patients that the 2 × 4 Model clinic 'has their back' through communicative actions can help build that trust. A major theme that should transcend the communications emanating from the 2 × 4 Model clinic is a thoughtful consideration of how communications should be best designed to benefit each patient and their situation, and the overall mission of the clinic. Often, these communications will represent the only real advocacy and outwardly directed support that many patients will receive from anyone, and patients will often be well aware of that. The therapeutic power of this support alone is substantial, not only in terms of making these patients feel they are valued and worth fighting for, but in terms of fortifying a stronger therapeutic bond that may need to be tested and leveraged at several points down the road to support persistence in care and better long-term outcomes. The four major categories of external threats to integrated dual diagnosis recovery that are addressed by 2 × 4 Model clinic communications are as follows:

1.   Adverse methods and interventions of the Criminal Justice System;
2.   Iatrogenic actions of the General Health Care System;
3.   Poverty: lack of shelter, income, or transportation; and
4.   Detrimental family, cohabitation, and other social contexts.

The following sections will describe these adverse forces and their subtypes in greater detail, and provide recommendations and templates for how addiction psychiatrists and other 2 × 4 Model program staff can best communicate with outside professionals and agencies to reduce them (**Figure 8.1**). In this effort, the 2 × 4 Model team keeps in mind that, just as patients present with individually distinct forms and comorbidities of mental illness and addictions that exist in their brains, they also will be externally pressured by different combinations and degrees of severity of one or more of these four major external detrimental forces and barriers.

The quality and intensity of externals forces can, like mental illness itself, be quite severe and complex and wax and wane over time, making treatment team members feel like the patients themselves: Overwhelmed and powerless to evoke improvement. Sometimes, 2 × 4 Model clinicians will find themselves wishing: "If only the societal dysfunction, social ills, and stigma that this patient has to live in, was only half as sick as their brain disease . . . then I could get somewhere!" Indeed, taking care of a complex dual diagnosis patient can sometimes feel like taking on two patients at once, one being the individual with the brain disease, and the other, the disturbed and unfortunately quite imperfect society they (and we all) live in. But, to avoid being overwhelmed by this realization, the addiction psychiatrist and 2 × 4 Model team members understand that they can and *should* effectively use their education, training, and social status—their professional power if you will—via smart, proactive, and discrete communication and educational work—to promote change not only in the patient but in his/her environment. Does this mean that the 2 × 4 Model clinic should see itself as being more than a health care entity? It probably should. The addiction psychiatrists and other team members should understand and embrace their work in the 2 × 4 Model design as contributing not only to individual's recovery but to positive social change—as acts of social justice, done one patient at a time—exerted not only through expert diagnosis and treatment delivery, but through outward communication.

Communications with the Criminal Justice System

The Context

There are many fine people and professionals that make up the many different components of the Criminal Justice System and law enforcement. Majorities of our people who work as police, guards, probation officers, judges, lawyers (on both sides of cases), and other court officials, do excellent work under often stressful and sometimes unsafe conditions to help keep the rest of us safe and our society as fair and peaceful as possible. However, the Criminal Justice System (like any system) is not perfect, and it is a system that ultimately must operate according to the laws, politics, and cultural currents of the governments, politicians, and voters who ultimately, if indirectly, determine the laws.

Two major cultural policy currents, commonly termed 'deinstitutionalization' and the 'war on drugs', have operated synergistically over the last several decades to i) inappropriately place undue responsibility on the Criminal Justice System for behavioral health concerns; and ii) to erode the viability and capability of the behavioral health system itself. While it was probably not anticipated that 'deinstitutionalization' and the 'war on drugs' would have these concerted effects, it was nevertheless practically unavoidable once these movements gained momentum, because the diseases of addiction and mental illnesses are fundamentally biologically linked in the brain, and, to a very great extent, happen together in the same populations (Chapter 2). Hence, if we make addictive behavior (including intoxication, use, possession, and acquisition of drugs for personal use) into serious crimes, we are criminalizing people with addictions. Then, since large fractions of people with uncontrolled, severe addictions have mental illness—and mentally ill people are no longer protected from ubiquitous access to addictive drugs by the old institutional system—these people become criminalized as well. The resulting criminalization of postinstitutional addicted mentally ill people has, over many years, created a self-perpetuating shift of human effort and capital out of the behavioral health, physical, and workforce infrastructure, toward criminal justice and incarceration industries (**Figure 8.2**). This has led to an increasing societal investment (at the expense of behavioral health and patient care) in the idea that we can, and should, punish brain-behavioral disorders out of patients, rather than treat them as biomedical problems. *The 2 × 4 Model clinic rejects the idea of punishment of mentally ill/addicted behavior as a legitimate medical treatment, and regards the shift toward this approach as a detrimental cultural policy movement that is inhumane, medically unethical, destructive to society as a whole, and contrary to the neuroscientific, clinical, and social science evidence.*

It seems ironic that criminalization and mass incarceration of mentally ill addicted people has grown to the extent that is has since 1970, given the tremendous advances that also happened during this time in understanding mental illnesses and addictions as brain diseases.

Perhaps the *momentum* for decline of the behavioral health system, and the association of addiction with criminality, was too much for the accumulating neuroscience to overcome. It's hard to translate a signal (neuroscience) effectively regardless of how clearly and elegantly it is expressed, when the receiver (behavioral health care system) is breaking down. Perhaps in part because neuroscience and pharmacological advances (*circa* 1980–2005) were so exciting and financially compelling, many leaders in academic psychiatry were not in touch with, or effected by the extent to which the breakdown in behavioral health care itself was occurring. In any event, as governments invested more into mass incarceration, behavioral health patients and their problems were being increasingly regarded and dealt with as criminal, recidivistic, and non-responsive to, or unworthy of evidence-based treatment. Ironically, even as the criminalization trend was actually not at all effective in reducing or curbing mental illness or addiction (and may have even exacerbated it in many ways), it was the psychiatric and addiction treatment sectors that often seemed to catch the blame for being ineffective, as they were increasingly considered too broken and too fragmented to deal with the problem. This dynamic, in turn, impacted the attitudes and culture of the health care system itself, which has viewed behavioral health, perhaps increasingly so, as more of an unprofitable activity and philanthropic mission, rather than being a core component of the house of medicine and public health. Hence, behavioral health would experience more defunding, degradation, and loss of prestige, with relative worsening of insurance reimbursement support, with more psychiatric clinics and hospitals closing, with fewer teaching faculty and time for teaching of medical students and residents, with proportionately fewer medical students entering psychiatry, fewer residency slots, etc. So, with drug use stubbornly not responding to some degree of mass incarceration, and behavioral health and addiction care being perceived as inadequate or incapable, and not really part of mainstream health care, the answer has been to move toward even more mass incarceration and even greater punishment for patients with addiction and mental illness.

In total, this history happening over about the last 50 years has created a dynamic where the Criminal Justice System has had to greatly overstep its area of expertise and capability, as compelled by mental health and addiction treatment systems that are increasingly broken, fragmented, and deficient of professionals and physical infrastructure. So, we have arrived at a situation where, as many commentators have observed, "the criminal justice and prison system have become the *de facto* behavioral health system."

Beyond the fact that judgement and punishment of mental illness and addiction do not offer effective, evidence-based ways to treat these brain conditions, the preoccupation of the police and the Criminal Justice System with vast numbers of current, future, or former prisoners with dual diagnosis conditions, has likely made it harder for them to actually apprehend, prosecute, and incarcerate dangerous criminals, or to efficiently process many offenses that actually have nothing to do with mental illness. In other words, as many professionals within law enforcement, the courts, and corrections are aware, the inappropriate assignment of responsibility of the Criminal Justice System for mentally ill addicted people, not only hurts mentally ill/addicted people, but it distracts and hinders the Criminal Justice System itself. By offering a new system of integrated mental health and addiction treatment services that is more proactive, comprehensive, and effective in taking of responsibility for mentally ill and addicted patients, and communicating that responsibility to the Criminal Justice System, the 2 × 4 Model system aims to reverse the trends that started with 'deinstitutionalization' and the 'war on drugs'. In this way, by improving the mission and function of behavioral health, the 2 × 4 Model system will produce an important, if indirect, effect of actually refining and improving the function of the Criminal Justice System as well.

Agenda of the 2 × 4 Model Program in Relation to the Criminal Justice System

In asserting its mission and communicating with the Criminal Justice System, the 2 × 4 Model system should keep in mind that as much as both these systems might share the same ultimate goal of reducing addiction, the means they use to this end are very different, and in some ways opposing. The 2 × 4 Model approach is a part of the medical tradition; its methods and efficacy are scientifically founded on and informed by the concept of positive reinforcement (e.g., offer humane and beneficial treatment to promote positive behavior, to reach a positive outcome). The criminal justice approach is part of the political–legal tradition. Its methods and efficacy are not nearly as scientifically based or motivated. It relies on more of a concept of the social contract and on a negative reinforcement model (judge and punish to stop negative behavior).

With these differences in mind, the 2 × 4 Model program should strive to keep itself clearly and firmly within the medical tradition; there simply is no aspect of the medical tradition either in its philosophical or scientific foundations that accepts or supports the idea that disease and suffering can be alleviated by punishment. A cornerstone of medical ethics and professionalism that addiction psychiatrists in the 2 × 4 Model clinic should hold onto is *'Primum non nocere'*—*'First, do no harm'*. Deviations by the clinic from this ethic into treatment approaches that intend to deliberately punish (or collude with punishing) patients for their addictive illness and behavior, produces an actual and perceived identification (from the perspective of the patient and society) of treatment with judgmental/punitive/criminal justice approaches. Conflating treatment with punishment contradicts multiple evidence-based approaches to addiction treatment. For example, the 'harm amplification' of punishment is quite the opposite of 'harm reduction' strategies; contingency management actually rewards progress instead of punishing failure; and, MET is neither a 'zero tolerance' approach nor one that uses judgement and punishment (see Chapter 6). Conflating treatment with punishment may also reinforce the aforementioned historical context of mass incarceration and criminalization that has grown at the expense of building a strong, evidence-based, integrated dual diagnosis care system. With this said, it should not be the approach of the 2 × 4 Model program to err toward the other extreme of ignoring or colluding with criminal behavior in patients. There should be an awareness that there are differential degrees of overlap between genuine, dangerous criminal behavior, and behavior driven by drug addiction (e.g., ranging from armed robbery to small time possession or failing a drug test). The 2 × 4 Model clinic seeks communication with the Criminal Justice System to support its own clinical mission, to enhance treatment compliance, to support individual's recovery, and to protect evidence-based treatment—in a way that is designed to educate and ultimately de-burden the Criminal Justice System of these responsibilities.

The usual scenario that produces a need for the 2 × 4 Model clinic to communicate with the Criminal Justice System, is when the two systems share common clients (we call them patients; they may call them clients, prisoners, parolees, or offenders). The Criminal Justice System essentially has only two categories of responses it can make to an addiction-related behavior: do nothing about it, or punish the person. When the decision is made to punish, there are at least five main forms of punishment that can have seriously adverse effects on the patient's recovery and the mission of the 2 × 4 Model clinic:

1. Incarceration and removal from care: For example, the patient has a 'dirty' drug screen and so, has to go to jail for days/weeks/months. *Adverse effect:* After this relapse they are removed (via incarceration) from psycho-therapies and/or medications prescribed by the 2 × 4 Model program, and are exposed to violence, overcrowding, drug use opportunities, and solitary confinement within the incarceration setting.

2. Financial penalties: For example, the terms of probation or pretrial agreements require payments to avoid jail, or to pay for required drug testing outside of medical/psychiatric practice, or to pay fines for the original offense, etc. *Adverse effect:* With financial penalties, patients have even less ability to afford medication or treatment co-pays, or transportation to treatment, or are forced to sacrifice treatment participation for income earning activities.

3. Loss of insurance: For example, with periods of incarceration and lack of employment produced via criminalization, patients lose their insurance and/or cannot afford insurance. *Adverse effect:* Without insurance, most patients cannot afford the out of pocket expenses of 2 × 4 Model pro-graming and their medications. Also, the 2 × 4 Model program cannot afford to treat patients without reimbursement.

4. Loss of employability: For example, soft incarceration (house arrest or work release) or full incarceration makes employment difficult, and a history of incarceration and addiction-related felonies can permanently damage a patient's long-term gainful employment. *Adverse Effect:* Patients are less likely to find a quality work life that gives them a reason to stay sober and to provide them with adequate health insurance coverage for needed treatment. Moreover, they are *more* likely to resort to income earning activities (prostitution/drug dealing) that put them at risk for worsening mental illness, drug relapse, victimization, and re-arrest.

5. Interference with treatment and improper referrals to care: For example, a prosecutor, probation officer, or judge may decide, without medical or behavioral health training or knowledge, what the standards, intensities, and durations of psychotherapies should be and what medication their clients can and cannot be on. *Adverse Effect:* Interference by the Criminal Justice System with evidence-based care and clinical decision-making for patients in the 2 × 4 Model clinic can undermine the therapeutic relationship needed to evoke recovery, and can lead to coerced acceptance of substandard levels of care.

The 2 × 4 Model *Guidelines for Communications with the Criminal Justice System* provides specific recommendations about how the team should communicate and interact with the Criminal Justice System to help protect patients against these types of punitive measures that can adversely interdict the treatment mission and patient recovery.

BOX 8.1 Guidelines for Communications with the Criminal Justice System

1. Do not communicate or interact with the Criminal Justice System in a way that renders the 2 × 4 Model a subsidiary or extension of the Criminal Justice System. For example, do not engage in a contractual agreement with a probation office or court that requires the clinic to lower a standard of care for a patient because he or she is a prisoner or on probation. Do not reduce standards of clinical care or standards of confidentiality that are routinely observed for patients with no legal involvement, for patients with Criminal Justice System involvement, even when those patients may have signed contracts with the Criminal Justice System, that reduce clinical and confidentiality standards. The 2 × 4 Model clinic should keep in mind that it is not ethical to agree to reduce its standards of care for patients who may have been coerced by threat of punishment, to accept lower standards.

2. Do not allow the Criminal Justice System to interfere with, or drive treatment decisions of the 2 × 4 Model program with respect to either medication or psychotherapeutic modalities. 2 × 4 Model team members should keep in mind that criminal justice officials are not educated, trained, qualified, licensed or employed to make health care decisions. The flow of expertise about mental health and addiction diagnosis and treatment should be from the 2 × 4 Model clinic to patients, and to the Criminal Justice System, and not in the reverse direction. While treatment planning can be made to accommodate legal sanctions that do not interfere with treatment, legal sanctions should not adversely dictate treatment.

3. The 2 × 4 Model clinic should not share specific clinical diagnostic information about patients with the Criminal Justice System, unless the clinic has been court ordered (by a judge) to do so. For example, the results of UDS in the clinic, regardless of the pattern of results, should not be shared with the Criminal Justice System without a specific court order (warrant/subpoena). The 2 × 4 Model team should keep in mind that such specific clinical information, when released to the Criminal Justice System is at risk of being used not to further treatment, but to punish the patient, which can result in separation of the patient from treatment. It is unethical to report the results of medical diagnostic tests and assessments ordered and utilized in the course of behavioral health treatment, to parties who would use the same information to harm patients or to separate them from treatment. Criminal justice officials are generally not professionally trained or qualified to interpret results of biomedical testing, including UDS testing collected in the 2 × 4 Model clinic, and this testing is not secured with the 'chain of custody', which is typically required for the court to take legal action on such testing results.

continued

BOX 8.1 **Guidelines for Communications with the Criminal Justice System**—*continued*

4. The 2 × 4 Model clinic should observe the same thresholds for divulging descriptions of criminal behavior or intent by patients to the Criminal Justice System, as is held in general psychiatric practice as guided by the Tarasoff Case. Generally, only an expression of a credible plan, intent, or ongoing action to harm or kill other specific adults or children, is the only obligatory breach of confidentiality that should be made. Patient's reports of criminal activity (e.g., using, possessing, and dealing drugs) that is related to or caused by addictive disease should be addressed through evidence-based treatment measures targeting addictive disease and mental illness, and not by turning patients over (or relaying this information) to the Criminal Justice System.

5. The 2 × 4 Model clinic should invite and encourage as much clinically relevant information as it can get from the Criminal Justice System about patients to drive treatment planning and decision-making. Communication channels between the 2 × 4 Model clinic and the Criminal Justice System should be active and collaborative, but the information flow is necessarily asymmetric. The exchange must be controlled and monitored by the 2 × 4 Model program to promote therapeutic engagement and efficacy for patients.

6. For patients with Criminal Justice System involvement who have been referred to treatment, it is acceptable and appropriate for the 2 × 4 Model clinic to disclose, in nonspecific terms, the overall severity of illness, the degree of clinical progress, and the extent to which the patient is demonstrating effort to engage in care. Such disclosure is typically made to inform the Criminal Justice System that treatment is beneficial and working; to advocate for more or continued treatment and less of a punitive strategy. Conversely, in cases where patients are not engaging in treatment at minimally acceptable levels to evoke therapeutic benefit, and are using the guise of treatment to avoid legal sanctions while not showing improvement, this information should also be communicated to the criminal justice systems in general terms.

Forms and Templates for Communications with the Criminal Justice System

Communications with an outside entity can take the form of verbal (phone or face to face) or written communications (email or regular printed letters). When communicating with the court (e.g., the attorneys, judges, or probation officers surrounding a patient's case), the preferred method is often the printed letter, sent on the clinic's letter head. For these types of communications, the central goal is often to ask the court to back away from pursuing a criminalized/punitive approach, and to instead support the 2 × 4 Model mission and the patient as they continue to engage in treatment or rebuild their lives while in recovery. At the core of such letters, the 2 × 4 Model clinic seeks to communicate i) that the core problem that led to the patient's legal charges have been caused by a brain and behavioral health disorder, and ii) that the patient is now engaged in optimal evidence-based treatment that can actually work to address the problem. This type of communication can give the court a level of confidence that something good and efficacious is being done about their 'client' and the root causes of their criminal activity, so that it doesn't feel so compelled to do something about it on its own—that is—to apply punitive measures. In a way, this type of communication aims to say, "Hey your honor, we got this", so that the Criminal Justice System can be reassured and relieved of the pressure to act that they might otherwise feel when there are no effective behavioral health options. Letters to the court in this vein will have the following key ingredients, appearing approximately in this order:

1. Statement of the patient's name and date of birth;
2. Purpose of the communication;
3. Broad diagnostic picture of the patient;
4. Brief description of treatment history and types of services being delivered to the patient (e.g., state that the patient is receiving care in a 2 × 4 Model clinic which emphasizes both medication and psychotherapeutic services for both mental health and addictive illnesses);
5. Statement acknowledging the patient's engagement and progress in care (avoid specific test results and medical data, which they are not trained to interpret);
6. Statement of the degree of concern about the potential impact of ongoing or additional punitive measures to harm the patient's recovery;
7. Statement about the patient's level of long-term commitment to treatment regardless of punitive sanctions; and
8. Signature and title of addiction psychiatrist with or without other psychotherapy staff.

Depending on the clinical details of the patient and the nature of the legal context and charges or convictions, points 3 through 7 may vary considerably in level of detail. The author should generally disclose as little information as possible, but as accurately as possible, to support the goal of the letter, while remembering that the target audience (a judge/prosecutor/defense attorney/ probation officer) is not usually medically or psychiatrically trained. Hence the letter should also be briefly and courteously educational as needed, and should not provide specific clinical details that only a well-trained physician or other psychiatric professional would be able to interpret. The following exemplar letters (A and B) are slightly modified examples (identifying information changed) of 2 × 4 Model clinic communications to the Criminal Justice System that string these elements together (see **Boxes 8.2 and 8.3**).

BOX 8.2 Exemplar Letter A: From the 2 × 4 Model Clinic to the Criminal Court

Dear Court Officials, X/XX/2015

This letter regards Mr. XY (DOB: XX/XX/XXXX), who I have been treating at the 2 × 4 Model clinic for his complex mental illness and addiction diseases for the past 6 months. With respect to his upcoming court date (on April XX, 2015), please let me convey in this letter that Mr. XY is receiving and engaging in treatment involving both medications and psychotherapies for these conditions and is responding very well to these treatments. We believe that the charges he faces from the incident and behavior in July of 2014, was a result of untreated mental illness and addiction, and hope the court will recognize this and understand that these issues are now being successfully addressed medically in our clinic. We hope the court will take this information into consideration in deciding the outcome of these charges in a way that facilitates, rather than disrupts his continued treatment with us, and optimizes his future well-being.

Thank you,

Aaa Bbbb MD

Aaa Bbbb, M.D.
Associate Professor of Psychiatry
Addiction Psychiatrist,
XXX 2 × 4 Model Clinic
XXX Street, Indianapolis, IN 46208
PH: XXX-XXX-XXXX

BOX 8.3 Exemplar Letter B: 2 × 4 Model Clinic Advocating for Expungement

Dear Court Officials, XX/XX/2012

This letter is written on behalf of our patient, Ms. QRS (DOB: XX/XX/XXX) who we have been seeing in our ZZZ-affiliated dual diagnosis clinic in Indianapolis for more than 3 years. During this time Ms. QRS has fully engaged in a comprehensive program of treatment services including group and individual psychotherapies and medication treatments for both her psychiatric illness and addictions. I am pleased to let you know she has recovered maximally in this treatment and has achieved full and sustained sobriety as well as about 95 percent remission of all her psychiatric symptoms. This exemplary recovery has made her able now to function at a high level as a mother to her 6-year-old son, and as a citizen of our society, while being a role model for other patients in our clinic who are also pursuing recovery.

We are aware that Ms. QRS has two felonies on her record dating from events happening in 1996 and 2002 (i.e., over 10 years ago) that clearly occurred as a result of behaviors caused by her psychiatric and addiction illnesses that at the time were not being treated. Unfortunately, although she has fully served her punishments for these offenses, and has achieved recovery from the brain illnesses that led to them, she continues to suffer from the presence of these felonies on her legal record both psychologically and as an ongoing barrier that is damaging her ability to acquire gainful employment, potential housing opportunities and other civil freedoms. Accordingly, our team wholeheartedly advocates that her criminal record be fully expunged as the right thing to do for her recovery, and for our society.

Thank you,

Aaa Bbbb, M.D.
Associate Professor of Psychiatry
Addiction Psychiatrist,
The XXX 2 × 4 Model Clinic
XXX Street, Indianapolis, IN 46208
PH: XXX-XXX-XXXX

Communication with Child Protective Services (CPS)

Many patients in need of addiction and dual diagnosis services will be parents, and more specifically, women with young children, presenting with or without reliable support from the father of the children or other male or extended family parental figures. In most families, where a CPS case has been opened, untreated or ineffectively treated mental illness and addiction is the primary context and root cause of the case situation and context. Identification of this context by CPS investigators can (and should) precipitate referrals to the 2 × 4 Model clinic.

Although the agency and mission of CPS is usually structured and defined more as a social services endeavor, rather than as criminal justice endeavor, many of the cultural and operational attributes and attitudes of CPS are often similar to those of the Criminal Justice System, and these two systems must necessarily work very closely together. Both CPS and the Criminal Justice System share the common ground of being government-funded agencies that are ultimately answerable to elected officials, instilled with a duty to protect the population (albeit in different ways), while being supervised and regulated by the courts. Because of these similarities, and a general lack of neuroscience or behavioral health background and perspectives within both the Criminal Justice System and CPS agencies, the 2 × 4 Model clinic will often experience parallels between how it has to communicate and interact with both of these systems in the interest of protecting the integrity of treatment and in supporting individual patient's recovery.

There can be two major problems with CPS (that may be present to different degrees depending on the case and the geographical location or government jurisdiction) that the 2 × 4 Model program has to be aware of and contend with. First, there is the cultural mentality (and resulting tactics) that may influence CPS services (and their supervising courts) that overvalues the idea that punishment is an effective way to control and improve the behavior of mentally ill and addicted parents. But, while the Criminal Justice System attempts to deter or reduce certain behaviors via incarceration and/or financial penalties, CPS uses the lever of separating parents from their children. While CPS is trying its best to conduct its primary mission of protecting children, there are times that, from the perspective of behavioral health professionals, CPS seems to be acting excessively by punishing mentally ill/addicted parents through withholding access to their children, or, by threatening those parents with permanent separation in the hopes of motivating them to 'shape up'. The perception of CPS as an agency that can be deconstructive rather than supportive of families can be reinforced in situations where the alternative placement of the children (e.g., in foster care) may also be a relatively high risk setting for the children, and, where despite substantial clinical improvement in the parents, CPS (or the court) persists in maintaining the separation and trajectory to permanent removal.

Certainly, in some instances, there is no alternative but to remove children from their parents for the short-term, or permanently. Children can be successfully placed in much healthier and nurturing environments with extended family members or adoptive parents. But there are also many cases where this is not the optimal outcome that could be achieved, and the goal should be to maintain the unity of the family and the attachments within it, as supported by a good standard of longitudinal integrated dual diagnosis care delivered to the family and the parents in particular. The long-term clinical, behavioral, and brain consequences of governmental actions to break up families and disrupt or destroy parental–children attachments (either through criminal incarceration of the parent, or CPS-enforced separation) can be far reaching, and ultimately, worsen mental illness and addiction diseases, in real time, or trans-generationally. More immediately, CPS interventions to separate parents from children may not only exacerbate current levels of affective and trauma-spectrum disorders in the parents and children (as a traumatizing stimulus), but they can also actually provoke worsening of addiction and relapsing activity. The instinct to protect one's children from *outside* threats is an ancient, deeply rooted, mammalian behavior that is usually fairly intact even in mothers with mental illness and addiction. So, the forced separation from children by a government agency is rarely welcomed and can be accompanied by anguish and hostility on the part of the parent. On top of this, the separation can produce new onset homelessness and loss of health insurance for the parent that further jeopardizes clinical stability and access to dual diagnosis services. These latter adverse consequences can occur as a result of social policies that require that the mentally ill/addicted parent has to be living with and acting as the guardian of the child in order to have social support income and/or to have public health insurance. Sometimes in a decision to keep the child at home with another relative, the mentally ill/addicted patient has no choice but to become homeless.

The second major problem for CPS across many jurisdictions is that they are seriously understaffed and underfunded agencies. This can happen even to the point where they are operating below government-set guidelines for staffing, where they cannot field the number of case workers they need (or are mandated to have) for the number of cases they are investigating. High staff turnover and burnout rates are partially to blame for this as well as deficient budgeting. Oversizing of CPS caseloads per case worker is also exacerbated by the lack of adequate behavioral health and dual diagnosis treatment services that exist in most parts of the country, which would otherwise help reduce the number of CPS cases arising in the first place. In any event, oversized caseloads and other resource shortages that CPS systems must often work with, likely have detrimental effects on the ability of CPS to nuance and individualize their approaches to specific cases and families, and their ability to provide constructive support (e.g., services that keep families together), instead of resorting to more destructive interventions (e.g., splitting families apart). Oversized caseloads and other resource shortages can result in CPS performance problems that are observable by behavioral health professionals (and sometimes the public at large via media stories), as a persistent inability to deploy measured levels of attention or interventions, according to differential degrees of risk. Thus, the same CPS agency may be observed to be performing too heavy-handedly in some cases, where the risk to the child is not that great, except for there being an unmet need for adequate mental health and addiction services. Other times, the same agency can seem unfocused and negligent in providing appropriate interventions, for example, when children are harmed or killed during open CPS cases due to inadequate protections, or, when children are removed from their parents to even more dangerous contexts.

The 2 × 4 Model clinic should expect to take on a number of patients who are parents with open CPS cases. The goal of the clinic should be to operate independently from CPS while maintaining appropriate communication with CPS, to provide mental health and addiction care to these patients as a means to restore and optimize their parental functions. This work should involve 2 × 4 Model team efforts to help patients keep their families united, and to improve and maintain healthy parent–child attachments and child rearing skills, leading to the successful closure of CPS cases. As with the Criminal Justice System, this work should involve careful and selective communication with CPS, done in a way that protects the standards of patient care, the mission of dual diagnosis recovery, and the independence of the 2 × 4 Model clinic in terms of treatment decision-making and nurturing the confidential therapeutic bond with patients. Of course, any and all information that CPS has about a given patient should be welcomed by the clinic, but, not all the information a clinic has about at patient should be disclosed to CPS. This is especially true when disclosure of detailed clinical information could be used needlessly or adversely, by CPS or the court (who are generally not trained to interpret that clinic information), to impair treatment or the opportunities for recovery.

For most cases, the 2 × 4 Model team would work with and on behalf of patients, to advocate for more treatment and services to keep the parents healthy and the family intact. In more rare instances, when there is more uncertainty in the minds of the patients and/or the clinical team about the desire or capability of the patient to be able to function as a parent, convergence to a solution of a co-parenting network or adoption may be sought. Either way, the goal of the 2 × 4 Model team is to support the mental health and addiction recovery of the patient, which ultimately, when done independently, will also benefit the mission and effectiveness of CPS. As with the Criminal Justice System, communications with CPS can be done in letters to CPS workers or the court, but may involve more in-person communication as a more impactful approach. CPS team meetings involving the patient, 2 × 4 Model professionals including the addiction psychiatrist can be immensely productive in getting all parties on the same page in terms of pursuing or maintaining parental–child unification and case closure. Team members and the addiction psychiatrist should also be prepared, under the right circumstances, when bolder action is needed and warranted to save a family, to attend court and testify on behalf of a patient. Exemplar letter C from the 2 × 4 Model program to CPS illustrates an often appropriate level of disclosure and advocacy. **See Box 8.4.**

BOX 8.4 Exemplar Letter C: From the 2 × 4 Model Clinic to CPS and Court

Dear Department of Child Services Official and Your Honor,
XX/XX/2014

We have received a recent request from your office for clinical information regarding Ms. ABC (DOB: XX/XX/XXXX). Ms. ABC has given us written permission to respond to that request. Ms. ABC has been in my care at the XXXX- 2 × 4 Model clinic since 3/3/2013. Over this past year and a half she has shown very strong clinical improvement with respect to both her mental illness and addictive disorders and has maintained an overall excellent level of treatment engagement with both medications and psychotherapies. While her treatment course has, as with many patients, been punctuated with rare, minor relapses and brief phases of worsening psychiatric symptoms, she has overall been improving and is from our perspective able to function well interpersonally and as a mother. She continues to engage in treatment with us and has expressed awareness and motivation to continue in treatment indefinitely as required for her chronic mental health conditions, after her CPS case is closed. Given her recovery, we hope the court will move to increase her contact with her children beyond supervised visits of 2 hours a week to full reunification as expediently as possible.

Thank you,

Aaa Bbbb MD

Aaa Bbbb, M.D.
Associate Professor of Psychiatry
Addiction Psychiatrist,
XXX 2 × 4 Model Clinic
XXX Street, Indianapolis, IN 46208
PH: XXX-XXX-XXXX

Communications with the General Health Care System

The Context

As mass incarceration and other criminal justice measures against mental illness and addictive disorders have grown in scope, the sector of health care that should be responsible for properly diagnosing and treating these conditions as informed by science (i.e., behavioral health), has been steadily degrading in terms of declines in professional workforce availability and training, physical infrastructure, and ability (or willingness) of health insurance to adequately cover treatments for behavioral health conditions. At the same time general (nonbehavioral) health care has become increasingly and unsustainably expensive, even as longevity and other public health measures of health care efficacy and quality are stagnant, or are in decline, particularly in the U.S. Two quite similar vicious cycles have likely contributed to this trend, one happening at the interface of criminal justice and behavioral health (as previously described), and the other, at the interface of behavior health and general health care (**Figure 8.2**). As described already, one of these vicious cycles may be outlined as follows: The misappropriation of addictionology to the Criminal Justice System produces the apparent need for incarcerating more and more addicted and mentally ill people. Then perhaps ironically, as this criminalization trend has no real benefit to curb addiction or mental illness, the trend has been to double down on this strategy (e.g., "if our current levels of punishment of addiction aren't working, then we must need more punishment"). Increasing emphasis on the criminalization approach then, has two major consequences on behavioral health and addiction treatment: 1) it increasingly deprives behavioral health of public resources (e.g., needed to build and maintain psychiatric facilities, professional training, and adequate insurance reimbursement); and 2) it causes addiction to be increasingly identified with criminal behavior, as something alien to mental health and general health care where, in a better world, addictionology should actually belong.

This context sets the stage for a second vicious cycle happening at the interface of behavioral health and general health care. As addiction treatment is not adequately valued, financed, or included within the domain of behavioral health care, and by extension, the general health care system, addictions go on underdiagnosed and untreated, producing all manner of psychiatric and medical consequences that are extremely challenging and expensive to treat. Adding to this dynamic, the general health care system has unfortunately (and mostly inadvertently) trended toward aligning its most lucrative interventions and business approaches toward the strategy of ignoring addiction while focusing on medical conditions and organ injuries that result from untreated addictions. To a substantial degree this has corresponded to a misalignment between the financial motives and approaches of the general health care system and the actual goal of keeping people healthy. Thus, to a very real extent (e.g., in the fee for service model) the health care system has fallen into a trap where it is not only *not* financially incentivized to treat addiction and other behavioral health conditions, but where it actually makes a lot more money by not treating these conditions. Hence, as general medical care becomes increasingly expensive (even as it is less effective in keeping more people healthy), it is being financially reinforced for having inadequate professional resources, treatment infrastructure, and expertise needed to treat addictions and related behavioral health problems.

At the heart of both of these somewhat causally inter-related vicious cycles, is the failure of our behavioral health care system to adequately integrate mental health and addiction treatment services and expertise, which is a problem that the 2 × 4 Model design aims to remedy. As behavioral health has degraded into increasingly disconnected fragments—inpatient rehabs, short-term psychiatric hospitals, therapists on one side of town and psychiatrists or primary care doctors on another, methadone clinics here, and 12-step groups there—how can any of these treatment systems take comprehensive, decisive, longitudinal responsibility for their patients? How can these disconnected fragments effectively speak with one convincing voice to the Criminal Justice System or the rest of the health care system, to advocate and make room for the best standards of integrated mental health and addiction care for their patients? With full integration of mental health and addiction expertise and services happening in the 2 × 4 Model, the clinical efficacy, responsibility, and communicative power of the treatment team is amplified and concentrated.

Agenda of the 2 × 4 Model Program in Relation to the General Medical System

As much as hope for positive change can emerge from the ashes of tragedy, the modern iatrogenic prescription drug epidemic in the U.S. is a public health catastrophe that should motivate real action needed for greatly expanding, rebuilding, and integrating addiction and mental health services and expertise. Over a 25 year period dating back to the early 1990s, the U.S. experienced geometric increases in the prescription of addictive drugs, most detrimentally, opioids, happening in a void of expertise or knowledge about the risks, pathophysiology, diagnosis, or treatment of drug addiction. This epidemic was created in part by conditions that gave major financial benefits to large health care companies that promoted high-throughput patient care (e.g., 'the 8 minute med check'), patients as consumer movements, and powerful pharmaceutical marketing to health care providers and the public. In the space of increasingly inadequate mental health services and expertise, chronic pain complaints that often accompany unrecognized or untreated mental illness was held up as a widely prevalent symptom and *vital sign*, that deserved and required aggressive, long-term opioid treatment. By 2010 in the U.S., there were enough opioids being prescribed by U.S. physicians to supply the entire adult American population with a month's supply of multiple daily doses of opioids, producing a prescription drug overdose death toll that had surpassed rates of homicides, suicides, car accidents, and all illicit/non-pharmaceutical drug overdoses. This epidemic even reached proportions to where it actually caused decreases in the life span of white Americans for the first time, and to where, in many regions of the country for many patients, contact with the health care system itself had become a major risk factor for acquiring a serious addiction. And, as many studies have confirmed since the mid-2000s, the victims of this epidemic were not randomly or evenly distributed across the general population. It was the mentally ill who were the most vulnerable to acquiring iatrogenic opioid addictions, just as they are most biologically vulnerable to other major addictions involving nicotine, alcohol, cocaine, methamphetamine, and other reinforcing drugs. Emerging in the later stages of the 'war on drugs', and 'deinstitutionalization', and concurrent with an increasingly broken and deficient behavioral health system, the iatrogenic opioid epidemic has actually further contributed to the criminalization and morbidity of mentally ill and addicted people. After becoming iatrogenically addicted, these patients face cycles of arrests, incarcerations, and probation, without access in most parts of the country, and especially in rural America, to adequate standards or expertise in integrated mental health and addiction care.

Toward reversing these trends, the 2 × 4 Model seeks to promote its mission and position as a vital part of the health care system, by working with other professionals and agencies to prevent and reduce iatrogenic addictions. This involves assisting nonbehavioral health trained physicians in their efforts to best care for patients with mental illness and addictions, for example, by helping them avoid over-prescribing addictive drugs. Further, this work involves, advocacy and promotion of adequate insurance coverage for the treatment of patients with mental illness and addictions on par to what is afforded to other medical conditions (i.e., *parity*). Accordingly, there are three main categories of communications that must occur between the 2 × 4 Model clinical team and the rest of the health care system: 1) pharmacological interdiction; 2) Consultative–liaison addiction psychiatry; and 3) interactions with health insurance companies.

Pharmacological Interdiction

Unfortunately, it is not uncommon that patients presenting for addiction treatment will have had substantial proportions of their addictive illnesses initiated, propagated, or worsened by contacts with health care professionals who have prescribed them controlled substances. The 2 × 4 Model clinic labels this phenomena as 'iatrogenic prescribing'. The iatrogenic prescription opioid epidemic is a large-scale and particularly devastating consequence (in terms of total public health impact) of this problem. As discussed in Chapter 7, the overprescription of OPs, BZDs and SITMs have all be been part of this problem, although OPs and OPs + BZDs combinations by far produce the largest overall morbidity and mortality.

The pervasiveness of iatrogenic prescribing, and its potential to keep patients with addictions and dual diagnosis disorders stuck in their illnesses is substantial. In some cases, there is no chance for recovery or real benefit for patients in attending psychotherapies in the 2 × 4 Model clinic, if iatrogenic patterns of prescribing persist after the patient enters treatment. For many patients who enter treatment and begin to make clinical progress, ongoing exposure to iatrogenic prescribing (from outside health care providers) is a continuous risk that can produce various degrees of relapse and clinical decompensation. In either case, it is absolutely the responsibility of the 2 × 4 Model team (and especially the addiction psychiatrists, because of their clout as physicians and addiction specialists) to directly intervene via communications with outside prescribers to stop and/or prevent iatrogenic prescribing.

In general, there are two main categories of prescribers that 2 × 4 Model physicians will encounter as contributing to iatrogenic prescribing: The malignant vs. the well-intentioned. The malignant category is composed of prescribers who run businesses that essentially sell controlled prescriptions (or the drugs themselves) outside the scope of legitimate practice, while operating under the guise and cover of legitimate medical practice. These operations are often variously described as 'pill mills' or 'legal' drug dealerships or 'quack' clinics. Often claiming to provide pain treatment services, primary care, or even addiction treatment, these operations are characterized by having not just one but several of the following attributes: Take cash only ('out of pocket') payments for all clinical services (even for patients who have insurance and have their meds paid for by insurance); follow high-throughput models of patient flow where patients are seen in herds; contact with appropriately trained professionals (e.g., physicians) or clinical evaluations are inappropriately brief or exceedingly rare; clinical charting and/or clinical practice that is relatively devoid of appropriate diagnostic assessment, individualized treatment planning, or medical decision-making; medical charting that is filled with contracts, forms, and rating scales filled out by patients (delegating the responsibility of medical charting and evaluation to the patients themselves); prescribing of high volumes and/or complex combinations of controlled substances to large numbers of patients while inappropriately minimizing other modalities of treatment (that don't involve controlled substances and require more time and professional expertise); lack of attention to medical or psychiatric symptoms that contraindicate the prescription of controlled substances.

For patients presenting with histories of recent or current contact with malignant iatrogenic prescribers, it is important for the 2 × 4 Model physician to educate the patient about the harm that these practices produce, and the need to cease contact with those practices moving forward. In addition, the addiction psychiatrist should consider making a direct contact to the malignant operation to ensure that the patient is no longer enrolled in that program and to communicate the professional opinion that the patient is not best served in that program. In some rare instances, enough evidence about the malignant program may be accumulated as reported by multiple patients and the particularly egregious or clinically harmful nature of the program (and as confirmed by prescription drug monitoring data) that consideration should be made to report that program or physician to the licensing board or DEA.

The well-intentioned category of iatrogenic prescribing is a much more common and routine type of adverse controlled substance prescribing. This type of prescribing happens as a result of quite genuine efforts to help patients. These practitioners may be relatively well trained in their specialties (e.g., in family medicine, internal medicine, emergency room medicine, surgery, dentistry, and advanced nursing) albeit they usually have little to no training in behavioral health care, psychopharmacology, and addictionology. Unlike malignant iatrogenic prescribers, they do not necessarily sell/prescribe a high volume of controlled substances to the majority of their patients as a key part of their practices or business models. Essentially, their contribution to iatrogenic prescribing might be attributable to a number of contextual problems that pervade the culture of modern medicine. These include widespread deficiencies of addiction training and awareness among physicians; a lack of time allowed to get to know patients; lack of continuity of care; and the over-marketing and raising of consumer expectations that promote aggressive prescribing of opioids for pain (and other addictive drugs for other indications).

When well-intentioned iatrogenic prescribing is encountered, as suggested by evidence that it is contributing to the addiction of the patient, or is harming their recovery (e.g., it is relapsing them), it is of course important for the 2 × 4 Model psychiatrist to directly communicate with the outside prescriber(s) in a collegial and tactful way. This communication should inform them about a) the patient's mental illness-based addiction vulnerability and their addiction(s); b) the necessity to cease and avoid future controlled substance prescribing (except under specific circumstances as agreed upon); and c) the general strategy the 2 × 4 Model team will use to foster the patient's recovery moving forward. The tone of these communications should be collaborative and educational to encourage continued constructive partnership between the 2 × 4 Model clinic and the outside physician in the comprehensive, coordinated care of the patient. Also, these communications should aim to help the outside physician avoid enacting similar iatrogenic prescribing patterns for other patients. Generally, these communications are done on the phone, as this helps the 2 × 4 Model physician know for sure that the communication was received by the outside prescriber. Also, the verbal conversation helps prevent misunderstandings of content or attitude (that could happen in a written email or letter) while allowing for a more two-way exchange of information. It can be helpful in these exchanges for the psychiatrist to encourage the outside prescriber to more routinely query the PDMP database on their patients, and to generally avoid situations where the patent is on more than one controlled substance drug class at a time. Again, because the 2 × 4 Model clinic aims to take care of patients comprehensively in terms of the psychopharmacology of both mental illness and addictions (while also avoiding the potential risks of split care), these communications should also be used to ask outside physicians to avoid prescribing psychoactive agents (e.g., to please leave this up to the 2 × 4 Model clinic prescriber).

In general, it is important for the 2 × 4 Model team to get written permission from the patient to make communications to outside physicians for pharmacological interdictions. This not only protects the patient in terms of confidentiality, but it recruits the decision-making of the patient (and thus their investment) in their own care. Notably, however, because certain iatrogenic prescribing patterns can be quite dangerous, the 2 × 4 Model physician may be justified in making communications to outside prescribers without formal written permission from the patient, as a matter of addressing the risk of a serious medical emergency. But, this override of consent should only rarely be used because it can introduce a breakdown of trust between the patient and the team, and it can rob them of the opportunity for a constructive therapeutic process that happens when planning, negotiation, and education are needed to arrive at a disclosure with the patient's consent. Sometimes patients want to make the disclosure themselves first to the outside physician. In other instances it takes time for the team to convince the patient that the disclosure needs to happen, and, that the 2 × 4 Model clinic is able to handle the aftermath and still offer benefit to the patient. Regardless of the timeline for this process, there are situations where the 2 × 4 Model psychiatrist should aim to secure permission for the disclosure and make the pharmacological interdiction before other therapeutic actions should be initiated. Patients who absolutely refuse to allow physician-to-physician disclosures and communications are conveying either that they cannot trust the expertise of the 2 × 4 Model physician, and/or that they are protecting an interest in maintaining the outside prescriber as a source of addictive drugs. In either case, these are potentially important prognostic indicators that the subsequent therapeutic efforts of the physician may not work. A reduction of these concerns through a successful process of consent, disclosure, and interdiction may be a justifiable prerequisite for any other therapeutic action (e.g., medication prescription) that the psychiatrist in the 2 × 4 Model may make. Exemplar letter D provides an example of a pharmacological interdiction communication from the 2 × 4 Model physician (see **Box 8.5**).

Consultative–Liaison Addiction Psychiatry

Given that addictions cause so many forms of injury and secondary diseases in multiple body organs, patients with addiction and dual diagnosis conditions tend to have greater need for medical care than people in the general population. Many patients with addictions and dual diagnosis actually show evidence for their brain illnesses first with an encounter with non-behavioral health care services (e.g., in the emergency room), with an injury or medical condition that was caused by an undiagnosed and untreated addiction that had been present for some time. Conversely, many patients engaged in dual diagnosis care may have addiction-related medical problems (e.g., hepatitis C) first diagnosed in the behavioral health setting. In either of these scenarios, it is crucial that the 2 × 4 Model and its physicians are communicative and collaborative with nonbehavioral health medical and surgical professionals and services.

BOX 8.5 Exemplar Letter D: From the 2 × 4 Model Physician to Interdict Iatrogenic Prescribing of Controlled Substances

Dear Drs. DDD and YYY, XX//XX/2013

Yesterday (XX/XX/2013) a patient of mine, who I see at our dual diagnosis clinic, Mr. JKL (DOB: XX/XX/XXX), presented to your ER, for evaluation after suffering a bruise to his back. I am writing to provide feedback and express concern about his disposition, specifically regarding the prescription of opioid medications to him as a result of this ER encounter.

Please be aware that Mr. JKL carries a diagnosis of schizoaffective disorder and has suffered with multiple addictions for many years involving opioids, alcohol, marijuana, nicotine, and benzodiazepines. His addictions, in the setting of his severe mental illness, have caused him significant harm resulting in repeated loss of housing, lack of disability support, requiring psychiatric hospitalizations, and recently, a suicide attempt involving prescription opioids.

I was concerned to learn from Mr. JKL that after evaluation for a bruise that did not involve any serious structural injury (breakage of skin, bones) he was prescribed 24 hydrocodone tablets out the door from the ER to take as needed, in addition to the recommended ibuprofen and cold packs. In general, the prescribing of multiple doses of opioids to take 'PRN', (e.g., on any schedule, and on an outpatient basis) without ongoing medical supervision or plan to manage the consequences of opioid prescribing, carries substantial risk, especially for persons already suffering from mental illness and addiction. In light of the fact that the ER context does not often afford the time or luxury to investigate the full psychiatric and addiction history of most patients, a useful rule of thumb is that in the absence of a significant structural injury, pain deemed not severe enough to require a standing (non-PRN) regimen of opioids, and not requiring ongoing medical supervision for care (e.g., admission), is not a level of pain that often warrants opioid prescriptions to fill after discharge from the ER.

Thank you for considering this feedback; my aim is to be as constructive as possible for the future care of this patient should he re-present to your ER, and to enact my consultative and educational duties in the prevention of iatrogenic addictions and its associated morbidity and mortalities.

Sincerely,

Aaa Bbbb, M.D.
Associate Professor of Psychiatry
Addiction Psychiatrist,
XXX 2 × 4 Model Clinic
XXX Street, Indianapolis, IN 46208
PH: XXX-XXX-XXXX

The integrated care movement and medical home models have enjoyed increasing popularity and attempts toward implementation by large health care systems. The worthy goals of these trends are to a) provide better comprehensive care to patients; b) to increase efficiency and reduce redundancies of services or testing that often happens in disconnected medical services; c) to reduce iatrogenic illness and injury to patients that can happen in the delivery of uncoordinated medical care. Of course, many barriers exist to realizing these integrative models, including the challenges of merging different treatment cultures (and professionals who are trained in different ways), and the geographical separation of physical infrastructures of different treatment lines (e.g., a primary care clinic, a dialysis center, and a community mental health center in a given community may be separated by miles). And then there is the arcane, arbitrary, and extremely complex reimbursement rules and mechanisms that differ between different domains of health care, that tend to favor the delivery of procedures and tests, instead of interactions between health care professionals and patients.

Two of the most immediately viable approaches toward integration include the establishment of better virtual and physical linkages, that is, the development of advanced communication platforms between doctors in different specialties, and the construction of clinics that put doctors and teams of different specialties in close proximity. Advanced EMR systems, doctor to doctor hotlines, and real time audio–visual 'telemedicine' technologies are all increasing the capabilities of doctors to consult with one another and to be aware of what each of them are doing and thinking about a given patient. Outpatient clinics that include behavioral health and primary care services side by side (in same building, on same floor) are becoming more frequent.

A pitfall in moving toward better integration, is the tendency to conflate the goals of integration with the need to resolve heath care shortages in primary care and behavioral health. This comes up when the idea of integration goes so far as to encourage doctors who are not trained or really interested in treating mental illness and addictions to take on responsibility for treating these conditions. The same can also happen for psychiatrists who, because of shortages of access to primary care for many behavioral health patients, feel compelled to step beyond their expertise in conducting internal medicine. Clearly, the adoption of clinical practices by physicians who are not really trained to perform those practices is not the aim of integration, and for integration of primary care and behavioral health services to work well, the approach still needs a critical mass of experts in *both fields*.

As discussed in Chapter 9, the 2 × 4 Model concept leverages (and seeks to enlarge) the already well-established cross-training pathway of addiction psychiatry, in which physicians are comprehensively trained and certified in the diagnosis and treatment of both mental illness and addictive disorders. Moreover, the neurobiological, phenomenological, and epidemiological connectedness of mental illness and addictions (Chapter 2) and their treatments, makes psychiatry (and mental health care as a whole) the most logical, natural home for addiction expertise and care. The 2 × 4 Model thus advocates for and achieves the integration of mental health and addiction services, so that once these two clinical domains are bound (i.e., via vertical binding in the 2 × 4 Model), the treatment team becomes a cohesive unit that can then be integrated with other primary care services via close communications and/or physical proximity. This approach is different from strategies to integrate behavioral health into primary care that promote the dismembering of behavioral health services and expertise, and their dispersion throughout primary care. The 2 × 4 Model suggests that we do not want to disintegrate the components of behavioral health (e.g., into siloed mental health vs. addiction services), in order to achieve an integration of these parts of behavioral health into primary care. This approach would merely maintain the way our current behavioral health system is broken (because it is so fragmented along mental health vs. addiction treatment services (**Figure 8.2**)), in which the integration of a broken behavioral health system into primary care, may have little benefit for improving behavioral health. By analogy, putting a broken engine into an otherwise new car cannot be expected to fix the broken engine, or make the new car better. Thus, the 2 × 4 Model views the integration of mental health and addiction expertise and services as a first priority and step, that should be followed by secondary steps to link and integrate the intact 2 × 4 Model team as a module into the rest of health care. Certainly, 2 × 4 Model physicians and team members can and should be engaged in consultation–liaison activities outside the walls of the 2 × 4 Model clinic (e.g., in hospitals, primary care clinics, ERs, etc.) to assist in the management of addicted/dual diagnosis patients in those arenas, and to facilitate the referral of new patients to the 2 × 4 Model clinic. But these activities should be just a portion of the work of 2 × 4 Model team members, who should also have substantial allocations of their time devoted to work within their home base of the 2 × 4 Model clinic.

Interactions with Health Insurance Companies

Lack of appropriate health insurance coverage for behavioral health treatments and expertise (e.g., lack of parity) persists as a pervasive and serious health care problem, driven by many forces including stigma, lack of understanding and acceptance of disease models for mental illness and addictions, and the relative lack of financial resources and political power of many behavioral health patients. This lack of parity perpetuates widespread deficits in access to addiction and dual diagnosis services by contributing to shortfalls in dual diagnosis treatment workforce and infrastructure. It also creates the false impression in the minds of the public that behavioral health is too expensive (because the cost of care is disproportionately pushed onto patients and families), when in fact, the failure to appropriately reimburse addiction and psychiatric services makes the rest of health care far more expensive and ineffective (**Figure 8.2**). But beyond these 'big picture' considerations, the most direct and pressing problems that result from lack of parity as routinely encountered in the 2 × 4 Model clinic, are the numerous methods insurance companies use to prevent or deny support for addiction psychiatry services and treatments.

In combating this problem, the 2 × 4 Model clinic should emphasize in its work with patients and the public that it strives to accept reimbursement via health insurance, and indeed, that it will work to protect the right of patients to have their care reimbursed appropriately by insurance as consistent with the scientific evidence base and on par with the treatment of other major medical conditions. Accordingly, there are times when the 2 × 4 Model physicians or other team members must devote time to conducting communications directly with insurance companies and stakeholders of insurance companies (e.g., the government or the public at large) to fight for appropriate and adequate health insurance reimbursement for treatment. Unfortunately, insurance companies that are blocking care (via 'prior authorization' or outright denials) are also not going to reimburse professional time needed to communicate with them to argue against or overcome the blockage of care. Nevertheless, it is a fight that must be fought if integrated dual diagnosis care is going to be understood and accepted as being an important part of the house of medicine, which health insurance is required to support. Multiple team members (case workers/ therapists/nurses) can participate in these communications, especially those that involve helping patients establish or maintain health insurance. However, physicians provide the most clout in situations where there is conflict with insurance companies. Being active in making phone calls and writing letters to insurance company representatives, and keeping notes on these communi- cations (and the time they take), can help build the case for treatment for individual patients, while also documenting the way the company is potentially harming behavioral health and even violating federal parity laws. Exemplar letter E pertains to a patient that was being denied appropriate medication treatment by a private insurance company contracted by federal Medicare to manage pharmacy benefits. The letter was effective in ending the insurance blockade of coverage for care (see **Box 8.6**).

Communications with Housing/Income Agencies and Employers

Poverty and homelessness have devastating effects on patients and families with mental illness and addiction, with growing evidence showing that these contexts may not only keep patients treatment refractory but contribute to brain pathologies that generate dual diagnosis conditions. The chaos, uncertainty, and break downs in attachments and social networks, and the multiple forms of health and educational depravities that poor families are exposed to are not good for the brain. It is therefore the responsibility of the 2 × 4 Model team and psychiatrists to understand the scope and status of socioeconomic challenges and deprivations patients are living with. Patients who cannot adequately provide for their own food, clothing, and shelter, and who do not have assistance with achieving these provisions, cannot be expected to respond reliably to

BOX 8.6 Exemplar Letter E: From the 2 × 4 Model Clinic to Health Insurance Companies Failing to Support Treatment

Dear Insurance Company XXX Representative, XX/XX/2013

This communication regards Ms. XXXX XXXXXX (DOB: XX/XX/1970; Member Number: B5555555)) who I have been treating since XX/XX/2013 for her complex addictions and neuropsychiatric disorders. In our clinic she is receiving comprehensive outpatient services encompassing individual and group psychotherapy and medication for her mental health and addictive diseases. Pertaining to the *appeal documentation request that your company is requiring me to justify my care for this patient*, Ms. XXXXXX suffers with *opiate dependence* that has unfortunately been contributed to by the prescription of various addictive drugs including opioids which your company has actually paid for as a subcontractor of Medicare. This activity is well documented by us as shown by prescription drug monitoring data, and in telephone interviews I have conducted with several of Ms. XXXXXX physicians. In this context, after having made the correct diagnosis of opioid dependence, and having ended the inappropriate prescribing of opioids that your company has been paying for, I have now initiated buprenorphine/naloxone therapy. *Buprenorphine is an evidence-based, FDA approved treatment for the diagnosis of opioid dependence. I, the prescriber of this medication, am a fellowship trained and board certified (ABMS/ABPN) addiction psychiatrist, with DEA privileges to prescribe this medication for this indication. It is the standard of care and of medical necessity to prescribe this medication for this patient.*

Thus far, your company has denied support for the reimbursement of this medication for this patient. This denial may not only be in frank violation of Federal Parity Laws (Mental Health Parity and Addiction Equity Act (MHPAEA; 2010)) but in this specific case, is a denial of indicated coverage that seriously jeopardizes this patient's health. Further, the time I am taking to convince your company to support the appropriate treatment of this patient, is distracting me from taking care of more patients in need while causing financial injury to my healthcare organization, because this time expended is not reimbursable. I encourage your team to move forward as soon as possible to provide coverage for this patient's medication, and to remove any further barriers that your company may impose at a later date that will prevent, delay, or unnecessarily complicate this patient's care under my direction, or others who are expertly trained and certified to do so.

Sincerely,

Aaa Bbbb

Aaa Bbbb, M.D.
Associate Professor of Psychiatry
Addiction Psychiatrist,
XXX 2 × 4 Model Clinic
XXX Street, Indianapolis, IN 46208
PH: XXX-XXX-XXXX

medications or psychotherapies that the clinic provides. Therefore, the need for satisfying these basics has as much priority as delivering evidence-based treatments. To help patients acquire these basics, 2 × 4 Model team members should be aware of the range of housing options for patients in recovery in the community; to be in communication with them to understand what they offer; to understand what their requirements are; and, to help patients stay in these units when they are symptomatic.

Connectivity and communications with food pantries, and programs that provide low cost child care, food assistance, or transportation options are important. Vouchers for public transportation provided to patients within the 2 × 4 Model clinic can be provided on an as needed basis or in a contingency management like format to facilitate treatment compliance. Communications and advocacy with assisted employment services, and directly, with certain employers can help patients find and keep jobs.

One of the more common and important duties of the 2 × 4 Model psychiatrist in terms of aiding in the financial support of patients and families is the filling out of paperwork in support of disability claims. Some amount of public income can be a game changer for many patients, allowing them to afford medication or treatment service co-pays, food, and housing.

Further, this assistance can help many patients stop occupations, or escape housing situations that put them in danger and represent illness reinforcing contexts, such as prostitution or living with an abusive partner. In filling out disability income forms it is imperative that the psychiatrist (or other team members) be diagnostically accurate and realistic in expressing opinions on the functional status and employability of patients. However, stronger arguments can rightfully be made in these reports for certain patients who are in very desperate need, and who would seem to benefit greatly from a recovery stand-point in receiving this support. Also, the psychiatrist should be aware that the reporting of substance use diagnoses must be done cautiously as this can adversely hinder the success of the application. In the eyes of the judge or other government reviewers, these diagnoses often carry major stigma of the patient being criminalistic, wasteful, and undeserving of the support. Of course, the psychiatrist should be reflective of the extent to which the disability support has the potential of being misused to support pathological behaviors or addictions (e.g., to support purchases of tobacco, alcohol, lottery tickets, hard drugs, etc.) for a given patient, with consideration as to whether or not the patient needs a money manager ('payee'). But, with these thoughts in mind, it is important for the clinician to give the patient the benefit of the doubt in considering their realistic options for employability, to keep in mind that disability support levels are often too minimal to live on for many patients, and that they do not necessarily preclude the option for patients to work on the side. It is also useful to remember that disability income levels are often less expensive for the government to afford per patient than it costs to incarcerate them.

Communications with Family and Cohabitants

While remaining sensitive to appropriate confidentiality protections, communications with family members and cohabitants of the patient via face to face encounters or phone can provide crucial collateral information not only about the clinical status and functioning of the patient, but the degree to which the patient's dual diagnosis illness is being contributed to by the people they live with. Abusive behavior, enabling, and untreated substance use disorders and/or drug dealing involving other family members and cohabitants can seriously impair chances for recovery, requiring consideration of strategies between the team and the patient about how they can escape these circumstances. More hopefully, these circumstances can also lead the patient to successfully encourage their attachments and cohabitants to get into treatment as well, which can result in significant stabilization of the whole group.

Fortunately in many cases, family members and cohabitants can be sources of support and strength in recovery, and communications with these people can facilitate strategies for recovery in the home setting. A series of formal family therapy sessions can serve many purposes for building trust with the patient's family and peer group, stabilizing relationships and providing education about the disease processes of addiction and mental illness to help families be better allies in the recovery process.

Vertical and Horizontal Binding and Modalities of Communications

As previously mentioned, communications from the 2 × 4 Model clinic to outside agencies or individuals will carry the potential to be more informative, persuasive, and effective in protecting and promoting the recovery of patients, than what segregated mental health and addiction services can provide, as allowed by the vertical binding in the 2 × 4 Model design. Because the 2 × 4 Model clinic embraces its ownership for the care of both mental illness and addictive disorders, it has the highest capacity to understand and convey how these illnesses are intertwined for a given patient, how treatment for both categories of these disorders should take place, and what may be expected in the course of recovery. In contrast, mental health services without addiction treatment are hindered by a major blind spot: Lack of awareness, attention, or strategy for treating addiction that many of their patients will also have. Similarly, the addiction-only treatment service can only speak to the addiction illness component, while operating in relative darkness about their patient's mental illnesses. Thus, as segregated services will have created for themselves a relatively incomplete picture of what is happening with many of their patients, communications emanating from these services will likewise be relatively incomplete and therefore less effective. Because the 2 × 4 Model clinic can accurately claim in its communications that it is using a comprehensive range of diagnostics, psychotherapies, and medications for both mental illness and addictions (i.e., creating a horizontal binding of the Therapeutic components with the Communication components in the 2 × 4 Model design), it is also able to communicate a greater sense of expertise, responsibility, and confidence in the recovery of its dual diagnosis patients.

As a final point for this chapter, the 2 × 4 Model clinician making a communication should not only be deliberate and precise in choosing the messaging content, but they should carefully select the optimal modality of the communication. In person, telephone, email, regular mail, or paper letters (that patients carry with them) all have their pros and cons. These different modalities vary in their impacts, time–costs, potential for engendering education, likelihood of creating two-way conversations and collaborations, and degree to which they give the author confidence that the message got through. Experimenting with and practicing different modalities of communications to different audiences is important for the team over time. At any rate, since well performed communications from the 2 × 4 Model are potentially just as important and impactful in the patient's recovery as are diagnostics and therapeutics, any communications made on behalf of a patient should be documented as if it were diagnostic or therapeutic in the medical record. This documentation should briefly detail the audience, goal, and content of the communication.

Background References and Further Reading

Alexander, M., and C. West. 2012. *The New Jim Crow: Mass Incarceration in the Age of Colorblindness.* Revised ed. New York Jackson, TN: New Press Perseus Distribution.

Becker, W. C., D. A. Fiellin, J. O. Merrill, B. Schulman, R. Finkelstein, Y. Olsen, and S. H. Busch. 2008. "Opioid use disorder in the United States: Insurance status and treatment access." *Drug Alcohol Depend* 94 (1–3): 207–213. doi: 10.1016/j.drug alcdep.2007.11.018.

Birnbaum, H. G., A. G. White, M. Schiller, T. Waldman, J. M. Cleveland, and C. L. Roland. 2011. "Societal costs of prescription opioid abuse, dependence, and misuse in the United States." *Pain Medicine* 12 (4): 657–667. doi: 10.1111/j.1526-4637. 2011.01075.x.

Boscarino, J. A., M. Rukstalis, S. N. Hoffman, J. J. Han, P. M. Erlich, G. S. Gerhard, and W. F. Stewart. 2010. "Risk factors for drug dependence among out-patients on opioid therapy in a large US health-care system." *Addiction* 105 (10): 1776–1782. doi: 10.1111/j.1360-0443.2010.03052.x ADD3052 [pii].

Carten, A. J. 1996. "Mothers in recovery: Rebuilding families in the aftermath of addiction." *Social Work* 41 (2): 214–223.

CDC. 2011. "Vital signs: Overdoses of prescription opioid pain relievers United States, 1999–2008." *Morbity and Mortality Weekly Report* 60 (43): 1487–1492.

Davis, L., A. Fulginiti, L. Kriegel, and J. S. Brekke. 2012. "Deinstitutionalization? Where have all the people gone?" *Current Psychiatry Report* 14 (3): 259–269. doi: 10.1007/s11920-012-0271-1.

Draine, J., M. S. Salzer, D. P. Culhane, and T. R. Hadley. 2002. "Role of social disadvantage in crime, joblessness, and homelessness among persons with serious mental illness." *Psychiatric Services* 53 (5): 565–573.

Els, C. 2007. "Addiction is a mental disorder, best managed in a (public) mental health setting—but our system is failing us." *Canadian Journal of Psychiatry 52* (3): 167–169.

Franklin, G. M., and American Academy of Neurology. 2014. "Opioids for chronic noncancer pain: A position paper of the American Academy of Neurology." *Neurology 83* (14): 1277–1284.

Galanter, M. 1993. "Network therapy for addiction: A model for office practice." *American Journal of Psychiatry 150* (1): 28–36. doi: 10.1176/ajp.150.1.28.

Gray, J. P. 2001. *Why Our Drug Laws Have Failed and What We Can Do About It: A Judicial Indictment of the War on Drugs.* Philadelphia, PA: Temple University Press.

Greene, M. S., and R. A. Chambers. 2015. "Pseudo addiction: Fact or fiction? An investigation of the medical literature." *Current Addiction Report 2* (4): 310–317. doi: 10.1007/s40429-015-0074-774 [pii].

Hartwell, S. 2004. "Triple stigma: Persons with mental illness and substance abuse problems in the criminal justice system." *Criminal Justice Policy Review 15* (1): 84–89. doi: 10.1177/0887403403255064.

Jensen, E. L., J. Gerber, and C. Mosher. 2004. "Social consequences of the war on drugs: The legacy of failed policy." *Criminal Justice Policy Review 15* (1): 100–121. doi: 10.1177/0887403403255315.

Johns, C. J. 1992. *Power, Ideology, and the War on Drugs: Nothing Succeeds Like Failure, Praeger Series in Criminology and Crime Control Policy.* New York: Praeger.

Kuehn, B. M. 2014. "Criminal justice becomes front line for mental health care." *The Journal of the American Medical Association 311* (19): 1953–1954.

Lavee, Y., and D. Altus. 2001. "Family relationships as a predictor of post-treatment drug abuse relapse: A follow-up study of drug addicts and their spouses." *Contemporary Family Therapy 23* (4): 513–530.

Lembke, A. 2012. "Why doctors prescribe opioids to known opioid abusers." *The New England Journal of Medicine 367* (17): 1580–1581. doi: 10.1056/NEJMp 1208498.

Lembke, A. 2016. *Drug Dealer, MD: How Doctors Were Duped, Patients Got Hooked, and Why It's So Hard to Stop.* Baltimore, MD: Johns Hopkins University Press.

Link, B. G., E. L. Struening, M. Rahav, J. C. Phelan, and L. Nuttbrock. 1997. "On stigma and its consequences: Evidence from a longitudinal study of men with dual diagnoses of mental illness and substance abuse." *Journal of Health & Social Behavior 38* (2): 177–190.

Mauer, B. J., and B. G. Druss. 2010. "Mind and body reunited: Improving care at the behavioral and primary healthcare interface." *Journal of Behavioral Health Services & Research 37* (4): 529–542.

McNiel, D. E., R. L. Binder, and J. C. Robinson. 2005. "Incarceration associated with homelessness, mental disorder, and co-occurring substance abuse." *Psychiatric Services 56* (7): 840–846.

Moore, L. D., and A. Elkavich. 2008. "Who's using and who's doing time: Incarceration, the war on drugs, and public health." *American Journal of Public Health 98* (5): 782–786. doi: 10.2105/AJPH.2007.126284

Mundt, A. P., W. S. Chow, M. Arduino, H. Barrionuevo, R. Fritsch, N. Girala, A. Minoletti, F. Mitkiewicz, G. Rivera, M. Tavares, and S. Priebe. 2015. "Psychiatric hospital beds and prison populations in South America since 1990: Does the Penrose hypothesis apply?" *The Journal of the American Medical Association Psychiatry 72* (2): 112–118. doi: 10.1001/jamapsychiatry.2014.2433.

Padgett, D. K., V. Stanhope, B. F. Henwood, and A. Stefancic. 2011. "Substance use outcomes among homeless clients with serious mental illness: Comparing housing first with treatment first programs." *Community Mental Health Journal 47* (2): 227–232. doi: 10.1007/s10597-009-9283-7.

Sentincing Project, Bureau of Justice Statistics. 2005. "New incarceration figures: Thirty-three consecutive years of growth." http://sentencingproject.org/Admin/Documents/publications/inc_newfigures.pdf.

Rich, J. D., S. E. Wakeman, and S. L. Dickman. 2011. "Medicine and the epidemic of incarceration in the United States." *The New England Journal of Medicine 364* (22): 2081–2083.

Richardson, L. P., J. E. Russo, W. Katon, C. A. McCarty, A. DeVries, M. J. Edlund, B. C. Martin, and M. Sullivan. 2012. "Mental health disorders and long-term opioid use among adolescents and young adults with chronic pain." *Journal Adolescent Health 50* (6): 553–558. doi: 10.1016/j.jadohealth.2011.11.011 S1054-139X(11)00644-6 [pii].

Simpler, A. H., and J. Langhinrichsen-Rohling. 2005. "Substance use in prison: How much occurs and is it associated with psychopathology." *Addiction Research and Theory 13* (5): 503–511. doi: 10.1080/16066350500151739.

Pew Center on the States. 2009. *One in 31: The Long Reach of American Corrections.* Washington, DC: The Pew Charitable Trusts.

U.S. Department of Health and Human Services (HHS), Office of the Surgeon General. 2016. *Facing Addiction in America: The Surgeon General's Report on Alcohol, Drugs, and Health.* edited by HHS. Washington, DC: HHS.

Vaillant, G. E. 1988. "What can long-term follow-up teach us about relapse and prevention of relapse in addiction?" *British Journal of Addiction 83* (10): 1147–1157.

Wasan, A. D., E. Michna, R. R. Edwards, J. N. Katz, S. S. Nedeljkovic, A. J. Dolman, D. Janfaza, Z. Isaac, and R. N. Jamison. 2015. "Psychiatric comorbidity is associated prospectively with diminished opioid analgesia and increased opioid misuse in patients with chronic low back pain." *Anesthesiology 123* (4): 861–872. doi: 10.1097/ALN.0000000000000768.

Wright, E. R., H. E. Kooreman, M. S. Greene, R. A. Chambers, A. Banerjee, and J. Wilson. 2014. "The iatrogenic epidemic of prescription drug abuse: County-level determinants of opioid availability and abuse." *Drug Alcohol Depend 138*: 209–215. doi: 10.1016/j.drugalcdep.2014.03.002 S0376-8716(14)00777-7 [pii].

9   Professional Team Composition and Physical Infrastructure

The human elements of the 2 × 4 Model clinic are its essential assets. It is the professionalism, formal training, and experience of the multidisciplinary, collaborative 2 × 4 Model team that allows the clinic to provide highly individualized and effective mental health, addiction, and dual diagnosis care. This chapter considers the required and optional professional members of the 2 × 4 Model team, and what some of their key responsibilities should be. In addition, an outline of the space they need to work in, that is, the physical infrastructure this team needs to operate in, is described. The purpose of this Chapter is thus two-fold: 1) to set the stage for Chapter 10 (All Together Now) and; 2) to provide a concrete list of 'raw materials' needed for a given health care system or psychiatry department to build a 2 × 4 Model program.

2 × 4 Model Team Composition

A fully operational 2 × 4 Model clinic must be staffed with the following professionals:

1. Addiction psychiatrist(s)
2. Nurses
3. Psychotherapists
4. Logistical specialists (administrative and support staff).

This core group of professionals, which forms a three legged stool that 'holds-up' the 2 × 4 Model clinic (**Figure 9.1**), may be augmented by other specialists including data managers, billing and insurance advisors, and attorneys. The following sections will describe these team members and their roles in more detail.

Addiction Psychiatrists and Other Physicians

The 2 × 4 Model program does not exist without the professional contributions and leadership of one or more addiction psychiatrists. These professionals are the only types of physicians that are formally trained (in psychiatric residency and fellowships accredited by the American College of Graduate Medical Education (ACGME)) and board certified (by the ABMS) in the diagnosis and treatment of both MI and SUDs. As such, they are the only type of professional that exists in health care that is fully trained and certified not only in both components of the Illness Dimension of the 2 × 4 Model, but also in all four components of the Treatment Dimension, spanning Diagnostics, Psychotherapeutics, Medications, and Communications. In this way, the addiction psychiatrist represents, on the individual professional level, the full integration of mental health and addiction expertise. This integration of expertise in the key physician leader and top clinical decision maker of the 2 × 4 Model program, is crucial for maintaining the clinic's operations and cultural orientation as a fully integrated dual diagnosis program. Further, the addiction psychiatrist role models and provides educational and supervisory support for other team members to promote the attitudes, values, and approaches that cross-trained behavioral health professionals need to be equipped with in their roles, to provide excellent, fully integrated dual diagnosis services. To a very real extent the addiction psychiatrist, more than any other professional on the team, can and should be able to perform any of the other team members role's at a highly competent level—and so could function, at least theoretically, as a 'one man band' of integrated dual diagnosis care, like a walking 2 × 4 Model clinic. Not that this should happen of course, because integrated dual diagnosis care is necessarily a 'team sport': an individual physician taking on a dual diagnosis population solo would soon lose their grip on their personal life and burn out, while still only serving too few a number of individuals in need. Moreover, the efficacy, interest, and fun of integrated dual diagnosis care in the 2 × 4 Model program comes from it being a team effort. All the team members provide mutual psychological support, force amplification, and valuable secondary and tertiary opinions and clinical perspectives that are often needed to take care of particularly complex cases. The unique capacity of the addiction psychiatrist to understand and perform virtually all the clinical roles in the 2 × 4 Model program, spanning all of its design components, optimizes their leadership potential for the clinic, and their capacity for designing individualized multi-component treatment plans as executed by a multidisciplinary team. In essence, the addiction psychiatrist is the indispensable 'play caller' of the 2 × 4 Model team.

There are at least three major reasons why having an addiction psychiatrist is a requirement for the 2 × 4 Model clinic. First, the medical community, and the public at large both reasonably expect that any health care system that provides a domain of health care at a high standard, and markets itself as doing so, should be staffed by physicians who are formally trained and certified to perform in the that area of practice. This is true for clinics and hospitals that provide cardiology, neurology, obstetrics, pediatrics, and surgical services, etc., and so it should likewise be true for a service that claims to provide integrated mental health and addiction care. The required presence of an addiction psychiatrist in the 2 × 4 Model clinic guarantees to patients, other physicians, health care stakeholders, and the public at large that the clinic, by definition, is equipped with physician expertise and leadership in the highest standard of addiction and dual diagnosis care. Second, and in a related vein, many programs that claim to provide 'dual diagnosis care' actually do not provide anything close to a real integration of mental health and addiction services, that encompasses adequate treatment provisions and capabilities from both the mental health and addiction sides. This insufficiency of services and inadequacy of integration, is often associated with there being a lack of physician interest or expertise in both addiction and mental health care in the clinic (i.e., there are no addiction psychiatrists). The presence and leadership of an addiction psychiatrist on staff makes it far more likely that the clinic actually provides a comprehensive integration of MI and SUD care, where the clinic is sufficiently enriched with many diagnostic and therapeutic tools from both illness domains, and where treatment plans are individualized according to particular dual diagnosis combinations. Conversely, a clinic equipped, for example, with two doctors, one being a family medicine doctor that is not trained in psychiatry but does addictionology, and a psychiatrist who is not trained or certified in addictionology, is more likely to provide segregated care, even if under one roof, where at best a given dual diagnosis patient might have to be seen or consulted by both doctors for some form of integrated addiction/mental health care to take place. Third, and as we will elaborate more on in Chapter 11, the 2 × 4 Model clinic will also serve as a key hub for the training of more addiction psychiatrists and other cross-trained professionals needed for the development of larger or more numerous 2 × 4 Model clinical operations. To maximize their potential as training sites in this way, that is, to host addiction psychiatry training missions, these clinics need to be equipped with addiction psychiatrists.

Does this requirement mean that all the physicians in the 2 × 4 Model program must be addiction psychiatrists? No. It means that a given 2 × 4 Model team must include at least one addiction psychiatrist, defined as someone who has completed formal training in a psychiatry residency, and a one year fellowship in an ABMS/ACGME accredited program (with certification in either addiction psychiatry or addiction medicine). Other physicians in the clinic might include psychiatrists with ABAM certification only (e.g., who were 'grandfathered in' and/or passed the ABAM test, but did not complete a formal addictions fellowship). Psychiatrists with interest and experience in addictionology (but no formal training or certification), can also serve on the team with the support and collegial co-supervision of the team addiction psychiatrist(s). Certainly, nonpsychiatric physicians (family medicine doctors, internists, etc.) with ABAM training or certification, can serve on the team as well, especially as they can provide the luxury of onsite collaborative primary care. However, these professionals are not regarded as essential or core players in the 2 × 4 Model design, since they are not formally trained in psychiatric care, making them unqualified to provide expert diagnostics and therapeutics across the mental illness components of the 2 × 4 Model.

The chief roles of the psychiatrists in the 2 × 4 Model program are to design, monitor, and sculpt medication regimens, provide backup psychotherapeutic support (as integrated with medication management), monitor overall illness trajectories (with diagnostics), and guide the overall treatment plan of individual patients in clinical encounters, all through the direction of collaborative team actions. Further, they orchestrate and conduct outside communications, and provide professional education, training, and mentoring support to the multi-disciplinary team and outside professionals and organizations.

Nurses

The nursing team, composed of at least one RN (Registered Nurse) with a LPN(s) (Licensed Practical Nurse) and/or medical assistant(s), is another criti-cally important and required component of the 2 × 4 Model team. In many respects, the nursing team is the glue that holds the various parts of the clinical mission together; they work closely with doctors, therapists, and patients, performing functions that span diagnostics, psychotherapeutics, medication management, and communications. In addition, the nurses link the DWT service and the LIDDT missions of the clinic together (see Chapter 7), while directly operating the DWT service with supervisory support of the psychiatrists. Much like the psychiatrists, the nursing staff of the 2 × 4 Model program are jacks-of-all trades; in many situations they are 'force amplifiers' of the psychi-atrists performing various activities delegated to them by the physicians.

The varied duties of the nursing team include, but are not limited to the following:

1. Performing assessments and follow-ups of new patients entering DWT who are entering the 2 × 4 Model clinic for the first time, and are beginning to engage in LIDDT. This work includes diagnostic and treatment measures for withdrawal symptoms, and psycho-education and persuasion to promote the bridging of patients from DWT into LIDDT.
2. Performing withdrawal checks for patients already engaged in LIDDT, who have been discovered to need a new round of DWT.
3. Fielding calls, sending and receiving messages to/from outside professionals or patients on behalf of the psychiatric physicians.
4. Assisting with brief clinical checks, supervised by the psychiatrists in the course of LIDDT, for unscheduled visits (e.g., 'walk-ins' or when physicians request unscheduled visits), vital signs, and weight checks.
5. Performing unobserved and more rarely observed UDS (rapid testing and/or confirmatory testing) as per the physician's direction.
6. Conducting verbal orders, as supervised by the psychiatrists, for short-term medication runs to ensure that patients do not run out of medications until the next appointment with the physician.
7. Delivering and tracking intramuscular medication injection series, including antipsychotics and injectable naltrexone; managing clinic supplies of these agents.

8. Performing pill counts and preparing medication boxes for select patients.
9. Coordinating and scheduling primary care and other diagnostic exams for patients that must occur outside the 2 × 4 Model clinic (e.g., neuro-radiology).
10. Contacting insurance companies to secure support for treatment and medications; working with psychiatrists to conduct communications that combat insurance company blockade of mental health and addiction treatment.

Therapists

The psychotherapy team is the third required leg of the clinical team in the 2 × 4 Model clinic. The therapists can be diverse in their training backgrounds but need a combination of postgraduate education, supervised clinical training experience, and one or more certifications (and licensure) in the field of mental health and/or addictions therapy. Masters level therapists, social workers, and psychologists with PsyD or PhD degrees would compose the psychotherapy team.

As a rule of thumb, all the psychotherapists in the 2 × 4 Model program should be competent and engaged in the basic modalities of psychotherapy of the 2 × 4 Model program (Chapter 5), with a balance of work in both groups and individual therapies. Typically, the patients on a given therapist's caseload would be the ones they are working with in 1:1 psychotherapy (but not always), and more often, there will be patients in groups run by a given therapist that are on a different therapist's caseload. In this way, the therapy team members are inter-collaborative, and back each other up with the care of specific patients.

Each patient in the 2 × 4 Model clinic, once they are engaged in LIDDT, will essentially have two clinicians assigned to their case: The therapist and the psychiatrist. In this way the therapist is a key set of eyes, ears, and hands, for the psychiatrist, collecting longitudinal clinical observations about patients on the psychiatrist's caseloads (made in the course of individual and group therapies), but also collaborating with the psychiatrists in terms of developing a design and focus of the individualized psychotherapeutic program for a given patient. The psychotherapists help determine the appropriate balance of 1:1 therapy vs. group assignment a given patient needs with consultation and advice of the psychiatrist (and other therapy team members). But as mentioned in Chapter 6, the psychiatrist should always see themselves as performing a combination of psychotherapy and medication management in their own encounters with patients. In this way, most patients in the 2 × 4 Model clinic will actually have *two or more therapists* on their cases, the major one being the primary therapist, the minor one the psychiatrist, and secondary minor ones being other therapists (that may encounter the patient in their groups), and nursing team members. This multi-therapist approach provides multiple eyes on a given patient, which allows for a more holistic and comprehensive assessment of the patient, while also modeling the multiple care giver/multiple attachment framework that research suggests is most beneficial in supporting the interpersonal growth and well-being of children and adults.

Clinical case managers are another important part of the psychotherapeutic team who do not necessarily require postgraduate education and advanced experience and training in psychotherapies, but who, nonetheless, need a psychotherapeutic orientation when engaging patients around a number of themes including housing and occupational opportunities. Case managers do tremendously important work performing the communications component of the 2 × 4 Model Treatment Dimension (Chapter 8), and take this work a step further by actually setting up and/or managing financial, housing, vocational, and transportation arrangements for patients. Case managers also tend to be the most mobile of the 2 × 4 Model team, in terms of venturing out of the clinic (with or without patients) to help make arrangements for patients. Case managers are also often engaged in representing the 2 × 4 Model program on client's behalf to the Criminal Justice System, most often via written and verbal communications. Whereas the psychotherapists, and perhaps more rarely the psychiatrists, may engage in face-to-face interactions with the Criminal Justice System and Child Protective Services (e.g., in inter-service meetings, hearings, or court).

Logistical Specialists

In support of the three types of front line clinical professionals of the 2 × 4 Model (psychiatrists, nurses, and therapists), a number of additional professionals that are key to the logistics of the clinic operate behind the front line. Depending on the size and resourcing of the clinic, these professionals can vary in number and hours committed. These positions are described as follows:

Administrators are required professionals of either the clerical or clinical varieties that manage patient scheduling, flow, billing, and the overall psychotherapeutic operation of the clinic respectively. The domain of the clerical team is typically in the waiting room, front office, and supply rooms of the clinic, while the domain of the clinical administrators is primarily in the clinical care areas (e.g., the group rooms and individual clinical offices). Ultimately, the highest ranking clinical administrators of the program would have authority over the clerical team, since the clinical mission is the primary mission for the 2 × 4 Model program, and the activities of the clerical service should be designed to optimize the effectiveness of the clinical administration.

The clinical administration should ideally be composed of individuals who are engaged in both administrative duties and some degree of direct clinical work, so that they can lead 'from the front, instead of behind', endowing them with greater respect by the clinical team and greater awareness of the particular problems and barriers the direct clinical staff may be facing. In general, the addiction psychiatrist of the 2 × 4 Model clinic should be understood as having fundamental administrative authority and influence of the clinical operations of the 2 × 4 Model clinic as well, but this authority may be couched as being either formal (e.g., as recognized in a medical director, or service line chief role) or informal. The right balance of administrative verses clinical work must be struck. Having the addiction psychiatrist doing too much administrative work that is not focused on direct patient care could be a waste of greatly needed clinical expertise and physician effort, but at the same time a 2 × 4 Model program that is devoid of big picture oversight and influence by addiction psychiatrists is one that could wander too far from the scientific evidence base, compromising clinical effectiveness. Typically, clinical administrators drawn from the psychotherapeutic team would do more of the hands on managerial work of the other therapists as well as representing the 2 × 4 Model program (along with the addiction psychiatrists) to the central leadership of the hosting clinical organization. Internal to the clinic, the clinical administrators would also be involved in developing and monitoring the activities and effectiveness of the individual and group psychotherapies. This would involve providing psychodynamically informed clinical supervision with content and process analysis for the entire psychotherapeutic team. Educational and independent scholarly career growth opportunities may also be provided by the clinical administrators.

Health insurance coordinators can be crucial elements to the 2 × 4 Model program, needed to help patients across the socio-economic spectrum find and maintain their best insurance options, whether that be from private or government-sponsored programs. The importance of these professionals rests in the fact that obtaining, keeping, and understanding health insurance has become incredibly arbitrary, arcane, complex, and endlessly evolving, to the point where even physicians and most other medical professional cannot operate as effective advisors to their patients on insurance matters. At the same time, it is very important for the financial solvency (and very existence) of the 2 × 4 Model clinic that it is proactive in making sure its patients are adequately and appropriately covered by health insurance. Additionally, this focus on securing health insurance for dual diagnosis patients, who may otherwise not have the psychiatric stability, cognitive capacity, or material resources to successfully obtain and keep their health insurance unassisted, is broadly important for advancing the cause of parity of health insurance for addictive and dual diagnosis illnesses.

Attorneys can serve as important and effective consultants to patients and clinical team members in the 2 × 4 Model program. Lawyers attached to the clinic can significantly force amplify the physician's efforts with respect to all facets of the Communications in the 2 × 4 Model (Chapter 8), particularly in terms of interacting with the Criminal Justice System. They can make up for the typically inadequate legal defense that many dual diagnosis patients suffer with due to their socio-economic standing, and the inadequate funding and staffing that limits many public defenders agencies.

Data managers are essentially research and development officers in the clinic who collect, compile, and analyze quantitative clinical data on the clinical census or certain subgroups of patients in the clinic. This data can be used to inform and refine ongoing clinical programming and human resource allocation in the 2 × 4 Model clinic, and even to test hypotheses concerning the effectiveness of differential clinical strategies. These individuals are graduate or postgraduate trained in data management and statistics, and/or public health and epidemiology with working knowledge of how to extract data from electronic medical records and other clinic sources. These professionals could be powerful assets for the clinic in terms of advancing its research mission (see Chapter 11), or in terms of collecting data needed to justify substantial changes (e.g., to a central administration) in clinical team composition or infrastructure that although requiring new expenses, could increase overall efficiency or clinical effectiveness.

Behavioral health pharmacists are pharmacists with specialized training in psychopharmacology. They can operate onsite in the 2 × 4 Model program to assist and support the physician team in designing optimal medical strategies for individual patients, and in increasing the efficiency of overall medication management provided by the clinic. Along with data managers, these professionals can be important assets supporting the psychopharmacological research and educational missions of the clinic.

Physical Infrastructure

The building (or building section) that the 2 × 4 Model operates in should have a design that reflects the different component missions and job profiles of the various professionals of the clinic. A mixed plan of individual/confidential therapy offices (each of about the same size) and group room spaces (of various sizes to accommodate different group sized) are needed. The following provides a rough sketch of the team member types and clinical space components for a small to medium sized 2 × 4 Model program. These human resources and physical space elements can be scaled up or down together to create a larger vs. more basic clinical program.

In general, the psychiatrists and nurses will be smaller in number compared to the therapists and logistical specialists, and to a large extent the space allocations to the different staff types will reflect this. So that the work of the clinic does not ground to a halt when someone goes on vacation or gets sick, the clinic should operate with *at least* two of each kind of clinical professional type (psychiatrists, nurses, and therapists) on staff. As a guideline, the ratios of staffing by professional type might approximate 2:2:10 (psychiatrists:nurses: therapists) in terms of raw full time equivalent units, with the actual numbers of these staff increasing with more part-time professionals in each category. A clinical staff of this size would be able to take care of from 200–400 patients longitudinally with a new intake rate ranging from 6–20 patients per week. Another 2–5 logistical specialists (administrators, health insurance advisors, etc.) not including front office staff, would complete the team. Of course, depending on the desired size and clinical reach of the program (and the skill, endurance, and health of the individual team members) the program can be scaled up and/or the proportions of the professional groups can be varied somewhat from the 2:2:10 rule of thumb.

But assuming the 2:2:10 ratio represents a basic staffing of a small to medium sized program, the *basic physical space infrastructure* would be composed as shown in **Box 9.1**.

BOX 9.1 Basic Physical Space Infrastructure

Staff Type	Space
Physicians	2–4 individual interview offices
Nurses	2 individual interview rooms (including 1 main office/med storage room) 1 physical exam room (including 2 bathrooms for UDS collection)
Therapists	8 individual interview offices 1 case management offices 2 small conference rooms (up to 16 seats) 1 medium conference room (up to 32 seats) 1 large conference room (up to 64 seats)
Logistics/Support	1 waiting room 1 front office 1 business supply/copiers room 2 administrators offices 2 staff bathrooms and kitchen

---

Based on this template, 2 × 4 Model clinics with significant research or training missions might have additional rooms. More sophisticated designs might also include physical infrastructure that houses both outpatient and inpatient missions. The latter could include full-locked dual diagnosis inpatient units capable of handling suicidal patients and basic medical services vs. less intensively monitored (voluntary) beds for supervised detoxification and short-term diagnostic and rehabilitation programming. An interesting design variation could also be built to conduct the full spectrum of *family integrated dual diagnosis care* in which three adjacent 2 × 4 Model clinics, one serving adults, another adolescents (10–18 years old), and a third program serving pregnant women/women with small children. As suggested in Chapter 8, the 2 × 4 Model program physical infrastructure as outlined above could also be a section or floor of a larger building that provides a large range of outpatient medical services, for example, in support of an integrative medical home model that includes addiction psychiatry.

Background References and Further Reading

Chambers, R. A. 2013. "The addiction psychiatrist as dual diagnosis physician: A profession in great need and greatly needed." *Journal of Dual Diagnosis* 9 (3): 260–266. doi: 10.1080/15504263.2013.807072.

Horsfall, J., M. Cleary, G. E. Hunt, and G. Walter. 2009. "Psychosocial treatments for people with co-occurring severe mental illnesses and substance use disorders (dual diagnosis): A review of empirical evidence." *Harvard Review of Psychiatry* 17 (1): 24–34. doi: 10.1080/10673220902724599.

Johnson, S. 1997. "Dual diagnosis of severe mental illness and substance misuse: A case for specialist services?" *British Journal of Psychiatry* 171 (3): 205–208.

Rosenheck, R. A., S. G. Resnick, and J. P. Morrissey. 2003. "Closing service system gaps for homeless clients with a dual diagnosis: Integrated teams and interagency cooperation." *The Journal of Mental Health Policy & Economics* 6 (2): 77–87.

Schulte, S. J., P. S. Meier, J. Stirling, and M. Berry. 2010. "Dual diagnosis among addiction treatment staff: Training levels, training needs and the link to retention." *European Addiction Research* 16 (2): 78–84.

10 All Together Now

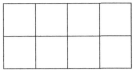

Vertical and Horizontal Binding in the Functioning 2 × 4 Model Clinic

The overarching goal of the 2 × 4 Model clinic is to provide the highest standard of longitudinal evidence-based care for patients with any major mental illness(s) in combination with any addiction(s), by one treatment team, under one roof. In achieving this goal, the 2 × 4 Model program is guided by *10 Core Directives* (see **Box 10.1**), which have already been described in various forms in prior chapters, but are now succinctly summarized here.

This chapter will describe the key operational aspects of the 2 × 4 Model clinic, which allow the 2 × 4 Model design to function as an effective and coherent clinical unit, that fully integrates its various professional roles and treatment missions for the optimal fulfillment of these directives.

Horizontal Binding of Treatment Dimension Components in the 2 × 4 Model

A central operational attribute of the 2 × 4 Model is the way that it binds together Diagnostics, Psychotherapies, Medications, and Communications into one integrated whole (**Figure 10.1**). This is made possible by both the multidisciplinary treatment team approach (where team members work side by side and collaborate in the same building) and the rejection of traditionally held views that it is acceptable for clinics to offer only medication management, or only psychotherapies, or only detoxification to addicted/mentally ill patients. In horizontal binding, both Psychotherapeutic and Medication management tools are to *some extent* provided to most if not all patients. At the same time, there is great flexibility in the quantity and type of psychotherapies and medications that are provided, depending on what the patient needs and/or can tolerate. In addition, horizontal binding implies there are interactive and synergistic effects between the psychotherapies and medications, and between these two components and Diagnostics. In fact, in the longitudinal course of treatment, there should be an iterative back and forth happening between diagnostics, psychotherapies and medications. Diagnostics are not only implemented at the start of care but are repeated over and over after segments of therapeutic interventions, to track trajectories of illness courses and recovery,

---

BOX 10.1 10 Core Directives of the 2 × 4 Model Clinic

1. Provide *longitudinal outpatient care* (treatment for weeks, months, and years), depending on patient's needs and not on arbitrary limits.
2. Provide care that encompasses both short term DWT and LIDDT.
3. Provide care that is local to where the patient's live.
4. Provide care that does not abandon or punish patients because they are sick and treatment resistant.
5. Provide multiple modalities of addiction treatment, not just one treatment for all.
6. Provide treatments for many types of addiction, not just treatments for only one type.
7. Provide treatments for all major co-occurring mental illnesses involving multiplicities of illnesses and treatment types.
8. Provide both medication and psychotherapeutic treatments, not one or the other.
9. Strive to accept health insurance, avoid and minimize out of pocket fees; protect patient's rights to excellent care via professional communications.
10. Provide care under one roof, by one team of cross-trained mental health/addiction treatment professionals comprised of physicians, nurses, and therapists.

---

and to individualize, optimize, and refine the application of the therapeutic tools. In this way, the addiction psychiatrist and the 2 × 4 Model team are like sculptors in the art of patient's recovery, making one intervention here and another there, then standing back to see what the result has been, only to return back to the work, to make more interventions as needed. Then, as horizontally bound with Communications with the outside world, these Treatment Dimensions are further protected and amplified in their power to create stability and recovery in the patient.

Horizontal binding occurs via multiple bidirectional interactions between all four Treatment Dimension components of the 2 × 4 Model as described in the examples provided below:

Diagnostics to psychotherapies: The initial and follow-up diagnostic evaluations will inform updates on the balance of individual vs. group therapies that patients should try, and what the focus areas of these treatments should be. Evolving symptoms of mental illness, the current stage of change, and acute life stressors would be assessed in clinical exams, as complimented by objective measures of substance use.

Psychotherapies as diagnostics: The behavior of the patient in individual and group therapies can further illuminate the psychiatric diagnosis the patient may have. These observations in turn should inform refinements in future psychotherapeutic approaches and medication management. Tracking of psychotherapy appointment attendance can suggest stage of change and level of motivation or capacity for attachment of individual patients, and/or other dynamics that may be in play in the treatment itself.

Diagnostics to medications: Of course, the initial dual diagnosis examination by the psychiatrist, along with assessments by other team members, will be used to make DSM diagnoses that provide medication treatment targets in both the addiction and mental illness components. Repeated diagnostic evaluations over time are used to refine and focus medication choices as the patient's illness course evolves or stabilizes over time.

Medications as diagnostics: Medications themselves can aid and clarify the diagnostic assessment. For example, application of monotherapy with an SSRI that precipitates a manic picture, points to a bipolar spectrum illness.

Medication impact on psychotherapies: Psychotherapists may observe patients frequently being drowsy in groups, suggesting that medication regimens are too strongly sedating. Conversely, patients with psychotic and or manic features may be too paranoid or disruptive in groups, suggesting the need for the addition of antipsychotic or mood stabilization medications to improve group participation. For some patients on opioid replacement therapies, their compliance with treatment appointments is observed to be too limited to only seeing the psychiatrist when they will receive scripts for the opioid (e.g., buprenorphine). This phenomena may inform a choice to delegate the delivery of controlled medications to the time of psychotherapy encounters.

Psychotherapy impact on medications: A goal of the 2 × 4 Model psychiatrist is to have the patient be on the most parsimonious and effective medication regimen possible for the treatment of mental illness and addiction, with as few meds as possible. Sometimes patients may present requesting more or different meds, including controlled substances that the psychiatrist is reluctant to prescribe due to unacceptable risks and side effect profiles. Patients not participating adequately in psychotherapies, with such treatment-refractory symptoms, can be reminded and encouraged to seek a psychotherapeutic solution for symptom relief, instead of seeking a 'pill for every ill'.

Communications to protect and enhance diagnostics/psychotherapies/medications: As reviewed in Chapter 8, communications with the Criminal Justice System can help protect the quality and integrity of treatment for the patient and limit other adverse effects of criminalization. Communications with the health care system can prevent or limit iatrogenic relapses, and secure appropriate insurance coverage for care. Communications with housing, financial, and occupational support services can help patients with basic needs to foster more reliable and secure participation in care. Across all of the communications, the capacity of the 2 × 4 Model clinic to speak relatively definitively and comprehensively about the patient's mental health *and* addiction diagnoses and treatment needs, enhances the potency of these communications compared to segregated service systems.

Building, Balancing, and Directing Treatment Strategies: Vertical Binding

Returning to the concept of vertical binding introduced in Chapter 3, and incorporating it with horizontal binding described above and in Chapter 4, we have depicted the fully integrated dual diagnosis clinic design that the 2 × 4 Model emulates (**Figure 10.2**).

Using the power of this design, the addiction psychiatrist and the multidisciplinary 2 × 4 Model team are able to pursue a clinical strategy that aims to flexibly treat the MI and SUD comorbidity comprehensively, at 'four points of attack' (**Figure 10.3**).

As reviewed in earlier chapters, most patients presenting to the clinic will have some combination of MI and SUD illness(s) that will vary across individuals by quality, severity, and number of DSM illness components. Each of these two main syndrome components, that is, the MI component and the SUD/addiction component, represent the two Direct Targets of attack of the 2 × 4 Model approach. But as described in Chapters 2 and 3, each of these illness components are also mutually and bidirectionally reinforcing of one another. The biology of the mental illness increases addiction risk and severity, and conversely, the addiction illness (and associated drug use) worsens mental illness. So, these interactive causal reinforcing dynamics that exist between the MI and SUD, are also treatment targets (we will call them Indirect Targets) of the 2 × 4 Model treatment strategy.

In general, the treatment strategy of the 2 × 4 Model clinic for a given patient will include some attention and focus on all four of these points of attack (as shown in **Figure 10.3**), although the manner, prioritization, force, and timing of these tactics will of course be individualized based on the unique diagnostic picture and other personal factors each patient carries. But, the 2 × 4 Model team is always keeping this 'four points of attack' model in mind, and patients should be introduced to and educated about it in the early stages of treatment and periodically as they continue their recovery. Even for patients who have succeeded in completely remitting their SUDs or their MI symptoms (e.g., for patients that are no longer classifiable as currently 'dually diagnosed'), the 'four point of attack' model remains relevant as a preventative conceptual framework. For example, the patient with depression who has successfully quit smoking can be reminded of the evidence that staying abstinent will help prevent new depressions or lessen their severity.

It is important to describe in some more detail here, what tactics are used by the team in pursuing these 'four points of attack', particularly with respect to the Indirect Targets. The Direct Targets, the MI, and addictions, are of course treated by the array of evidence-based psychotherapies and medications already reviewed in Chapters 6 and 7. Attacking the Indirect Targets, that is, intervening in ways that reduce the way the MI and addictions mutually reinforce one another, also involves psychotherapies and meds, but in more nuanced ways as described below.

Reducing the Capacity of SUDs to Produce or Worsen MI Symptoms

The most immediate effect of substance use is to generate or worsen MI symptoms during intoxication and/or withdrawal states. For example, cocaine and amphetamine intoxication can drive psychoses and mania, while their withdrawal states can produce acute suicidality and look indistinguishable from depression. Alcohol and opioid intoxication can impair cognition and consciousness, while their withdrawal states can produce severe anxiety, insomnia, and psychosis. Accordingly, pharmacological interventions that reduce the severity of intoxication and, more commonly, withdrawal states are relevant to interdicting the capacity of addiction to worsen MI. In essence, DWT is a prime example of the Indirect approach to breaking the linkages from SUD to MI.

Later in the course of recovery when LIDDT is well underway, new interventions are frequently needed that seek to minimize the effects of the lingering damage that the addiction has caused the patient, which could still precipitate more psychiatric symptoms. For example, a long history of addiction often has the effect of 'burning bridges' in the patient's life, producing serious damage to relationships, particularly with family members. In addition, many patients have selected social contacts as mechanisms to acquire and use drugs, so that they are more likely to have lost a relatively high number of friends to drug related medical illnesses, accidents, and overdoses. Thus in sobriety, many patients 'wake up' to a world of significant loss of connection in their familial and broader social networks. And of course, we know this impoverishment of social network is a major risk factor for more depression and suicide. So, to combat this, a major focus of the treatment team is to re-connect the patient to a new and healthier social network, not only through the act of participating in psychotherapies in the 2 × 4 Model clinic, but through volunteering, occupational, group recreational, or religious community membership, etc. A related phenomena, which in some ways manifests like a form of trauma or PTSD that is a direct result of the cumulative addiction history, is the tendency of recovering people to genuinely believe that they are educationally and occupationally incapable of success, because this is pretty much all they have experienced. In fact, the more likely scenario has been that they would have been quite competent in these domains, if they hadn't been chronically using—but, they don't have the insight to realize this. In other words, they have so identified who they are with drug use, and the consequences of drug use, that they see themselves as a failure, rather than understanding they are a potentially successful person, who caught a disease that caused them to fall far short in realizing their potential. These patients tend to believe that they have turned to using substances because they are failures, when actually, their ongoing heavy substance use was a cause of their failures. Obviously, patients stuck in this form of 'drug history trauma/grief', need targeted supportive and insight oriented psychotherapy from all 2 × 4 Model team members to prevent further psychiatric consequences of harmful re-enactment and expectation of failure.

Reducing the Capacity of MI to Produce or Worsen Addiction and Relapse

Experiencing psychiatric symptoms and then adopting the drug use rationalization that the self-medication hypothesis provides is a common dynamic that can fuel and propagate drug relapses. Steering clear of, and rejecting the self-medication hypothesis through insight-oriented and MET approaches, are important to supporting patients' sobriety while they experience mental illness symptoms. In addition, pharmacological management in the 2 × 4 Model clinic should involve due caution and awareness on the part of the psychiatrist, of the potential pitfalls of prescribing controlled substances to dual diagnosis patients who are attempting to make a compelling case for these substances while using a 'self-medications' like argument. As reviewed in Chapter 7, a helpful rule of thumb for the 2 × 4 Model psychiatrist to adhere to is to avoid prescribing (or allowing more than one physician to prescribe) a combination of two or more controlled substances on a long-term basis.

Two other clinically observable aspects of mental illness that can provoke vulnerability to relapse are impulsive decision-making and psychiatric vulnerability to stressful events. A range of affective syndromes, PTSD spectrum illness, and personality disorders render patients impulsive and more prone to use despite secondary consequences. At the same time, stress intolerance, high emotional reactivity, and re-victimization that go with these disorders, can drive craving and drug-seeking behavior in these patients. While solid pharmacological treatment of these underlying psychiatric disorders (e.g., with lithium, which can reduce impulsivity) is probably helpful here, targeted psychotherapies delivered by the psychiatrists and the therapists that use motivational enhancement and CBT approaches are important for training patients how to navigate psychiatric symptoms and distress that function as relapse triggers. Insight to how psychiatric symptoms can lead to relapse (and how that relapse in turn often ends up worsening the psychiatric picture) can often be gained through a careful collaborative review and situational narrative and mapping of the pathway to relapse, by the patient and clinician together.

Again, with the 'four point of attack' framework in mind, it is up to the psychiatrist and the 2 × 4 Model team to design the best overall strategy to manage the particular dual diagnosis combination a given patient presents with. This strategy should be expected to evolve over the course of care, just as the patient's illness components are expected to evolve in quality and severity. Thus, the horizontal binding of diagnostics with psychotherapeutics and medication treatments, through continuous re-assessment and diagnostic testing is important for allowing the treatment to evolve with the patient. It is important for the psychiatrist and the 2 × 4 Model team to have the operational flexibility and freedom to take on the MI vs. addiction illness components via Direct and Indirect approaches in whatever order the team believes is in the best interest of the patient. Typically, but not always, this will involve simultaneous targeting of both the MI and the SUD(s), in some relative proportion or another. The psychiatrist will take a lead role in guiding the balance of this strategy in collaboration with the rest of the 2 × 4 Model team, much like the coaching staff and quarterback of a football team (see 'NFL analogy', Chapter 3) make decisions about the balance and ordering of 'passing' vs. 'running' plays during the course of the game. Based on what is generally known about the opponent (dual diagnosis syndrome) and assessing in real time how successful these plays (MI and SUD treatments) are proving to be during the course of the game (longitudinal treatment), a constant stream of minor adjustments are made to the strategy to increase the margin of victory (recovery).

Flow of Care in the 2 × 4 Model Clinic

The timeline for care in the 2 × 4 Model clinic should be based on two principals: 1) individualization; and 2) persistence in care for as long as it takes to generate and maintain substantial gains in recovery. Arbitrary limits on durations of treatment programming, although pervasive in many treatment cultures and reinforced by people who conflate addiction treatment with achieving educational degrees or completing terms of punishment, are not well evidence based and tend to ignore the reality that addictions and mental illnesses are often chronic diseases. With these points in mind the 2 × 4 Model clinic accepts patients into care with no preconceived notion of how long they will be there, until substantial clinical results are achieved and consolidated, and for as long as it is felt by the patient and team that some level of maintenance treatment is needed. Thus, a key value of the 2 × 4 Model clinic is that from the very start with each patient, the clinic is interested in forming a long term vision and therapeutic relationship for helping patients achieve an enduring recovery at the highest level with respect to both their addictive disease(s) and mental illness(s). Notably, this level of commitment and continuity of care for the patient is made possible by the 2 × 4 Model design, because in distinction to segregated mental health or addiction treatment services, the patient will not have to be referred out to another service regardless of how the patient's mental illness and addictive disorders evolve over time.

Certainly some patients may stay in treatment for only a few days and others for many years; some may do intense work for a short period of time and others may pursue a very long but sporadic course of encounters. There is no absolute right or wrong about any of these trajectories, and no evidence exists to suggest that one size fits all. Rather, the most important factors are whether the patient is getting better or not, and is the clinic doing what it can to take long-term responsibility for the patient. This is not to mean that the clinic should not recommend concrete schedules of individual and/or group psychotherapy regimens and psychiatrist appointments, or that tracking attendance to these are not important. It simply means that the clinic should expect and accept a diversity of temporal trajectories of recovery, given the diversity of diagnostic combinations, demographics, and external barriers to treatment that the clinic will encounter in its census.

With this philosophy, the 2 × 4 Model clinic provides the full spectrum of early, middle, and late stage dual diagnosis and addiction care. Unlike rehabs or addiction hospitals, the 2 × 4 Model program is not just a beginning of treatment, or more unfortunately, 'a bridge to nowhere', as in the case of many patients who travel long distances from smaller cities and rural towns to attend high-end rehabs, only to be discharged back into their treatment-impoverished local communities where they quickly relapse.

In the early stages of treatment, the focus is more on initial evaluations, introducing the patient to the culture of the clinic and treatment team members, and of course, to provide DWT. In this stage of care, the psychiatrist and nursing team collaboration will play a more prominent role, while the psychotherapy staff are working more independently to orient the patient and on building therapeutic relationships. In middle to later stages of treatment, the psychiatrist and psychotherapy staff collaboration becomes more dominant as LIDDT progresses, while the nursing team collaboration becomes more secondary. Thus, in the clinical professional triangle (psychiatrists/nurses/therapists) that patients in the 2 × 4 Model clinic recover in (**Figure 9.1**), the intensity of interactions and collaborations between professionals (and between each professional type and the patient) will normally shift over time. As treatment progresses to even more advanced maintenance stages (e.g., where they are quite stable), they may gravitate to hanging on to more of a psychotherapy based foundation (no longer, or only rarely seeing the psychiatrist, or the nursing team), or to more of a psychiatrist-based foundation, where they only see the psychiatrist every 3–6 months for check-ins, maintenance medications, and brief psychotherapies. Sometimes, before it ever gets to this stage, some patients will drop out of care entirely for any number of reasons, most optimistically, being that they are too well to need care any longer, which is definitely a fine and desirable goal for care. But then there are those that drop out for detrimental reasons (e.g., they are forced out by the Criminal Justice System, have lost insurance, have relapsed and given up, have moved away, have died due to illness, suicide, or homicide, etc.). For this group, that is, for the ones who are still alive, the hope is that they will return to treatment, and that when they do so, they will be even more successful and persevering in treatment the next time around. For this reason, when patients who left care eventually do return, it is very important for the addiction psychiatrist and the 2 × 4 Model team to take on an attitude of welcoming, celebration, and congratulation toward the patient for their return, rather than to stand in judgment and condemnation for the mistakes they may have made that led them to leave.

For new and returning patients. The 2 × 4 Model clinic should develop its own procedure or set of procedures for taking new and returning patients into the clinic. Precisely how this is done, how soon a new patient can see the addiction psychiatrist, and how flexibly all this can occur across different patients (as indicated by individual needs and acuity), depends on the overall magnitude of clinical demand the clinic faces, its professional staffing levels, and other local conditions. Typically, the psychotherapy and nursing staff (in the course of DWT) see patients first and for some period of time before the psychiatrist, until an open initial evaluation slot emerges with the psychiatrist. A caveat to this is that the psychiatrist can and should see patients briefly very early on in the course of DWT, as the addiction psychiatrist should always avoid prescribing controlled substances of any kind to any patient they have not seen. In general, it is appropriate for returning patients to be processed more rapidly than totally new ones, and, fast-track pathways can and should be set up for patients in certain other circumstances, like for pregnant patient intakes, and people who are highly motivated after experiencing a life threatening overdose. An important consideration to be aware of for new patients with opioid addiction is that starting an opioid maintenance treatment is usually never an emergency in and of itself (in distinction to how urgently the patients may suggest they need an opioid), especially for the majority of these patients who have been using for years and have easy access to heroin and diverted prescription opioids. Accordingly, patients can be entered into the DWT and psychotherapy components of treatment well before they are started on buprenorphine or naltrexone. Some patients should be considered for treatment in the affiliated methadone maintenance program (if there is one) which can often start patients on opioid replacement more rapidly after the date the patient first presents.

For patients needing DWT while already engaged in treatment. It should be kept in mind that DWT is not only needed for patients first entering treatment, but it may be needed for patients who are well known to the clinic and have been engaged for months or years. For example, an alcohol addiction could be discovered by the team quite a while after a patient starts care, or, patients in care for some time could enter sustained relapse phases on opioids. In either case, DWT can be piggy-backed onto the LIDDT as part of the overall treatment plan. In the same vein, certain new or well-known patients may need more intensive DWT than what the 2 × 4 Model clinic can provide in house. Patients with very complex and acutely symptomatic dual diagnosis conditions, patients who are medically complex or fragile (e.g., with brittle hypertension), those with histories of seizures or delirium tremens, patients who have previously failed outpatient DWT, and those who simply cannot refrain from using while they are living at home or are homeless, should be considered for inpatient or quasi-inpatient (supervised) detoxification unit beds for 1–4 weeks. Regardless of when DWT is needed, it should be understood that DWT really only has impact when it is offered as a complimentary service and subsidiary of LIDDT that the 2 × 4 Model provides. Without LIDDT, DWT operates as a relatively costly and largely ineffective 'bridge to nowhere'.

The 2 × 4 Model Team Meeting

The 2 × 4 Model team approach requires a regular forum for the team to meet as a whole to discuss strategies in individual patient's care and the functioning of the clinic. It is recommended that a regularly scheduled hour per business day be reserved for this purpose on at least three, and as many as five days per week. A clinic leader (administrative, psychotherapist, or physician) should facilitate the meeting and guide the team in drawing the agenda. The team meeting, when operating well, will serve several specific purposes as outlined below:

Discuss specific cases. Collaborations between psychiatrists, therapists, and nurses will be routine in the clinic, and most of this interactive work will not need airing in the team meeting. However, there will be complex patients and situations that require the input and participation of three or more team members for decision-making and treatment plan implementation. In our experience, the patients that most often require this attention are people who have strong comorbidities of robust Axis I mental illness with robust Axis II (personality disorders) and multiple addictions. Often, these patients can be very difficult (and sometimes impossible) to manage in the outpatient setting, serving as reminders to the team that for a small but standout minority of patients, total deinstitutionalization is probably a failed policy. For these and other challenging patients that are not progressing well and make the team feel stuck, creative team brainstorming on the next therapeutic move is sorely needed. Sometimes there is controversy or splitting on what direction the care should take, and the team has to find a way to have a healthy, productive debate, and/or to address the splitting in the team. Healthy strategic work on patients should strive to achieve a consensus on the plan and optimal integration of psychotherapeutic/case management, medication, and communicative elements. If two competing plans emerge, both with merits and downsides, it can be possible to agree on trying both as a hybrid or compromise plan, or, to try plan A first followed by plan B if the first one fails. In any event, decision-making in the course of care for patients should ultimately rest with the addiction psychiatrist. But for this to work well, the addiction psychiatrist has to earn the respect of the team; he/she needs to listen and look to the other team members for their thoughts, observations, and inputs. Good leadership skills are required, and subtlety in this leadership is a virtue; if the team can generate a sound strategy without the verbal input of the psychiatrist (except for an "I agree . . .

sounds good"), that is a good thing. At the same time, there should be a good amount of collegial 'help calling' and advice-seeking from the psychiatrist to the other team members, and conversely, from the therapists and nurses to the psychiatrists. Asking for help and advice on cases not only gets the work done, but it shows how professionals appreciate and enjoy their collaborations with each other. In this work, care should be taken to keep the tone professional and even appropriately lighthearted and certainly not accusatory where one team member feels like another is calling them out for doing an inadequate job. In general, disciplinary or critical appraisals of any team member has no place in the treatment team meeting.

Conduct whole team interventions on specific patients: There are times when it is beneficial to patients and their therapeutic process, to bring them into the team meeting to discuss where their care has been and where it is going. Generally the patient's lead therapist, the psychiatrist, or a clinical administrator leads the discussion with other team members chiming in at appropriate intervals. This group intervention can be helpful in addressing splitting, miscommunication, motivating greater change, and providing constructive feedback from and to patients about their care. But this can be a quite stressful and intimidating experience for patients and they should be supported, not punished for their participation in it. Although fact finding and problem solving with the patient's input can and should be an important goal, this type of meeting should not veer into becoming an interrogation or trial of the patient for their behavior. Hearing from the patient as one team, and speaking to the patient as one team, can be an important move to make, but one that has to be managed with care.

Analyzing and working through systematic problems or changes in the 2 × 4 Model clinic: A gift that many of our most challenging patients can bring the team, especially those with strong Cluster B personality components, is their remarkably acute talents for showing the team the weaknesses and failures of our systems and approaches to care. Certainly, these cases are very good to discuss and work though in the team meeting, as being illustrative of broader, more pervasive problems that may affect many other patients. Similarly, any one team member may be seeing things happening to reduce the effectiveness or efficiency of care for multiple patients that is happening on a system level, and these should also be brought up. Internal or external changes and pressures impacting the team in either positive, negative, or unknown directions should also be aired. Again, in this forum, care should be taken not to use the team meeting to single professionals out for fault (i.e., scapegoating them). Instead, the discussion should stay on analyzing the operation and proficiency of the team as an organizational unit, in which the course of care of groups of patients or individual patients are discussed.

Monitoring team process and professional group health: The team meeting is also an important venue for the addiction psychiatrist and other team leaders to monitor morale and the healthiness of communication patterns, collabor-

232 All Together Now

ations, and other dynamics. Treating dual diagnosis patients and dealing with the social barriers and challenges they face, can be very hard and emotionally taxing work. The ripple effects of extremely sick patients and the social problems they live in, can radiate through the team to cause burnout, conflict, and other stress responses that degrade excellence in care provision and prevent the work from being as gratifying and fun as it should be. It is the job of the addiction psychiatrist and other team leaders to monitor for these problems as they arise and to address them over time. Essentially, the addiction psychiatrist should be mindful to take care of the team in parallel to their work in taking care of the patients. Maintaining good humor and collegiality in the team meeting is of course fundamental in this effort. But other approaches such as hosting organized team retreats to discuss team dynamics, and to increase interpersonal familiarity among team members can be important tactics. 'Social grooming' segments (e.g., celebrating a team member's birthday or new baby with a luncheon) during or outside the team meeting are important. As with any well-functioning group, maintaining a sense of professional safety and freedom to express thoughts and concerns among all members of the team is important.

Other team strengthening activities can include educational segments, such as brief journal article reviews, or evidence-based presentations by team members to support intellectual and professional growth and capability. Helping people feel they are learning and growing while being part of the team can do wonders to make up for other professional stressors and even low pay. Finally, the team meeting should be used to give the professional group a sense of control and ownership of its own composition. Team interviews and discussion about potential hires that may come on board, and conversely, collective goodbyes for members leaving are important.

Conflicts and Incompetence on the 2 × 4 Model Team

Conflicts and differences of perspective are of course inevitable in any human group or team effort. When resolved through healthy discussion and debate, these conflicts can actually allow the group to arrive at a solution that is better than what any individual had originally intended or could execute on their own. The 2 × 4 Model team is no exception to this axiom, and some of the specific 'conflict zones' that can arise in it, are worth outlining below.

First, there is the multidisciplinary nature of the team that requires strong collaborations between different professionals who are trained in diverse ways and to different levels. Inter-professional fault lines tend to be less of an issue for psychiatrists and nurses (who are essentially both trained in the Western Medical tradition) and have often been trained together (as disciplines). Fault lines tend to be larger between the therapists and the physicians. Unfortunately, divisions between the latter two groups can be exacerbated by the mentality of some psychiatrists that medications are all that have value for their patients, and that psychotherapy is nonsense. Conversely, therapists particularly from the addiction side can sometime harbor anti-medication attitudes (e.g., 'medications are crutches') while over idealizing the primacy of therapy in addiction treatment. Obviously, there cannot be a solid horizontal binding of the psycho-therapeutic and medication components of treatment in the 2 × 4 Model clinic, if the psychiatrists and therapists on the team really felt this way, and held each other's roles on the field of play in such mutual disrespect. For this reason, the 2 × 4 Model encourages and thrives on comfort with some degree of role diffusion, especially between the psychiatrists and the therapists. For example, the psychiatrist should absolutely view themselves, and should be viewed by the other team psychotherapists, as being competent and active participants in the patient's psychotherapies. This means incorporating psychotherapeutic techniques into medication management appointments, and being attuned to and supportive of efforts by the other therapists on the team to conduct individual and group psychotherapies on the patients. Similarly, the psychiatrists should also invite the therapists into the processes involved in medication management, including inviting and listening to the observations of therapists about patient's symptoms, and occasionally delegating/linking the delivery of scripts or collection of UDS to the therapist's appointments. It is most helpful for the psychiatrists and psychotherapists alike to realize that both medications and psychotherapies are effective, evidence-based treatments that often work very well together. In addition, they both carry risks and side-effects, and neither are meant for every patient. While most patients will benefit and need a balance of both these modalities, some will just need, or be able to accept a lot more of one or the other. In any event, what is key is that the 2 × 4 Model team is able to deliver on whatever combination of medication and psycho-therapy works best for a given patient.

A second conflict zone relates to the potential for the traditional split between addictionology and mental health (training and treatment cultures) to rear its ugly head and produce divisions on the team. Often, the resolution of these kinds of conflicts can depend quite a bit on the leadership and guiding input of the addiction psychiatrist, since he or she is essentially the most well-trained professional on the team in both the fields of addiction and mental health care. For example, addiction-only trained professionals sometimes tend to want to blame choppy treatment compliance or resistance to care demonstrated by patients, purely on 'addicted thinking' and manipulation, when a major part of the problem is the co-occurring mental disorder. The addiction psychiatrist can help the team develop a more effective treatment plan and decrease judgement of the patient, by discussing the case more comprehensively with respect to the mental illness.

Third, there are professionals who cannot seem to let go of 'old school' approaches to addiction which tend to see the disease as resulting from lack of spiritual fortification, and/or reflecting a lack of moral integrity. Professionals stuck in this thinking in its most severe forms often advocate for treatment plans that seek in some way to punish or eliminate the patient from care, or to blame the patient for their poor progress, rather to examine and change what the team could be doing that is not effective. Obviously, this perspective could create conflict with more medical model disease-based approaches to treatment that the 2 × 4 Model generally espouses. While it is certainly the case that antisocial patients with addictions can unfortunately contribute to old-school thinking (not to mention training histories of professionals based in abstinence only models and criminal justice contexts), it is up to the addiction psychiatrists and other 2 × 4 Model team leaders to support the disease model of mental illness and dual diagnosis. Emphasis on supporting nonjudgmental motivational interviewing approaches, and supervision to help staff members recognize and control their own counter-transferences are also important. A more minor, but more common 'old school' line of thinking from the addiction field that can drive treatment planning conflict, can take the form of an over-idealized belief that group therapies are the only modality of value or efficacy in addiction care. Therapists can get caught up in thinking that patients who are not in groups, but may be doing 1:1 therapy, and may be in medication management with the psychiatrist once a month "are not participating in treatment!" Again, understanding the importance of flexible, balanced, multimodal integration, and individualization of medication and psychotherapeutic services, which is core to the 2 × 4 Model design, can help the staff resolve conflicts from 'old school' thinking.

Fourth, there are inter-professional jealousies and power struggles that have little to do with differing professional skill sets or knowledge bases, but have more to do with human dynamics surrounding power, envy, competition, and ambition. To some extent, working teams and groups of all kinds need time to 'jell' for these dynamics to settle out, which puts the onus on the team leaders to do their best to prevent rapid turnover on the team, especially among the leaders themselves. Then again, there is the potential that real trouble is irrefutably connected with individual professionals.

Fifth, raw incompetence and/or malignancy of personality is a problem that effects a small minority of any professional type, and can be a source of persistent conflict or dysfunction on the 2 × 4 Model team. As in any modern health care organization, the clinic and its hosting institution should have well thought-out and workable mechanisms in place to remediate or remove professionals with these issues. 2 × 4 Model leadership meetings, happening outside the team meetings (and typically involving only the physicians and other administrative leaders), can be very helpful in dealing with these types of issues and sorting out conflicts and professional behavior that reflect serious personal issues vs. routine differences that can be resolved. Unfortunately, when the addiction psychiatrist is incompetent and/or malignant, the consequences for the 2 × 4 Model program and patient care can be especially catastrophic and hard to deal with, given the level of responsibility, authority, and impact they normally have on patients, and the treatment team as whole. To protect against this possibility, the team approach does provide somewhat of a system of checks and balances, multiple eyes on patients, and cross monitoring of care, where bad events can get caught. Moreover, the presence of more than one professional of each type in the clinic, including the psychiatrists, and ideally, the presence of more than one board certified addiction psychiatrist, can help the clinic be resilient to weathering professional malignancies and necessary terminations. Of course the best protection against the wayward addiction psychiatrist comes from addiction psychiatry fellowship program directors, who do their best to accept and train the most talented and emotionally intelligent professionals and leaders they can find. Also, they should include team leadership training and supervision in addiction psychiatry fellowship training (e.g., in a 2 × 4 Model clinical setting as described in Chapter 11).

Specific Issues in Patient Care

One of the major decision points for the 2 × 4 Model team is the question of when, if ever, is it appropriate to transfer patients out of the program or terminate their care. Unfortunately terminating/transferring patients is resorted to all too often in segregated mental health vs. addiction treatment systems, as they can always label dual diagnosis patients as being too diagnostically complex and beyond their expertise for them to handle. This urge to transfer patients out can also result from patients being viewed as too treatment refractory or labor intensive. The 2 × 4 Model design offers a level of care that is better than what segregated mental health vs. addiction treatment systems can provide for the large majority of behavioral health patients who are dual diagnosis cases. Part of this capability rests on the capacity and willingness of the 2 × 4 Model clinic to accept and be more than competent at treating patients from across the entire spectrum of addicted, mentally ill, and dual diagnosis conditions. The goal is to provide a longitudinal continuity of care regardless of whether patients go through phases of MI-intensive or SUD-intensive treatment or both, over time. In doing this, when patients are not progressing as well as the team would like, the responsibility of the team is to look at what it is doing, and how it can change and improve the treatment plan, to match it to the patient's needs, rather than taking the 'easier road' of just deciding "the patient is not right for our service" or somehow blaming the patient for poor results and then discharging them out. The 2 × 4 Model clinic should view itself as the best there is, and the end of the line for outpatient psychiatric care in terms of handling complex behavioral health patients. So, if the decision is to transfer patients out, the team should be aware that this decision, short of transferring the patient to an inpatient detox unit, hospital, or long term institution, cannot often be well supported with the rationale that the team is "moving the patient to a higher level of care." The 2 × 4 Model clinic is flexibly designed to provide a full spectrum of *different levels* of outpatient care in addition to being able to handle diagnostic diversity.

236 *All Together Now*

Yet, there are circumstances where it is necessary to end treatment, to transfer patients out, or, to accept when patients make their own decision to walk away. Probably one of the most important and clinically valuable caveats to the longitudinal commitment that the 2 × 4 Model clinic makes to take care of mentally ill/addicted patients, is that the psychiatrists and the team should not hold on to patients at all costs. More specifically, if a medication regimen and/or treatment plan is recommended that the team firmly believes in and the patient refuses it, the team should not change that plan, to an ineffectual or potentially harmful regimen in response to the patient threatening to leave the clinic if they don't get what they want. Basically, the idea is that the clinic should not fire patients for refusing to follow certain treatment plan recommendations, but it is certainly ok for patients to fire the clinic if they don't agree with what the psychiatrist or the team is willing to do. In reality, outpatient, voluntary treatment nearly always happens to some degree as a compromise, and as a process of unanimous decision-making in the partnership between patient and the clinician. If either the patient or the psychiatrist disagree with a treatment plan element then it pretty much won't happen. But, it is up to the 2 × 4 Model team to be offering the patient many therapeutic elements and tools, so the failure to agree on a few, or even many treatment plan ideas should not bring down the whole house of care for the patient. For example, when the patient is expecting the psychiatrist to prescribe them alprazolam, testosterone, and amphetamine salts "or I'll leave because these are the only things that I know help me", then the psychiatrist should stick to their integrity, their clinical knowledge, and the evidence base, and let this patient walk. At some point, if that same patient reaches a point where they realize they need to stop using doctors as drug dealers, and that they need real treatment, they will come back (to where they know the treatment is real), and they will be willing to follow the team's lead.

On occasion, there are situations where there are no treatment plan options left except for one next step that has to be implemented before more care or other treatment plan elements can take place. In these situations, the psychiatrist may have to be prepared to not move until this next step happens first. For example, in a case where a patient is not allowing the psychiatrist to contact outside physicians (who are prescribing that patient harmful regimens of addictive drugs), their psychiatrist is rather stuck until the patient gives the permission. This is because the refusal to allow the disclosure represents a strong signal that the patient is not really interested in the judgment of the addiction psychiatrist, and is more interested in maintaining the utility of doctors as drug dealers. Under these conditions, there is very little the addiction psychiatrist and the 2 × 4 Model team can do other than to effect a breakthrough with the patient to agree to the disclosure. This may require some time and a concentrated effort of the whole team, and singularity of focus of the treatment plan to achieve this goal. Once it is achieved, it can lead to many other therapeutic efforts; but if it cannot be achieved, it is likely best to let the patient walk away.

Another situation where the team and the patient can get stuck, and a 'one door solution' arises, is where the patient, for example, a person with opioid addiction, is demonstrating no progress in care, and is treatment refractory to meds in large part because he is living with family members that are all using and dealing prescribed opioids and other drugs. In this situation, the only move that can produce a better result is for the patient to move into a supportive sober environment (e.g., like a rehab house). If the patient cannot make this move when such options are presented, then the team can reasonably hold off from other therapeutic actions until they do.

Other than letting patients 'fire the team' and walk away, there are very few situations where patients should be terminated proactively by the team. But they do exist, and they happen as one of two contexts:

1. The patient has shown significant intimidation and/or aggression toward one or more team members (or patients) generating genuine fear. In well-trained behavioral health professionals, real fear is real threat, and a sign of danger. Plus, behavioral health professionals working in real fear cannot do their job. In these situations, which are thankfully extremely rare, the team members have to protect themselves and the patient has to go. Whether the patient is permanently banned from the clinic for this behavior should depend on a team and administrative decision (with input from team members put in fear), with consideration of whether or not the mental health condition that led to the aggression was transient and genuinely reversible with appropriate treatment.

2. The patient has in some way utilized the clinic to commit a significant crime that may or may not harm other patients, and demonstrates an intent to fake being in treatment for the sake of accomplishing the offence. Extreme examples of this might include conclusive evidence that the patient is dealing weapons or heroin in the clinic, or is recruiting or running prostitution. We say significant crime here because merely sharing prescribed meds, although technically illegal, is unfortunately extremely common. Also, patients with petty vendettas against one another can leverage false accusations or exaggerations, and the team should beware that its energies can easily be sapped into investigating 'crimes' of all kinds, instead of operating as a health care team. Fortunately, significant crime that requires termination is also quite rare in a well-run dual diagnosis clinic like the 2 × 4 Model where the team and the physicians know the patients well, and build enough rapport through group and individual psychotherapies to know what patients' motives are. If the clinic shows integrity and expertise, and makes it clear to patients that it cares about them and wants them to get better (as opposed to acting like its main goal is to make money, by not individualizing care and operating like a pill mill), then patients with integrity and genuine intent to get better will tend to persist in care. There will be a proportion of antisocial patients in the dual diagnosis patient

population but many of these folks actually are trying to get real treatment too. Given that the 2 × 4 Model clinic will be staffed by well-trained psychiatrists and other behavioral health professionals who are well versed in identifying, observing, and managing a spectrum of anti-social symptoms and other personality disorders that can involve pathological manipulation, the team should be adept in deciding as a unit when a given patient has crossed the line into needing termination. Again, this should be extremely rare, and most antisocial patients with only nontreatment seeking motives will avoid the 2 × 4 Model clinic altogether, or will get themselves out on their own soon enough when they realize being in the clinic is all about treatment.

A final issue for patient care that is important to mention here, and one that is far more common than the more extreme scenarios listed above surrounding termination, is the issue of split care. As mentioned in Chapter 7 with respect to pharmacology, the idea and design of the 2 × 4 Model clinic fundamentally opposes split care. The clinic seeks to integrate mental health and addiction-ology, and it seeks to integrate psychotherapies and medication management. Accordingly, for patients identified as being prescribed multiple psychiatric medications by different physicians, the clinic should strive to take it all over and have it all happening 'by one team under one roof'. The same should generally be true for psychotherapies, so that the clinic should not engage in doing psychotherapy for a patient who is getting their psychiatric meds from an outside physician. Similarly the addiction psychiatrists should not engage in prescribing meds to a patient who is predominantly getting their psycho-therapies on the outside. There can of course be minor exceptions to this anti-split care stance (e.g., when the outside medications or therapies are playing a helpful but very *minor* role; when transitions in care are taking place, etc.). But the overall goal is for the 2 × 4 Model team to be in charge of, and serve as the final authority of the patient's mental health and addiction care. Striving to achieve unified–integrated care of the dual diagnosis patient in the 2 × 4 Model requires good horizontal binding of all of the clinic's treatment dimension components (Diagnostics, Psychotherapies, Medications, and Communications). This biding does not have to happen all at once or up front, but over time it should be aimed for and happen in the care of every patient.

A *top-10 list of Guiding Principles for Patient Care in the 2 × 4 Model Clinic* is shown on the facing page (**Box 10.2**).

BOX 10.2 **Guiding Principles for Patient Care in the 2 × 4 Model Clinic**

1. Do not fire or turn away patients because they have a certain kind(s) of major mental illness or addiction.
2. Do not fire patients because they are sick, treatment refractory, or prone to relapse.
3. Do not fire patients because they are compliant with meds only, or groups only, or individual psychotherapy only.
4. For difficult and challenging patients, look at what the team can do better; do not focus on how the patient has failed.
5. Expect that individual patients will end up with different allotments of therapies and meds, and different balances of therapies and meds, which will change over time.
6. Expect that different patients will need different tempos and intensities of recovery activity and participation over time.
7. Always accept the once lost but returning patient back with open arms. Celebrate the return as their success and yours.
8. Treat patients in every interaction like you want them to come back, even if they quit, relapse, and give up in the short term.
9. Only terminate the rare patient that frightens or directly harms the program with no intent to achieve genuine recovery.
10. Oppose split care; enact integrated mental health–addiction care, and integrated psychotherapy and medication treatment by one team under one roof.

Background References and Further Reading

Carey, K. B. 1996. "Substance use reduction in the context of outpatient psychiatric treatment: A collaborative, motivational, harm reduction approach." *Community Mental Health Journal* 32 (3): 291–306; discussion 307–310.

Carroll, K. M., and B. D. Kiluk. 2012. "Integrating psychotherapy and pharmacotherapy in substance abuse treatment." In *Treating Substance Abuse Theory and Technique*, edited by S. T. Walters, and F. Rotgers. New York: Guilford Press.

Carroll, K. M., T. R. Kosten, and B. J. Rounsaville. 2004. "Choosing a behavioral therapy platform for pharmacotherapy of substance users." *Drug Alcohol Dependence* 75 (2): 123–134. doi: 10.1016/j.drugalcdep.2004.02.007 S0376871604000456 [pii].

Carroll, K. M., B. J. Rounsaville, L. T. Gordon, C. Nich, P. Jatlow, R. M. Bisighini, and F. H. Gawin. 1994. "Psychotherapy and pharmacotherapy for ambulatory cocaine abusers." *Archives of General Psychiatry* 51 (3): 177–187.

D'Souza, D. C., E. Perry, L. MacDougall, Y. Ammerman, T. Cooper, Y. T. Wu, G. Braley, R. Gueorguieva, and J. H. Krystal. 2004. "The psychotomimetic effects of intravenous delta-9-tetrahydrocannabinol in healthy individuals: Implications for psychosis." *Neuropsychopharmacology* 29 (8): 1558–1572.

Farren, C. K., K. P. Hill, and R. D. Weiss. 2012. "Bipolar disorder and alcohol use disorder: A review." *Current Psychiatry Reports* 14 (6): 659–666.

Kranzler, H. R., and R. N. Rosenthal. 2003. "Dual diagnosis: Alcoholism and co-morbid psychiatric disorders." *American Journal on Addictions* 12 (Suppl 1): S26–S40.

McLellan, A. T., A. I. Alterman, D. S. Metzger, G. R. Grissom, G. E. Woody, L. Luborsky, and C. P. O'Brien. 1994. "Similarity of outcome predictors across opiate, cocaine, and alcohol treatments: Role of treatment services." *Journal of Consulting & Clinical Psychology* 62 (6): 1141–1158.

Osher, F. C., and L. L. Kofoed. 1989. "Treatment of patients with psychiatric and psychoactive substance abuse disorders." *Hospital & Community Psychiatry* 40 (10): 1025–1030.

Pettinati, H. M., R. D. Weiss, W. Dundon, W. R. Miller, D. Donovan, D. B. Ernst, and B. J. Rounsaville. 2005. "A structured approach to medical management: A psychosocial intervention to support pharmacotherapy in the treatment of alcohol dependence." *Journal of Studies on Alcohol* (Suppl. 15): 170–178; discussion 168–169.

Riba, M. B., and R. Balon. 2005. *Competency in Combining Pharmacotherapy and Psychotherapy: Integrated and Split Treatment.* Washington, DC: American Psychiatric Publishing.

Rognli, E. B., and J. G. Bramnes. 2015. "Understanding the relationship between amphetamines and psychosis." *Current Addiction Reports* 2 (4): 285–292. doi: 10.1007/s40429-015-0077-4.

Sajid, A., A. Whiteman, R. L. Bell, M. S. Greene, E. A. Engleman, and R. A. Chambers. 2016. "Prescription drug monitoring program data tracking of opioid addiction treatment outcomes in integrated dual diagnosis care involving injectable naltrexone." *American Journal on Addictions* 25 (7): 557–564. doi: 10.1111/ajad.12441.

Sankaranarayanan, A., V. Clark, A. Baker, K. Palazzi, T. J. Lewin, R. Richmond, F. J. Kay-Lambkin, S. Filia, D. Castle, and J. M. Williams. 2016. "Reducing smoking reduces suicidality among individuals with psychosis: Complementary outcomes from a healthy lifestyles intervention study." *Psychiatry Research* 243: 407–412. doi: 10.1016/j.psychres.2016.07.006.

Ziedonis, D. M., D. Smelson, R. N. Rosenthal, S. L. Batki, A. I. Green, R. J. Henry, I. Montoya, J. Parks, and R. D. Weiss. 2005. "Improving the care of individuals with schizophrenia and substance use disorders: Consensus recommendations." *Journal of Psychiatric Practice* 11 (5): 315–339.

11 Professional Training and Research in the 2 × 4 Model Clinic

The final two chapters of this book address the approaches needed for advancing the capacity, technical capability, and reach of the 2 × 4 Model system through professional training, research, and infrastructure development. An established 2 × 4 Model clinic should be viewed as a setting not only for conducting excellent standards of addiction, mental health, and dual diagnosis care, but also as the ideal place for workforce creation and training, and research on dual diagnosis illnesses. Clearly, a clinic that is focused on both mental illness and addiction diagnoses and treatment with equal prioritization that is also well equipped with the expertise and clinical tools to integrate this focus, is a clinic that is optimized to provide cross training for physicians, nurses, and therapists in both mental health and addiction care. Moreover, since the 2 × 4 Model design emphasizes and relies on the work of an integrative multidisciplinary team, the professional training that can take place in the 2 × 4 Model clinic is both intra- and inter-disciplinary, where professionals not only learn and refine their own roles and expertise, but how they can best collaborate and 'force amplify' one another as a cohesive team. Similarly, with respect to the research mission, a clinic that is fundamentally interested in i) how mental illness and addiction diseases interact biologically and phenomenologically; ii) how new and more effective treatments can be developed, tested, and implemented for dual diagnosis patients; and iii) how treatment outcomes for different forms of dual diagnosis illnesses can be tracked—is a clinic that is ideally suited to conduct research on addictions and dual diagnosis disorders.

Professional Training

Physicians

Without physician leadership, and the clinical and scientific expertise the profession of addiction psychiatry entails *with respect to knowing both mental illness and addiction diseases*, integrated dual diagnosis care and the 2 × 4 Model system itself cannot really work. Fortunately, the field of addiction psychiatry has been well established for many years. However, it is represented by a physician workforce that is far too small in proportion to the clinical need and it is a medical specialty that has not previously been linked to a specific kind of clinical mission or design. The 2 × 4 Model aims to remedy this situation by being a key clinical model and professional setting where addiction psychiatry training and practice can take place. A commonly held misunderstanding or misapplication of addiction psychiatry is that it is, or should be, a highly specialized field that focuses primarily on treating addictions. Rather, *addiction psychiatry is more accurately understood as being more general, and less specialized in focus than is general adult psychiatry.* This point is clear because while general psychiatry represents professionals who are well trained to treat one domain of behavioral health (principally, mental illnesses), addiction psychiatrists are professionals that are well trained to treat *both* mental illnesses and addictions. Thus, addiction psychiatry is a more broadly capable field that can treat a wider variety of behavioral health patients and illness combinations; the specialization of addiction psychiatry is actually about being better trained generalists! Unfortunately, because of the widespread segregation of mental health and addiction treatment training and services, many addiction psychiatrists, after training, find themselves working in siloed systems of care. Due to the lack of team or institutional support for integrated dual diagnosis care, they are often not able to perform integrated dual diagnosis care even if they wanted to, and instead, are mostly utilized in terms of only half of their professional potential, as either mental health, or addiction treatment physicians. The 2 × 4 Model addresses this problem by serving as a home base, natural habitat, recruitment center, incubator, and training ground for the field of addiction psychiatry. As a system of 2 × 4 Model clinics might grow, so would the field of addiction psychiatry grow and become more clinically empowered and accessible to the public.

With this union of addiction psychiatry and the 2 × 4 Model in mind, a key aim of the 2 × 4 Model clinic system is that it would represent an excellent clinical context for departments of psychiatry to support and conduct addiction psychiatry fellowship training programs. At present, it is not known to what degree each of the 45 or so addiction psychiatry fellowship programs in the U.S. conduct their training in settings that approach the 2 × 4 Model design. Moreover, there really are no clear standards (or methods or infrastructures set up to check these standards) that have been established for how integrated dual diagnosis care systems should be built, operated, and staffed by physicians with training in dual diagnosis care.

As described in this chapter and in Chapter 12, the 2 × 4 Model design could fill this gap, if implemented by psychiatry and the health care system as a whole, as both a training context and clinical standard for addiction psychiatry and integrated dual diagnosis care. The ACGME has established professional training standards and goals for all the major American medical specialties that lead to ABMS board certification including addiction psychiatry. These training standards, known as the *ACGME Milestones*, serve as guide posts and criteria (i.e., competencies) by which addiction psychiatrists and other specialists should be trained and evaluated by during their postgraduate training leading to board certification. Generally, training directors maintain a running appraisal of how far each of their residents and fellows have progressed with respect to expected levels of mastery on a one (beginner) to five (expert) scale. For addiction psychiatry, there are 16 competencies spread among six milestone domains as listed in the box below.

Figure 11.1 shows the addiction psychiatry ACGME milestones map to the 2 × 4 Model, with a corresponding listing of chapters in this book that most directly contain content material relevant to each sub-competency. All of the Patient Care (PC) sub-competencies, and some of the Medical Knowledge (MK) and System-Based Practice (SBP) sub-competencies (six total), map well to one of the four treatment components of the 2 × 4 Model. The remaining ten sub-competencies involve a significant degree of an integrative understanding of the two illness dimension components (mental illness/addictions) and four treatment dimension components of the 2 × 4 Model design, meaning they are relevant to descriptions of the vertical and horizontal binding inherent in the 2 × 4 Model design. Figure 11.1 thus provides a framework for how addiction psychiatry fellows and training directors may use this book as a textbook for addiction psychiatry, and how this training can be optimally based in a medical school or residency that supports or is affiliated with a 2 × 4 Model clinical program.

BOX 11.1 Addiction Psychiatry ACGME Milestone Structure

Domain Name (Acronym)	No. of Sub-Competencies	General Description
1. Patient Care (PC):	3	How to practice/clinical skills
2. Medical Knowledge (MK)	3	Scientific knowledge of disease/treatment
3. System-Based Practice (SBP)	4	How to leverage the system for care
4. Practice-Based Learning/ Improvement (PBLI)	2	How to increase skills, knowledge
5. Professionalism (PROF)	2	How to practice with integrity and ethics
6. Interpersonal Communication (IC)	2	How to interact with people and the record
	16	

Nurses and Therapists

Although workforce deficiencies in nurses and therapists who are cross trained in addiction and mental health are also an issue in behavioral health, the remedy for this is somewhat less complicated than for addiction psychiatrists, because the formal training of these professionals does not require medical school, psychiatric residency, and fellowship (i.e., it is not as long and expensive). However, their training and implementation into a 2 × 4 Model design is still fairly dependent on the presence of an addiction psychiatrist.

Cross training for nurses and therapists in integrated dual diagnosis care is more of an 'on-the-job' endeavor, and therapists can be certified in either or both mental health and addiction counseling somewhat independently from their work in an integrated dual diagnosis clinic. Accordingly, it is easier for a 2 × 4 Model team to be 'trained up' on the job from the guidance and supervision of the addiction psychiatrist leadership, than it is for a team to be formed and operate adequately as a dual diagnosis program, when the therapists are adequately cross trained but the psychiatrists are not. This is because of the tendency for psychiatrists that are not formally trained or motivated to treat addictions, to be relatively hard to 'convert' into practicing integrated dual diagnosis care. Moreover, nonaddiction psychiatrists do not often have the experience and training needed to provide the nurses and therapists with guidance and supervision to conduct integrated dual diagnosis care. Thus, the optimal training context for nurses and therapists in integrated dual diagnosis care is a setting where the clinical team has addiction psychiatrist(s) on board, and there are the appropriate mentors and supervisors for those disciplines on the team. In this context, the nurses and therapist will receive supervision and training support from both the addiction psychiatrist(s) and the administrative leadership of the team in charge of the psychotherapy staff. This training support would happen in supervision sessions as well as in the course of routine clinical care involving both multidisciplinary clinical care meetings, and the team meeting.

Typically, if the 2 × 4 Model clinic is a training site for an addiction psychiatry fellowship program associated with a medical school and/or psychiatry residency, then those institutions will often also be resources for students in medicine, nursing, psychology, and social work, allowing the 2 × 4 Model program to operate as a multidisciplinary clinical and training program (e.g., as a comprehensive 2 × 4 Model workforce pipeline). Such connections between a given 2 × 4 Model program and local professional training programs are thus encouraged as they will be important for enlarging the clinical expertise and human capital needed to build a robust system of 2 × 4 Model clinics across a given region. It is conceivable that in parallel to addiction psychiatry board certification for physicians, the various nursing and psychotherapeutic disciplines of social work and psychology should consider developing mental health and addiction cross-training practicums and certification pathways that could be based in 2 × 4 Model clinics.

Research

A strong research mission in a psychiatry clinic can be synergistic with, and enhance both the clinical and training missions. Given the need to develop more effective prevention and treatment strategies for all behavioral health patients, including the majority of them who have current or histories of *both* mental health and substance use disorders, the 2 × 4 Model clinical system would readily serve as a natural home for integrated dual diagnosis research. Assuming that NIDA and the NIMH could eventually look beyond their segregated missions and start supporting dual diagnosis research more collaboratively (with each other and NIAAA) in proportion to the unmet clinical need, human subjects and clinical treatment research funded by these agencies could become quite usual *and translational* at the point of care in 2 × 4 Model clinics. This of course, will have to involve some degree of culture change in these agencies (and the thinking of scientists whose expertise they rely on), where committees that review grants for either agency don't penalize grant applications for having what is often perceived as a divided or too complicated a focus on both mental illness and addictions. Further, study designs should be encouraged and not penalized for being *clinically realistic*, so that studies can actually seek out, instead of excluding, the entry of subjects with complex comorbidities of both mental illnesses and addiction. Although such a change to accept MI–SUD comorbidities into NIMH, NIDA, and NIAAA research portfolios will introduce some new methodological complexities, sometimes including the need for higher numbers of research subjects and more complex analytic approaches, it will result in research that is much easier to recruit into, more scientifically revealing and honest, and more accurate to real world clinical questions and problems that behavioral health clinicians are trying to solve everywhere, every day. As pointed out in Chapter 9, clinical researchers and data analysis professionals embedded in the 2 × 4 Model clinic could work well with the clinical team on projects funded by NIH, private endowments, nonprofits, biotech companies, and of course, the pharmaceutical industry to develop better treatments for patients across the real-world spectrum of MI–SUD comorbidities. Following the 2 × 4 Model design, the following research topics and approaches can and should be pursued across a system of 2 × 4 Model clinics:

Diagnostics

New Technologies in Drug Testing

Integrated dual diagnosis care would greatly benefit from advances in *integrated MI- and SUD-relevant drug testing* where not just the major addictive drugs are tested for, but also the psychotherapeutic drugs being prescribed in the clinic (for MI indications) are tested for in the same assay. This would not only be helpful for assessing the reliability of the sample, but it would provide a much higher level of information about the causes behind a clinical decompensation.

For example, are the symptoms worse because the patient a) is using; b) is non-compliant on psychiatric meds; or c) both; or d) neither of these?

Other than the need for testing to be sensitive and specific, new testing technologies should also find ways to become less expensive, to have more rapid turnaround time, and to be impervious to cheating. Routine drug screens in the $100 plus price range, although common in forensic and other medical treatment settings, are not really acceptable in the 2 × 4 Model clinic given the high volume of regular testing each patient will need. While rapid (immunoassay tests) can deliver results in minutes, they are weak in accuracy and do not give quantitative values. In the meantime, more definitive and quantitative testing using chromatography methods suffers from more expense and time delays. To address these problems and to improve ways to circumnavigate patients cheating on testing, new technologies are needed that can perform small blood volume assays in the clinic, analogous to a glucometer. Noninvasive tests that detect trans-dermally, or on the breath for substances other than alcohol, are also needed. There is also room for advances in technology and the expansion of more testing labs to reduce bulk testing costs and time-to-results.

Advanced Multi-Modal Real-Time Diagnostic Telemetry

Smart phones and wristwatch/wearable monitoring technologies are now available that can monitor, in real-time or in multi-day summaries, a number of biological and behavioral variables including heart rate, wake/sleep time, motor activity, and location. Further, these technologies can prompt and query patients multiple times a day/week about psychiatric symptom levels and craving, and even warn patients when they are entering a geographical 'trigger zone'. Such bio-patterns downloaded and analyzed in the 2 × 4 Model clinic could provide new insights about patients' diagnoses, particularly how their MI and SUDS are clinically intertwined over time. Treatment responses could be more objectively tracked outside the clinic with these technologies, complimenting regular in clinic interviews. If paired with noninvasive methods for drug and alcohol use monitoring, these technologies could be especially useful in the early stages of treatment including outpatient DWT.

Neuroimaging and Neurocognitive Testing

Patients with different patterns of neuroimaging and neurocognitive testing profiles may be differentially vulnerable to addictions, and/or differentially responsive to certain medication and psychotherapy treatments for their dual diagnosis conditions. Thus, clinical research on how these methods could predict addiction risk in young adults with emerging mental illness may be helpful for indicating preventative/protective therapies and medications, even before a severe addiction begins to occur. At the same time, these methods could shed more light on the extent to which a wide variety of mental illnesses and various levels of traumatic experiences may differentially set up addiction risk or severity, indicating the need for specific treatment interventions.

Genotyping and Ecophenotyping

While progress in defining a solid evidence base for using gene arrays to inform psychiatric diagnoses and medication selection based on genotype is still underway, a similar effort to estimate the biological results of the cumulative exposure to developmentally impactful abuse, neglect, trauma, and attachment experiences (i.e., the ecophenotype) may also inform both medication and psychotherapeutic treatment approaches. Sorting out which of these genetic and environmental factors contribute to both MI and addiction phenotypes (e.g., multifinality) and identifying these in patients may help drive parsimonious medication strategies for dual diagnosis disorders.

Psychotherapies

Preventative Strategies (Family/Trans-Generational Integrated Treatments)

Exposure to early abuse, neglect, trauma, and attachment disruption are contributory to dual diagnosis disorders in adulthood. Moreover, these experiences can lead to parenting behaviors that repeat these adverse experiences (and propagate dual diagnosis conditions) in the next generation of children. Accordingly, new individual and group therapies (e.g., the Circle of Security) that support healthy attachment formation and parenting behavior in dual diagnosis patients with young children, will be important for breaking trans-generational recurrence of dual diagnosis disorders. New lines of longitudinal research in 2 × 4 Model clinics are needed to refine and quantify the effects of such therapies.

Experiential Therapies

The 2 × 4 Model clinic would be an excellent research setting to explore the design and efficacy of any number of experiential therapies using either individual or group formats. For example, treatment plans might test the use of cardiovascular workout regimens and training on top of routine medication and psychotherapeutic management. Art therapies and interactive cognitive therapies (e.g., using video game or virtual reality experiences) might be tested in their capacity bolster prefrontal cortical function, and fortify the individual against specific craving triggers, stimuli, and related psychiatric symptoms.

Medications and 'Neuromechanical' Interventions

New Drug Development and Testing

The 2 × 4 Model clinic would be an ideal setting to test the development of any novel psychotropic agent for either a mental illness or addiction indication, because the clinic is so well geared to diagnosing and treating both of these classes of illnesses, and is thus capable of detecting beneficial or harmful effects of a given medication in either illness domain. This capability would have major benefits in preventing postmarketing surprises that can happen for medications developed and studied in the traditional approach, where MI-only or addiction-only subjects are allowed (or recognized) in the pre-FDA approval studies. For example, new medications for addiction could be better screened for psychiatric side effects (and vice-versa) helping to prevent the assignment of false causal associations between certain medications and certain behavioral side effects, or, to better identify true risks along these lines.

Parsimonious Drug Development

Another benefit and positive flip side of being able to detect side effects for a mental illness diagnosis in a treatment for addiction (and addiction-related side effects from a mental illness treatment) is the capacity of the 2 × 4 Model clinic to be able to identify novel medications that are beneficial for preventing and treating *both* mental illness and addiction disorders. To the extent that both MI and SUDs are intimately inter-related and share common genetic and experiential etiologies, it is likely that many more medications beyond the first PDDA bupropion have parsimonious efficacy for certain dual diagnosis combinations. Expansion of pharmacological treatment trial research in settings with dual diagnosis capability and expertise, such as what 2 × 4 Model clinics can provide, could make parsimonious dual diagnosis medication development far more common and routine, making it much more likely that advanced treatments for dual diagnosis conditions will be developed.

Neuromechanical Interventions

Deep brain stimulation (DBS), repetitive transcranial magnetic stimulation (rTMS), ablative or neurotrophic neurosurgical interventions, and eventually, even biological or artificial neural network prostheses could also be tested in 2 × 4 Model research clinics as optimal settings to track both mental illness and addiction-related outcomes. As is the case with new medication development, whether the primary indication to be tested is a mental illness or addiction condition, the eventual clinical deployment of the technology will inevitably involve large fractions, if not majorities of patients, with dual diagnosis conditions.

Medication Development for Specific Stages of Recovery

The longitudinal commitment to recovery that the 2 × 4 Model clinic makes to patients with dual diagnosis disorders allows the clinic to not only have expertise in specific recovery phases (e.g., as in the Stages of Change, or in terms of DWT vs. LIDDT programming), but also in transitioning and progressing patients successfully through each of these stages. Beyond having MI or SUD-specific indications, novel medications may also be found to have efficacies for specific stages and transitions in recovery. While ECT and ketamine seem to show more rapid and profound efficacy in the early stages of treatment for severe major depression, similar treatments may be specifically powerful in early abstinence or the transition between DWT and LIDDT. For example, a medication treatment that facilitates success rates in the transition from methadone or buprenorphine maintenance to long-term naltrexone therapy, could be readily tested in the 2 × 4 Model setting.

Research to Advance Horizontal Binding in the 2 × 4 Model

Integration of Medications, Psychotherapies, and Experiential Treatment Approaches

A very exciting frontier of treatment research for which the 2 × 4 Model clinic is well suited, because it directly integrates (i.e., horizontally binds) medication management and psychotherapies, is investigation and clinical trials of medications that are designed to be given in conjunction and synergy with psychotherapeutic and/or experiential interventions. The scientific rationale for these types of integrated treatments is based on the concept that for substantial recovery to occur in many addicted/mentally ill patients, there needs to be medication/neuromechanical interventions that are *profoundly neuroplastic*. That is to say, these treatments should be capable of profoundly changing and/or growing neural networks that are effected by mental illness and addictions (i.e., the axonal-dendritic connectivity architectures of frontal–cortical striatal–temporal–limbic networks). Based on fundamental principles of neuroscience, this kind of 'super-plastic-therapeutics', would require concurrent environmental data input (e.g., of a psychotherapeutic or experiential nature) to ensure that the revision and growth of the new network connectivity architectures are optimally guided by and adapted to healthy motivational–behavioral sets, environments, and lifestyles. Thus, given that a network architecture that is not adaptive to the environment is what mental illness and addiction are on their most fundamental levels, 'super-plastic-therapeutics' would be designed to biophysically remodel the network into a state that is better suited to the psychosocial–environmental context. The risk is that if such super-plasticity is induced without feeding the brain optimal information (experiences) that it can adapt to and build internal representations around, there is a danger that a profound network revision will increase, rather than decrease psychopathology. But, the potential benefit is that such plasticity, if guided by the best or most appropriate experiences, could have a quite profound therapeutic effect for many of our sickest and most treatment refractory patients.

The concept that a combination of medications and psychotherapies is the best standard and most effective approach for most patients with mental illness and addictions is of course not new, and is an assumption that is built into the

2 × 4 Model design. But the idea of 'super-plastic-therapeutics' is to push this concept biologically and therapeutically much further than we have before, to exert more rapid and more profound recovery in a greater number of patients with serious mental illness and addiction diseases. Already, a number of lines of basic neuroscience and clinical research are advancing treatment possibilities in line with super-plastic-therapeutics. For example, might certain types of psychotropic medications or drugs of abuse (e.g., benzodiazepines or alcohol) be harmful to psychotherapy approaches while others (SSRI's) are more capable of enhancing psychotherapies? On the other hand, might analogs of LSD, MDMA or ketamine be particularly therapeutic and have longer lasting effects if they are administered in the context of particular experiences and psychotherapy approaches? Is it possible to use video games and virtual reality experiences in combination with neuromechanical interventions like rTMS to 'ablate' brain representations of craving and to help extinguish the intensities of triggers to PTSD symptoms or drug relapse? Might particular schedules of cardiovascular exercise work synergistically with certain mental illness and/or addiction medications to boost dual diagnosis recovery? For all of these types of investigations, the 2 × 4 Model clinic is ideally suited because it specifically emphasizes and has expertise in not only the horizontal binding of medication and psychotherapeutic treatments, but also the assessment and tracking of both mental illness and addiction-related symptoms. The latter is particularly important in terms of advancing 'super-plastic-therapeutics', because of the high degree to which mental illness and addiction are intimately inter-related and overlapping within cortical-striatal-temporal-limbic networks. Just as their disease processes are inter-related, so will be their more definitive cures; advancing super-plastic-therapeutics in 2 × 4 Model clinical research settings will be of high importance.

Binding of Diagnostics and Treatments: Advanced Dual Diagnosis EMR Systems

Unfortunately, most current Electronic Medical Record (EMR) systems used in psychiatry suffer from three serious flaws that end up hurting the quality of patient care and the work-satisfaction of clinicians: They are typically 1) not user friendly; 2) not well designed for behavioral health applications; and 3) designed more for extracting maximal billing at the expense of empowering clinicians in the care of patients. Accordingly, there is a substantial need for research and development of behavioral health-specific EMR systems, particularly those designed specifically for the 2 × 4 Model system.

Research on the best EMR system for the 2 × 4 Model clinic would aim for two goals:

1. Provide the most accurate and efficient means for clinicians to document clinical data, (i.e., to cut down on painful documentation time and increase patient interaction time).

2. Provide the highest quality clinical data summary and longitudinal analysis review functions that can best inform treatment planning and addiction psychiatry medical decision-making.

Goal two would be realized by the design of a 2 × 4 Model EMR that efficiently and fairly automatically tracks and summarizes multiple strands of clinical diagnostic data (described in Chapter 5), with information pertaining to participation in psychotherapies (types, durations, intensities) (Chapter 6), and of course medication regimens (Chapter 7). Such information, when compiled and displayed in user friendly (e.g., visual-graphical) but mathematically rigorous formats, could be used by the addiction psychiatrist and the treatment team to drive evidence-based treatment planning (and facilitate more automatic documentation of treatment planning changes). Moreover these systems would represent clinical research data bases, *allowing for the collection of clinical diagnostic and outcomes data* in a fairly automatic way, as programmed by the addiction psychiatrist and other 2 × 4 Model clinic-based researchers, *whenever new psychotherapeutic and/or medication treatments are introduced.* Thus, research and development of 2 × 4 Model-specific EMRs are expected to not only improve clinical outcomes directly by enhancing treatment plan decision-making, but also by enhancing the power and efficiency of clinical diagnostic and treatment research for mental illness, addictions, and dual diagnosis disorders.

Background References and Further Reading

Bellack, A. S., M. E. Bennett, J. S. Gearon, C. H. Brown, and Y. Yang. 2006. "A randomized clinical trial of a new behavioral treatment for drug abuse in people with severe and persistent mental illness." *Archives of General Psychiatry 63* (4): 426–432.

Buckley, P. F., and V. Madaan. 2008. "Leadership and professional workforce development." *Psychiatric Clinic of North America 31* (1): 105–122. doi: 10.1016/j.psc.2007.11.007.

Chambers, R. A., and S. C. Wallingford. 2017. "On mourning and recovery: Integrating stages of grief and change toward a neuroscience-based model of attachment adaptation in addiction treatment." *Psychodynamic Psychiatry 45* (4): 451–474.

Chambers, R. A. 2008. "Impulsivity, dual diagnosis, and the structure of motivated behavior in addiction." *Behavioral and Brain Sciences 31* (4): 443–444.

Fireman, M., K. Kamphman, R. Ronis, A. J. Saxon, and J. J. Wilson, Eds. 2015. *The Addiction Psychiatry Milestone Project*, edited by C. P. Thomas. Washington, DD: The Accreditation Council for Graduate Medical Education (ACGME) & American Board of Psychiatry and Neurology (ABPN).

Galanter, M., H. Dermatis, and D. Calabrese. 2002. "Residencies in addiction psychiatry: 1990 to 2000, a decade of progress." *The American Journal of Addiction 11* (3): 192–199. doi: 10.1080/10550490290087956.

Gonzales, J. J., and T. R. Insel. 2004. "The conundrum of co-occurring mental and substance use disorders: Opportunities for research." *Biological Psychiatry 56* (10): 723–725.

Hall, M. N., M. Amodeo, H. J. Shaffer, and J. Vander Bilt. 2000. "Social workers employed in substance abuse treatment agencies: A training needs assessment." *Social Work* 45 (2): 141–155.

Herrold, A. A., S. L. Kletzel, B. C. Harton, R. A. Chambers, N. Jordan, and T. L. Pape. 2014. "Transcranial magnetic stimulation: Potential treatment for co-occurring alcohol, traumatic brain injury and posttraumatic stress disorders." *Neural Regeneration Research* 9 (19): 1712–1730. doi: 10.4103/1673-5374.143408.

Hulvershorn, L. A., T. A. Hummer, R. Fukunaga, E. Leibenluft, P. Finn, M. A. Cyders, A. Anand, L. Overhage, A. Dir, and J. Brown. 2015. "Neural activation during risky decision-making in youth at high risk for substance use disorders." *Psychiatry Research* 233 (2): 102–111.

Kavanagh, D. J., L. Greenaway, L. Jenner, J. B. Saunders, A. White, J. Sorban, and G. Hamilton. 2000. "Contrasting views and experiences of health professionals on the management of comorbid substance misuse and mental disorders." *Australian & New Zealand Journal of Psychiatry* 34 (2): 279–289.

Krystal, J. H. 2007. "Neuroplasticity as a target for the pharmacotherapy of psychiatric disorders: New opportunities for synergy with psychotherapy." *Biological Psychiatry* 62 (8): 833–834.

Murphy, S. A. 1989. "The urgency of substance abuse education in schools of nursing." *Journal of Nursing Education* 28 (6): 247–251.

Rao, K. N., A. M. Sentir, E. A. Engleman, R. L. Bell, L. A. Hulvershorn, A. Breier, and R. A. Chambers. 2016. "Toward early estimation and treatment of addiction vulnerability: Radial arm maze and N-acetyl cysteine before cocaine sensitization or nicotine self-administration in neonatal ventral hippocampal lesion rats." *Psychopharmacology (Berl)* 233 (23–24): 3933–3945. doi: 10.1007/s00213-016-4421-8.

Rassool, G. H., Ed. 2002. *Dual Diagnosis: Substance Misuse and Psychiatric Disorders.* London: Wiley-Blackwell.

Renner, J. A., Jr. 2004. "How to train residents to identify and treat dual diagnosis patients." *Biological Psychiatry* 56 (10): 81–816. doi: S0006322304004755 [pii] 10.1016/j.biopsych.2004.04.003.

Sturgess, J. E., T. P. George, J. L. Kennedy, A. Heinz, and D. J. Muller. 2011. "Pharmacogenetics of alcohol, nicotine and drug addiction treatments." *Addiction Biology* 16 (3): 357–376.

Tiet, Q. Q., and B. Mausbach. 2007. "Treatments for patients with dual diagnosis: A review." *Alcoholism: Clinical & Experimental Research* 31 (4): 513–536.

Williams, J., M. Steinberg, M. H. Zimmerman, and E. Salsberg. 2009. "Training psychiatrists and advanced practice nurses to treat tobacco dependence." *Journal of the American Psychiatric Nurses Association* 15 (1): 50–58. doi: 10.1177/10783903 08330458.

Zhang, X., E. A. Stein, and L. E. Hong. 2010. "Smoking and schizophrenia independently and additively reduce white matter integrity between striatum and frontal cortex." *Biological Psychiatry* 68 (7): 674–677.

12 Building 2 × 4 Model Clinics and Systems
Local to International

Goals and Limits of Building a National System of 2 × 4 Model Clinics

The building of a national network of 2 × 4 Model clinics has the potential to decisively raise the standards of addiction and dual diagnosis care, while making behavioral health care as a whole far more accessible, efficient, and effective for a much wider portion of the general population. The public health impact of such a rebuilding and renaissance of integrated behavioral health would not only increase the health and well-being of the population, but it could significantly reduce the unsustainable overgrowth and expense of the both the Criminal Justice System and general medical surgical care (Chapter 8).

The creation of a national network of 2 × 4 Model clinics would change psychiatry and mental health care, by effecting a major merger of mental health and addiction infrastructure, treatment and expertise, and making this treatment mainstream—the rule rather than the exception. Of course there would still be a need for more specialized psychiatric clinics, hospitals, and private practices involving independent psychiatrists and other psychotherapists that do not provide integrated mental health/addiction care, or addiction care at all. The goal of a national system of 2 × 4 Model clinics would not be to lead to the demise of these more specialized venues, but to compliment them. In essence, the 2 × 4 Model system would aim to be a new backbone and core of behavioral health, existing in academic, community, and private venues, operating as 'the primary care of psychiatry', being generally capable of longitudinal care for the majority of patients with mental illness, addiction, and their combinations. As suggested in **Figure 12.1**, the creation of a system of 2 × 4 Model clinics in a given region, state, or nation, would help transform a behavioral health infrastructure from one that is highly fragmented and unevenly equipped with resources and expertise, into one that is better integrated and more reliably expert at managing real world complex comorbidities. Then, while able to care for the full spectrum of patients with mental illness and addictions at a high standard of care, clinics qualifying as (and declaring themselves to be) 2 × 4 Model clinics would be clearly transparent in what they offer, how they are equipped and staffed, and how they operate, because these features are explicitly described in the 2 × 4 Model design as characterized in this blueprint book. Notably, this would be a major departure from the status quo in the U.S. where, for any given treatment clinic that says it offers mental health or addiction services, or dual diagnosis services, there is no reliable existing standard or expectation on the part of the public for what such a system can or should actually provide or offer in terms of evidence-based care. Thus, the 2 × 4 Model design is a shorthand descriptor of a clinic design, professional team composition, and method of operation, which reliably and transparently indicates a high standard of addiction and dual diagnosis care, so that health insurers, the courts, other medical professionals and ultimately, patients and their families, know what they are getting into, and what they should expect from any clinic so named. Based on a set of essential qualifying criteria needed to designate a clinic as a 2 × 4 Model clinic (e.g., as listed at the end of this chapter), it is possible to build a distributed system of 2 × 4 Model clinics that can be reliably referred to and understood by referral sources and the public at large for what they offer.

With this vision in mind, a goal could be for every major city (e.g., with >100,000 population) and/or community mental health center (that may serve a collection of smaller cities) in a given region, state, or country, to have at least one 2 × 4 Model clinic. Or, an alternative goal may be to establish at least one 2 × 4 Model clinic within an hour's driving time from 75 percent of the population. Regardless of how it is formulated, the goal would be to establish a system of 2 × 4 Model clinics that are reasonably reachable by the majority of the population for up to three times a week of clinical encounters. In larger cities that may host particularly large 2 × 4 Model clinics, or several of them, it would be possible to create a system of satellite residential facilities surrounding them to house special populations of patients (e.g., pregnant women; young people from rural areas who have no access to legitimate standards of behavioral health or addiction care in their communities). These residential centers, which might be termed 2 × 4 Model recovery campuses, could be designed to house people on the intermediate long-term basis (e.g., six months to four years), allowing enough time for patients to significantly consolidate their recovery.

In any event, the 2 × 4 Model is not intended to represent a corporate chain, rather it is a description of a clinic design, team composition, and operational clinical method; a wide variety of nonprofit or for-profit clinical systems, VA (Veterans Administration) facilities, community mental health centers, academic medical centers, and departments of psychiatry could freely build and operate one or more 2 × 4 Model clinics, as long as they are accurate in adherence to the required design features.

Replication and Expansion of the 2 × 4 Model System

So the question becomes, how does a system of 2 × 4 Model clinics get built? With this blueprint and operations manual in hand, the remaining critical resource that is needed is the human capital (workforce and expertise). Then, within the human resource, the key pieces are the addiction psychiatrists, because they will be uniquely fully capable, formally trained, and certified for maintaining focus and expertise on both the mental illness and addiction components of the illness dimension (managing their vertical binding), and the treatment plan components (diagnostics, psychotherapeutics, medications, and communications). This collection of professional attributes and skill-sets are critical, not because the addiction psychiatrist is expected to run the 2 × 4 Model clinic solo; they actually cannot and should not do this because operating the 2 × 4 Model design has to be a team effort. Rather, the key is that the addiction psychiatrist can act uniquely as a supervisor and trainer for the entirety of the rest of the clinical team, including nurses and therapists, who can then be secondarily cross trained. Thus, the addiction psychiatrist is the essential seed upon which any 2 × 4 Model clinic can be grown. It's not that cross-trained nurses or therapists can't be critical catalysts and leaders in this effort, it's just that the most necessary human element is the addiction psychiatrist.

On this basis, it becomes clear that the growth and vitality of a distributed system of widely available 2 × 4 Model clinics will depend heavily on the condition of the addiction psychiatry workforce. Considering the U. S. for example, as of 2015, only about a third of all 120 or so psychiatry training programs in the county, and half of the 50 states, were equipped with addiction psychiatry training programs. Among the 45 or so active addiction psychiatry training programs, typically, anywhere from zero to three new addiction psychiatrists are being trained at any point in time (with many slots and programs going unoccupied), creating national annual production levels of between 30 and 60 graduates per year. These numbers mean that formally trained and certified addiction psychiatrists represent less than 5 percent of the entire workforce of practicing psychiatrists. From these numbers, it becomes clear that the building of a robust system of 2 × 4 Model clinics for the U.S. will require a significant and sustained increase in the production of addiction psychiatrists. To the extent that addiction psychiatry training occurs in, and is joined to 2 × 4 Model clinics (Chapter 11), the momentum for growth in the profession and the 2 × 4 Model treatment system would be intertwined.

If 2 × 4 Model clinics become more usual as training settings for addiction psychiatrists, and a strong system of such clinics is built, it is likely that these clinics and their physician workforces (and training missions) will be self-sustaining. But the questions remain: By how much and by what means do we increase the production of addiction psychiatrists? A goal could be to increase this workforce production by 3–4 fold above current levels so that 15–20 percent of psychiatrists are trained as addiction psychiatrists. At these levels, if every addiction psychiatrist was paired with (or closely consulting to) one or two general psychiatrists (e.g., as in a 2 × 4 Model program or other consulting arrangement), then such dual diagnosis capable physician work-groups would make up 40–60 percent of the overall psychiatric physician workforce. This dual diagnosis capability would be in line with epidemiological data indicating that 40–60 percent of all behavioral health patients have dual diagnosis comorbidities.

Increasing and maintaining the production of addition psychiatrists on this scale will likely require expansions in three areas: 1) number of training programs; 2) number of training slots per program; and 3) number of trainees entering available slots.

Increasing the number of training programs through which psychiatrists can be trained in addictionology is already occurring via the development and expansion of formal addiction medicine fellowship programs (sponsored by the ABAM), which, along with addiction psychiatry fellowships can lead to ABMS certification in addictionology (via either addiction medicine or addiction psychiatry). Specific expansion of addiction psychiatry fellowships (the American Board of Psychiatry and Neurology (ABPN) pathway) will also be important however, as this path into addictionology requires completion of general psychiatry residency, thus guaranteeing that all physicians trained in addiction psychiatry are fully cross trained in both mental illness and addictions (the ABAM route is open to both psychiatrists and other nonbehavioral health physicians). In addition, addiction psychiatry training and certification is required for a person to become an addiction psychiatry fellowship training director. Thus because the clinical and professional training missions of the 2 × 4 Model clinic are a degree more in line with the ABPN pathway, expansion of addiction psychiatry training programs across more departments of psychiatry will more directly pertain to the expansion of 2 × 4 Model clinics. In the U.S., a 50 percent increase in the number of psychiatry residencies that host addiction psychiatry fellowships (e.g., up from about 45 to 67 programs) could help equip nearly all the U.S. states with addiction psychiatry fellowships well above current levels, where only about half U.S. states are so equipped. Since a given 2 × 4 Model clinic could operate as a training context for an addiction psychiatry program, colonizing a department, city, or state with both at the same time would be practical. The American Academy of Addiction Psychiatry (AAAP), the ACGME, the ABPN, and local departments of psychiatry can work together to create a new addiction psychiatry training program.

Increasing addiction psychiatry training slots in an already established program is readily achievable as long as training stipends, faculty time, and general institutional support are sufficiently abundant. A well-motivated addiction psychiatry training director can often find partners in clinical care systems that are affiliated with their academic departments to make such expansions happen, because addiction psychiatry fellows are 1) a relatively cost-effective way for institutions to host fully trained board eligible (or certified) psychiatrists and 2) institutions that provide training settings and stipends to fellows often have a major advantage on recruiting these professionals for longer term positions.

Recruiting more graduated psychiatrists into addiction psychiatry fellowship slots is one of the more challenging chores for the addiction psychiatry training director. Extreme shortages of general psychiatrists everywhere virtually guarantees that graduating psychiatrists do not need any fellowship training to garner high starting salaries. Extremely high (and historically unprecedented) educational loan debt burdens, reaching into the multiple hundred thousand dollar range per psychiatrist, has made doing another year of fellowship training (and accepting the relatively low pay of a fellowship year) untenable for many talented physicians. The difference in one year's salary for a starting general psychiatrist vs. that of a full time addiction fellow can range from $100,000 to $200,000. This means it is virtually this much money a graduating resident must be willing to forgo to become an addiction psychiatrist.

A quite effective strategy for overcoming this financial barrier against addiction psychiatry training and workforce enlargement is the offering of unconditional loan repayment programs. Local (hiring) clinical institutions as well as government agencies interested in addressing workforce shortages in addiction psychiatry, can often be extraordinarily supportive by designing loan repayment options in cooperation with training directors and departments of psychiatry that could offer such incentives as recruitment tools. Medical schools and large health care systems that wish to create new addiction psychiatry training missions and 2 × 4 Model clinics, could do so relatively quickly by using total loan debt recruitment incentives for new addiction psychiatrists trained elsewhere. They can also create or enhance new pipelines of trainees by forgiving educational loan debts for current students who are committed to addiction psychiatry training at the institution, and are later hired on with the institution as addiction psychiatrists.

Additional issues that may prevent more general psychiatrists from entering addiction psychiatry training include stigma against addiction within the profession, and the lack of exposure to addiction neuroscience and clinical care. Both of these problems go hand in hand, and reflect the paucities of addiction psychiatrists (teachers and role models), fellowship programs, clinical care sites for addiction, and dual diagnosis treatment that exists at most medical schools and psychiatry residency training programs. Expanding the number of faculty members who are addiction psychiatrists, and increasing the number of addiction psychiatry training programs across more psychiatry departments, will of course help address these problems. For example, more addiction psychiatry faculty members in a given department will allow more general psychiatry residents (and medical students) to have more intensive, frequent, and earlier exposure to addiction neuroscience and clinical care. Obviously, a 2 × 4 Model clinic where medical students and residents can rotate, would provide an excellent environment for training and recruitment into addiction psychiatry. As previously mentioned, a common misunderstanding held by many professionals, including general psychiatry residents, about addiction psychiatry is that the training and the profession aims to overspecialize the psychiatrist so that all they will see is a very narrow diagnostic band of patients with addictions. Again, the 2 × 4 Model and the addiction psychiatry practice it supports not only busts this myth, but achieves quite the opposite, as it is about psychiatric care that is far more flexible, individualized, and diagnostically broad than what mainstream segregated mental health-only or addiction-only care provides. There actually is no other type of clinic in behavioral health care that welcomes and is clinically capable of treating a broader diversity of patients than the 2 × 4 Model clinic, which is all about treating any major mental illness(s) comorbid with any addiction(s) by one team under one roof.

Barriers to Overcome

Building a 2 × 4 Model clinic in a given new location and replicating this model across a geographical landscape will take time, investment, and effort to overcome a number of barriers beyond the aforementioned limitations in addiction psychiatry workforce. These barriers may be classified broadly as *cultural, professional,* and *financial.*

As covered in the earlier chapters in this book, the cultures of addictionology and mental health have predominantly been largely segregated from one another across nearly every domain in which they have missions, spanning basic and clinical research, professional training, clinical care, and certainly funding. The expansion of 2 × 4 Model clinics will require more of a broad-based awareness of the failings of the segregated status quo and recognition of the scientific, clinical, and social benefits of creating much more of an integrated addiction and mental health *culture* across all these domains. While the first four chapters of this book make the case for why this integration is needed from the perspective of basic neuroscience, epidemiology, and clinical evidence, the latter chapters describe explicitly how it can happen in a working model of an individual clinic.

Professional barriers refer here to the human resistance to change needed to build and implement a system of 2 × 4 Model clinics, which is bound to happen with many professionals in either the mental health or addiction fields who do not accept the ideas, science, or clinical rationale behind integrated dual diagnosis care or more specifically, the 2 × 4 Model itself. Some professionals may reject the 2 × 4 Model because they were trained in the segregated system, have operated for most of their careers in it, and find the prospect of participating in the change (e.g., treating both mental illness and addiction) unacceptable, undesirable, or intolerable. Certainly, it is not the goal of the 2 × 4 Model design to recruit any professional into it who does not see its value, or, who is not interested in practicing addictions and integrated dual diagnosis care. However, it is expected that more 2 × 4 Model clinics will create more interest and capacities for trainees and professionals in practice to work in them. Other professionals, especially those in academia, may feel like the 2 × 4 Model is not in line with their own hyper-specialization, not just in mental illness or addiction, but in one type of mental illness (e.g., the PTSD expert) or addiction (e.g., the nicotine expert), which the academic environment tends to favor. Beyond academic and clinical professionals, many stakeholders in the behavioral health industry will be concerned about the costs of transforming their currently segregated system of care into integrated 2 × 4 Model (or like systems), or the potential losses their own segregated systems could take should they remain as offering only segregated care. Ultimately, it will be the responsibilities of the behavioral health science and clinical professional communities that will determine to what extent they find the 2 × 4 Model compelling and convincing, and in the best interest of the patients they serve.

Financial barriers refer to methods used by the *health insurance industry* across its various governmental and private-for-profit segments to maintain arcane and sometimes illogical and clinically counter-productive rules that not only make the reimbursement of behavioral health care inefficient and difficult, but seek to maintain and support the segregation of mental health from addiction services. Significant reform will be needed to build new behavioral health reimbursement models that incentivize rather than penalize integrated dual diagnosis care, for example, when some systems require each patient to have either a primary mental health or a primary addiction diagnosis (but not both), or when health care for the treatment of both disorders simultaneously is considered 'double dipping' of reimbursement. This reform will not only require parity of mental health with medical care, but parity of addiction care with mental health care. The alignment of adequate insurance reimbursement with care delivered by the appropriate clinical expertise, and the delivery of sound, evidenced-based standards of care in addiction and dual diagnosis care will also be important. Psychiatric hospital beds should no longer be reserved only for gravely impaired psychotic and suicidal people, but for people who are at equally grave risk for dying due to overdoses, serious intoxications, or episodes of withdrawal. If the insurance industry, the government, and ultimately the public are able to recognize the public health, social, and economic advantages of creating and supporting a cross-trained dual diagnosis professional workforce and clinical infrastructure as *a mainstream* standard of behavioral health, creating a national system of 2 × 4 Model clinics could happen surprisingly rapidly.

2 × 4 Model Fidelity: Team, Tools, and Techniques

As 2 × 4 Model clinics are replicated across a geography in the building of a dual diagnosis capable system, it will be important for health care providers, insurance companies, government agencies, and the public to know if a given clinic qualifies as adhering to 2 × 4 Model design. The idea is that if a clinic does qualify as a 2 × 4 Model clinic based on the blueprints and operational guidelines described in this book, and publicly identifies itself as such, then there is instant transparency as to exactly what the program offers, how it is staffed, and the spectrum of patients it can serve (i.e., virtually the entire spectrum of mentally ill, addicted, and dual diagnosis patients). Thus, the 2 × 4 Model clinic is also a description of a standard that addresses the significant and widespread problem that patients, families, and other stakeholders of behavioral health care face. Although treatment systems often claim they are 'dual diagnosis capable' or that they provide both addiction and mental health services, these unstandardized terms can mean a very wide range of things and capabilities, which actually often fall far short of representing comprehensive integrated dual diagnosis care and expertise.

In a 2 × 4 Model clinic, patients and the public have access to clinical standards described in **Box 12.1** below, *Guaranteed Clinical Capabilities of the 2 × 4 Model Design.*

To ensure the accuracy of a claim that a given program is in fact a 2 × 4 Model clinic, it is necessary to outline a minimum set of required 2 × 4 Model features that the clinic must be equipped with (or operate by) to qualify as a 2 × 4 Model design. These features, as described in much more detail in prior chapters of this book, are reprised at the end of this chapter as a reference check list that can be efficiently used for verifying 2 × 4 Model fidelity. This list of minimum required features, which are handily broken down into categories of 'The Three T's' (Team, Tools, and Techniques), can help external observers determine how a clinic may be rated with respect to fidelity to the 2 × 4 Model design. Four ratings (or classifications) are proposed in **Box 12.2**, *Classification Ratings of Clinics Approaching the 2 × 4 Model Design.*

For building a system of 2 × 4 Model clinics (**Figure 12.1**), a region or state could start the process with building and operating an *academic 2 × 4 Model clinic*, affiliated with a medical school and psychiatry training program. This academic 2 × 4 Model clinic would then serve as a 'development hub' by establishing contacts with the regional network of medical centers, psychiatric

---

BOX 12.1 Guaranteed Clinical Capabilities of the 2 × 4 Model Clinic

1. Care provided and/or directed by physicians that are formally cross trained and certified in both mental health and addiction;

2. Access to the highest available standards of multiple evidence-based psychotherapeutic and medication modalities for both mental illness and addiction;

3. Individualized treatment planning and execution, instead of one-size fits all, pill mill approaches;

4. Longitudinal care, which does not fire patients for being sick or too complex, which is committed to the long-term success of the patient, regardless of the type of mental illness, addiction, or comorbid combinations;

5. Proactive defense against anti-behavioral health treatment practices of the Criminal Justice System, the insurance industry, and the broader health care system that can interfere with achieving and sustaining recovery or access to proper care.

BOX 12.2 Classification Ratings of Clinics Approaching the 2 × 4 Model Design

1. *Non-2 × 4 Model clinic*: Any behavioral health clinic that provides segregated mental health or addiction care that does not meet the minimum required features of the 2 × 4 Model design, and has no intent to become a 2 × 4 Model Program.

2. *Developing 2 × 4 Model clinic:* A behavioral health clinic that offers a substantial number of required 2 × 4 Model design features *and* is explicitly aiming (via dedicated institutional and leadership support encompassing the recruitment of an addiction psychiatrists) to become a 2 × 4 Model clinic in the near future.

3. *2 × 4 Model clinic:* A behavioral health clinic that actualizes *all* the minimum required features of the 2 × 4 Model design, described in The 'Three T's': Team, Tools, and Techniques.

4. *Academic 2 × 4 Model clinic:* An established, qualifying 2 × 4 Model clinic that is engaged in professional training (of other physicians (addiction psychiatrists), nurses, or therapists), and/or is involved in clinical research (contributing to research publications within the last 5 years). This 'enhanced' form of the 2 × 4 Model clinic will typically be affiliated with academic medical centers and psychiatry residency training programs. Academic 2 × 4 Model clinics are expected to be involved in spawning/developing new 2 × 4 Model clinics in nearby regions, growing 2 × 4 Model professional workforces, and advancing new diagnostic and treatment technologies for mental illness and addictions as implementable in the 2 × 4 Model design.

BOX 12.3 Minimum Requirements: Team

1. **Physicians**: There should be at least one addiction psychiatrist on staff. An addiction psychiatrist is defined as a physician (MD/DO or British Medical System equivalent) with formal training in general psychiatry (and ABPN board certification) and completion of 1 year of formal training in addiction psychiatry (ABPN pathway) or addiction medicine (ABAM pathway) with certification in either or both.

2. **Nursing**: At least two nursing (RN/LPN) staff.

3. **Psychotherapists**: At least three psychotherapeutic staff; therapists (MA, LCSW, and PhD level) capable and trained to deliver individual and group psychotherapies.

BOX 12.4 Minimum Requirements: Tools

1. Diagnostics: (Routine and frequent use of the following)

   - Initial (1 hour) and follow-up (15–30 minute) dual diagnosis examinations (by psychiatrists) (ranging from once per week to once every 4 months);
   - Rapid (on site) UDS testing;
   - Confirmatory UDS (send out) UDS testing;
   - Breath alcohol screening kit;
   - PDMP data checking;
   - Rating scales: COWS, CIWA, Folstein MMS, SOGS, ACES; and
   - Routine medical equipment: Scales, vital sign kits, pregnancy tests, onsite blood draws.

2. Psychotherapies:

   - Multiple modalities of individual psychotherapies: MET, CBT, interpersonal, psychodynamic, supportive; and
   - Multiple modalities of group therapies: 12-step based, psychoeducational groups based on stages of recovery, tolerant to presence of mental illness.

3. Medications:

   - Full array of evidence based medications for all forms of major mental illness that is routine in psychiatric care: Including capacity for oral and depot (IM) medications;
   - Full array of evidence-based medication management for DWT; and
   - Full array of evidence-based medications for longitudinal addiction treatment including all FDA approved medications available.

4. Communications:

   - Informatics and EMR systems for rapid communications, clinical data entry, compilation and analysis, regular communications with Criminal Justice System, child protective services, elements of the broader health care system, insurance companies, housing and disability agencies, and families of patients.

BOX 12.5 Minimum Requirements: Techniques

1. **Vertical binding**: Full, balanced, and flexible focus and attention of the program on both mental illness and addiction, based on the patient's diagnostic picture and dual diagnosis combination.

2. **Horizontal binding**: Full integration of diagnostics (as initial and repeated longitudinal measures), psychotherapies, medications, and professional communications to generate dual diagnosis recovery.

3. **Treatment team meeting**: Whole 2 × 4 Model clinical team meeting to discuss cases and clinical programming: 1 hour, 3–4 times a week.

4. **Leadership meeting**: Physician and administrative leaders meet 1–2 times a month to discuss clinical programing, 2 × 4 Model design or flow issues, professional issues, educational, and research agendas.

5. **Engagement in both DWT and LIDDT missions**: Emphasis on full continuity of care from withdrawal–stabilization to long-term recovery. Resources for referral and treatment planning engagement with inpatient units for mental health crises and supervised inpatient detoxification and stabilization.

6. **Longitudinal commitment to care of the patient**: Clinical decisions made with both short- and long-term visions of recovery in mind. Philosophy held that for any given patient that walks in the door, the clinic aims to make a long-term commitment to care, until the patient is fully or sufficiently recovered or chooses to leave. Avoidance of arbitrary limits on durations of treatment. Avoidance of practices that blame or discharge patients for being ill, treatment refractory, or diagnostically complex.

7. **Delivery of flexible, individualized care**: Avoidance of one size fits all approaches, pill mill like practices, and over-reliance on rule-based care. Avoidance of arbitrary requirements that patients must take predetermined amounts, intensities, or durations of individual or group psychotherapies, or specific medication types. Provision of multiple treatment options for any one MI or addiction illness type; provision of treatments for all MI–addiction comorbidities.

hospitals or clinics, or community mental health centers that are interested in building up current (or new) teams and venues into 2 × 4 Model programs. The development hub would thus identify developing 2 × 4 Model clinics and help them move toward qualifying as full 2 × 4 Model programs. Some of these in turn could then evolve further into new academic 2 × 4 Model clinics, further increasing the capacity to facilitate the development of more 2 × 4 Model programs.

It is certainly the case that a number of addiction treatment programs and/or community mental health centers equipped with addiction psychiatrists in the U.S. would already qualify (or come close to qualifying) as 2 × 4 Model programs. Modifying these programs so that they would qualify (or identifying those that already do qualify) as having 2 × 4 Model fidelity would be helpful to starting a regional or national network of 2 × 4 Model clinics. Defining this network would help local, regional, and national level organizations create strategies for expanding 2 × 4 Model clinics toward the goal of achieving near universal access and for easy coordination of referrals. Certainly, it will be possible for some 2 × 4 Model clinics to have many more types of team members, tools, and techniques than those listed in the minimal requirements. These 'enhanced' 2 × 4 Model programs might also specialize in certain demographic groups, for example, focusing on pregnant women/women with young children, or adolescents and young adults. Over time, the minimal requirements for the 2 × 4 Model program might also be modified or grow, based on new scientific evidence or technologies in diagnosis and treatment. But the core principal of the 2 × 4 Model design, allowing the longitudinal treatment of any major mental illness and any addiction, in any combination, by one team under one roof, should remain unchanged. As made possible by the vertical binding and integration of team expertise and attention to both mental illness and addiction, and, the horizontal binding of diagnostics, psychotherapies, medications, and communications, the 2 × 4 Model design holds considerable potential for rebuilding and modernizing behavioral health into a system that is far more clinically effective, efficient, neuroscientifically informed, and readily accessible by all people in need.

Background References and Further Reading

Arnaudo, C. L., B. Andraka-Christou, and K. Allgood. 2017. "Psychiatric co-morbidities in pregnant women with opioid use disorders: Prevalence, impact, and implications for treatment." *Current Addiction Reports 4* (1): 1–13. doi: 10.1007/s40429-017-0132-4.

Brewer, S., M. D. Godley, and L. A. Hulvershorn. 2017. "Treating mental health and substance use disorders in adolescents: What is on the menu?" *Current Psychiatry Reports 19* (1): 5. doi: 10.1007/s11920-017-0755-0.

Brousselle, A., L. Lamothe, C. Mercier, and M. Perreault. 2007. "Beyond the limitations of best practices: How logic analysis helped reinterpret dual diagnosis guidelines." *Evaluation and Program Planning 30* (1): 94–104. doi: 10.1016/j.evalprogplan.2006.10.005.

Canaway, R., and M. Merkes. 2010. "Barriers to comorbidity service delivery: The complexities of dual diagnosis and the need to agree on terminology and conceptual frameworks." *Australian Health Review 34* (3): 262–268.

Carra, G., F. Bartoli, G. Brambilla, C. Crocamo, and M. Clerici. 2015. "Comorbid addiction and major mental illness in Europe: A narrative review." *Substance Abuse 36* (1): 75–81. doi: 10.1080/08897077.2014.960551.

Carra, G., and M. Clerici. 2006. "Dual diagnosis—policy and practice in Italy." *American Journal on Addictions 15* (2): 125–130.

Hawkins, E. H. 2009. "A tale of two systems: Co-occurring mental health and substance abuse disorders treatment for adolescents." *Annual Review of Psychology 60*: 197–227.

Mowbray, C. T., M. Solomon, K. M. Ribisl, M. A. Ebejer, N. Deiz, W. Brown, H. Bandla, D. A. Luke, W. S. Davidson, 2nd, and S. Herman. 1995. "Treatment for mental illness and substance abuse in a public psychiatric hospital. Successful strategies and challenging problems." *Journal of Substance Abuse Treatment 12* (2): 129–139.

Ridgely, M. S., H. H. Goldman, and M. Willenbring. 1990. "Barriers to the care of persons with dual diagnoses: Organizational and financing issues." *Schizophrenia Bulletin 16* (1): 123–132.

Timko, C., K. Dixon, and R. H. Moos. 2005. "Treatment for dual diagnosis patients in the psychiatric and substance abuse systems."*Mental Health Services Research 7* (4): 229–242.

Index